THE VIOLIN AND VIOLA

History, Structure, Techniques

SHEILA M. NELSON

DOVER PUBLICATIONS, INC.
MINEOLA, NEW YORK

TO
FRANK HOWES

Bibliographical Note

This Dover edition, first published in 2003, is an unabridged reprint of *The Violin and Viola*, first published by Ernest Benn Limited, London, and W.W. Norton & Company Inc., New York, in 1972. A new "Preface to the Dover Edition" has been specially prepared by the author.

Library of Congress Cataloging-in-Publication Data

Nelson, Sheila M.
    The Violin and Viola : history, structure, techniques / Sheila M. Nelson.
        p. cm.
    Originally published: London : E. Benn, 1972, in series: Instruments of the orchestra. With new pref. by the author.
    Includes bibliographical references and index.
    ISBN 0-486-42853-2 (pbk.)
    1. Violin. 2. Viola. I. Title.

ML800.N44 2003
787.2—dc21

2003043998

Manufactured in the United States of America
Dover Publications, Inc., 31 East 2nd Street, Mineola, N.Y. 11501

Contents

Preface to the Dover Edition

SINCE THE AGE OF SIXTEEN, when I taught my first violin group, string teaching has been my constant interest. For this new edition in a new century I feel the need to update my view of the string learning world as contained in Chapter 10.

Although cheap instruments were widely available, a shortage of string players became very noticeable in the West during the latter part of the twentieth century, while wind playing became ever more popular. This was partly blamed on the difficulty of string playing and on the expense and isolation of traditional one-to-one teaching. The attention of string educators was drawn to group learning as a possible remedy, and parents today can choose from a number of new approaches.

Paul Rolland's contribution to the understanding of the physical aspects of string playing is surely the most original and comprehensive of the century. As President of the American String Teachers' Association he directed a research project in string teaching at the University of Illinois with special reference to the teaching of physical techniques to groups. Beginners in school classes were included and films were produced. The progress and enjoyment displayed by large numbers of children were remarkable. Rolland's work on avoiding tension and conveying the balanced movements so vital in sport, ballet, and music-making has already affected standards of string achievement to conservatory level and beyond.

Children started on the earlier Suzuki Method have sometimes been found to have difficulties later with rhythm reading and part playing due to the fact that their playing skills developed so far beyond their reading in the early stages. This can discourage them from joining in with the chamber music and youth orchestra activities that are so important to keep teenage students interested. The method is still widely used, but many teachers have found adaptation advisable.

Géza Szilvay's Colourstrings method, originating in Finland in the 1970s, chose the opposite approach to Suzuki, and is becoming well known as an alternative for the youngest beginners. Three-year-old children are helped to attain a good recognition of pitch and rhythm through

v

Kodály-based singing and movement before starting instrumental lessons from about the age of five. Note-reading is helped by using a different color for each string, and films, recordings, and brightly colored books are specially designed for the very young. Szilvay's aims, like mine, are centered on chamber music as the ideal experience for learning and future enjoyment.

My chance to see Rolland at work came when he read this book and invited me to visit the United States in 1976, a memorable trip made possible by a Churchill Fellowship. On my return, I was invited by the Inner London Education Authority to join a new string teaching team in the east end of London where school opportunities were sparse. The Tower Hamlets String Teaching Project was born. Mixed-string team teaching for whole classes plus smaller single-instrument group lessons became a normal part of the school timetable in participating schools. Weekly in-service teacher training and discussion sessions allowed more than sixty teachers and hundreds of children from the age of seven to benefit from the work of Rolland and of musicianship specialist Adrian Thorne. Appropriate new repertoire was produced, and before the final breakup of the ILEA many visitors from abroad had carried away plans for developing similar group instrumental work in their own countries. A detailed research report was produced by London University's Institute of Education.

The shared experience from this Project was taken up by the Guildhall School of Music & Drama in an attempt to clarify a logical progression of string learning and assessment in the GSM examination curriculum. One end result was the Essential String Method, written jointly during 1995–2000 by four of the Project's leading teachers—Nelson (violin/viola), Howard (cello), Elliott (bass), and Thorne (musicianship)—and published in collaboration with Boosey and Hawkes. Its aims are broadly based but clearly defined. The instrumental teacher is in charge of all aspects of the pupil's early development, and teacher, parent, and pupil can be aware of the ground already covered at any stage. Only the early learning stages are covered in four books for each instrument, sufficient to include sight-singing and sight-reading using the most common rhythms and keys, and touching on some technical features often left until much later—such as double-stops, left-hand pizzicato, shifting, spiccato, and sautillé bowing.

In contrast to the methods of Suzuki and Szilvay, playing and music-reading skills are tackled from the beginning, but separated from each other at first. Each lesson contains some playing, by copying, inventing, or using charts. Pulse and rhythm are developed by tapping and speaking, then playing from homemade cards or by ear. An understanding of pitch comes from a special repertoire of songs which gradually covers all the intervals of the major scale. These are memorized with words and in *solfa,* then made at first on a one-line staff with pebbles, feet, or disused CDs, later using the full staff. The ability to sustain different simultaneous actions is built up until the children are ready to read music and play at the same time. This may take a long time for very small children, but they can have the elements of performance in place before formal schooling begins. Older children actually progress faster when the playing and musicianship skills are separated at first to provide easily attainable targets.

The repertoire within the books is designed to be merely a skeleton, supplemented by specially written material for mixed instrumental groups and from other sources. New notes, rhythms, and bowings are introduced one at a time to avoid confusion. Three-and-four-note songs are played at different places on the instrument to explore different positions or new hand patterns. Partly based on Kodály (but already taken up in translation in some countries teaching the fixed *doh*); the reading material is made more instantly applicable to strings by an early introduction of the semitone. Games and visual aids clarify scale-building without reference to a keyboard; this fits neatly into work with hand-pattern families as different keys are explored in Book 4.

The best things in music learning are often caught, not taught. Any string learner who is lucky enough to have a group lesson as well as individual help has a good chance of finding a lifelong interest. I no longer worry about the violin family's survival; its roots are long and deep.

Sheila Nelson
October, 2002

Introduction

THE UPPER MEMBERS of the modern string family have over nearly five centuries acquired such an extensive repertoire and literature that any attempt to cover more than one aspect within a single book must present problems of what to leave out rather than what to include. Certain aspects have been covered in great detail by modern musicologists, the book to which I am most indebted in my early chapters being David D. Boyden's immensely thorough *History of Violin Playing to 1761*. The circumstances under which *The Violin and Viola* has been written, over a fairly long period during a busy professional life as performer and teacher of both instruments, have prevented much of the original source-seeking of the full-time musicologist, and my aim has been to avoid concentration on single aspects and to try instead to give a historical perspective to the role of these two instruments, their makers, performers, teachers, and composers, in musical life.

The simplest arrangement for such varied material seemed to be chronological, generally in periods of fifty years, and as descriptions of the modern instrument and bow fitted most logically into the period when their dimensions became standardised, I inserted a separate chapter on violin structure (Chapter 4), but included the bow in Chapter 7. The chapter on acoustics, a subject which practising musicians tend to shun although it explores such topical questions as whether we play in tune and why some instruments sound better than others, is left to the end only because of its perpetual relevance. Musical forms are described only when they have dominated the history of either instrument at certain periods, and for obvious reasons no attempt has been made to provide even basic lists of repertoire, makers, or performers. As I am neither a violin-maker nor an acoustician I have been grateful for advice on Chapters 4 and 11 from Mr Dietrich Kessler and Mr Philip Bate respectively.

Against the disadvantages of part-time musicology I can set the very practical advantage of being in close touch with the music and instruments under discussion, and the fact that my particular interest for many years has been the possibility of new approaches to the training of string performers and teachers; in Chapter 10 I have tried to relate some suggestions in this field to the historical progress covered in the earlier chapters, without making didactic statements about how the instruments should be taught or played. The book is intended to provide easy consecutive reading; in order to avoid interrupting this I have limited my footnotes to numerical indications of my sources in the Selective Bibliography at the back, with page references wherever possible. For the student who wishes to explore any single aspect in more detail, I have tried to indicate modern lines of research and sources of information. For the practical music-maker and listener, I have kept in mind the relevance of historical fact to modern practice; my hope is that the book will prove to be of interest to all concerned with music-making on stringed instruments.

I am indebted to the many friends and colleagues who helped with the preparation of the final manuscript and with proof-reading. In particular I should like to mention Mr Robert Masters, Mr David Nalden, and other members of the Menuhin Festival Orchestra; Dr Anthony Lewis (Principal of the Royal Academy of Music), Mr Frank Howes, Mr Emanuel Hurwitz, Mr Ivor McMahon, Miss Jean Middlemiss, Dr John Padel, and Mr Edward Selwyn. I am grateful to them all.

S. M. N.

London
December 1971

Acknowledgements

ACKNOWLEDGEMENT for kind permission to reproduce illustrations is made to the following, to whom copyright belongs:

Accademia, Venice (photograph by Osvaldo Böhm): 19
Alte Pinakothek, Munich: 18
Ashmolean Museum, Oxford: 2, 4C, 12C, 14, 20
Bibliothèque Nationale, Paris: 1
F. Bruckmann Verlag, Munich: 13
David Buckton: 24
German National Museum, Nuremberg: 9
Kunsthistorisches Museum, Vienna: 4A, 4B, 8, 11
Mr Yehudi Menuhin (photograph by F. R. Herrmann): 21
National Gallery, London: 3, 10
The Director, Royal College of Music: 15, 17
Service de Documentation Photographique de la Réunion des Musées
    Nationaux, Versailles: 5
Victoria and Albert Museum, London: 12A, 12B, 13

and quotations:

Barrie and Jenkins Limited: *Memoirs* by Carl Flesch
Cassell and Company Limited and Praeger Publishers Inc: *Szigeti on the Violin*
Faber and Faber Limited: *On Playing the Flute* by Johann Joachim Quantz
Carl Fischer Inc: *The Art of Violin Playing* by Carl Flesch, translated by F. H. Martens
Oxford University Press: *The History of Violin Playing from its Origins to 1761* by David D. Boyden
A Treatise on the Fundamental Principles of Violin-Playing by Leopold Mozart, translated by Editha Knocker

THE PITCH OF individual notes is indicated in the text by the following widely accepted scheme, which gives the open strings of the violin as *g d' a' e"*.

BB C D   c d   c' d' c" d" c''' d''' *etc.*

The position of the left hand on a stringed instrument affects the pitch range of notes covered. In the first position, the first finger covers the note one tone or semitone above the open string, giving the following stopped notes on the violin. Various keys are possible.

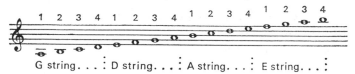

G string. . . : D string. . . : A string. . . : E string. . . :

In the second position the whole hand is shifted one note higher.

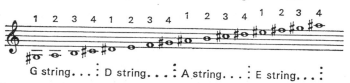

G string. . . : D string. . . : A string. . . : E string. . . :

The third position is one note higher still 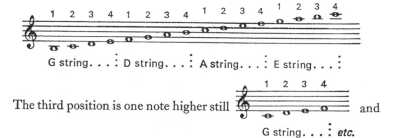 and

G string. . . : *etc.*

so on up to the eight or nine positions; higher still, only the top notes on the *e"* string are normally used, and these are often fingered by extensions rather than shifts of the whole hand.

The half position places the second finger one tone above the open string, leaving the first finger for the intervening semitone.

G string. . . : D string. . . : A string. . . : E string. . . :

Early violin methods in English often referred to second position as the 'half shift', third position as the 'whole shift', sixth position as the 'double shift', and seventh as the 'last shift', although Geminiani, familiar with the French practice, calls the positions 'Orders'. Violin and viola fingering does not use the thumb, 1 is therefore the index finger.

List of Plates

xiii

PLATE I The Old Men Surround the Lamb (13th-century miniature)

PLATE 2   Arion playing a rebec

PLATE 3   Angel playing Renaissance fiddle (*c.* 1500)

A

B

C

PLATE 5   Henriette de France playing the viola da gamba

PLATE 4   *Lire da Braccio*

PLATE 6   *Madonna of the Orange Trees* (*c.* 1529–30) by Gaudenzio Ferrari (detail)

PLATE 7   Fresco by Gaudenzio Ferrari

PLATE 8   Musical Still Life by Bartolommeo Bettera (1600)

PLATE 9   Musical Society at Nuremberg by F. von Falckenburg (1619)

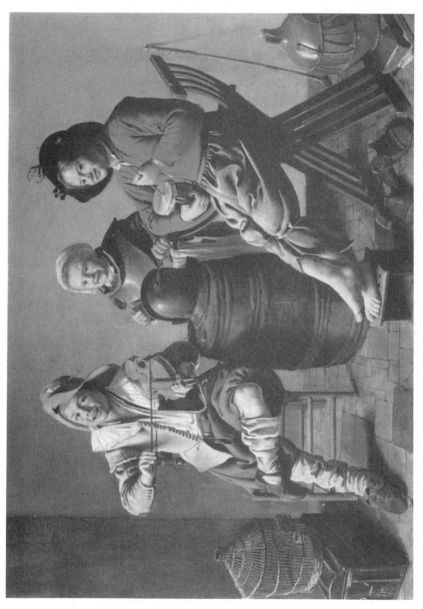

PLATE 10   Three Young Musicians by J. M. Molenauer (1629)

PLATE 11   Musical Company (c. 1600–30) by Valentin de Boulogne

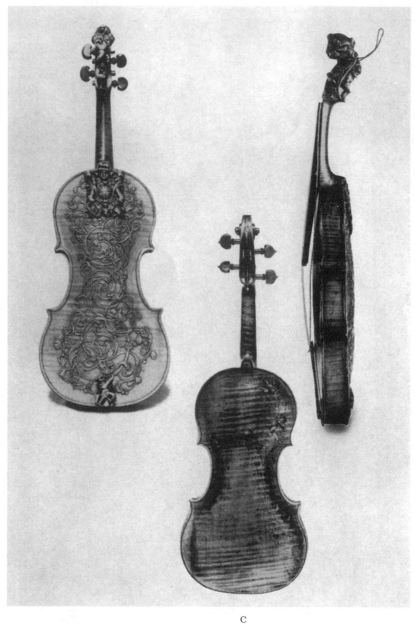

A   B

C

PLATE 12   A and B Two views of a carved English violin, C Violin
by A. Amati (1564)

PLATE 13　Three views of a violin with modern neck by Antonio Stradivari

A

B

PLATE 14   Lira-viola and viola by Gasparo da Salò

PLATE 15   Self-portrait by Gérard Dou illustrating the French bow-hold

Some General Rules for the TREBLE VIOLIN.

FIrst, The *Violin* is ufually plaid above-hand, the Neck thereof being held by the left hand ; the lower part thereof is refted on the left breaft, a little below the fhoulder : The *Bow* is held in the right hand, between the ends of the Thumb and the three firft Fingers, the Thumb being ftaid upon the Hair at the Nut, and the three Fingers refting upon the Wood : Your *Bow* being thus fixed, you are firft to draw an even ftroke over each ftring feverally, making each ftring yield a clear and diftinct found.

Secondly, for the pofture of your left hand, place your Thumb on the back of the Neck, oppofite to your Forefinger, fo will your Fingers have the more liberty to move up and down in the feveral Stops.

Thirdly, for your true fingering, obferve thefe directions, which will appear more eafie to your underftanding, if in your firft practice you have your *Violin fretted*, as is before mentioned, that where you skip a *fret* or *ftop*, there to leave a finger, for every *ftop* is but half a Tone or Note, for from ♭ to ♮ is but half a Note, but from ♭ to ♯ is a whole Note, therefore the leaving of a finger

PLATE 17   Leopold and Wolfgang Amadeus Mozart

PLATE 16 A Page from Playford's *Introduction to the Skill of Musick*
B Cantata performance in south German church

PLATE 18   Concert in a Venetian *ospedale* by Francesco de' Guardi

PLATE 19   *Concert* by Pietro Longhi (1702–85)

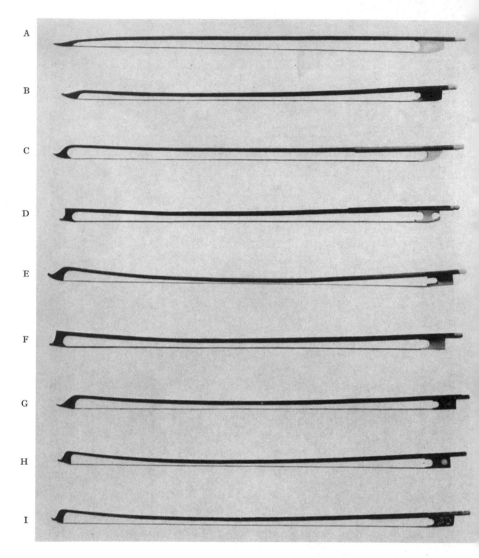

A

B

C

D

E

F

G

H

I

PLATE 20   Viola and violin bows (1740–1820)

THE MODERN ORPHEUS.

Opera House – June 3ᵈ 1831.

Sketches of the Musical World N°10 to be continued

Lithog.ry Published by Tho.ˢ M.ᶜ Lean June 6ᵗʰ 1831 26 Haymarket.

PLATE 21   Niccolò Paganini

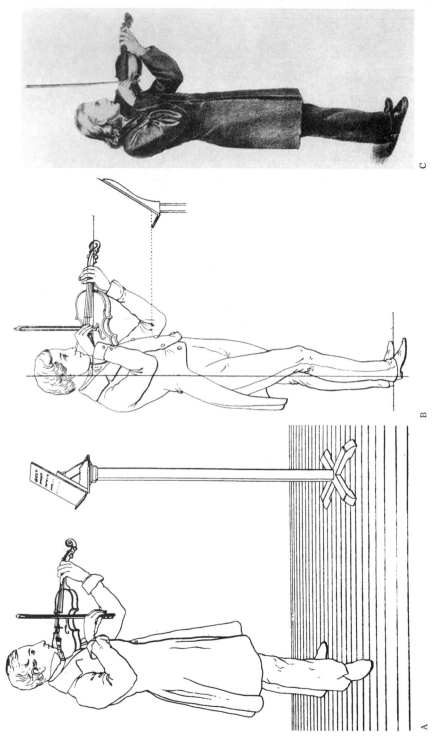

PLATE 22   Violin postures as recommended by Spohr, de Bériot, and F. David

PLATE 23   Joseph Joachim and Clara Schumann

PLATE 24   Japanese students demonstrate Suzuki Method

The Braccio Family: 1500–1600

THE VIOLIN FAMILY, which has formed the basis of our orchestra for the past three and a half centuries, emerged almost complete during the later Renaissance. The musical application of a vibrating string was recognised by primitive peoples, and resonating boxes in the form of gourds or merely bark-covered holes in the ground were added many thousands of years B.C. Variety of pitch obtained by using strings of different length on the same instrument was well known to the ancient Egyptians (a harp is depicted on a vase dated *c.* 3000 B.C.) and the Bible contains many references to plucked or struck stringed instruments (harps, psalteries). But bowing appears to have been a much later development.

Werner Bachmann, who has made a detailed study of the origins of bowing,[1] finds the earliest evidence in Islamic and Byzantine writings and paintings of the 10th and 11th centuries. Bowing probably spread to Europe from the East and after the Islamic conquests; the famous picture of a 'bowed' instrument in the Utrecht Psalter (A.D. 860) is discredited by Bachmann on the grounds of the excessive length of the line said to represent a bow, the unlikely playing position, and the fact that the player is also burdened with a triangular harp. If the minstrel in the picture is meant to be bowing, he must be producing a rather unsatisfactory sound, as the bow lies between the bridge and the tail-piece. Bachmann convincingly explains the origin of the long rod in the musician's right hand by referring to Psalm 108, for which it is an illustration, and finding that the Psalmist (identified by the musical instruments he carries) is helping another man in the picture who carries a similar measuring rod, to 'divide Shechem, and mete out the valley of Succoth'.

Up to the end of the 10th century bowing seems to have been confined to the Arabic and Byzantine Empires: during the 11th century it spread from Spain into Europe. The Welsh crwth, often described as one of the earliest bowed instruments, was undoubtedly plucked during the first centuries of its existence. Another reputed early source of the principle of bowing, Odo of Cluny's description of the hurdy-gurdy with its rosined wheel setting strings simultaneously in motion, has been found to be misdated; it was written not by Odo in the tenth century, but by an anonymous author of a later period. The earliest known representations of the hurdy-gurdy occur in carvings over Spanish cathedral doorways, suggesting an Islamic origin. Even the Spanish guitar came from the East.

The strings of the hurdy-gurdy could be 'stopped' by wooden bridges, making possible melodic progression in consecutive fourths, fifths, or octaves, over a drone bass-note. Almost undoubtedly, early bowed instruments also played several strings at once – bowing on individual strings was a later development, when drones and consecutive perfect intervals became less popular. Strings stopped by fingers on a finger-board were used before the discovery of bowing; Bachmann points out that the artist who drew some of the earliest known pictures of bowing in Spain (in the Beatus manuscripts dating from early in the 10th century)

> seems to have gone out of his way to draw attention to the process of bowing, as if representing something new and special in the musical scene, whereas the stopping of the strings is treated casually and with no attention to detail.[2]

Tuning pegs were found on the mediaeval stringed instruments: indeed after the appearance of the bows almost all the components of the violin were known in a rudimentary form. The small *vielle* had its strings attached to a special board at the base of the instrument, pointing to the violin's tail-piece, and its circular sound-hole (a characteristic of plucked instruments) was bridged by a small bar, parallel to the strings, forming two semicircular sound-holes. The crwth anticipated the functions of a sound-post by extending one foot of the bridge through the sound-hole to the back. The incurved waist of the violin began to appear on the *vielle* during the 12th century, allowing one string to be bowed without a continuous drone accompaniment from the others, and the other main developments up to A.D. 1500 were in the refinement of structural methods and ease of performance. A half-pear shape carved from a solid block of wood and given a flat belly, was found to resonate more fully if constructed from many strips glued together, and when bowed instruments were held on the shoulder instead of the knee, a flat back was found more comfortable than the bulging one: only the rebec family clung to the old shape instead of adopting side-walls or ribs and an almost flat back.

In some ways the rebec family, tuned in fifths and held on the shoulder, points most directly to the violin, but its already old-fashioned club-shaped structure in 1500, with finger-board unseparated from the body and bulging back (see Plate 2), prevented any extension of technique. The rebec's sound-rose, which is acoustically unsuited to bowed instruments, was rejected by the violin family, but the slightly reflexed angle of the peg-box which the rebec had adopted from the mandola became a feature of both violins and viols. The three members of the rebec family were bass, alto, and soprano (tuned *g d' a'*), and it was bowed with the hand held over the bow, like the violins but unlike the viols. It had no frets, no sound-post, and a nasal, penetrating sound.

The Renaissance fiddle, a matured version of the early *vielle* or *fiedel*, looked more like a rudimentary violin by 1500, having adopted an incurved waist, a flat or slightly curved back with straight ribs joining it to a flat belly, and a separate neck and finger-board (see Plate 3). But unlike the violin family it used frets (ridges on the finger-board against which the string was stopped, often movable pieces of gut), it had no overhanging edges, and its five front pegs were set vertically into a flat peg-box. Its tuning was probably in fourths, with the lowest string possibly acting as a drone, and it was held on the arm or breast like the rebec and violin.

The 15th century *lira da braccio* (Plate 4) most closely resembles the violin family in appearance, as here we find a similar body outline, and the overlapping edges, arched back and belly, pointed corners, and f-holes which are familiar properties of the modern violin. But the pegs were vertical to the plane of the belly, as in the Renaissance fiddle, and there were seven strings – two acting as the already obsolescent drones, the others tuned (according to Praetorius) to *g g' d' a' d''*. The sound-post would increase the instrument's sonority, and except for the old-fashioned drones, awkward fingering caused by the irregular tuning, and the inefficient peg-box, the *lira da braccio* might have led directly to the violin. Instead, the violin family combined the best points of these three main lines of ancestry, and an instrument emerged with a potential for sonority, blending power, agility, and personal expression which has never been bettered.

The viol family (Plate 5) may have emerged simultaneously with or a little before the violins: the two families existed side by side for two centuries, and the viol is in no sense the ancestor of the violin. This common assumption may have arisen from the fact that viols were widely accepted into serious music-making for a century before the violins, which in their early days were considered unsuitable for 'virtuous people', being used by dancing-masters and wandering professional fiddlers.

In tuning, construction, and sound the viols were quite different from the violins; they had six strings tuned either in fourths or with a third between the middle pair and fourths on either side, and were fretted in semitones. (This would facilitate learning for the amateurs with whom the viols were so popular.) Played downwards held on or between the knees, the viol used an underhand bow-hold which gave even pressure on up- and down-bows, but allowed little variety, while the thin wood and slacker, thinner strings of the instrument, compared with the violin, gave a more husky but sweet sound with considerable blending power but far less volume, contrast, and vitality.

The viol is easily distinguishable from the violin by its sloping shoulders, flat back, deep ribs, and lack of overhang on belly and back. C-holes were characteristic of the viol instead of f-holes, and a carved head rather than a scroll. The Italians differentiated between the two families by referring to the downward-held instrument as *viola da gamba* (*gamba* = leg) and the violin as *viola da braccio* (*braccio* = arm). The bass viol proved during the 17th and 18th centuries to be a more manageable instrument than the double-bass of the violin family, and a certain amount of cross-fertilisation took place: we can see in the modern double-bass clear derivations from the viol, such as sloping shoulders, a flat back, lack of overhang over the ribs, and tuning in fourths. Even underhand bowing is still used by some bass-players today. But instances of mutual influence between the other members of the two families (such as viols with f-holes, cellos played with an under-hand bow-grip, and five- or six-string cellos) were fairly infrequent, to judge from 17th-century paintings.

The varied nomenclature in use during the 16th century has caused some confusion among musical historians, and it is still not clear in all cases whether viols or violins were referred to. The use of the French term *violon* or earlier *vyollon* to apply solely to violins, while *violone* in Italian, literally 'big viola', refers to viols, thoroughly complicated the whole issue at an early date. The French term for viol was *viole*, and they found no need for the qualifying terms *da gamba* or *da braccio*. The word *violino* may have been used before the French *violon*, but its first known use is in 1538, whereas *vyollon* appeared in a French reference to Italian violinists in 1523.[3]

This late appearance of the actual title *violino*, coupled with the fact that the earliest violins had no *e″* string and that the word *viola* was used much earlier to denote different stringed instruments, led to a long-standing theory that the viola was the parent instrument of the violin family. It is in fact difficult to state definitely whether an instrument which no longer exists but which is known to have had three strings tuned *g d' a'* was a violin without an *e''* string or a viola without a *c* string, especially when these instruments are most commonly painted in the hands of angels of unspecified dimensions. David Boyden[4] points out that there is no real evidence putting one member of the family before the others: four sizes of a hybrid leading to the violin were depicted together in a woodcut by Champier (1516), and Gaudenzio Ferrari (*c.* 1480–1546), who painted the earliest known picture of a violin, held by a small angel, depicted possibly all three members of the violin family together a few years later (Saronno, 1535). Winternitz, in his essay on Ferrari's violin paintings,[5] doubts that the artist was intending to portray a complete consort of violins in the Saronno frescoes, and he points out the presence of a fourth peg-stem inside the peg-box of the alto-sized one (although only three peg-heads are shown). But the artist's earlier painting known as 'The Madonna of the Orange Trees' shows an undisputed three-string violin which Winternitz describes in detail:

> Most striking are the proportions: its body is compact, very wide, and its upper half is almost mirrored by its lower, slightly wider half; also, the double curve of the shoulders is repeated at the bottom of the body. This is a shape as different from all the Saronno fresco violins as it is from the modern violin. The marked bulge of the sound-board does not begin near the edges, but is confined to a rather narrow middle section. The f-holes slightly diverge towards the neck; they are cut precisely into the rims of the strong middle bulge of the sound-board. There is a heart-shaped string-holder. The long finger-board terminates in a long peg-box with a scroll and three pegs. The instrument is played with the head pointing downward, the bow is short, and the bowing and stopping hands, with the thumbs visible, are depicted most carefully and convincingly.[6]

The earliest extant references to violins are in French: payment was made in Savoy, December 1523, for the services of 'trompettes et vyollons de Verceil'.[7] Although French was the official language of Savoy, 'Verceil' is the Italian town of Vercelli where Ferrari's earliest violin painting originated.

Francis I of France, an artistically-inclined monarch who wished to possess Milan and spent considerable energy and money in winning and losing this city as well as Savoy and Piedmont, had violinists travelling with him who are mentioned in his accounts of 1533 and 1534.[8] This might account for the close link with France in the early history of the violin – one of the suggested 'inventors' of the violin, Gaspar(d) Duiffoprugcar, worked in Lyons from c. 1533 to 1571.

But there seems little doubt that the violin family appeared in northern Italy around Milan, and that most claims to name its inventor can be fairly easily disproved. Duiffoprugcar's violins were found to be 19th-century forgeries,[9] although Woeriot's engraving of him points to the manufacture of violins in Lyons by 1562;[10] Gasparo da Salò was born ten years after the first violin painting and Andrea Amati, who is now known to have been born c. 1511, would still have been rather young to have designed and made the instrument painted by Ferrari. No inventor can be named with certainty, and it seems very probable that an earlier generation of makers produced the first violins. Certainly Giovanni Maria dalla Corna of Brescia, who made the beautiful *lira da braccio* (Plate 4) now in the Ashmolean Museum, possessed sufficient technical skill to have contributed to the rise of the violin family, and Zanetto Montichiaro (1488–c. 1568) or Girolamo Virchi (teacher of Gasparo da Salò) were Brescian makers who may have produced three-string violins, though we possess no direct reference to them.

Lanfranco's *Scintille di musica* (1533) was published in Brescia, and although he does not mention violins by name, he speaks of 'little bowed violas without frets' which could be violins or rebecs.[11] One year later Pope Paul III brought *violini Milanesi* (violinists from Milan) to a Peace Conference at Nice: this is the earliest use of the term *violino*. *Milanesi* could mean the city or the area around it – including Brescia, Vercelli, Cremona, and Turin.

In 1545 the violin family is included in a German publication, the revised edition of Agricola's *Musica Instrumentalis Deudsch*. He speaks of '*kleine Geigen* without frets from Poland',[12] with strings tuned in fifths, stopped with the fingernail. He considers their tone more beautiful than that of the viola, and says that they are played with vibrato (*Zittern frey*). Rebecs are clearly differentiated, and the tuning of bass, alto-tenor, and discant is given as F G $d\,a'$, $c\,g\,d'$, and $g\,d'\,a'$. Praetorius in 1619 also refers to the Polish *Geige*, but it seems probable that the Poles imported the violin from Italy and contributed their own manner of performance.

By 1550 the four-stringed violin family was sufficiently established to be described in the *Epitome musical* of the Frenchman Jambe de Fer, who gives the modern tuning for violin and viola. He also firmly places the violinist in the servant class.

The Italians call it *violon de braccia* or *violone* because they support it on the arm, some with a scarf, strings or other thing; the bass is very difficult to carry because of its weight, for which reason it is sustained with a small hook in an iron ring or other thing, which is attached to the back of the said instrument very exactly so that it does not interfere with the player. I have not illustrated the said violin because you can think of it as resembling the viol, added to which there are few persons who use it save those who make a living from it through their labour.[13]

The social climate of the Renaissance was ideal for the ready acceptance of the viols, which could be fairly easily learned by the leisured amateur. Playing the viol involved less physical strain than the arm-held instruments, its tone was quiet and genteel and blended easily with voices, for which most music had so far been written, and it fulfilled a deepening harmonic sense by being produced in various sizes. This tendency was manifest in all types of instrument – those capable of playing chords like the lute, harp, great organ, and keyboard instruments (clavichord, spinet, and harpsichord) becoming a most important means of personal expression, while the single-voiced instruments (even flutes and bassoons) were produced in all sizes to form harmonically blending families.

At the same time, certain facets of 16th-century life were leading towards the final dominance of the loud, vital, expressive violins with their emotional vibrato and virtuoso capacities. The division of Europe into states ruled from wealthy Courts led to the provision of costly entertainments for the princes and their followers. Dancing was an important feature of these entertainments, and the Italians were leaders in the earliest history of the ballet. Lorenzo de' Medici, famous patron of the arts, had a favourite dancing-master called William the Jew, who was knighted by the Holy Roman Emperor, and King Charles VIII of France is said to have been astonished by the wealth of dancing at the Courts when he visited Italy in 1494. The violin became the dancing-master's instrument probably because of its very considerable carrying-power – the very quality which kept it out of refined drawing-rooms for so long, but made it a concerto soloist and virtuoso instrument at a later date.

During the 16th century we can follow the gradual movement towards freedom of personal expression in the arts, which resulted in a search for increasing contrast and dynamic range. With the growing importance of the secular order in European culture came the dramas of Hans Sachs, which broke away from the church mystery-play tradition, and the priest-baiting essays of Rabelais. Drama and contrast were sought in the startling lighting effects of the late Renaissance painters Tintoretto and Caravaggio, and in the antiphonal choirs of instruments and voices used by Venetian composers. St Mark's, the chapel of the Doges in Venice, with its two choirs and two organs, led the field of musical development within the Church. There Willaert (*c.* 1490–1562) followed by Andrea and Giovanni Gabrieli, experimented with multiple choirs, orchestras of various instruments, echo effects, solos and duets with instrumental accompaniment, and orchestral interludes. Claudio Merulo's virtuosity on the organ drew admiring crowds to the chapel, and his toccatas for the keyboard provide some of the earliest examples of instrumental virtuosity, a realm in which the violin was later to hold such a pre-eminent position.

Until the 16th century the human voice remained unrivalled as a vehicle for musical expression, and composers turned to it naturally for both secular and sacred compositions. But the voice is unsuited to dancing, and as Petrucci's method of printing with metal type began to spread instrumental compositions abroad, we find groups of dances for lute, strings, or other instruments – usually at first *pavan, saltarello*, and *piva*. The *saraband* followed, with the *galliard, pavane, courante, basse-danse*, and *branle* in France. Normally instruments apart from the lute were unspecified, but these compositions where instruments were freed from the restraint of doubling the vocal part paved the way for the more exciting and athletic range of the violin family.

The addition of an *e″* string to the violin increased its range and carrying power, so important for dancing, and complete string harmony was produced by using two viola lines. The viola varied greatly in size, and probably in tuning: pitch in the 16th century was so variable that the tuning of a stringed instrument often began with screwing up the top string as 'high as it can bear' (Agricola, 1528),[14] and tuning the other strings or instruments downwards from this rather arbitrary top note. But it seems unlikely that two distinct types of viola, the alto and tenor, regularly existed with different tunings. Zacconi (1592)[15] refers to four tuning-registers for the violin family (including F *c g d′* for the tenor) but always to *groups* of three tunings: it seems likely that the alto and tenor instruments were most frequently given the same tuning, while playing different parts. A string ensemble might even have three viola parts to one each of soprano and bass.

The smallest violin, *violino piccolo*, could be tuned a third, fourth, or even an octave above the violin and the cello was found in various sizes until the time of Stradivari. A double-bass to the family was made, but its clumsiness prevented it from becoming popular.

All the strings on these earliest members of the violin family would be made of gut, and tuned with far less tension than on today's violin, owing to the slightly shorter neck of the instrument, which projected straight out in the same plane as the belly, instead of being thrown back at an angle as it is today. A wedge was inserted between neck and finger-board to permit the latter to slant upwards towards the bridge. 16th-century violin and viola necks were broad and comparatively clumsy, and their peg-boxes slanted back at a more acute angle than on later instruments. Finger-boards were short, as the playing position of the violins held against the breast or shoulder and not gripped by the chin made the use of high positions a risky and difficult business: doubtless the technique was used experimentally, however, as it was well established on the viols.

To judge from 16th-century paintings, the position and shape of violin bridges was very varied; quite often they were placed much further towards the tail-piece than today, which would radically change the tone. The sound obtained from the slacker gut strings would be less penetrating than modern violin or viola tone, and the lowest string of each instrument was rarely used (owing to its coarse sound) until the 18th century when strings wound with wire became widely accepted. Vibrato, used almost continuously in modern technique, was an ornament reserved mainly for long notes, and the short bow with yielding hair would make impossible the kind of legato-playing obtainable today.

We have no bows from the 16th century, only pictures, as bows were cheap enough to discard when improvements took place. Bows were convex, like the archer's bow, until the end of the century, held palm downwards for the violin family, at the frog or some distance towards the middle of the bow. The manner of holding probably varied widely according to the size and balance of bow used and the type of music performed. Sometimes the thumb would be placed on the hair of the bow, allowing the player to regulate the hair tension. Three fingers were then placed on the stick; this hold becoming known as the 'French grip' and persisting in France until the middle of the 18th century. The Italians preferred a hold somewhat similar to the modern method, as shown in some sketches by Lodovico Carracci (1555–1619). The four fingers and thumb are placed on the stick itself, at the nut, with the thumb straight and the bow running across the second joint of each finger.

The violin and viola, unlike the viol, would obtain a natural accentuation on the down-bow. This happens on all instruments using overhand bowing: on the viol, the up-bow is if anything a little stronger. The give of the bow-hair would cause a slight break before each new bow-stroke succeeded in making the string speak, giving a more detached style than today. Bows were usually short, especially the dance-music bows, and as straighter sticks began to replace the unwieldy convex bows, part of the hair at the point could not be used without the stick touching the string (Plate 20). A rudimentary nut appeared earlier than the bow 'head' which held the hair away from the stick at the point, and which is first depicted c. 1600. Most bow-hairs were fixed in tension, and they were tied or fixed to the stick in ways which would not produce such a broad ribbon of hair as on the modern bows. This too would affect the tone production, emphasising the upper partials and reducing the lower.

A typical 16th-century violinist or viola-player would in all probability be a professional, and therefore classed among the servants. He would play mainly for dancing in the European Courts, propping his short-necked instrument just above the breast and using only the top three strings in the first position. His tone would be quiet, reedy, and pure by present-day standards, lacking a true legato on account of the shortness of bow and a slight delay in making the gut strings speak, but possessing an articulation and accentuation ideal for dancing. He would avoid his lowest string because its tone was poor, and he might use a fingering nearer to the modern cello or to the viol than to the modern violin, especially if he played on one of the very large violas being made at the time. Using mainly separate bows, he might employ a semi-legato kind of *portato* stroke joining two or three notes into one bow, sometimes bringing the strongest beats on to a down-bow in this way. The size of his violin might vary from 13¾ inches to almost 14½ inches body-length instead of the 14 inches standard today, and if its appearance was particularly beautiful it could have been made in Brescia by Gasparo da Salò (1540–1609) or in Cremona by Andrea Amati (c. 1511–79).

Northern Italy was undoubtedly the centre of 16th-century violin-making, and leadership in the field passed rapidly from Brescia, home of the earliest violin painting and of Gasparo da Salò and his pupil Giovanni Paolo Maggini (c. 1580–1632), to Cremona. Here Andrea Amati founded a violin-making tradition culminating in the late 17th and early 18th centuries, when the house of the Amati family stood close to those of A. Stradivari, Guarneri del Gesù, Carlo Bergonzi, Francesco Ruggieri, and Lorenzo Storioni.

Andrea Amati's date of birth was proved by Carlo Bonetti (1938) to have been before 1511, and his death before 1580: in spite of this, almost all modern reference works on the violin give 1535–1611 as his dates. His violins therefore precede those of Gasparo da Salò, and although it is just possible that he served some kind of apprenticeship in Brescia as tradition has it, all his known instruments were made in Cremona. However, the three-string violin painted at Brescia by Ferrari in 1530 might just conceivably have been made by Andrea Amati or by his unknown teacher. Two violins, attributed to Amati, dated 1542 and 1546, were reported during the 19th century to have been converted from three strings to four, but there is no proof of this. Some early four-string instruments still exist in playing order, however, a large viola (1574) and a small violin (1564; Plate 12) in the Ashmolean Museum, and a violin in Carlisle City Museum. All these instruments have the arms of France on the back, and may have been members of a set of thirty-eight instruments (twelve large- and twelve small-pattern violins, six violas, and eight basses) which are said to have been ordered by Charles IX of France (1560–74), showing the extent of Andrea's fame.

The surviving instruments show Andrea's work to have been very beautiful, with rather high arching, wide purfling, and a small but very sweet, pure tone. His translucent varnish varied from golden-brown to amber, and the maple he used for ribs and back had a beautiful marbled grain. F. Farga[16] points out that this wood, which came mainly from the Balkan forests, was imported by the Venetians for oar-making. Amati, a rich man, could afford to visit Venice and buy all his requirements, as eastern resins and dyes of all kinds were obtainable in this great commercial market. Andrea Amati took great care in choosing the wood for his instruments, and in preparing and applying a varnish which has lasted until the present day. His meticulous work laid the foundations of the greatest school of violin-making, and Corelli is said to have preferred his Andrea Amati violin, made before 1580, above all others.

The great Brescian makers, Gasparo da Salò and his pupil Maggini, aimed at producing a large sound rather than the sweetness and purity obtained by A. Amati, and their instruments are therefore often larger and flatter. Gasparo Bertolotti, called Gasparo da Salò, made more violas than violins, using a more massive outline than the Amatis, with strong wood and a dark, glowing varnish. His sound-holes were long, wide-open, and upright, and he occasionally used the double purfling favoured by his pupil Maggini (Plate 14).

By the end of the 16th century these manifestly superior instruments were replacing the shrill rebecs, not only in Italy but all over Europe, as accompaniments for weddings, festivals, and court dancing, and even in the churches as an accompaniment for the Mass. Their function at first, like their technique, would be derived from their nearest ancestors, the rebec and *lira da braccio*, and music would be handed down from player to player or from instrument to instrument, or read from vocal parts when voices were doubled. Music printing was still costly, and many musicians could not read music, but probably most of them could improvise upon well-known melodies. Very little music for violins was written down before 1600, and our knowledge of the amount and type of music played is derived from such sources as contemporary pictures, descriptions, and account books.

In Italy, for example, there are records from mid-century of payments made to violinists at weddings, and in theatres, where they supplied *intermedi* between scenes or acts. The accounts of Emmanuele Filiberto, Duke of Savoy (1528–80), quoted by David Boyden,[17] show frequent references to violinists, who must have played at dinners and social occasions. There is one reference to a woman violinist in Germany. Music-making was clearly an important aspect of the Duke's Court at all times, and it is likely that similar circumstances in various Courts of Italy enhanced that country's lead in musical fashion.

Perhaps the most important centre of musical progress was Venice, where Giovanni Gabrieli became organist of St Mark's, succeeding his uncle, Andrea, in 1586. Giovanni was the first composer to exploit the contrasted sonorities of choirs of instruments balanced with or opposed to choirs of voices. By doublings at the octave he produced wind sonorities which sound exciting even today, and his *Sonata pian' e forte* (1597) alternates instrumental groups for dynamic contrast, uniting them for a climax; a revolutionary step in instrumental writing. He only once used the two-instrument continuo, in the *Sonata con tre violini e basso se piace*, but his works belong more to the Baroque than to the Renaissance: the fact that violins rather than viols were often specified in this very forward-looking music was a significant pointer in the history of the violin family.

The marriage of Catherine de' Medici to the Duc d'Orléans in 1533 strengthened an already considerable artistic link between Italy and France, especially after she became Queen in 1547. Italian dancers led by Pompeo Diobono of Milan were brought to Paris in 1554 by the French Marshal, and the following year they were joined by a group of Italian violinists. Among these was one Baltazarini di Belgiojoso, who was known as 'the finest violinist in Christendom'.[18] Beaujoyeulx, as he became known in France, brought the Milanese tradition of court festivities to France and absorbed the theories of the Académie de Musique et de Poésie, which aimed at combining music, verse, and movement. Probably his most spectacular undertaking was the ballet for a royal wedding in 1581, the *Balet Comique de le Royne*. An illustrated description was printed and distributed afterwards, so we have a good idea of the lavishness of this spectacle, which cost 3,600,000 francs and was made up of a mixture of music, song, dance, and declamation. The earliest known printed violin music survives from this performance, two sets of dances being for ten 'violins' (presumably violins I and II, violas I and II, and bass). The players were dressed in white satin decorated with golden tinsel and provided with egret plumes. At this date musicians in the employ of the French Court were listed as part of the *écurie* (= literally stable), but during the reign of Charles IX the band of violins moved up one social step, so that by 1609 they were referred to as the twenty-two 'violons ordinaires de la chambre du Roy'.

Although Italian violins were the most famous and costly, and used all over Europe, France had already well-established centres of violin-making during the 16th century, at Paris, Mirecourt, and Lyons. Jambe de Fer's treatise containing the earliest printed description of a four-string violin was printed in Lyons, a town with very close trade connections with Milan, and in Gaspar Duiffoprugcar Lyons had a famous instrument-maker who may have made violins.

In England there is no record of violin-making as early as this, although after 1550 Italian violins and violinists became established as part of *The King's Musick*. Some of the musicians, like Ambrose Lupo, played both viol and violin. 'Musicke of Violenze' preceded a performance of the play *Gorboduc* given before Queen Elizabeth in 1561, and the Earl of Leicester owned a 'chest of five violens' in 1583. 'Apt for voices or viols' was the English equivalent of 'per cantar e sonar', a frequent 16th-century caption showing the close link between instrumental and vocal writing of the period. But by 1599 (very soon after Gabrieli's *Sonata pian'e forte* which calls for a single violin within a wind ensemble) we have an English collection of dances mentioning the violin in its title, *Pavans, Galliards, Almains and other short Aeirs both grave and light in five parts for Viols, Violins or other Musicall Wind Instruments*.

Shakespeare's contemporaries Byrd, Morley, and Gibbons were more interested in vocal than instrumental forms, favouring the madrigal when it was already in decline in Italy. But British keyboard works showed a new emancipation of instrumental writing unrivalled in

Europe, as early as 1575 (The Mulliner Book), and Britain's leading instrumentalists, John Bull (*c.* 1562–1628) on organ and virginals and John Dowland (1562–1626) on the lute, opened new vistas of instrumental potentiality, as brilliant soloist or subtle accompaniment to a solo vocal line.

If Brantôme is to be believed, violins were quite common in Scotland as early as 1561, when Mary Queen of Scots arrived in Edinburgh from France. He reports that 'five or six hundred scoundrels of the town serenaded her with wretched violins and small rebecs'.[19] But in Spain and Germany references to violins before 1600 are surprisingly rare. Spain's domination of the Italian states after 1559 must have led to cultural exchanges, but the only traces of a violin-playing tradition are found in a few paintings towards the end of the century. However, it would be surprising if a cultural climate which produced Cervantes and El Greco did not have its outstanding musicians as well: Morales and Vittoria were important composers of church music and Antonio de Cabezón (1510–66) a pioneer of keyboard composition, particularly in his use of unbroken variations.

A famous German painting by Mielich (between 1565 and 1570) shows that the violin family was in use at the Bavarian Court, but no evidence has been found of a violin-making tradition in Germany, Poland, or the Netherlands before 1600 – indeed, such small indications as have been found point to the importing of violin traditions from Italy, except for Agricola's unexplained reference to the 'Polish fiddle' in 1545, and the Stralsund burgomaster's four 'polnische Geiger'[20] mentioned in 1555.

By the close of the 16th century the violin family was still considered unsuitable for the hands of the gentry, but it was gaining in importance as an adjunct to court and town festivities. The exact size and pitch of the various members were not finally established, but the tradition of holding the instrument on the shoulder and using overhand bowing clearly separated the violin from the viol, and gave a lively accentuation which was part of its special appeal.

Other instruments were already giving a lead in breaking away from the vocal domination of the previous centuries, and with the birth of opera and ballet, and the Venetian experiments in orchestral tone-colours, the way was open by 1600 for the emergence of the violin family as the basis of Western instrumental composition.

NOTES

1 10 Bachmann.
2 ibid. p. 29.
3 21 Boyden, p. 21.
4 ibid.
5 194 Winternitz.
6 ibid. pp. 17–18.
7 21 Boyden, pp. 21–2.
8 ibid. p. 25.
9 ibid. p. 18.
10 107 Leipp, p. 31.
11 21 Boyden, p. 25.
12 ibid. p. 28.
13 ibid. p. 32.
14 ibid. p. 70, again in 137 Playford, p. 112.
15 ibid. p. 42.
16 54 Farga, p. 29.
17 21 Boyden, p. 60.
18 68 Guest, p. 16.
19 21 Boyden, p. 59.
20 ibid. p. 40.

CHAPTER 2

Founders of the Violin Tradition: 1600–50

THE 17TH CENTURY and the first half of the 18th cover roughly the period now referred to as the Baroque Era: a period during which the violin family took a position of pre-eminence in Western music which it has never lost.

Although it would be a mistake to imagine any clear dividing-line between Renaissance and Baroque, there was definitely a feeling, about 1600, of the introduction of a new style of musical composition, referred to as *stile moderno*, as opposed to *stile antico* which was preserved after the style of Palestrina. Composers consciously selected their style of writing, in much the same way as Richard Strauss and Arnold Schönberg chose the old and the new styles of the early 20th century.

This conflict of styles, the old, contrapuntal, strictly regulated church idiom and the new expressive representation of the meaning of words, made composers truly style-conscious for the first time in musical history. From the sense of contrasting vocal styles the transition was rapidly made to a contrast between vocal and instrumental idiom, between church and secular writings, and between group-writing where all voices held an equal, interweaving importance and group-writing where the upper melody was related to the bass alone, with the middle parts merely filling in harmonies (as with the *basso continuo*). Mersenne mildly indicated the new feeling for instrumental style with the words

> For although each instrument can serve for playing whatever piece one wishes, nevertheless experience teaches that some succeed better than the others, when they are played on certain instruments, and that what is good on one is not so agreeable or so suitable on another,[1]

while Agazzari is already much more definite about violin-writing in 1607 (*Of Playing upon a Bass with All Instruments*):

> The violin requires beautiful passages, distinct and long, with playful figures and little echoes and imitations repeated in several places, passionate accents, mute [Boyden gives 'changing'] strokes of the bow, groups, trills etc.[2]

In the new style, tonality, with a home key to which each piece or group of pieces returns, gradually replaced the less tonic-centred key-systems of Renaissance modes, and harmonic progressions gravitated towards a tonal key centre, instead of resulting from the intervals produced by linear modal writing. This harmonic progression became the basis of musical tonality and form for the next 300 years, and modern audiences have to free themselves from this habitual urge towards a tonal centre fully to enjoy Renaissance and pre-Renaissance music.

Rhythmically the Baroque composers emancipated themselves first of all from the even flow of beats and mathematical rules of proportion in the *stile antico* by making the music subservient to the written word, and the voice also led the way to idiomatic writing in the discovery of its remarkable virtuoso qualities during the early Baroque. Vocal declamation and recitative (one of the rare instances where theory preceded practice, as it was created by a group of intellectuals, the *Camerata* of Florence) opened the way to monodic writing and opera, from which the violins were to gain a new unity as accompanists and a new virtuosity in imitation of the solo singers.

The viols suffered from this increased interest in a melodic line set against a harmonic bass, as the consort of viols was the ideal instrumental group for the old concept of equally blending linear counterpoint. By 1650 the viol family was clearly being overtaken in importance by the violins, although viols lingered on for a long time in England and longest of all in France.

In 17th-century scores it becomes increasingly obvious that members of the violin family are required, in spite of a persistent vagueness of nomenclature. The term *viola da braccio* still separated the violins from the viols, but could include the *violino piccolo*, a small instrument tuned higher than the violin, as well as the violin proper; the viola tuned as today and referred to as 'alto' or 'tenor'; the bass (cello) of the family tuned C G *d a* (Praetorius) or BB flat F *c g* (Mersenne); and another 'tenor' instrument sometimes called a 'bass', but tuned upwards from F or G. This was probably like a small cello in appearance, was played like one, and was very occasionally substituted for the cello. By the end of the 17th century it had pretty well disappeared, and the middle parts of a normal string ensemble might consist of two or three parts for violas of different sizes, tuned identically but using the register most effective for their size. Gradually a second violin part was to replace the highest viola line, so that the modern quartet consists illogically of two sopranos, alto, and bass instead of paralleling the vocal quartet.

The violin might be referred to as a treble, soprano, or descant *viola da braccio* or *Geige*, but a *Discant-Geig* tuned a fourth higher than the violin and another tuned a whole octave higher are mentioned by Praetorius. It is not advisable to make definite deductions from the clefs used, as Monteverdi, for instance, used both treble and soprano (first line = C) clefs for the ordinary violin parts. The violas might find middle C on the third or fourth line, while in France the normal practice for the violin was to use the G clef first line instead of second. Occasionally tablatures were used, but this practice never became fashionable as it did with the lute.

A source of considerable conjecture has been Monteverdi's listing of instruments for the orchestra of his opera *Orfeo* (1607) with its reference to *violini piccoli alla francesca*; but more momentous than the detail of the instruments required is the fact that the orchestra was listed and imaginatively exploited, as it was to an even greater extent in his *Scherzi musicali* of the same year. This was the leap forward into the stylistic exploration of the Baroque which first asserted the coming importance of the violin family and heralded the vital part Italy was to play in all aspects of the violin's development.

In musical matters the acknowledged leader of Europe was Italy. Other countries took over pre-eminence in the visual arts, with Rembrandt, Poussin, and Rubens becoming the leading 17th-century painters, and the French theatre blossoming into prime importance with Corneille, Molière, and Racine, as the English and Spanish traditions declined. But Italy had a musical tradition which abounded in experiment and discoveries, leading to the new feeling of personal expression sought in the Baroque era, and Italy's leading composer, Claudio Monteverdi (1567–1643), was a man of genius who could unite the experimental ideas and creations of his contemporaries into musical forms of lasting value.

No other country was so far producing violins to rival those of Italy, where in Brescia, Gasparo da Salò's pupil G. P. Maggini was making more refined and ornate instruments, usually on a similar pattern to those of his teacher (to whom he is said to have been apprenticed at the age of seven) but occasionally copied from Girolamo Amati. His models tend to be long and broad, with long upright sound-holes, but some of the violas are slender. Double purfling and ornaments on the back of his violins were characteristics frequently copied by 19th-century forgers: the backs of genuine instruments being made sometimes of poplar or pear-wood instead of maple, and the scrolls rather small with half a turn less than became the later tradition. The tone of

Maggini's violins is often powerful and suited to concert work, but the few extant violas vary very considerably as to size, tone, and proportions.

In Cremona, Andrea Amati's two sons, Antonio (Antonius; 1540– ?) and Girolamo (Hieronymus; 1561–1630),[3] continued their father's tradition, often signing their instruments together. They used lower arching than Andrea, and well-seasoned wood, particularly maple with a small curl, often cutting the back in one piece. The arching slopes down to a concave chamfer towards the edges, and the purfling is elegantly finished, reaching almost to the ends of the corners. Earlier instruments have a reddish varnish; later they preferred a thin, light amber colour. The size of their instruments is sometimes a little below today's standard length, although the violas vary enormously, and the tone, while very beautiful, is not always powerful enough for modern concert performance.

The most important of all the Amatis, Nicola (1596–1684), not only produced violins famous today for their superb workmanship and tone (particularly his 'grand pattern' instruments) but exerted possibly the widest influence of any single maker through his unique position of eminence in the craft. An interesting letter[4] to Galileo, the astronomer, from Father Micanzio of Venice points out, in 1637–38, that a violin for his nephew should preferably originate from Cremona, not Brescia, and it was to Nicola Amati in Cremona that the most brilliant violin-makers came to learn their craft. Among his pupils were Andrea Guarneri (c. 1626–98), founder of a dynasty comparable to that of the Amatis; G. B. Rogeri; Francesco Ruggieri; Paolo Grancino (founder of his own dynasty in Milan); and the greatest of all: Antonio Stradivari (c. 1648–1737).[5]

Although a number of instruments made before 1650 are in use today, their appearance and sound would differ in several respects when the Amatis were working. The approximate body-length of 14 inches was already fairly standard, although Maggini exceeded this and the Amatis sometimes reduced it a little; but violas were infinitely variable, as indeed they still tend to be. The string tension on the bridge would be considerably less than today, because all strings were made of gut and the old-style short neck projected straight out from the body of the instrument; so the bass-bar was thinner and lighter, and probably the sound-post narrower. Not until 1800 was the neck lengthened and tilted back on almost all old violins to give the extra power required for modern performance.

Peg-boxes might have a carved head instead of a scroll, after the viol

fashion, and bridges shown in contemporary paintings vary considerably, not only in design but in position: instead of being placed between
the central notches of the f-holes as today, they were often further down
towards the tail-piece. Mersenne, Kircher, and Praetorius all refer to the
existence of metal strings, but they were apparently not used on violins
until after 1700: this must have greatly reduced the speaking power of
the G string of the violin and the C string of the viola, especially as they
were slacker than today. Moving the bridge back to lengthen the string
would allow greater tension and reduce this weakness, but change the
tone-colour of the instrument.

17th-century violinists were fully aware of the use of high positions
(see above, p. xii) from the more advanced left-hand technique of the
viol-players, but on these early violins the finger-board was some $2\frac{1}{2}$
inches shorter than today: it was to be gradually extended as the higher
registers were explored, just as the bow was gradually lengthened when
greater sustaining power was required.

Unlike the violins, early bows were discarded as they went out of
fashion, and almost no specimens exist. From pictures, however, we
can trace a development in length from about 15 inches of playing hair
to the present $25\frac{1}{2}$ inches between the years 1600 and 1800. With the
division of styles emerging in the Baroque we see bow-lengths varying
for different purposes: dance bows needed to be short and light, as the
performer would be playing for extended periods and using mainly
quick strokes; while the new explorations into idiomatic violin-writing
encouraged a greater playing length capable of sustaining notes and
slurring groups of notes. Screw-knobs (Fig. 1) to alter the hair tension
and a head instead of a point at the tip (Plate 20) may have been devised
before 1650, but cannot definitely be claimed until the latter part of the
century, when the *crémaillère* (notched) bow was also used (Fig. 6A). The
hair was narrower than on the modern bow; Mersenne suggests eighty
to a hundred hairs, as opposed to 150 to 200 today.

The bow-stick was either straight or convex, round or octagonal, and
occasionally fluted. Snakewood was favoured, but brazil-wood and even
ebony are mentioned as early as *c.* 1631, in Pierre Trichet's *Traité des
Instruments de Musique*. Gradually the convexity was reduced and
strength with flexibility was sought, by experiments with various woods,
to add to the subtlety of bow-strokes obtainable on the violin. As it
became generally recognised that the stronger bow-stroke with the hand
held above the bow is the down-bow, the first instance of a bowing
discipline appeared with the 'Rule of Down-Bow' which held that down-
bows should be used for stressed notes, often the first in the bar. The

Italians and French followed this rule during the early 17th century, but as the Italians explored more rhapsodic forms, it became chiefly a characteristic of French dance music.

Monteverdi, himself a professional string-player, left a remarkable variety of techniques and effects requested in his scores considering the comparative youth of the violin and bow, but it must be remembered that the viol-players had already explored many of the possibilities of a basically very similar instrument, and that some of Monteverdi's virtuoso contemporaries, without having his creative musical genius, equalled or surpassed him in technical invention.

Two of these violinists, Carlo Farina (c. 1600–40) and Biagio Marini (c. 1597–1665), spent part of their lives in Germany, which was to be the main centre of technical exploration during the following half-century (1650–1700). Farina worked in Dresden and later Danzig; Marini moved from Venice to Brescia where he was director of music at the Church of Sant' Eufemia, before joining the household of Ferdinando Gonzaga in Parma. Four years later he moved to Munich, then to Düsseldorf, but he returned to Italy to spend the rest of his life in Ferrara and Milan.

A singer-composer in the service of the Medicis of Florence, Giulio Caccini (1545–1618) had a very strong indirect influence on violin composition: his affective embellishments and use of the *basso continuo* were rapidly imitated by string-composers, and he was one of the pioneers of opera before Monteverdi. Monteverdi himself, son of a physician, and pupil of the strict contrapuntist Ingegneri, was both a string-player and a singer, serving in these capacities at the Court of Vicenzo Gonzaga in Mantua. His dismissal from Mantua was closely followed by his appointment to the most coveted musical position in the country, that of chapel-master at St Mark's, Venice, where he took holy orders and remained until his death. His sense of vocal and instrumental colour infused new dramatic impact into the 'new music' styles used by Peri and Caccini, and he not only laid the foundation of the traditional Baroque orchestra, with a string and continuo nucleus, but employed it for dramatic effect by using tremolo and pizzicato effects in *Il Combattimento di Tancredi e Clorinda* (1624), and brought the opera orchestra into the church with his Vespers of 1610.

Farina's *Capriccio Stravagante* of 1627 uses technical devices which one rarely meets before 19th century scores – *col legno, sul ponticello, sul tastiera,* and *glissando* – in his efforts to imitate animal and bird sounds. Low positions were most commonly used, but Uccellini, who became chapel-master in Modena, wrote as high as the sixth position (see above,

p. xii). The Italians favoured the custom of resting the violin on the shoulder, and probably steadied the instrument with the chin as they shifted downwards. If the thumb supports the violin and always shifts before the fingers do, however, it is possible to make most shifts without holding the instrument with the chin.

Left-hand techniques derived from the viols and imitating keyboard writing were the double and triple stops used particularly by Marini and referred to by him as *a modo da lira*. The Germans were particularly interested in this form of virtuosity, and Marini's opus 8 (composed 1626, published 1629) is an outstanding example of the early recognition of the violinist's ability to produce fairly rapid successions of thirds and sixths, sometimes using *scordatura* (the retuning of one or more strings) to aid the fingering. The fourth finger was not very popular at this period, owing to the rather fat neck of the violin, but it must have been used with considerable agility in the double-stop passages of Marini, Farina, and Grandi. After these virtuoso compositions, multiple stops fell out of favour with Italian composers for about fifty years.

Caccini, in his introduction to the *Nuove Musiche* (1602), lists a number of effects with which the human voice could more movingly express the meanings of the written word, and the Italian violinist with his gradually lengthening and more responsive bow was not slow to imitate these effects. The two methods of holding the bow mentioned in Chapter 1 persisted during the 17th century, as French violinists continued to be interested mainly in dance music and preferred the firm grip with the thumb on the hair, while the Italians were experimenting with *portato*, *tremolo*, and swelling and dying within a note; techniques made easier by their more subtle finger contact with the wood of the bow. Not that the Italian string-playing was necessarily quieter and less resonant in sound than the French: Rognoni (1620) speaks of the bow being 'well pressed to the *viola da brazzo* as the good players do'.[6] And as he mentions as many as fifteen notes slurred within one bow-stroke, the shorter bow at that time would require steady pressure to make all the notes speak.

Rognoni also gives directions for a *portato* arm-movement within a slur, 'the motion of the bow arm beat every note as if it were skipping along',[7] possibly imitating an effect described in Caccini's *Nuove Musiche* and occurring fairly frequently in vocal music of the period.

Syncopated slurrings were used by Farina, Lombard rhythms (♩♩.) were often slurred, and measured and unmeasured *tremoli* were written out in the works of Farina and Marini long before 1638, when Monteverdi claimed to have invented the measured *tremolo* to express warlike emotions.

Most ornaments were written out in full before 1650, the shorthand signs not being generally known, but 'tr' was used as an abbreviation for *tremolo*, which meant our modern trill using two notes. Confusion is increased by the fact that the word *trillo* referred to what is now called *tremolo* – rapid repetition of the same note.

Vibrato and slurs were regarded as ornaments during the 17th century; Mersenne uses the sign —꜔꜔— to indicate vibrato for violin or lute, and suggests that on the lute, the thumb should not touch the instrument's neck, as this would impede the vibrato. The same technique applied to the violin, however, would leave the instrument unsupported, unless it was allowed to fall into the crook of the thumb. This could be one of the reasons for the rarity of singing melodies in violin-music of the period, which copied the human voice in so many other ways. The short bows were another factor making rapid passagework (*passaggi*) and leaping patterns (often added *extempore* to a given melody) more characteristic of 17th-century violin-music than was the *cantabile* melodic line. Occasionally the direction *come sta senza passaggi* was added to restrain the performer from adding his own ornaments.

Mersenne greatly admired violin tone with vibrato, which must have been in his mind when he wrote the description

> The tone of the violin is the most ravishing, for those who play it perfectly . . . sweeten it as they wish and render it inimitable by certain tremblings which delight the mind.[8]

Although dynamic markings apart from *piano* and *forte* were rare in the early 17th century, the subtlety of nuance obtainable on the violin was soon recognised and compared favourably with contemporary keyboard instruments by Mersenne and others. Monteverdi's use of *forte* and *piano* 'within one bow-stroke' is probably an early way of writing a *diminuendo*, as is his reference to a 'diminishing bow-stroke' in *Il Combattimento di Tancredi e Clorinda*, but the most frequent use of printed dynamics was the indication of echo effects; otherwise, performers were left to supply their own nuance.

17th-century composers inherited a system of rhythm and tempo based on the *tactus*, a generally accepted steady beat, probably about M.M.60, usually represented by a written semibreve. Unlike the modern time-signature plus tempo indication, the signs used at the beginning of the music were to indicate the relationship of the printed notes to this stable beat: they were therefore indications of tempo rather than of number of beats in a bar. *Alla breve*, for instance, meant that the notes should be played twice as fast as with the time-signature **C**.

With the pervasive increase in freedom of expression during the 17th century came a natural impulse to shake off this tradition which restricted composers to speeds which were multiples or divisions of **o** = M.M.60. The first tempo indications to appear were fast or slow, the moderate tempo of the *tactus* being implicit if no contrary indication was made. Banchieri (1605)[9] lists *adagio, allegro, veloce, presto, più presto, prestissimo*. Mersenne suggests a kind of pendulum for fixing relative speeds, an idea realised by Maelzel nearly two centuries later.

Certain traditions of accent and of rhythmic alteration of note-values persisted throughout Baroque music, until the more precise musical language of the Classical period produced ways of indicating these patterns in the notation. Dotted notes might be lengthened to double dots or shortened to make a triplet effect, according to the mood of the piece, and the practice of dividing two groups of three beats into three of two beats, especially before a cadence, was a favourite rhythmical device emphasised by the bass line and known as the *hemiola*, often brought out by use of the 'Rule of Down-Bow'.

During the 20th century determined efforts have been made to explore these lost traditions of rhythm, tempo, and notation, with a resulting increase in accuracy of interpretation of early music. But opportunities of hearing 17th-century music as the composers must have conceived it are very rare. Even when the violin is restored to its original condition and stringing, it is difficult for a modern instrumentalist to play within a pitch-system where a sharp is lower than its enharmonic flat. The actual pitch of keyboard instruments varied enormously from country to country or even from church to church during the 17th century, and Mersenne speaks of viol music being played a tone lower in England than in France 'so as to render the harmony softer and more charming'.[10]

Played on modern instruments, however, Monteverdi's music has been restored to the concert and opera repertoire of the 20th century, and there is instrumental music by his contemporaries which is worthy of revival. To the modern ear many of the early groups of dances and pieces entitled 'sonata' lose appeal on account of the extreme brevity of their movements, but the fugal movements soon acquired a quite substantial length, and Marco Uccellini (*c.* 1603–80) extended his sonatas to more than one hundred bars by the use of variation techniques. Dance movements were played in pairs, usually one of a moderate duple metre contrasting with another of a quicker triple metre: later a third might be added in a still faster tempo. *Passamezzo* and *saltarello, pavane* and *galliarde*, and later *allemande* and *courante*, were popular pairings which were to appear as part of the *sonata da camera* later in the 17th century.

The terms *sonata da camera* (chamber sonata) and *sonata da chiesa* (church sonata) emerged before 1650, but served at first to differentiate the places suitable for their performance rather than to indicate any recognised form or grouping. The earliest pieces entitled *sonata* were mainly one-movement works derived from the contrapuntal but light-hearted *canzona*, whose themes were occasionally derived from popular songs. As the term became more generally applied to works for one, two, or three melodic instruments and continuo, however, the practice of grouping contrasted movements under the one title increased, and the form became especially associated with the violin family. The custom of counting the keyboard and cello or other bass instrument as one continuo line resulted in a puzzling system of nomenclature, persisting into modern terminology, as the 'trio sonata' usually requires four players.

Giovanni Gabrieli's sonata for three violins and continuo (1597) may have been the model for the sonata-composers of the next fifty years, of whom Merula, Rossi, Grandi, Marini, Farina, Uccellini, and Fontana were probably the leading composers for violin. Sonatas for two violins usually opposed the two players contrapuntally or united them in a high register with closely spaced chords and frequent part-crossings. In sonatas for four violins the two pairs might be opposed in the style of the later concerto, but it was the 'solo' sonata for one violin and continuo which allowed the fullest extension of the instrument's technical capabilities referred to earlier.

Variations on a ground bass formed an important part of early Italian Baroque chamber music, providing movements much longer than the simple binary or ternary forms of the dances. Popular Italian melodies such as *la Romanesca, il Ruggiero, la Scatola,* and *la Bergamasca* would frequently be found repeated in the bass, sometimes in the treble. The very repetitiveness of the basic material led to extra ingenuity in devising lively figuration, a pastime enjoyed by composers of instrumental chaconnes and passacaglias in later centuries. Sonatas were sometimes named after the ground-bass theme, more rarely given imaginative titles such as Tarquinio Merula's *La Gallina*, based on the clucking of a hen, and Farina's *la Cingara, la Capriole,* and *la Desperata,* all of a programmatic nature.

Italian composers for the violin before 1650 are already too frequent to consider in detail, whereas a violinist-composer from any other

European country before 1650 holds an automatic position of eminence owing to his lack of rivals. Such a composer was the German, Kindermann, who wrote solo sonatas after the Italian style, probably influenced by Farina who lived in Dresden, using basic violin techniques and effectively contrasting movements. One of his solo sonatas uses *scordatura* throughout, a practice favoured in Germany longer than in other countries.

Germany was the country closest to Italy in the advancement of violin technique, although during the early part of the 17th century the Thirty Years War impeded cultural development. Leading composers such as Hassler and Schein were not especially interested in the new forms and sounds conceived by the Italians for the violin, but Moser[11] refers to the violinist-composer Schop as making great technical demands on the violinist. Heinrich Schütz (1585–1672), a German pupil of Gabrieli and Monteverdi, requests musicians unfamiliar with 'modern music and its notes of lesser value, and also the steady broadened way of bowing which we Germans have'[12] to take lessons before performing his *Symphoniae sacrae*, opus 10. This may indicate that the rapid passage-work used by Italian violinists was until then not widespread in Germany: certainly, published works by German composers were mainly in dance forms using older techniques, and only in double-stopping techniques were they to take the lead later in the century.

No German, French, or English violin-maker of repute emerged before 1650, and the French and English traditions of violin performance lagged far behind those of Italy. Fewer Italian musicians were active in France than in England or Germany during the 17th century, and in contrast to the rival cultures of the many Italian Courts, Paris was France's sole cultural centre. The solo sonata did not reach this centre until Couperin introduced it in 1692, and although the violin gained in respectability with the formation of the *24 Violons du Roy* in 1626, Trichet (1631) speaks of the violin as 'principally used for the dance, balls, ballet, mascarades, serenades, aubades, feasts and other joyous pastimes'.[13]

Mersenne refers to the violin as 'the King of Instruments', and tell us 'Those who have heard the Twenty-four Violins of the King avow that they have never heard anything more ravishing or more powerful.'[14] He also mentions the use of fourth position, but points out that French violinists played on the top two strings most of the time. This would give a very limited compass, and it is evident that French violinists did not explore virtuoso passage-work, since the violinist Maugars was astonished by the fast violin-playing he heard in Italy in 1639.

In England, the situation was somewhat similar: there was one central Court, where the violin was used mainly for dancing. In 1621, Thomas Lupo was appointed 'Composer for the violin' by James I, and by 1631 there were fourteen players of 'violins' (including the lower members of the violin family) in the Royal Band of Charles I. Court masques were a favourite diversion, with violins prominent among the accompanying bands, and violins were sometimes called for in printed music such as Dowland's *Lachrimae* (1604) and Adson's *Courtly Masquing Ayres* (1611 and 1621). Although the Italian sonata did not appear in England until much later, there is evidence of violinistic writing in some of the chamber music collected in *Musica Britannica*, and it seems likely that the violin's role as a chamber-music instrument was explored sooner in England than in France. John Jenkins (1592–1678) showed the gradual influx of Italian influence as he ceased to write elaborations on *canti firmi* for groups of viols and turned to three-part fantasias in which the viols were replaced by violins. A later critic (Roger North in *The Musicall Gramarian, c.* 1726) was to complain of his lack of 'fire & fury, such as the Itallian music affects. In their stabbs & Stoccatas', and of 'the manner of movement' which was 'cheifly (as it were) going up & downe staires, and had less of the sault or Itterations than ye Itallians have'.[15] But Jenkins, Lawes, and Coperario wrote some chamber music idiomatically suited to the violin, without knowledge of the Italian technical developments which were to astound them on Baltzar's visit to England *c.* 1655, and without regard to those who, like Mace, complained of the violin's '*High-Priz'd Noise* . . . rather fit to make a Mans *Ears Glow*, and fill his *Brains full of Frisks*, &c., than to *Season, and Sober his Mind, or Elevate his Affection to Goodness.*'[16] Only after the period of political unrest covering the Civil War and the Commonwealth was the cultural climate in England to become settled enough to absorb the new Italian notions of sonata and opera.

In the other European countries before 1650, with the possible exception of Austria, which was closely linked to Germany and accepted the sonata form without producing any outstanding violinist or violin composer, the picture regarding the violin was much the same: until the new Italian principles could be copied and absorbed, the violin remained in the hands of the dance-musicians.

NOTES

[1] 117 Mersenne, p. 235.
[2] 175 Strunk, p. 429.
[3] 21 Boyden, p. 109, n. 3.

[4] ibid. p. 109.
[5] ibid. pp. 505–7.
[6] ibid. p. 153.
[7] ibid. p. 165.
[8] 117 Mersenne, p. 24.
[9] 21 Boyden, p. 184.
[10] 117 Mersenne, p. 41.
[11] 21 Boyden, p. 136.
[12] 175 Strunk, p. 437.
[13] 21 Boyden, p. 137.
[14] 117 Mersenne, p. 235.
[15] 130 North, p. 24.
[16] 113 Mace, p. 236.

CHAPTER 3

The First Virtuosi: 1650–1700

THE SECOND HALF of the 17th century shows the main musical initiative still held by various Italian Courts, while Germany, Austria, France, and England were to produce composers of genius who imparted a distinctive national flavour to forms originated by the Italians. For the first time an outstanding non-Italian violin-maker emerges in the Austrian Jacob Stainer (1617–83), whose violins fetched a higher price than those of Nicola Amati or Stradivari in early 18th-century London, and were used by Veracini, Locatelli, and J. S. Bach.

With the gradual increase in tonality apparent in Corelli's music we have the first violin literature which is easily appreciated by modern audiences educated mainly within a tonal system, and the Italian *bel canto* style, which freed the melodic qualities of the voice from the dictatorship of the words, was to pave the way for songlike melodies now considered so much a part of the violin's repertoire. In opera, cantata, and oratorio, Italian composers such as Carissimi, Cavalli, and Scarlatti developed the violin family's importance in the orchestra and as obbligato instruments, while an Italian, Lully, gave Paris a leading reputation for orchestral precision with ballet and opera. England produced a genius of her own in Henry Purcell, whose melodic invention outshone even the Italians, while Austria and Germany took the lead in exploring certain aspects of violin technique with the complicated double stops and *scordatura*, bariolage, and high positions found in the sonatas of Biber and Walther.

The musical consolidation of the sonata and the development of *concerto grosso* and solo concerto forms appear to have occupied Italian violinist-composers more than the further exploration of the instrument's technical capabilities during the second half of the century: it is probably no coincidence that Stradivari was seeking to make a violin of more powerful tone without loss of beauty to the ear at the time when one solo violin was first required to stand out against a group of violins in the concerto. The bow, too, was the object of wide experimentation at this time, and rare specimens remain, showing that Corelli would have available a bow of considerable subtlety on which great attention to detail of balance and ornamentation had been lavished.

The other principal change in the role of the 17th-century violin was its final emancipation from dance music and acceptance as a 'respectable' instrument, as amateurs in most countries (France being the notable exception) forsook the viols and took to playing violins. Simple music and treatises for amateur violinists became available, but the viola was falling into disrepute, as it was not included in the most popular chamber form, the trio sonata.

Before 1700, when Corelli's twelve solo sonatas (opus 5) were published, the sonata had taken a recognised form with four or five contrasting movements, of abstract forms in the *sonata* or *sonata da chiesa* but including dances in the *sonata da camera*.

At first Venice, the main publishing centre, continued to hold a principal role in sonata development. One of the homes of the new *bel canto* style with its very simple, tonal harmonies, Venice was quick to accept the new ideas in Cavalli's operas and Carissimi's oratorios: from these and the vocal cantatas chamber music received fresh life. Alessandro Stradella (1642?–82) and Giovanni Legrenzi (1626–90), both eminent composers in the vocal forms as well as of violin music, composed string sonatas using basic violin techniques without any of the stunts favoured by Farina, and raised the form to a new musical importance by their use of thoroughly instrumental themes treated with fugal ingenuity and considerable harmonic interest. The sonata's derivation from the *canzona* can be seen in Legrenzi's use of the same thematic material in the first and last movements; the influence of *bel canto* is apparent in his slow movements – particularly the sarabandes, and his skilful use of chaconne basses set an example for many later composers. That Bach and Handel were impressed by Legrenzi's chamber music is apparent from the fact that they borrowed his fugue subjects.

During the latter part of the century Bologna became even more important than Venice as the centre of violin music, for here were the music chapel of San Petronio, famous for its instrumental accompaniments to church services, the *Accademia di Filarmonici* (founded in 1666), and two renowned publishers, Monti and Silvani. Cazzati, appointed director of the San Petronio chapel in 1657, left a considerable literature of string chamber music and greatly stimulated instrumental activity in Bologna, while his pupil G. B. Vitali wrote instrumental music which skilfully combines idiomatic instrumental writing with serious fugal technique. The first solo cello music by Domenico Gabrielli (*c.* 1659–90) was another product of 17th-century Bologna, Corelli's birthplace.

G. M. Bononcini in Modena, G. B. Bassani in Ferrara, and A. Veracini in Florence all contributed to the advancement of the trio sonata, Bononcini adding optional viola parts, as did some of his contemporaries; but the first peak of Italian chamber music was reached by a Bolognese composer who moved to Rome at the age of eighteen, Arcangelo Corelli (1653–1713).

Corelli was one of the few composers fortunate enough to be recognised as a master on the publication of his opus 1 (1681) and to live a life of luxury and renown thereafter. His output was singular in its restriction to certain categories; in all he published six collections, four of trio sonatas, one of solo sonatas (opus 5, 1700), and one of *concerti grossi* (opus 6). In the last category he may have been an innovator, as Muffat reports that Corelli's *concerti* were played in Rome as early as 1682; but in the sonata he took an already established form and gave to it a personal significance which has made his works part of the standard violin repertoire up to the present day.

In opera 1–4, Corelli refers to himself on the title-page as *il Bolognese*, probably referring to his four years of training which culminated in membership of Bologna's *Accademia di Filarmonici* in 1670. Most of the rest of his life was spent in Rome where he was held in the highest esteem, although he made little use of his wealth, and Handel considered him somewhat miserly in his habits. It was in Rome that Handel and Corelli met, and Corelli had to admit himself baffled by the fiery style of one of Handel's overtures, when Handel in a fury snatched Corelli's violin and played the part himself. On this occasion Corelli remained amiable, modest, and polite, and these characteristics are evident in his compositions. Important as a teacher as well as performer and composer, he taught many of the notable violinists of the next generation, including Francesco Geminiani, Pietro Locatelli, G. B. Somis, J.-B. Anet, and Pietro Castrucci.

Corelli's sonatas achieved no fewer than seventy-eight reprints during his lifetime, an unparalleled success. And although they may seem somewhat sedate to modern ears, there is little doubt that his performances of his own works aroused great excitement: Hawkins writes:

> A person who had heard him perform says that whilst he was playing on the violin, it was usual for his countenance to be distorted, his eyes to become as red as fire, and his eyeballs to roll as in agony.[1]

For the first six sonatas of opus 5 we are fortunate in having a set of ornaments 'composez par Mr. A. Corelli comme il les joue', published by Estienne Roger (Amsterdam) *c.* 1710, shortly followed by Walsh in

London. If these are not actually by Corelli they are at least representative of the practices of his time, as they were printed in about 1710. Bearing in mind that these particular ornaments were decried by Roger North in 1728 as 'vermin'[2] and a publisher's trick, it is still well worth the time of any student of Baroque chamber music to obtain the Joachim-Chrysander edition of opus 5 which reproduces these ornaments and see how much it reveals of 17th-century practice in composition, presentation, and performance in Italy.

Of the twelve sonatas in opus 5, the first six are of the church type, the next five of the chamber type, the very last being a set of twenty-three variations on the popular tune '*la Follia*'. The sonatas have four or five movements, and although movements in the church sonatas normally carry no dance titles, there are two obvious jigs, one of which (in sonata 5) is so entitled.

The continuo is described variously as *Violone o Cimbalo* and *Violone e Cimbalo*. This may have been because 'and' and 'or' were used indiscriminately, but there is evidence that the bass viol was sometimes used alone as a continuo line. However, in opus 1 and opus 3 Corelli specifies that viol and organ should be used, and it is clear from the words *tasto solo* found at various points in opus 5 that both instruments must be present, for here the keyboard-player leaves the violist alone and no figures are given. Probably an organ would be the keyboard instrument expected for all of Corelli's church sonatas, a harpsichord or spinet for the chamber sonatas.

From the beginning of opus 5 we can see the ways in which Corelli has sought increased length of movement without losing interest. The opening movement of the first sonata contains six short sections: *Grave, Allegro*, and *Adagio*, repeated with the violin silent in the repetition of the *Allegro*. In the first bar of the *Grave* we meet with the 17th-century Italian custom of placing a cross (+) above a note to indicate that an ornament would be appropriate. The player is free to choose the type of ornament, within the traditions of Corelli's time. For the modern interpreter, therefore, it is important to know that ornaments were usually slurred, that a repetition of the same phrase calls for the same ornament, that trills normally started on the upper note and sometimes ended with a turn or *Nachschlag*, and that consecutive trills were rare before 1700. The mordent normally started with the written note and used a semitone or tone below. Vibrato was also considered an ornament, but rarely indicated by a sign.

The practice of adding embellishments like those in the slow movements of opus 5, nos. 1–6 must have been widely accepted: in one instance in the Christmas Concerto Corelli finds it advisable to write *come sta* – play it as it stands – to prevent this practice. Sometimes quick movements as well as slow ones were decorated in the repeats, although the printed ornaments for opus 5 are limited to the slow movements of his church sonatas. His pupil Geminiani's edition of the same opus gives an opportunity of comparing a typically ornamented quick movement with the original.

From the beginning of opus 5, no. 1, it is apparent that Corelli either played his embellishments extremely quickly and lightly, or that he had a bow of considerably more length and sustaining power than was seen before 1650: there are sixteen notes within a slur in the second bar and twenty-three later. Pictures of bows are comparatively rare during this period, but a few actual specimens remain showing the experimentation and rapid development which was taking place. The bow used for the Italian sonata was much longer than the dance bow, and being longer was sometimes held further from the nut: it was light and strong, and in some ways more sensitive than the modern Tourte bow; modern violinists sometimes prefer to play 17th-century music with a replica of a contemporary bow. The Italian bow-hold with the thumb on the wood was gradually replacing the French method, while devices for tightening the hair were becoming more common.

By 1700 slurs were frequently indicated by the composer, especially in the slower movements: probably in the dance movements the violinist was expected to conform to the 'Rule of Down-Bow', still strictly held in France, which brought up-beats on to up-bows, down-beats on to down-bows. With the old bow, to judge from contemporary treatises, it was more common to use two consecutive down-bows than it is today. Corelli gives no signs for up- or down-bows, but certain of his contemporaries used initial letters such as T (*tirare*) and P (*puntare*), d (down) and u (up), N (*Niederzug*) and A (*Aufzug*), and T (*tiré*) and P (*poussé*).

On reaching the *allegro* section of the first movement of Corelli's opus 5, no. 1, the modern interpreter needs to be aware of the more detached sound produced on separate bow-strokes by the Corelli-period bow, without lifting it from the string. An ultra-smooth *détaché* has been part of violin technique only since the Tourte bow. This *allegro* covers almost the whole range of the violin as used by Corelli, starting on the G string and ascending into the third position. He used the G string rarely except at the bottom of chords, or to give the effect of big leaps as in the *Allemanda* of opus 5, no. 7, and the two notes above third position on the E string very rarely indeed, but third position must have been used freely on the three upper strings to make the multiple stops possible. The fourth finger, which was still not popular owing to the wider neck of Corelli's violin, must also have been used for the double stops, although open strings were preferred in first position. Corelli would probably hold his violin on the shoulder and steady it with his chin on downward shifts, but holding the instrument against the breast was still the practice with dance musicians. In this first *allegro*, he would probably go into third position on either the ninth note of the third bar or the second note of the fourth bar, as open strings and repeated notes were favoured opportunities for shifting.

The second movement, a fugal *allegro*, shows the solo sonata's origin in the trio sonata, whose two violin parts have been contracted to one by using double stops. Here we find typical attributes of the Baroque sonata: chord progressions gravitating towards a tonal centre, especially through sequences in fifths as in bars 35–38; chords of the seventh on any note of the scale, as in bars 6–7; and a diminished seventh chord at the climax just before the cadence (bar 58). A series of suspended sevenths, a favourite Baroque device, occurs in bars 11–13, while bars 42–53 show how fugal movements were lengthened by interpolating idiomatic instrumental episodes, and variety of key obtained by the use of modulating sequences (bars 47–51). The meantone system of tuning keyboard instruments, with its 'pure' thirds and flat fifths, made it inadvisable for a composer to move from a sharp to a flat key; when G. B. Vitali did so he may have been writing for an instrument tuned in a then exceptional equal temperament. Corelli goes as far afield as F-sharp minor and B major from the home key of D major in this movement by using sequences.

The tempo of the movement can be deduced as a rather steady *allegro*, from the complications of the double and triple stops, and from the fact that the harmony occasionally changes on the second quaver of a beat. That the continuo has become a melodic part can be seen in the imitative phrases of bars 5, 11–13, 20, etc., and the final *adagio* is a clear forerunner of the cadenza.

For the modern performer, a technical question is posed by the mixed two- and three-note crotchet chords of bars 6, 7, and elsewhere. The function of these chords is clearly to continue the contrapuntal texture, not to make a startling rhythmic, homophonic effect, as for instance in the modern use of chords in Walton's viola concerto. With the present-day bow and instrument, three-note chords may be played together with ease at the heel of the bow, and with more difficulty on the up-bow, provided that the bow is placed further than usual from the bridge and that the chords are not quieter than *mezzo-forte*. To play quiet smooth chords with three notes sounding pleasantly together is impossible, as the bow must be dropped from above on to the middle string of the three with a certain amount of strength in order to depress it to the level of the two outside strings. Repeated down-bows are therefore preferred for groups of three-note chords like those in the first movement of Max Bruch's G minor violin concerto – while the bow is retaken, the left hand has time to prepare the next chord.

It is not known whether or not Corelli and his contemporaries would attempt to play three- and four-note chords together. Some (though not all) of the violin bridges used in the 17th century were flatter than those of today, and should have made sustained chords easier, but the Italians used a straight bow and Sol Babitz, in comparing modern and 18th-century bows and instruments, found the modern bow capable of sustaining chords for about twice as long as the old one.[3] It seems likely that attempts to sustain the chords in this *allegro* movement would cause a sudden increase in volume and probably a deterioration of tone-quality which would be alien to the structure and mood of the piece, and the 17th-century performer probably considered the printed score as an idealised version to be interpreted according to his skills as a violinist, by splitting or arpeggiating the chords. Sometimes (as in bar 14) it would be physically impossible to sustain the notes as printed. Quite often the direction *Arpeggio* is given at the beginning of a chain of chords, as in bar 31 of this *allegro*, in which case the violinist would hold down the chord-notes with the left hand and produce *arpeggio* patterns with the bow to suit his own taste, after the style of the following examples:

Rapid arpeggiation from bottom to top of three- and four-note chords, with a slight dwelling on the bottom note, was probably the recognised method of performance, as it is described in Simpson's *The Division Viol* and later by Quantz and Rameau: the latter suggests

downward arpeggiation should the melody be in the lowest part.
J.-J. Rousseau remarked in 1750 that

> there are instruments on which there cannot be formed a full
> accord but thro' the Arpeggio. Such are the violin, the violincello,
> the viol, and all those which are played with the bow; for the
> convexity of the bridge hinders the bow from fixing itself at once
> on all the strings[4]

and it appears that the favourite modern method of dividing chords with
two notes sounding at a time was a 19th-century innovation.

Another passage which cannot be performed as written occurs in bars
11–13 of this *allegro*. Chains of suspensions could only be played if
included under one long slur – often impossibly long – and no slurring
is indicated. The performer must therefore break the bowing to fit either
the top or the bottom line exactly, choosing between dividing one of the
parts into repeated notes or inserting rests instead of sustaining the note.
In this movement

would probably be played as

or

or

but

would be possible, although this way we lose the tied suspension.

Other double stops have to be approximated by shortening certain notes, e.g. bar 14

becomes

and slurs must be added occasionally to make sustained notes in another part possible. Completely consistent bowing is usually unattainable in these contrapuntal movements unless one is willing to sacrifice the sprightly character given by the use of separate bows in the opening theme, and adopt a bow-per-beat system throughout the movement, except for repeated notes of fractions of a beat. A more satisfactory plan seems to be to adapt the slurring and note values to suit the character of whichever line seems most important at any point in the movement: the violinist can waste frustrating hours in seeking a logical bowing pattern which was not even considered by the composer.

The third movement of Corelli's opus 5, no. 1, is again an *allegro*, but of a *perpetuum mobile* instead of a contrapuntal character. Stradella and Torelli had already made impressive use of this kind of violin passage-work; Corelli's contribution was in the conciseness and balance of his movements. The last eight bars reveal another favourite harmonic formula of Baroque composers, the descending series of sixth chords, often used by Bach in a slightly more complex form as in the opening *tutti* of the Fifth Brandenburg Concerto. Corelli introduces the only dynamic marking of this sonata, a *piano*, in the penultimate bar of this movement.

The sparsity of dynamic indications in 17th-century scores has led some interpreters to consider them an anachronism in performance, but sufficient indications were in use (*fortissimo, forte, mezzo piano, piano, più piano* [=*pp*], and *pianissimo* [=*ppp*]) to indicate that graded dynamics were known and expected from the interpreter, if rarely dictated. Simpson speaks of growing louder towards the middle or the end of a single note, and the short crescendo and diminuendo now sometimes referred to as a 'hairpin' on a long note were traditional by Corelli's time, using vibrato, and known as *messa di voce*. A diminuendo could be indicated by *f–p–pp*, as at the end of Corelli's opus 6, no. 8, and David Boyden quotes a contemporary description of a diminuendo by Scipione Maffei:

> . . . when with artful degree the tone is diminished little by little, and then resumed in a loud manner; and this artifice is used frequently, and with marvellous effect, in the great *concerti* at Rome.[5]

The earliest known clear indication of a crescendo occurred in England, in the storm music of Matthew Locke's incidental music for *The Tempest* (1672). The storm rises with the indication 'louder by degrees' and fades again with 'soft and slow by degrees'. In performing 17th-century music, it seems reasonable to follow the practice of a contemporary writer, Christopher Simpson, who says 'We play loud or soft, according to our fancy, or the humour of the Musick', or again 'Playing also sometimes loud or soft, to express Humour and draw on Attention',[6] rather than to follow any dogmatic preconceived ruling.

The fourth movement of Corelli's opus 5, no. 1, offers plenty of opportunity for vibrato and *messa di voce*: its *cantabile* style indicates how the greater performers must have been able to produce a singing tone with the longer bows and more powerful instruments now at their disposal. Vibrato was becoming increasingly popular towards the end of the century, judging from contemporary descriptions. Roger North complains

> I must take notice of a wrist shake, as they call it, upon the violin, which without doubt is a great art, but as I think injured by overdoing; for those who use it well never let a note rest without it. . . .[7]

The final movement contains problems of interpretation of multiple stops similar to the fugal *allegro*: it is not possible to play bars 15–16 exactly as written, for instance. Bar 17 and the final cadence bars contain examples of a typical Baroque formula in triple-metre movements: the hemiola. This is a rhythmic harmonic device emphasising a cadence, the two groups of three beats immediately preceding the cadence being divided into three groups of two, with the harmony changing on every second instead of every third note. Bar 17 is thus a $\frac{3}{4}$ bar in a 6/8 movement, while the equivalent of a $\frac{3}{4}$ bar crosses the penultimate bar-line.

Rhythmical conventions which persisted well into the 18th century and provide endless ground for musicological argument, concern the lengthening or shortening of dotted note-patterns and rests (particularly where triplets and duplets occur within a movement), and the alteration of running passages to make *notes inégales*.

The appeal of this problem to the argumentative lies in the fact that we can never definitely know the answer, although in simple and consistent movements like the *Giga* from Corelli's E minor sonata, opus 5, no. 8, for instance, we can be fairly sure. We notice at the start that the time-signature for the violin-line differs from that of the continuo in that a $\frac{12}{8}$ is added after the **C**: presumably, therefore, the **C** bears its old function of indicating a moderate tempo. But the continuo line is written throughout in $\frac{4}{4}$ notation across the steady $\frac{12}{8}$ of the violin, giving two notes against three occasionally as in bar 3, and $\begin{smallmatrix}12\\8\\4\\4\end{smallmatrix}$ in bars 22–24.

As this movement is consistent throughout, it seems reasonable to follow the 17th-century convention of adapting to the dominant rhythm of the movement, making pairs of quavers into ♩ ♪, and ♩. ♪ into ♩. ♩ ♪. But an over-generalised application of this particular convention can result in an ironing-out of rhythmic subtleties which may well have been intended by the composer. To the musician who quotes C. P. E. Bach's ruling[8] that ♩.♪ should be adapted to ♩ ♪ when there are triplets in the melody, one may immediately oppose Quantz's dictum of one year earlier (1752):[9] that the dotted note should be doubly dotted in this circumstance. If, as C. P. E. Bach claims, ♪♪ and ♩.♪ both equal ♩ ♪ one wonders why composers bothered to write the dotted formula at all. Corelli's use of simultaneous $\frac{4}{4}$ and $\frac{6}{8}$ (see the *Giga* from opus 4, no. 4, where only the second violin has a C time signature) can be explained both as an economy in engraving costs and as a result of old traditions; but the persistence of these traditions into the early work of Haydn, Mozart, and even Schubert, and the apparent inconsistencies of interpretation, are much harder to explain.

Attempts to make a general ruling on dotted notes and triplets fail when one encounters a movement such as the *Giga* from Corelli's opus 2, no. 9. It would be possible to perform the whole movement in $\frac{12}{8}$, but as the other jigs in this opus are written out in compound time, why should this one be the exception? Bar 21 in the *Tempo di Gavotta* of opus 2, no. 5 shows that Corelli would use a triplet and a duplet on consecutive beats and this *Giga* could be an elaboration of the same idea, making true cross-rhythms. Even in Corelli's time, the movement would probably be performed differently in different places: the practical musician today takes a decision, having studied the score, on the way he will interpret the rhythms, and uses his rehearsal time to bring out the qualities of this particular interpretation. The less practical interpreter can all too easily use up his rehearsal time in deciding the length of each individual quaver.

Occasionally Corelli used the old form of proportional time-signature, as in the *Giga* of opus 3, no. 10, where the changes from compound to

simple time and back again are indicated by 12 or 8 over the beginning
of the bar, showing that eight notes are to be played in the time of twelve
or vice versa. The $\frac{9}{8}$ time-signature in the third movement of opus 5,
no. 2, has a similar meaning – nine quavers in the time of the previous
six – and instances of C placed before a time-signature are frequent in
Corelli's sonatas. Often a tempo indication is given as well: presumably
'C$\frac{3}{8}$ Vivace' in opus 5, no. 11 requires a slight quickening of the rather,
steady $\frac{3}{8}$ indicated by the C.

By 1700 the mensural, proportional time-signatures were already dying out, and *andante* occasionally appearing to indicate a moderate speed
(e.g. Corelli's opus 3, no. 5). *Accelerando* and *ritardando* were still not
written into scores, but the practice was known, because Muffat complains about it.

Georg Muffat, a south German composer and organist of Strasbourg
and later Salzburg Cathedrals, is one of our principal sources of information on the 17th-century French school of string-playing, as he spent
some years in Paris studying Lully's style and on his return to Germany
published collections of suites for strings and continuo. These had fore-
words containing discussions of French and Italian styles, and instructions about the execution of ornaments and the playing of instruments.

Muffat rejects, like Lully, the 'immoderate runs as well as frequent
and ill-sounding leaps'[10] in vogue with the 17th-century Italians, and
gives five basic instructions to string-players performing ballets in the
Lullian-French manner.

> First, one must, for purity of intonation, stop the strings accur-
> ately. Second, the bow must be drawn in a uniform way by all the
> players. Third, one must bear constantly in mind the time signature,
> or tempo and measure, proper to each piece. Fourth, one must pay
> strict attention to the usual signs of repetition introduced and also
> to the qualities of the style and of the art of dancing. Fifth, one
> must use with discernment certain ornaments making the pieces
> much more beautiful and agreeable, lighting them up, as it were,
> with sparkling precious stones.[11]

He gives clear instructions in his *Florilegium Primum* about the use of
first- and second-time bars, and not-so-clear indications regarding the
interpretation of his mensural-proportional time-signatures with additional tempo markings. A reference to 'notes inégales', a French practice
of rendering ♫♫♫ as ♪.♫.♪ in running passages, infers that this was
not the habit of the Italians, and Loulié in 1696 gives clear descriptions

of *notes inégales* both ♪♪ ♪♪ and ♪. ♪., stipulating that only French music must be interpreted this way.[12]

Muffat does not mention the practice of double-dotting described by Quantz in 1752, although it is now considered particularly applicable to Lully's slow French-overture style, which was widely imitated during the following century. Leopold Mozart used actual double-dot notation for the first time after 1752, but Quantz makes it quite clear that the short note after a dot was often considerably delayed to give a more vivacious effect.

French string-music in the 17th century was connected mainly with the ballet and the opera, in both of which Lully (1632–87) was the principal composer. Possibly the only French contribution to technical development at this time was indicated in Muffat's second injunction to the performers of his *Florilegium Primum*, i.e. that the bowing should be the same throughout the group. This is a form of orchestral discipline which gives extra attack and cohesion to the sound, and has remained a part of orchestral tradition up to the present day.

17th-century French violin-music rarely goes more than a semitone above the first position, and double stops or complex bowings were used only on the viol, which was still the recognised string instrument for solo and chamber music in France. Rousseau's *Traité de la Viole* appeared in 1786, and Marin Marais was enjoying considerable fame at that time as a viol virtuoso and composer. The rich string sound obtained from Lully's orchestration for two violin sections, two viola sections, and bass (or three violin parts and one for viola) made French orchestral playing internationally famous: the 24 *Violons du Roy* having proved too inefficient for the ambitious Lully, he persuaded Louis XIV to create a new band known as *Les Petits Violons*, and drilled it in his disciplines of uniform bowing, marked rhythms, and limited ornamentation.

Most 17th-century French music was intended for the Court alone, and was therefore never published. Some manuscripts remain with only the bass and treble lines shown; others with the middle parts filled in apparently by a less competent hand than Lully's own. Suites of string pieces drawn from the works of Lully and his most talented contemporary, Charpentier, are occasionally performed today; but although their sonorities and rhythmic vivacity are pleasing to the ear, one tends to agree with Bukofzer's statement that 'Lully handled his keys with striking monotony'.[13] Almost all of the string music was designed as an adjunct to or background for a stage performance. Only the string interludes from the operas would be performed between scenes, and these would probably be regarded as background music for the audience's discussions of the action.

Lully was trained as a dancer as well as a violinist and composer, and possessed political guile which, combined with his undoubted talents, gave him a virtual monopoly over music in Paris and made him one of the most wealthy composers ever. The austerity of his style appealed to the French far more than the emotional accents of the Italian Baroque: Corneille, Racine, and Molière reveal a similar tendency in drama strictly to regulate the content of their plays by adhering to the Aristotelian unities and dignity of language. Although Italian by birth, Lully was trained by French composers, and he was able to suit the French taste while borrowing from the Italians touches of pathos, chromaticism, and dissonance which made his operas more effective. It is possible that the French Court might have been won over to the Italian style of opera by two commissioned operas from Italy's great composer, Cavalli, had not Lully interpolated ballets, instead of the choruses and between the acts, which completely overshadowed the drama.

Two instrumental forms were considerably developed in Lully's hands: the French overture, which gradually acquired the pattern of a solemn opening with dotted rhythms and a fugal *allegro*, usually in triple metre (the return to the opening tempo was a later development) and the chaconne. Orchestral chaconnes were the longest instrumental pieces commonly written, and they were given contrast by the interpolation of wind trios. The strict ground bass did not always persist throughout, although its basic sarabande rhythm gave a similar sense of unity. Gradually, the extended chaconne began to fall into three large sections, the outer two in the same key, the centre in the tonic minor or relative major. J. S. Bach was later to use this plan in the chaconne from his D minor partita for violin alone, a D minor movement with a D major central section.

Although the violin played such an important role in the entertainment of the French Court, the French violinist was still low on the social scale, and a species of guild or union grew up to protect his rights to fees and privileges. The leader of this union was entitled *Roi des Violons*, and recognised by the King; but the instrument was still considered noisy and unsuitable for chamber music or for the recreation of well-bred amateurs.

In England, during the Civil War and Commonwealth years (1642–60) chamber music at home increased in popularity, for as Roger North said, 'many chose rather to fidle at home, than to goe out & be knockt in ye head abroad'.[14] This may be one reason for the acceptance of the violin into amateur music-making in England while it was still rejected in France: another factor was the influence of Italians attracted to England by the possibility of financial rewards. In 1713 Mattheson wrote: 'He who wishes to make a profit out of his music betakes himself to England',[15] and this reputation must have been held for many years to have attracted such an array of foreign talent in London.

John Playford complains in *Musick's Delight on the Cithren* (1666) 'Nor is any Musick rendered acceptable or esteemed by many, but what is presented by Forreigners',[16] and John Evelyn, while thoroughly admiring the technical feats of Baltzar and Matteis on the violin, is not so charmed with 'a Consort of 24 violins betweene every pause; after the *French* fantastical light way, better suiting a Tavern or Playhouse than a church'.[17] This innovation was introduced by Charles II (1660–85) whose French blood and long exile in France encouraged him to model the English court music on the pattern of the French, with a large band entitled '24 Violins of the King', and a small one called the 'Private Musick' in direct imitation of Lully's *Les Petits Violons*. Pepys considered King Charles 'a little musicall' because he 'kept good time with his hand all along the anthem',[18] but there were those who bewailed his 'utter detestation of Fancys' (North)[19] and the resultant decline in chamber music for the viols. Dances after the French style became very popular, and the earliest published violin-music in England is made up mainly of dances and variations. The Italian sonata was very soon to make its presence felt, however, and by 1683 Purcell was consciously imitating the Italians and turning his back on the French with the words 'tis time now . . . to loath the levity, and balladry of our neighbours'.[20]

English music was not so completely monopolised by the monarchy as French, although Purcell's teacher, Pelham Humphrey, had been sent to Paris to study the French style. Purcell himself was clearly acquainted with the Italian trio sonatas, probably brought over by the German violinist Baltzar and the Italian Matteis. English violin technique must have been fairly elementary on Baltzar's arrival c. 1655 for him to have made such a resounding success. Evelyn reports (4 March 1656) that 'he played upon that single Instrument a full Consort, so as the rest flungdowne their Instruments, as acknowledging a victory';[21] while North attributes the new popularity of the violin to him.

One Baltazar a Swede, about ye time of ye Restauration came over, and shewed so much mastery upon that Instrument that gentlemen, following also ye humour of the court, fell in pesle mesle, & soon thrust out the treble viol, and not without ye greatest reason, for the former hath of ye Latter multuple advantages.[22]

Up to this time, according to North, 'the use of the violin had bin litle in England except by comon fidlers'.[22]

In 1674 the Italian Nicola Matteis came in for similar praise, as 'that stupendous violin, Signor *Nicholao* . . . whom certainly never mortal man Exceeded on that Instrument: he had a stroak so sweete, and made it speak . . . like a Consort of several instruments'[23] in the words of Evelyn, and 'an excellent musitian . . . [who] in one respect excelled all that had bin knowne before in England, which was the *arcata*; his *stoccatas*, *tremolos*, divisions, and indeed his whole manner was surprising, and every stroke of his was a mouthful'[24] according to Roger North. The best of the English violinists, Davis Mell, sounded tame by comparison, and Anthony Wood reports that after Baltzar's arrival Mell 'was not so admired, yet he played sweeter, was a well-bred gentleman, and not given to excessive drinking as Baltzar was'.[25]

Baltzar's compositions as compared to Mell's show virtuoso passage-work, high positions, and double stops which must have been virtually impossible for violinists holding the instrument against the breast or low on the shoulder, as was still the tradition in England. Matteis, according to North, 'taught ye English to hold ye bow by ye wood onely & not to touch ye hair which was no small reformation',[26] after 1670.

Matteis attempted to simplify his compositions for the less able English players by printing the double stops as optional notes, engraved in dots, and evidently his printed Ayres for the violin were technically more moderate than his performances, as North again comments that they 'shew much of his air, & skill, but nothing of his manner of playing, wch made them much richer than ye prints shew and now it is Impossible either to find out or describe the musick he made of them'.[27] Music could be idiomatically suited to the violins without attaining the higher feats of technical virtuosity, however, and from the mid-century onwards there is increasing evidence of the violin's acceptance as a chamber-music instrument and one suitable for amateurs in England.

Several of the Fancies or Fantasias in *Musica Britannica* show treble lines which must have been intended for the violin, first in the works of William Lawes (1602–45), later in pieces by John Jenkins (1592–1678), Matthew Locke (1630–77), and Christopher Simpson (d. 1669), whose fantasias entitled *Months and Seasons* are for violin, two bass viols, and *basso continuo*. The Italian trio-sonata style becomes increasingly recognisable in the later English fancies, especially those using variations or 'divisions'.

Simpson's *The Division-Viol* (1659) was a much-imitated work carrying into string music the Elizabethan virginalists' practice of creating variations by splitting the theme into ever smaller note-values. Playford brought out *The Division Violin* in 1684, with some moderately difficult dances and variations, including the occasional use of third position by two foreign composers and one fourth position e''' in an anonymous piece. The variations on the *Follia* theme (entitled *Faronells Division on a Ground*) precede Corelli by fifteen years.

Following Playford's publication of *The English Dancing Master* (1651), a collection of airs for dancing designed for performance on the violin which was frequently reissued over the next eighty years, came several collections of violin dances suitable for amateur performers, and some of the earliest violin tutors. At the same time, enterprising English publishers were beginning to bring out Italian violin-music, but the tutors, essentially 'teach-yourself' books, only aimed at elementary standards and used methods already considered old-fashioned by professional violinists. John Playford's *A Brief Introduction to the Skill of Musick* does not refer to the violin in the first edition (1654), but the second revised edition of 1658 already contains a section entitled *Playing on a Treble Violin*. In 1695 two more English tutors appeared: *The Self-Instructor on the Violin* and *Nolens Volens or You Shall learn to Play on the Violin whether you will or no*. The latter is probably the earliest tutor devoted solely to violin-playing, as it appeared about six months before the *Self-Instructor*.

Henry Purcell (1659–95) composed both dances and viol fancies in his youth, but absorbed Italian influences possibly from the works of William Young (an English composer living abroad, d. 1672) and John Jenkins; certainly from hearing the violinist Matteis and the sonatas of Lelio Colista – he quotes from a sonata by 'Lelio Calista, an Italian' in his section entitled *Double Descant* contributed to the tenth edition of Playford's *Introduction to the Skill of Musick*. Purcell's sonatas could not be mistaken for Italian works: they contain typically English modal harmonies and some very complex counterpoint reminiscent of the fancy. The themes are a mixture of Italianate mottoes and more angular English tunes; the technique requires rapid figuration without higher positions or multiple stops. In Purcell's only solo sonata the bass-viol part is freed from the keyboard line; this occurs less often in the two groups of trio sonatas (published 1683 and 1697).

The main reason for England's assimilation of the violin before France appears to be that amateur music-making was less monopolised by court favour than in Paris. Amateur performers have long been the main arbiters of England's musical taste, and it is significant that the earliest public concerts in London sprang up between 1650 and 1700. One organiser of such concerts, a man who 'for a livelihood sold small-coal about the streets'[28] (Thomas Britton, 1644–1714), left us an example of the kind of library amassed by the enthusiastic amateur of the period: church music and madrigals, catches, English fancies, Italian sonatas by Bassani, Corelli, Vitali, and Uccellini, and concertos by Corelli and Vivaldi. From the German school were sonatas by Biber and Rosen-müller, and almost all contemporary English composers were well represented.

Schools and dancing academies often advertised music as part of their curriculum, and Purcell's *Dido and Aeneas* was written for one such establishment. At the same time the masques and stage productions of Charles II's Court were stimulating some dramatic orchestral writing by John Blow (*c.* 1648–1708), and Matthew Locke, who was Purcell's most able theatrical precursor. The death of Purcell put a sudden end to England's chances of founding a national school of opera composers; he left no successor.

Germany, torn by wars during the first part of the century, turned to church music as the main region of interest. Here the Italian influence was felt most strongly, as the leading composer of religious music, Heinrich Schütz, had studied in Venice under G. Gabrieli. The intense drama of his oratorios and Passion-settings was probably the most significant German contribution to 17th-century musical development, but the German instrumental school made its own impression without leaving a great deal of music which has remained in the repertoire, except for some important music by the keyboard virtuosi. Sweelinck, Scheidt, Buxtehude, Froberger, and Pachelbel established several forms used by Bach; the organ fugue, the chorale prelude, and the clavier suite.

Dietrich Buxtehude (*c.* 1637–1707) transformed the Italian trio-sonata pattern into something completely individual by using a viola da gamba for the second line, sometimes giving his *concertante* instruments entire solo movements, uniting them only for the outer movements. The Italian names for his trio-sonata movements do not indicate any direct imitation of Italian patterns, and the sonatas are made up of contrasted movements with no recognisable scheme, containing extremes of diffuse structure and fugal craftsmanship.

Formal structure was not widely explored by the string-composers of 17th-century Germany, the principal interest between 1650 and 1700 lying in the exploration of the violin's technical capacities. Although works of this period are now considered historically rather than musically interesting, it would be a mistake to underrate them. Without the explorations made by J. P. von Westhoff (1656–1705), J. H. Schmelzer (*c.* 1623–80), Heinrich von Biber (1644–1704), and J. J. Walther (*c.* 1650–1717), J. S. Bach's unaccompanied sonatas for violin would probably never have been written.

Some of Biber's music might have remained longer in the repertoire if the practice of altering the tuning of certain strings (*scordatura*) had not rapidly fallen out of favour during the 18th century. *Scordatura* was a favourite device of Schmelzer, who may have taught Biber, and Biber explored the sonorities obtainable from this technique with remarkable ingenuity and effect. Each of his *Mystery* (or *Rosary*) *Sonatas* (obtainable in a modern edition) is prefaced by a picture showing a scene from the life of Christ, and an indication of the string tuning required.

The violinist who wishes to explore any but the first of these sonatas requires some gut strings and a not-too-valuable violin (as the string tension may be far greater than usual), the patience to unravel key-signatures such as ♯♯♭♯ in Sonata 7, and the strength of mind to play the notes in front of him as though they were written for a violin of normal tuning. The results are surprising and dramatic: although these sonatas lack the tonal drive and formal cohesion of Corelli's, they have an impact and excitement which are not solely due to technical virtuosity, but more to Biber's ability to portray moods in music.

Comparison of the *Mystery Sonatas* (*c.* 1674) with Walther's *Scherzi* (1676, reprinted 1953 in *Das Erbe Deutscher Musik*) shows that the two composers shared certain technical characteristics such as the use of high positions (up to seventh) and advanced cross-string bowings with separate bows, with dots over notes and with dots under slurs. Biber uses twenty consecutive thirds in one up-bow in Sonata 8, separating them with dots above the notes: Walther in a later work asks for thirty-two single notes to be played consecutively with up-bow *staccato*. Walther does not use *scordatura*, but his multiple stops are often complex, and instructions for *Harpeggiando* (as used by Corelli), *bariolage* (a rapid alternation of notes on two strings, one stopped, one usually open, which was occasionally used by Corelli, as in the opus 5, no. 2 *allegro*), and *ondeggiando* (indicated by a wavy line under a slur, meaning that the

bow is waved back and forth between two strings while travelling in one
direction) occur fairly frequently. Biber uses the same devices but often
writes them out instead of using the printed term or sign. Two of these
techniques are prominent in Bach's solo violin-writing, *bariolage* in the
E major prelude for violin alone, *arpeggiando* in the D minor chaconne.

Biber's feeling for form was greater than that of Walther, especially in
the inter-relationship of movements: an example is the rondo-like interpolation of variants on the first *adagio* movement between each of the
following four quicker movements in a sonata of *c.* 1682. The German
preference for darker tone-colourings is evident in Biber's scoring for
larger groups: he writes for two violins and four violas in his *tam aris
quam aulis* sonatas of 1676, but the lowest 'viola' line has a bass clef and
extends beyond the viola range: it was probably played on a cello, the
continuo line on a violone. Georg Muffat, already considered as a
specialist in the French rather than the German tradition, used two
viola lines in his string group.

Walther shows Italian influences derived mainly from Farina, who
lived in Germany. These include programmatic effects and technical
stunts, imitations of cuckoos, nightingales, bagpipes, etc., in the *Scherzi*
and of a whole orchestra including organ, timpani, and harp in the
Hortulus Chelicus of 1688. This work covers the complete range of available technique on the 17th-century violin in one set of variations,
adding wide leaps and rapid shifts to the technical devices already
mentioned. Walther's sonatas are his most serious works, employing
neither programmatic effects nor *scordatura*, but they are formally unsatisfying, often containing strings of different short ideas with no
unifying factor, or over-lengthy variations with static basses. Occasionally Walther uses the sign *m* to indicate vibrato, and a wavy line above
repeated notes to indicate the *slurred tremolo* also used by Purcell. In this
stroke the bow does not actually stop between the notes, as it does in the
examples given by Muffat with dots beneath the slurs. Dots above or
vertical dashes beneath slurs, according to Muffat, can indicate that the
interval should be filled with notes of the scale, e.g.

played

dots over a slur indicating a distinct separation of the notes of the scale.

Pizzicato for whole movements was used by the Germans, but other
effects used by Farina, such as *sul ponticello*, *sul tastiera*, and *col legno*

seem to have disappeared for a time. Some of the ornaments explained by Muffat[29] are shown below.

played   or   played

played   played

German professional violinists undoubtedly held the violin and bow after the Italian style, and used the longer bow associated with the Italian sonata, but, as in England, the early treatises teach an old-fashioned style of playing for amateurs. Georg Falck's *Idea boni Cantoris* (1688) advocates holding the violin against the left breast, and curving the fingers over the finger-board. He recommends holding the bow at the nut with the French grip (thumb on hair); in fact the style of his instructions is approximately that of the French dance violinist rather than the German or Italian professional, although he refers to high positions (including the sixth) which were not normally used in France.[30]

Falck's reference to tone-production, producing a deep stroke and sound from the strings, is frequently reiterated by writers about the violin during the latter half of the 17th century. Volume and sonority became a preoccupation of composers, performers, and violin-makers, with variety of tone-colour obtained by the use of the mute, vibrato, *scordatura*, and *bariolage*. Harmonics were not a recognised additional colouring, but the G string's individual sound was gradually employed for contrasted effects. Grouping several instruments to play the same line of music was advocated by Muffat after the style of the French dance orchestra, and more surprisingly in works such as Buxtehude's *Sonatina forte con molti violini all unisono*. With the beginnings of the *concerto grosso* the solo violin needed to stand out in contrast to the *ripieno* group, and violins with the greatest carrying-power allied to sweetness of tone were matched with bows of greater length and strength than ever before: this was a period which saw the constant explorations of Antonio Stradivari towards perfecting the violin's proportions, and the building of an unsurpassed school of violin-making at Cremona.

NOTES

1 76 Hawkins.
2 129 North, p. 161.
3 7 Babitz.
4 152 Rousseau, article on 'Arpeggio'.
5 21 Boyden, p. 291.
6 165 Simpson, p. 56.
7 129 North, p. 165 note.
8 8 Bach, p. 160.
9 144 Quantz, p. 68.
10 175 Strunk, p. 447.
11 ibid. p. 448.
12 49 Donington, p. 390.
13 25 Bukofzer, p. 160.
14 ibid. p. 190.
15 115 Mattheson.
16 42 Demuth, p. 35.
17 52 Evelyn, 21 December 1662.
18 133 Pepys, 22 November 1663.
19 129 North, p. 250.
20 143 Purcell.
21 52 Evelyn.
22 130 North, p. 28.
23 52 Evelyn, 19 November 1664.
24 129 North, p. 355.
25 21 Boyden, p. 236.
26 130 North, p. 36.
27 ibid. p. 36.
28 76 Hawkins.
29 21 Boyden, p. 287.
30 ibid. p. 245.

CHAPTER 4

Violin Structure and Violin-Makers: 1650–1750

THE HISTORY OF music between 1650 and 1750 is as intimately bound up with the great violin-makers as with the violinist-composers. So closely did violin-music and violin-building interact that they pose a hen-or-egg problem: did the composers write music to suit the new more powerful instrument, or was the instrument made more powerful to suit the soloistic demands of the music? Although the evidence slightly favours the latter theory, it is quite possible to imagine Stradivari aiming to produce the most perfect instrument in every respect – craftsmanship, proportions, sweetness, and power of tone – without reference to its position in musical literature. Against this we have the fact that Stradivari was trained in Nicola Amati's workshop, where the greatest musicians came for their instruments: Corelli had an Andrea Amati violin; and prominent musicians visiting Cremona would doubtless specify what they desired from an instrument – power to stand out over a body of strings or sweetness to rival the soprano on the operatic stage.

The amount of time taken for violins to reach their full, mature sonority must have affected quite considerably the relative popularity of their makers during this hundred years. The Hill book[1] on the Guarneri family estimates the seasoning period required for Stainer's violins as from ten to fifteen years; Amati, Stradivari, and Guarneri del Gesù each progressively longer, with larger models taking longest, so that the most massive models of del Gesù and Bergonzi might take eighty years to reach their peak of performing power. Amount and intensity of use must be an important and variable factor affecting this maturation, for the sound of an unplayed violin does not mature at all (Spohr tried two almost unused Stradivaris and estimated that they would take ten years of playing before they began to speak properly) and the hard wear given by a concerto soloist would considerably accelerate the process. Various attempts, either unsuccessful or positively damaging, have been made to shorten the seasoning period. Very old wood for new violins does not help, and the practice of thinning down the bellies of the heavier models to make them vibrate more easily destroyed some very fine instruments. Hill quotes a paragraph from the *Public Advertiser* of 1778: 'Mr. Merlin . . . continues to alter the tone of the most common fiddle to that of the finest "Cremona" for one guinea each improvement.'[2] Catch-penny or well-intentioned 'improvements' in the form of cutting down, building up, thinning, or revarnishing old violins have ruined some of them for ever.

Only an expert can distinguish at sight the hand of a particular maker on a violin, and labels became unreliable as soon as a trader in violins realised that he could double his profit margin by moving a label from one instrument to another. It seems odd to imagine a dealer putting a Stainer label inside a Cremona fiddle, but this quite probably happened in the early years of the 18th century, when Stainer violins were prized very highly for their sweetness of tone and ease of tone-production. Stainer himself profited little from the popularity of his instruments, although during his lifetime (*c.* 1617–83), their merit was already beginning to be appreciated: he lived a life of debt and misery. His violins resemble A. Amati's in their high arching, but there is no evidence of his apprenticeship in the Italian workshop. Probably he copied the Amati violins owned by the members of the Innsbruck court orchestra. By the age of eighteen he was selling his violins on a market-stall in Hall, and by the early 18th century his violins were fetching more than instruments by Amati or Stradivari in London. Biber, J. S. Bach, Pietro Locatelli, and Francesco Maria Veracini spread the fame of Stainer's violins, and Pietro Guarneri of Mantua showed his admiration by copying certain characteristics.

The clarity and bite of Stainer tone, which gave an illusion of carrying-power, were not sufficient to maintain their popularity against violins which combined quality and real strength of tone, and as the violins of Stradivari matured, they became prized more highly than any others, a position which they have held ever since. During Stradivari's lifetime the normal length of a violin became standardised at 14 inches. In order to make the details and changes in violin-construction more comprehensible, it would perhaps help to list at this point the parts and dimensions of the violin as we know it today (see Fig. 1).

The dimensions of the 'Messiah' Stradivari are commonly quoted as standard, although a glance at the tables of comparative dimensions of violins made by Stradivari and his contemporaries, shown in the works of the Hill brothers and of Jalovec, show that it is hardly possible to find two instruments with identical dimensions. The 'Messiah' measurements are generally given as

	millimetres	inches
Length of belly and back	354	14
Upper width	166	6·9
Lower width	206	8·2
Middle width	109	4·3
Height of sides, upper bouts	30	1·2
Height of sides, lower bouts	31	1·25

In the Talbot Manuscript in Christ Church Library, Oxford,[3] we have detailed measurements of the violin as it was generally found in the late 17th century. Not all the details seem to be accurate, but many are confirmed by the very rare instruments preserved in their original state until today, such as a Stainer in the possession of W. E. Hill and Sons of London. The pegs, bridge, and fingerboard of this violin are not original, but the bass-bar (small and slight compared with today's) is. The neck is not shorter than the modern neck; but although Talbot also gives the same length of neck as on the modern violin, there is evidence that many violin necks were about ⅛ inch shorter. Instead of sloping back at an angle (an innovation dating from c. 1800) it is set in the same plane as the belly, and the fingerboard raised with a wedge to follow the line of the strings (see Plate 12).

Talbot makes the playing length of the string 13 inches, as it is today, and like us places his bridge between the notches on the f-holes: evidence of a shorter string-length is given in *Nolens Volens* (1695), but the Stainer of W. E. Hill and Sons is very little shorter than a modern violin. Boyden casts doubt on Talbot's height of bridge (1 inch) which would seem very low, and depth of violin (3½ inches) which is incredibly high; possibly 2½ inches, which would fit a highly arched Stainer or Amati, was intended. If Talbot's sound-post was really the thickness of a goosequill, it would be considerably more slender than the present one, the position 'under treble string . . . under bridge or there about accordg. to discretion of Artist'[4] not necessarily differing from Heron-Allen's 'within ¼ inch behind the right foot of the bridge'.[5]

The frontispieces to Veracini's *Sonate accademiche* and the violin treatises by Leopold Mozart and Geminiani all clearly show fingerboards which approximate to the 8 inches in length suggested by Talbot, as compared with today's 10½ inches. The neck was probably rather thicker, as the nut end of his finger-board is ⅛ inch wider than today, but the bridge was narrower.

Talbot suggested the same disposition of types of wood as that used by the Italian makers: maple for back, neck, ribs, and bridge; belly and bass-bar of pine; finger-board and tail-piece of finest Russian ebony

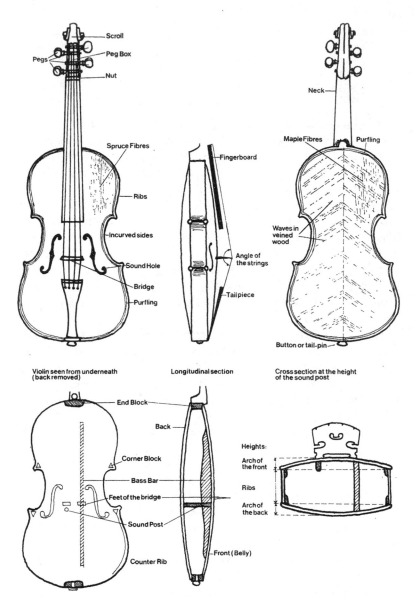

Scroll
Pegs
Peg Box
Nut
Spruce Fibres
Ribs
Incurved sides
Sound Hole
Bridge
Purfling
Fingerboard
Angle of the strings
Tail piece
Neck
Maple Fibres
Purfling
Waves in veined wood
Button or tail-pin

Violin seen from underneath (back removed)
Longitudinal section
Cross section at the height of the sound post

End Block
Back
Corner Block
Bass Bar
Feet of the bridge
Sound Post
Counter Rib
Front (Belly)

Heights:
Arch of the front
Ribs
Arch of the back

Fig. 1   The interior and exterior structure of the violin

(although today ebony does not come from Russia); pegs, nut, and button of 'dryd Box Ebony or any hardest wood':[6] the whole description being couched in specialised wood-workers' terms which have been explained by Hart, Galpin, and others.

Heron-Allen gives details about the selection and cutting of violin wood, and it is interesting to note the qualities of wood used by the great makers. Those whose instruments were in demand during their lifetime like the Amatis and Stradivari could afford to choose the most beautiful cuts, whereas the members of the Guarneri family who worked in Cremona and catered more for the working musician than the aristocracy, owing to the overshadowing presence of Stradivari, used serviceable rather than extremely beautiful wood. Guarneri del Gesù and Bergonzi at one time used pine cut from the same tree, the sap-mark being traceable today in several instruments. But Pietro of Mantua was the only member of the Guarneri family to obtain truly handsome wood for his violins, having moved away from Cremona and secured his income by becoming a performer as well as a violin-maker.

The term 'pine' is used to describe wood from various trees, the one most favoured by violin-makers being the ordinary spruce, which has low density, straight fibres, and does not easily warp. Trees grown on mountain slopes exposed to the sun are preferred, with growth-rings one to 2 mm apart; Switzerland, the Tyrol, Savoy, Romania, and Hungary are reputedly the best sources. Maple of suitable quality for violin-making is also found in Switzerland, the Tyrol, Hungary, or Bohemia – Heron-Allen preferred the southern slopes of the Carpathians and some parts of the eastern Alps. The main types of maple are the plane maple and the sycamore maple, which have medium density and transmit vibrations more slowly than pine. Besides being very beautiful in appearance, maple has extra resistance to deformation.

English violin-makers are put at a disadvantage by the fact that the wood needs to be fully exposed to sun and air but not rain for at least five or six years before it is dry enough to use: otherwise it might shrink and warp as it dries out after the violin is made. Artificial preparation of the wood has so far not proved an adequate substitute for this drying period – Vuillaume's early instruments for which he used artificial methods have deteriorated. The grain of the pine is not too close in fine Italian instruments, and the maple needs an even grain; wavy grain and knots or cracks have to be avoided.

Backs cut on the slab (i.e. in one piece from a plank cut as in Fig. 2) were nearly always used by the early Brescian makers. Inside the tree figures appear, in concentric lines, then in a horizontal or slanting curl which will reach right across the instrument. Slab-cut backs gradually became less popular than those built from two adjacent wedges (Fig. 3). This method gives a pattern which is symmetrical about the centre joint. Marbled wood is taken from closer to the roots, bird's-eye maple was rarely used by the old Italians. Heron-Allen points out that the wood should be split with an axe, not a saw, to show up defects of grain,

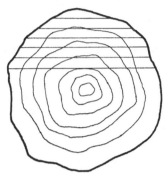

Fig. 2   Planks cut for backs in one piece

and it is suggested that the tone-producing qualities of maple are best when the wood is cut in December or January (when the sap has ceased to flow), from the south side of the tree, and when it is neither too hard nor too soft.

The early Brescians often used softer woods – lime, pear, or poplar – for the backs, sides, and heads of their instruments, but by the time of Maggini and the early Amatis, maple was preferred. Foreign maple, which would be more expensive than the local kind, was used in Cremona when it was available, and when the maker expected to be well paid for the instrument. Both pine and maple of adequate quality were available locally, and must have been used for the larger number of old Italian violins.

Violin-making varies among craftsmen as playing methods vary from performer to performer: only a general outline can be given here. The violin-maker shapes his instrument within a frame-like external mould or more commonly round a solid internal one (Fig. 4). This allows the positioning and shaping of the corner and end blocks which strengthen the corners, support the neck and tail-pin, and leave a guitar-shaped block of air to resonate within the instrument. Heron-Allen suggests that this volume of air should resonate at 512 vibrations a second (=256 c.p.s.). Blocks and side-linings are usually of pine, but Stradivari used willow. The ribs, of maple $\frac{1}{24}$ inch thick, are dipped into water and bent to the shape of the mould with hot bending-irons, and wedge-shaped linings which strengthen the ribs and increase the area of glued joint with belly and back are bent in the same way. It was a Stradivari–Guarneri habit to extend the linings into the centre blocks. The sides of the violin graduate in height from $1\frac{1}{4}$ inches in the lower bouts to $1\frac{5}{32}$ inches in the upper. Maple is difficult to plane, and especially

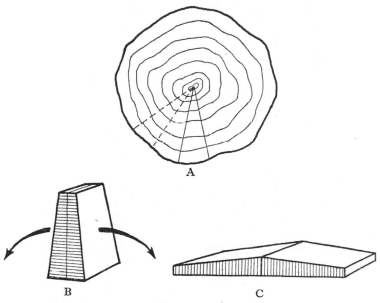

Fig. 3   Wedges (A) cut, (B) divided, and (C) joined so as to give symmetrical properties in relation to a centre join

difficult when possessing a fine curl, but patterned maple is sometimes considered the best for the sides. An old violin will sometimes show a fine join about $\frac{1}{8}$ inch below the top of the ribs: this shows that at some time a repairer has considered that the tone would be improved by the presence inside of a greater volume of resonating air, and has built up the sides to provide this. It can detract from the sound or value, or both, but has occasionally improved the sound.

The back and belly are shaped with saws, gouges, and planes from solid blocks of wood. Thicknesses at various places on the belly and back are crucial, and the work has to proceed very slowly and cautiously for fear of over-thinning, which tends to impair the tone more than a little too much thickness. Different thicknesses shade imperceptibly into one another, and the thickest part of the belly lies above the sound-post. The

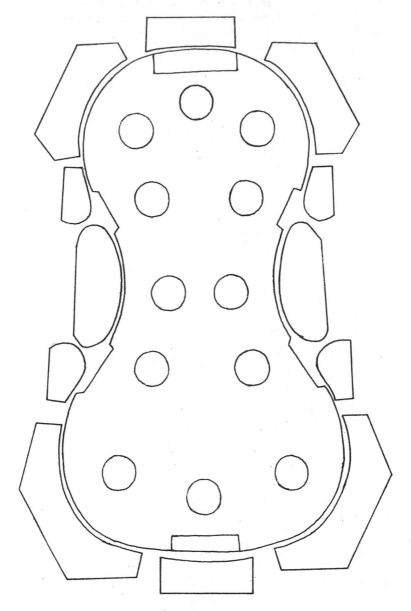

Fig. 4   The mould and its counterparts

overlapping edges do not affect the tone and are finished according to the aesthetic requirements of the maker. Heron-Allen points out[7] that when the back of a violin is held in a clamp and caused to vibrate with a bow, the note produced is approximately a tone higher than that given by the belly with f-holes cut and bass-bar in position.

The back is ready to be glued on to the sides and end- and corner-blocks as soon as it is fully carved and smoothed. The belly awaits f-holes and bass-bar: purfling was usually carried out later, but modern makers often add the purfling before glueing the belly and back on to the sides. Sound-holes present some problems of execution, as pine splits easily: their design and placing on old violins is one of the most individual factors. Hill writes of del Gesù:

> He simply relied upon a rough and ready determination of the position of the top and bottom holes, and the rest depended upon the fancy of the moment. And what an astonishing result! Sound-holes of diverse form and varying length, some cut very open, others moderately so; some placed upright, some slanting; yet, however cut, shaped, or placed, we never fail to recognise that strong impress of the man.[8]

Stradivari, although never repetitive in the design of his sound-holes, was nevertheless absolutely meticulous about their proportions and placings. He fixed the exact position for their top and bottom openings by using compasses, and with the aid of a template he traced the long opening, depending on his eye and skill with the knife to finish the designs. The shape of sound-holes is made necessary by the arching of the violin: they influence the vibrations of the whole instrument and thus affect the whole tone. It is also claimed that they enable the belly to support the very high tension (about 24 lb) of the strings on the bridge. Their position cuts down after-vibrations, required in plucked but not bowed instruments. The bridge and sound-post are positioned from the centre notches on the f-holes, which must therefore be a correct distance from the nut and from the thick part of the belly over the sound-post.

The bass-bar also has a vital effect on the tone of an instrument, and much has been written about its precise dimensions and position within the violin. It may not have originated until 1500–50: Hill suggests that before this the belly was left thicker on the G string side. The bar runs below the left foot of the bridge and may be set parallel to the join of the belly or slightly obliquely, the finger-board end closer than the tail-piece end. Gasparo da Salò is said to have used this oblique positioning, but his bass-bar would be very considerably more slender than the modern one, which is about 10½ inches long, $\frac{3}{16}$ inch broad, and $\frac{3}{8}$ inch deep in the centre, sloping away to nothing at the ends. A few of the measurements given by the brothers Hill[9] show how old bass-bars compared to the modern ones.

	Date	Length in inches	Length in mm	Height in centre inches	Height in centre mm	Thickness in inches	Thickness in mm
Modern bar	—	10½	267	$\frac{7}{16}$	11·11	$\frac{4}{16}$	6·35
N. Amati	1650	8⅝	219	$\frac{4}{16}$	6·35	$\frac{3}{16}$	4·76
Stradivari	1704	9½	241	$\frac{4}{16}$	6·35	$\frac{3}{16}$	4·76
J. B. Guadagnini	1760	9⅞	251	$\frac{5}{16}$	7·94	$\frac{3}{16}$	4·76

Exact proportions and placing are a matter for the expert craftsman: the bar is slightly sprung into place to give maximum pressure beneath the foot of the bridge, where otherwise the string pressure might cause the belly to subside. The right-hand side of the belly is supported by the sound-post. The old, slender bass-bar would be insufficient to support present-day increased string tensions: the modern one can cause a muffled tone on the lower strings if it is too strong and reduces the vibrating freedom of the left foot of the bridge.

Once the bass-bar is in place and the sound-holes have been cut, the whole interior surface being smoothed with glass-paper, the belly is stuck on to the ribs and back, making sure that all glued joins are air-tight. Small gaps in the glue can seriously affect the sound and cause mysterious buzzing noises which all violinists occasionally experience.

Purfling – the three narrow strips of wood (of which the outer two are dyed black or made of ebony) inserted into a groove following the outline of the violin on belly and back – may be mainly decorative or may strengthen the overhanging edges and increase the elasticity of the board, as some makers claim. Certainly it protects the main body of the instrument from damage and is one of the details revealing personal traits of the maker. The groove, having been measured from the edge with a purfling tool, is then deepened by hand with a gouge, and Guarneri del Gesù in his haste would often gouge deeply at the corners. Many Amati violins have the most perfectly finished purflings, and until very late in life Stradivari was a perfectionist in this as in all other techniques. Makers characteristically finish their purflings at the corners in different ways, running them far towards the edge in a graceful point or joining them more bluntly to give a less fragile effect. Some purfling characteristics are nearly as good as a signature on the violin. Dutch and Flemish makers often used whalebone, Giuseppe Guarneri *filius Andreae* used poorly-stained wood, Maggini preferred a double purfling, P. A. Testore and Peter Walmsley would sometimes substitute a painted line for the back purfling. Beautiful ornamental purflings were occasionally given to a violin meriting special attention: there are well-known examples by Andrea Amati, Maggini, Pietro Guarneri of Mantua, and Stradivari himself (the Hellier and Greffuhle violins).

The purflings are tapped into the groove with a small hammer and smoothed to the surface level of the belly. The old makers had to use pegs to fill the holes left by bradawls inserted to secure back and belly when glueing them to the sides, and Stradivari often made the purfling cover half of the peg.

The final stage in preparing the body 'in the white' is to add the ebony rest or saddle over which the tail-gut passes. Once this is glued in place, the body is ready for the addition of the neck and scroll. Originally these were carved from one piece of wood, glued on to the body, and secured by nails driven from inside the block into the base of the neck. Today the neck is morticed into the block, and tilted back at an angle to increase the tension on the string. The amount of tilt affects the angle at which the strings pass over the bridge, which has an effect on the tone produced. 17th- and 18th-century violins have had the necks replaced in the modern manner, usually with the original scroll grafted on (Plate 12), and a modern, long finger-board fitted. The carving of the scroll particularly reveals the artistry and craftsmanship of the maker, and an old violin to which a later scroll has been fitted loses a good deal of its market value. Some of the great makers, like Stradivari, almost invariably produced an exactly symmetrical scroll, while others, although probably starting from a similar premise of a pattern drawn with templates, like Guarneri del Gesù rarely made one side balance the other. Stradivari initiated the practice of picking out the curves of the outline of the head in black: he never replaced the scroll with a carved figure, a practice of viol-makers occasionally followed by violin-makers.

A smooth, even finger board is essential to the intonation across the strings of a violin: if strings which are properly tuned will not give perfect fifths higher up the finger-board, it may be because of grooves worn in the ebony by the constant tapping of the fingers, or because of incorrect relative thickness of adjacent strings. The production of suitable strings for instruments has been the subject of considerable experiment over the years, and at times their cost has seemed disproportionately high. A royal warrant was issued in October 1662: 'To pay John Bannister £40 for two Cremona violins bought by him for his Majesty's service, and also £10 for strings for two years ending June 24th 1662.'[10]

At this time all the strings would be gut, and would frequently break, although their tension was lower than today. Both pitch and tension varied from place to place, but in the early days of violin-playing there seems to be evidence that the Italians and Germans used thicker strings strung more tightly than the French, in order to produce a stronger and more brilliant sound. 17th-century writers were aware of the different qualities of thick, thin, true, and false strings, and Mersenne (1636) explains how strings are made and where the best ones come from. Silk, steel, brass, and copper are all mentioned for strings during the 17th century, but without acceptance by the violin family until after 1700. Boyden quotes Brossard's mention of a G string wound with silver, c. 1712, and a reference to the D string 'at present almost always partially wound with silver'[11] in the same work.

Except for the G string, gut seemed to be preferred by most players, and even the gut E string with its constant breakages persisted into the 20th century. In 1925 Bachmann could still state that 'The fourth or G string is the only covered string used on the violin'[12] and make no reference to metal strings; but today it is rare to see a professional violinist using an uncovered gut string, and with the improvement to all-metal strings given by the flexible woven core, complete sets of metal strings are increasingly popular. They have the advantage of long wear, easy tuning with adjusters, very little stretch so that a replacement may be used immediately without going out of tune, and precise grading of thickness to give perfect fifths. Against these properties stand the extra pressure and strain put on the instrument by strings with very little 'give', and the metallic sound sometimes given by the open strings. The metal-wound string with a gut or nylon core stands midway between the two and is often preferred for old violins; gut becomes frayed with heavy professional wear and rough to the fingers when sliding into new positions, while plain nylon tends to squeak. The problems of procuring gut are increasing, and with the advent of suitable synthetic materials it is no longer worthwhile for the string-maker to seek out young (but not too young) slim animals, detach their entrails while they are still warm after being killed at the slaughterhouse, separate off the necessary fibrous sections, and carry out the numerous processes laid down for the production of the ideal violin string. Gut strings are still produced, but less laborious processes are rapidly vanquishing the traditional.

The point where the strings pass over the end of the finger-board into the peg-box is clearly marked by a separate piece of wood, called the nut,

Fig. 5 The shape of a bridge made by Stradivari (above) compared with a modern viola bridge

which stands higher than the finger-board to allow free vibration of the string, and has grooves to keep the strings equidistant. It must be a separate piece of wood, as the grain of the finger-board runs along its length, whereas the nut needs a cross-grain to withstand the wear of the strings. The tail-piece needs a cross-grain for the same reason: it is occasionally made of rosewood instead of ebony to match a set of rose-wood pegs. Heron-Allen recommends these '. . . to amateurs, and especially to ladies, who should always use them, as they reduce the operation of tuning from a tiresome and lengthy to an instantaneous one'.[13] Peg-holes on old violins have often been filled in owing to wear, and a new set made – the head is then said to have been 're-bushed'.

The bridge, which is fitted after the finger-board in order to make the strings the correct height above it – close enough to be pressed down in the high positions, but not so close that the G string will rattle against the finger-board when bowed strongly – has changed little in design since the time of Stradivari, whose bridges were a little lower and more cut away (Fig. 5). A bridge attributed to N. Amati by Fétis shows a similar basic outline: the details of height, thickness, and width of shoulders all being related to the angle of finger-board, depth of belly, and tonal characteristics of the instrument.

The feet of a bridge must fit the belly exactly, and the hardness of the wood used will affect the sound: the same being true of the sound-post, which is made of pine and usually set with the grain running across that of the belly. Too tight a post will prevent the transmission of vibrations and also increase the contained air by pushing belly and back apart, too short a one can cause weak upper notes.

The effect of varnish on violin tone is a source of considerable argument: the Hill family estimate its effect very highly, pointing out in their book on Stradivari the tonal contrast between Stradivari's violins and those of his contemporary imitator Daniel Parker, who achieved in England a similar structure to Stradivari but used a harder varnish. Other experts, however, place the tonal influence of varnish at a good deal less: it is probably just one more of those factors, like the judging of hardness in relation to thickness of belly and back, which make each violin different in sound yet often recognisably representative of its maker.

Oil varnish of a recipe which fell into disuse about the middle of the 18th century was used by the great Italian makers, and many attempts have been made to imitate it. Spirit varnishes, sometimes used later for their quick drying properties, are less durable, may affect the tone adversely, and are usually less beautiful. The Cremonese makers probably used a variety of resins and vegetable colourings some of which would be imported: Venice was an important trading centre with Eastern countries. Jalovec[14] endorses a theory that bee-glue, used by bees to stop the crevices in their hives, provided the yellow grounding which was applied before the varnish on old Italian violins: this initial sizing of the wood must affect the tone, as the density of the wood will change according to the extent to which the pores are filled in. Although Bachmann[15] states that only two layers of oil varnish are necessary, Heron-Allen[16] recommends seven or eight, and it is probable that varnishing in Stradivari's time was a fairly lengthy business (at least twenty-four hours are needed for each coat to dry), otherwise such distinguished makers as Andrea Guarneri would not have resorted to the use of dryers to accelerate the hardening process.

The body of the violin is varnished after the setting of the neck but before the addition of the finger-board: the neck is left unvarnished so that the violin may be held by the neck and a spike run into the tail-pin hole during the varnishing process. Between each coat dust and flies are removed, and the neck is finally varnished when the instrument is dry and the finger-board fitted. Heron-Allen recommends the removal of varnish beneath the feet of the bridge, but this is unsightly, not a characteristic of old violins, and prevents the player making adjustments to suit his own taste.

The tone-producing qualities of a violin are naturally only fully exploited in the hands of an expert performer: even a good player who does not properly understand his instrument may lose part of the characteristic quality. It takes some weeks or months really to discover the individual traits of a fine violin, and this makes choosing one particularly difficult – a player needs to wean himself from his former violin before he can adapt his playing to a different one, especially if he changes from a French to an Italian fiddle, for instance. The interaction of a brilliant violinist and his first fine instrument brings out the qualities of both: Paganini must have taken great pleasure in discovering the potential of the Guarneri del Gesù violin he was given at the age of fifteen and played for the rest of his life, just as Corelli probably enjoyed the resonance of his Andrea Amati, more than a hundred years before. A good violinist can make a poor violin sound pleasing to the ear – most people have met the modern counterpart of Giardini who

> produced . . . a tone more powerful and clear than any of his contemporaries and even on an indifferent fiddle he displayed nearly the same admirable qualities. This knack . . . proved very profitable to Giardini, enabling him to sell his inferior instruments at a large price to gentlemen who, in his hands, admired the powerful tone, though they found afterwards, to their great surprise, that they could draw forth very little, apparently not aware that the tone came from the skill used, not from the fiddle.[17]

But today's large concert halls need the power and penetration of the fairly flat and massively constructed instrument in the tradition initiated by the early Brescians, da Salò and more particularly Maggini, and fully explored by Stradivari in his long-pattern period, when he enlarged the overall dimensions to increase the tone.

All the 'long-pattern' instruments are dated by the Hill brothers between 1690 and 1700, with a subsequent return to the 14-inch length and a more Amati-influenced pattern, followed by the fusion of characteristics which produced the violin now generally accepted as the ideal – Stradivari's 'Golden Period' model.

The Cremona school was undisputed centre of Italian violin-making for almost 200 years, until the mid-18th century; first through the supremacy of the Amati family, later through a teacher–pupil tradition which caused such famous makers and families as Stradivari, Guarneri, Bergonzi, Storioni, Ruggieri, Balestrieri, and Guadagnini to work in the same small town. Cremona traditions spread abroad, partly through admiration of the beautiful craftsmanship of the best violins, partly through the display of their tonal powers by famous violinists (such as Visconti, who introduced Stradivari's violins to London, probably giving rise to the first Strad-pattern English violins, made by Daniel Parker).

Certain makers felt that the competition in Cremona was overshadowing their own abilities, and moved to other towns to follow their trade. Cremona was, after all, a small provincial town. The musical centres where violin-making and repairing would be constantly in demand were

COMPARATIVE MEASUREMENTS FROM ANTONIO STRADIVARI BY THE BROTHERS HILL[18]

	Length A–A		*Width* B–B		*Width* C–C	
	inches	mm	inches	mm	inches	mm
Grand Amati 1658	14	355·6	$8\frac{1}{8}+$	206·4	$6\frac{5}{8}$	168·3
Small form Amati 1671	$13\frac{7}{8}$	352·4	$7\frac{15}{16}$	201·6	$6\frac{3}{8}$	161·9
Stradivari 1669	$13\frac{7}{8}$	352·4	$7\frac{7}{8}$	200·0	$6\frac{1}{4}+$	159·0
Stradivari 1679 (The Hellier)	$14\frac{1}{8}$	358·8	$8\frac{3}{8}+$	213·0	$6\frac{13}{16}+$	173·3
Stradivari 1690 (Long pattern)	$14\frac{5}{16}$	363·5	$8\frac{1}{16}$	204·8	$6\frac{7}{16}$	163·5
Maggini (Small pattern)	$14\frac{1}{4}$	362·0	$8\frac{3}{16}+$	208	$6\frac{5}{8}-$	168·0
Stradivari 1700	$14+$	356·0	$8\frac{1}{4}$	210	$6\frac{11}{16}$	169·9
Stradivari 1709	14	355·6	$8\frac{1}{4}+$	210·5	$6\frac{11}{16}+$	169·4
Stradivari 1720	$14\frac{1}{16}$	357·2	$8\frac{1}{4}$	210	$6\frac{5}{8}$	168·3

Sides D–D		*Sides* E–E	
inches	mm	inches	mm
$1\frac{3}{16}+$	30·2	$1\frac{3}{16}-$	29·4
$1\frac{3}{16}$	30·15	$1\frac{1}{8}$	28·6
$1\frac{3}{8}+$	35·0	$1\frac{3}{8}-$	29·4
$1\frac{1}{4}+$	32·0	$1\frac{3}{16}+$	30·5
$1\frac{1}{4}-$	31·5	$1\frac{3}{16}$	30·16
$1\frac{1}{8}$	28·6	$1\frac{1}{8}$	28·6
$1\frac{1}{4}$	31·75	$1\frac{3}{16}$	30·16
$1\frac{1}{4}$	31·75	$1\frac{3}{16}$	30·16
$1\frac{1}{4}$	31·75	$1\frac{3}{16}$	30·16

Measurements taken exterior to the instruments.
+ indicates a full, — a bare measurement.
millimetre conversions approximate.

still the big Courts of noblemen, and towns like Venice where the Church and orphanages kept a flow of performing traditions. The Dukes of Mantua, where Monteverdi first demanded violins in an opera-score (*Orfeo*, 1607), attracted a considerable array of musical talent to their Court for the performance, in particular, of opera. Pietro Guarneri (1655–1728) left Cremona to join the orchestra at the Court of Mantua, where he was appointed Master of the Violins by virtue of his skill as a performer. Camillus Camilli and Balestrieri also worked as violin-makers in Mantua.

Venice, for many years the musical centre of the world as well as a market for much of the wood and other necessities for the violin-maker, naturally attracted its own craftsmen besides dealing with Cremonese makers. Another member of the Guarneri family settled here after leaving Cremona: Pietro (1695–1762), brother of Giuseppe Guarneri known as del Gesù, and nephew of Pietro of Mantua. Violins for the many opera-houses, for the orchestras of young women from the orphanages (one of which had Vivaldi as musical director), and for the innovatory school of church music at St Mark's would be provided and repaired by a flourishing school of craftsmen including Domenico Montagnana (c. 1690–1750) and Santo Seraphin: Matteo Goffriller producing beautiful cellos during the same period.

The schools of Venice, Florence, Rome, and Bologna flourished, like Cremona, until the mid-18th century. The Carcassi family worked in Florence, the Tecchler family, of German origin, worked in Rome and produced particularly excellent cellos, while the Tononi family produced the most outstanding instruments of the Bologna school. Corelli used two violins, a new one by Matthias Albani of Rome which he probably played when leading orchestras, and an older Amati which he may have used for chamber music and solo work. Probably many busy musicians would follow his practice of patronising a local violin-maker for their second instrument.

The schools of Naples and Milan flourished longer, until c. 1800. Neopolitan violin-makers often used Stradivari as a model, and the large Gagliano family of makers became internationally famous. Milan, the cultural centre of an area including Brescia, Cremona, Saronno, Vercelli, and Turin, homes of the earliest important violin-makers, had sometimes a reputation for producing cheap violins for the poorer musicians, but some Milanese violins (often in the Guarneri style) bring very high prices today – especially those by Landolfi or members of the Grancino and Testore families. Another very famous family of makers was the Guadagnini family whose main representative, Joannes Baptista, lived and worked variously in Turin, Milan, Parma, and Cremona, strongly influenced by Stradivari.

In the Tyrol the first of a long line of instrument-makers, Matthias Klotz of Mittenwald, began a tradition of producing violins fairly cheaply in large numbers which later became an industry and still later mass production on a large commercial scale. Hendrik Jakobs in Holland copied Nicola Amati but used whalebone purflings: Dutch paintings before 1700 show that the violin was in use in Holland, but probably most instruments were imported. England's first important maker, Barak Norman, was born about 1678: his probable pupil Daniel Parker was producing copies of Stradivari's long-pattern violins by 1720, but this is unfortunately an isolated example. Most of the European makers, including the lesser Italians, adopted either Stainer or Amati patterns, and their instruments lack the power of flatter models. Peter Walmsley (c. 1715–60), William Forster (1739–1808), Benjamin Banks (c. 1725–95), and Joseph Hill (1715–84) made English violins which have a pleasant sound and are of good appearance, but not until John Lott (1775–1853) did the English violin rival the power of the best Italians. A John Lott copy of a Guarneri violin was used by a well-known concert artist for some years during the present century.

French violin-making only assumed international importance with F. L. Pique, N. Lupot, and Vuillaume, but Claude Pierray (1698–1726) and his pupil Louis Guersan had a local following in Paris, and Nicolas Médard (b. 1628) of Nancy had a considerable reputation. In Belgium Hendrik Willems was making violas and cellos before 1700.

The practice of inserting labels showing the name of the maker's teacher, or of the originator of the model copied, has made the label of least value today in helping to identify the maker of an instrument. Hill[19] quotes a petition of 1685 made by Tomasso Antonio Vitali, who complained that he had paid 12 pistoles for a violin by Francesco Ruggieri labelled 'Nicola Amati': the true maker being named underneath the Amati label, and the price paid being therefore four times too high. This type of labelling would not be done with any attempt to defraud, just as an indication that a certain model was being followed: often the real maker's name was also placed inside. Cappa, Andrea Guarneri, and some members of the Gagliano family are known to have labelled their fiddles after the style of the greatest makers, and later makers such as Vuillaume, Duke, and Joseph Hill did so in order to complete their copies in every detail. Copies marked 'Stainer' were numerous during the 18th century.

A more dishonest practice of forging labels or of removing them from genuinely fine instruments to insert them in inferior ones has obscured the origin of many old violins whose workmanship does not clearly reveal the hand of a famous maker. Some of these are composite violins, the expert forger making two violins out of one by adding a new belly to an old back and sides, putting the old belly with a new back. Others may have been worked by the master as well as an apprentice in a workshop, or had a portion replaced early in life, so that the added section looks as old as the rest. The famous Tarisio (? –1854), a travelling chair-mender with an infallible eye for a good violin, who amassed the greatest collection of old Italian violins ever known and sold many of them in London and Paris, was also a collector of old labels, and was possibly responsible for separating many of them from their original instruments. On his death, Tarisio's heirs sold the contents of his room to Vuillaume for 80,000 francs – not appreciating that the value of the 150 instruments must have been more than twenty times that sum, as they included twenty-five violins made by Stradivari, including the unplayed 'Messiah' violin; four by del Gesù; four by Nicola Amati; a viola by Gasparo da Salò; and Bergonzi's greatest violin, as well as instruments by other great makers.

Violas were made in disproportionately small numbers compared to violins during the 18th century, owing to the musical bias towards trio-sonata instrumentation, and to the fact that there were a fair number of instruments already available as a result of the 16th–17th-century habit of using two viola-lines in the string ensemble. Only ten violas by Stradivari were known to the Hill family when their monograph on that maker was published. The rich, the distinguished, and the successful did not play the viola; therefore large prices would not normally be paid for the instruments unless they were part of a set as occasionally ordered by a king or duke. Large- and small-pattern instruments were still made, although parts at different pitches were no longer written for them: the big ones ($17\frac{1}{2}$ inches–$18\frac{5}{8}$ inches) must have been very uncomfortable to play. This was the da Salò (Plate 14) and Amati model, taken to even larger dimensions by Stradivari. Andrea Guarneri preferred the smaller dimensions (c. $16\frac{1}{2}$ inches) which were also used by Stradivari and Stainer: the small model may have originated with Antonius and Hieronymus Amati. Many violas have been cut down during the last two centuries, destroying the balance of the original proportions.

While the violin was undergoing fluctuations of size and arching in the search for a more powerful and satisfying tone, the bow must have received similar attention, for every violinist is aware that a good bow can make an instantly audible difference to the sound drawn from a violin. Developments in the bow are hard to trace, as bows tended to be discarded rather than preserved, but there remain a few 17th-century and early 18th-century specimens which differ widely from each other, and many pictures which again serve to point to a variety of fashion rather than any single line of development. For a long time the fashion in bows was related to the musical fashion in the different countries: short, straight bows for the dance musicians in France; long, more curved bows for the Italian sonata; and even more outwardly curved bows for the Germans. As the national styles began to mingle during the 18th century, however, longer bows became the general rule, and straight sticks became more common than outwardly curved ones. It is often taken for granted that the inwardly curved stick and the hatchet-shaped head appeared together, but this is not so; there are instances of a concave stick with a pike's head in the late 18th century (see Plate 20).

David Boyden[20] describes a very beautiful bow dating from *c.* 1700, which is nearly as long as the modern bow, is made (like Tourte's bows) of Brazil Pernambuco wood, and has a screw for tightening the hairs similar to today's system. The lighter, more pointed head brings the point of balance further towards the hand than in a Tourte bow, but the difference in 'feel' of an 18th-century bow is not so great that violinists are unable to change from one type to the other. Players lucky enough to possess a pre-1780 bow usually find it superior for the performance of Baroque music, even though the violin has been somewhat altered since then.

It was not customary for the bow-maker to sign his bows until the late 18th century, when John Dodd was among the first to do so. But from drawings and inventories we know that Stradivari and Pietro Guarneri of Mantua probably made bows, and as the bow was considered a part of the violin, it seems likely that most of the great makers lavished attention on it. Oversimplified accounts of the bow's history need to be disregarded. So much experimentation took place that widely differing bows were in use at any part of the 17th and 18th centuries (Plate 20): standardisation only came with the Tourte bow, developed simultaneously by Dodd in England, towards the end of the 18th century.

The frontispieces to Violin Schools and to Veracini's *Sonate accademiche* (1744) show national trends: Veracini's bow is very long (longer than the modern bow). Geminiani (in the frontispiece to the French edition of *The Art of Playing on the Violin*, reproduced on the O.U.P. facsimile[21]) has a shorter one, about as long as today's bow; Leopold Mozart's[22] is shorter still and has a marked outward curve. 18th-century bows were generally lighter than the modern bow, and often fluted. Snakewood was the most used, but Pernambuco wood, used invariably since 1800, was also known.

François Tourte (1747–1835) is generally considered the 'Stradivari' of bow-making, but like Stradivari, his genius was employed in amalgamating the best aspects of the work of his predecessors rather than in radical redesigning. Tourte, like Stradivari, was a perfectionist in his craft, and he standardised the bow to give 25½ inches of playing hair, separating the hair from the concave stick by a deeper hatchet-head than had been used before, weighting the nut with metal inlays to balance this heavier head, widening the band of hair, and fixing it with a ferrule (see Fig. 7B). Tourte was followed by a line of makers, many of them trained by Vuillaume; including Voirin, Peccatte, Lafleur, and Sartory. Italy does not seem to have contributed to the bow-making tradition: a fact which underlines the gradually diminishing importance of that country in violin-making, playing, and composing. Leadership was by the turn of the 18th century in the hands of the French – a Milanese writer mentioned in 1823 that Italian violin-necks were being lengthened 'according to the fashion prevailing in Paris'. The highest-ranking violinists of today will almost undoubtedly play German concertos on Italian violins with French bows.

NOTES

[1] 85 Hill.
[2] ibid. p. 112.
[3] 48 Donington.
[4] ibid.
[5] 82 Heron-Allen, p. 150.
[6] 48 Donington, p. 29.
[7] 82 Heron-Allen.
[8] 85 Hill, p. 82.
[9] 84 Hill, p. 190.
[10] 103 Lafontaine, p. 150.
[11] 21 Boyden, p. 321.
[12] 10 Bachmann, p. 150.
[13] 82 Heron-Allen, p. 188.
[14] 93 Jalovec, p. 24.
[15] 10 Bachmann, p. 110.
[16] 82 Heron-Allen.
[17] 132 Parke.
[18] 84 Hill, pp. 291–5.
[19] ibid. p. 211.
[20] 21 Boyden.
[21] 65 Geminiani.
[22] 123 Mozart.

CHAPTER 5

The String-based Orchestra: 1700–50

THE LATER YEARS of the Baroque period are often referred to by musical historians as 'the age of Bach and Handel': from the viewpoint of the history of the violin and viola, they would be more aptly named 'the age of Vivaldi'.

Born *c.* 1678, Antonio Vivaldi became a leading figure on the Italian musical scene at a time when the *concerto grosso*, orchestral and solo concerto forms were occupying the attention of his composer contemporaries, and when Italian opera was in constant demand. String accompaniment was becoming increasingly accepted as the problems of balancing wind-groups were realised. The *concerto grosso* writing of Corelli and his contemporaries had already stimulated the development of violins with sufficient tonal power to stand alone in contrast to a group and Vivaldi, as Musical Director of the Pietà in Venice, had at his disposal a large and capable band of instrumentalists with which he could make experiments in orchestration. He was responsible for the development of one of the most typical and lasting forms of violin composition, the solo concerto, and for revealing the wealth of orchestral effects obtainable from a small string band with or without wind. His extension of the technique required by the concerto soloist was very considerable as compared with Corelli, and was governed by a sense of style and unity which made his concertos stand as a model for J. S. Bach.

The system of musical patronage prevailing at this time made court operas, chamber music, and church music the most popularly pursued branches of the art. Opera was the great status symbol of rival princes, supported by heavy taxation of the poorer classes or even (as in the case of the Duke of Brunswick) by selling subjects as soldiers. Noblemen who could not afford to support a standing opera would employ the newly-formed commercial opera companies and almost every Court would support its own composer and group of chamber musicians, who also provided music for official church services. Vivaldi's position at one of the four orphanages in Venice where girls were given a thorough musical education was unusual in its scope, for although he, like most of his contemporaries, was continually required to produce music for special occasions, he was less limited by the caprice of his particular employer, and the forces at his disposal were larger than usual. His considerable output of opera is mostly forgotten today, but the importance of the virtuoso male soprano singers, the *castrati*, in this medium must have affected his conception of the role of the violin soloist. While the visual arts moved away from the serious atmosphere of the Baroque towards the more frivolous, pleasure-seeking themes of the Rococo, music retained its seriousness during the first part of the 18th century, and seemed for a time to be the most deeply expressive of the arts. With Bach the contrapuntal style reached a peak of achievement when already the general trend of music was towards Rococo airs and graces. International exchanges of musical style were by now more rapid and frequent as music-publishing increased, and as musicians discovered that foreigners were almost invariably better paid and more favourably received than native musicians. Italy exported *castrati*, violinists, and violins to England, Germany, and France; such a notable composer as Handel spent much of his life abroad, and as many as twelve German violinists are mentioned in an 18th-century English orchestra.

> The band has received the addition of twelve *German* musicians, *imported* some years since, to complete the *Queen's* band, and put the natives of poor Old England out of countenance, as much as possible.[1]

The social rank of musicians was very gradually rising, but court musicians throughout the 18th century wore livery and sat with the servants 'below the salt' at table. Musicians' incomes were generally small, but those employed in households had the benefit of bed, board, and often such things as wood for their fires in winter as part of their terms of employment. Periods of mourning, when music and dancing were banned, could mean real hardship for musicians, and they were not slow to form unions to protect the distribution of work and pay for their services.

As music-publishing firms sprang up in the larger commercial cities, the works of leading Italian composers became available throughout Europe. An astonishing collection of European music was sold in London in 1714 on the death of Thomas Britton, the small-coal merchant who organised some of London's earliest concerts. He owned not only sonatas but concertos by Corelli, and (already) concertos by Vivaldi. Other Italian composers mentioned in the catalogue quoted in Hawkins's *History of Music*[2] are Albinoni, Vitali, Merula, Veracini, and Uccellini, while in addition to the music by Englishmen or foreigners living in England there are unexpected items such as 'Biber's Solo book finely engrav'd' – which poses the question of who in England at that time was capable of performing Biber's works. It seems that new music was heard abroad very soon after its initial publication, and publishers who were anxious to be up to the minute had no scruples about pirating editions.

During the 18th century, and particularly under the patronage-system, music tended to be composed for a specific audience on a specific occasion, often in a great hurry to meet the deadline. Inner string parts were sometimes left incomplete. Occasionally they were filled in by a different hand or added by a publisher, often to the detriment of the original concept. Theatre music by Purcell and by French composers was commonly left without middle parts, and Vivaldi would reduce his four parts to two by making the violins play one line, the violas and cellos doubling the other.[3] Probably originating as a short cut when pressure was high, this lighter orchestration now gives a refreshingly Baroque flavour.

Another time-saving habit of the hard-pressed Baroque composer was plagiarism – from himself or from others. Pincherle mentions one work by Vivaldi which contains fragments of operas by Micheli, Paganelli, Pampino, Mazzoni, Hasse, Handel, and others, while certain of his own movements reappear several times. Handel's self-plagiarisms sometimes reveal traces of the Renaissance concept of 'apt for voices or viols': the second movement of his D major violin sonata, for instance, appears as the fugal section of a chorus in *Solomon*, with the words 'Live, live for ever pious David's son'.

Young composers who had not yet established a sufficient reputation to obtain a post in a wealthy household, might publish their opus 1 at their own expense with a flowery dedication to a patron, who was expected to acknowledge the compliment with a sum of money. Compositions for special occasions would be commissioned by wealthy patrons, churches, or councils, and quarrels between union and non-union members, especially in Italy, but also in France, over providing music for weddings, etc., were frequent, particularly in places where the church employed its own group of performers. These musicians would be outside the union, as at St Mark's, Venice.

The composer was unlikely to gain any profit from his work except for the fee for its first performance, unless he was unusually astute, financially, and like Lully obtained a monopoly of music-printing, or like Schütz retained works in manuscript and only allowed the parts out on hire. A composer working under the patronage-system had definite advantages to offset his subservient role in the household. His position released him from worry about personal day-to-day expenses, and provided him with performers and an audience for every composition. A court Capellmeister stood higher in the social scale than a municipal musician, although employment by collective patrons was hotly competed for, and often gained by bribery or influence. Some cities and churches, like St Mark's, Venice, employed musicians for life after making sure of their highest musical competence; this gave maximum security without the indignity of having humbly to request their own dismissal, as from a noble household: municipal musicians were free to resign. Vivaldi's position was greatly coveted.

Patronage in England was less fashionable than on the continent, yet music itself was the height of fashion. Perhaps this was why England had a reputation for paying so well for her music: in 1713 Mattheson wrote: 'The Italians exalt music; the French enliven it; the Germans strive for it; and the English pay for it well.'[4] Many of the greatest composers and performers came to England during the 18th century: not on account of court patronage, which waned after the time of Charles II, but because of a growing concert life. Performers could claim high fees for single engagements in wealthy households, and composers whose music became fashionable began to make a profit on the entrance money for concerts of their works. Concert prices occasionally sound high even by today's standards; a letter from Lady Irwin of 1733 recounts

> Last week we had an oratorio composed by Handel out of the story of Borak [sic] and Deborah. . . . Handel thought, encouraged by the Princess Royal, it had merit enough to deserve a guinea, and for the first time it was performed at that price, exclusive of subscribers' tickets; and there was but 120 people in the House.[5]

The musicians themselves, lacking the ready-made audiences provided by the patronage-system, organised the earliest concerts in taverns, dancing schools, and theatres; Britton the small-coal dealer held free concerts in a room over his coal-store in Clerkenwell. An English soprano at the opera could command £500 per season, yet English artists were far less esteemed than foreigners: Joseph Addison wrote in *The Spectator* (21 March 1711)

> At present our Notions of Musick are so very uncertain that we do not know what it is we like; only, in general, we are transported with anything that is not English.

Handel, like many others, lost money heavily by putting on his Italian operas in London; a letter of his refers to engaging 'Sr. Senesino on the footing of fourteen hundred Guineas'.[6] London was becoming the home of the freelance musician.

Lists of instrumentalists employed by noble households in the 18th century give us some picture of how quickly the string basis of violins 1 and 2, violas, and cellos became accepted once the *concerto grosso* had become an established instrumental form. Robert Donington[7] lists over a dozen household orchestras around the middle of the century: all except one have at least one viola, one or more cellos, and a bass. Often wind-players would double on stringed instruments and it is likely that the repertoire of each of these orchestras would include *concerti grossi*, with a *concertino* section, usually of two solo violins and cello, alternating with the *ripieno* section of string quartet (doubled *ad libitum*) and continuo. The 'double bass' mentioned was often the *violone*, as the real bass of the violin family was not very popular. Mattheson (1713) describes playing on it as 'labour fit for a horse'.[8]

The viola was also an unpopular instrument in the early 18th century, although its importance was recognised for the completion of four-part string harmony in the *concerto grosso*. Corelli even inserted *ripieno* viola entries into the fugal *concertino* sections of his concertos, and Geminiani added a viola to the *concertino* group; but in spite of a gradual recognition by Bach, Handel, and Stamitz of the viola's particular tonal qualities, not until the trio sonata was replaced by the string quartet was the viola considered worthy of attention by the better performers. Quantz summed up the situation in 1752

> The viola is commonly regarded as of little importance in the musical establishment. The reason may well be that it is often played by persons who are either still beginners in the ensemble or have no particular gifts with which to distinguish themselves on the violin, or that the instrument yields all too few advantages to its players, so that able people are not easily persuaded to take it up. I maintain, however, that if the entire accompaniment is to be without defect, the violist must be just as able as the second violinist.[9]

Possibly Geminiani's unusual interest in the viola was stimulated by his stay in Naples, where according to Burney he was found to be 'so wild and unsteady a timist'[10] that he was restricted to playing viola parts.

Vivaldi wrote 454 concertos of which 27 are for cello and 7 for viola d'amore, even 37 for bassoon, but none for the viola, and Torelli says in the preface to his *concerti grossi* that the viola part may be omitted in all but numbers 3, 5, 6, 7, and 12. The lack of interesting repertoire for viola discouraged musicians from playing it, and as there were no reputable performers, the composers had no occasion to produce works for them. This vicious circle was only gradually destroyed by the composers of the Classical period, several of whom (Carl Stamitz, Haydn, Mozart, Schubert, and Beethoven) played the viola themselves.

With the publishing in several countries of *concerti grossi* by Corelli and his contemporaries, all Europe was once again under the spell of the Italian violinist-composers. Roger North's comment (1710) 'It is wonderful to observe what a skratching of Correlli there is everywhere – nothing will relish but Corelli'[11] could apply to several countries. Later he was to describe this vogue from a historical viewpoint in the *Musicall Gramarian*:

> . . . then came over Corellys first consort that cleared ye ground of all other sorts of music whatsoever; by degrees the rest of his consorts & at last ye conciertos came, all wch are to ye musitians like ye bread of life.[12]

Even France, though still occupied with dance music, began to accept the Italian sonata given a French flavour by Couperin, Leclair, and Mondonville: François Couperin wrote a trio sonata entitled 'l'Apothéose de Corelli' in 1724.

From the first half of the 18th century we have our first standard orchestral repertoire. Although earlier orchestral music exists and can still be performed, it was nearly all written to accompany theatre, vocal, or church performances of one sort or another. The Church was undecided during the 17th century as to the suitability of violins for religious services, but the existence of a serious style of composition, the *sonata da chiesa*, intended for performance in church, finally convinced most European bishops that the violin family was no longer to be solely associated with such frivolous pursuits as dancing and opera, and c. 1749 Pope Benedict XIV approved the use of the violin family in churches, while excluding wind instruments apart from bassoons.[13]

The 18th-century orchestra would today be referred to as a 'chamber orchestra', as it normally consisted of less than thirty players: often less than twenty. A gathering of more than thirty instrumentalists was a very special attraction in 18th-century concert life, to be mentioned in advertisements in much the same was as we see Tchaikovsky's 1812 Overture with 'orchestra of 120 players, brass band, and cannons' occasionally advertised today. In early English concerts, if the music was rehearsed beforehand, this would be mentioned in the advertisements too!

The exact size of Vivaldi's orchestra at the Pietà is not known, but we have details of one which he directed in Amsterdam in 1738. This had 7 first violins, 5 second violins, 3 violas, 2 cellos, 2 double-basses, 2 trumpets or horns, 2 bassoons. Pincherle[14] suggests that probably an oboist, timpanist, and harpsichordist played as well. Throughout the century a harpsichord was considered an indispensable part of the orchestra, and sometimes two harpsichords would be used, one with the *ripieno*, the other with the *concertino* strings: Quantz writes in 1752 'I assume that the *harpsichord* will be included in all ensembles, whether large or small',[15] and suggests that two harpsichords may be used with extra-large string-groups. But in church music a small organ often replaced the harpsichord, even in chamber works, and the use of a chamber organ with the *ripieno* of *concerti grossi* and a harpsichord with the *concertino* was probably a recognised method of adding contrast. Quantz's *Versuch* gives detailed instructions for the layout of an orchestra with harpsichord(s), placing the *concertino* players right in front of the harpsichord, then the first violins, second violins, and violas in that order behind,

> . . . so that the middle parts do not stand out above the principal part, for this produces a poor effect. . . . For how can a composition sound well if the principal parts are drowned out and suppressed by the bass or even the middle parts?[16]

By this time (1752) the string-quartet basis of the orchestra was firmly established, although the middle parts were to become far more important in the scores of Haydn and Mozart. While Vivaldi was not the first to use the orchestral quartet with pairs of wind for additional colour, he probably played the greatest individual part in establishing the strings as the orchestral nucleus. Operatic and oratorio accompaniments were the first to use orchestras similar to the Classical pattern, particularly in works by Marc' Antonio Cesti, Alessandro Scarlatti, and Giovanni Legrenzi during the second half of the 17th century; but the *concerto grosso* composers led by Corelli (whom Vivaldi greatly admired) were responsible for exploiting the possibilities of the orchestral quartet alone. Vivaldi did not accept Corelli's orchestration and develop it along a straight line towards the Classical orchestra: he was an experimenter and an innovator. Probably he often orchestrated according to the available personnel, as Bach sometimes did later: some strangely assorted orchestras may have been designed to use only his best players, while the orchestral concertos without solo parts were probably written for the students at the Pietà. Up to 1710 his orchestration was similar to Corelli's opus 6, although his use of the instruments was more daring: Pincherle[17] points out that Giuseppe Torelli (1658–1709) at this period was far more advanced in the contrasting of wind and string timbres.

Vivaldi occasionally added plucked instruments to the orchestral quartet, but no percussion except for an occasional work performed outside the Pietà. He frequently authorised substitutions – *pizzicato* violins for mandoline, bassoon or violin for oboe, and so on. Doublings were more common than today: Alessandro Marcello suggests that for his concertos of 1738 two oboes or flutes should double the *concertino* parts, which should be played by two violinists per part if the wind were not available.

Among the orchestral string-colourings explored in Vivaldi's concertos we find accompaniments for harpsichord alone, violins with violas, or violins alone, sometimes in unison providing a simple bass-line with no harmonic filling, sometimes in three-part chords *tremolando* or in semiquavers. Any of these methods of cutting down accompaniments provides a rest from four-part string harmony and causes the solo tone to ring out without danger of obliteration – a fact of which Vivaldi as soloist must have been very aware. Where several soloists are used, far from alternating blocks of *ripieno* and *concertino* like most of his predecessors, Vivaldi introduces his soloists by turn, varying the pairings and only occasionally combining them all. The *larghetto* of his concerto for four violins, opus 3, no. 10, is a pure experiment in orchestral colour, being a harmonic progression decorated throughout by a different (clearly indicated) arpeggiation for each soloist, while the two *ripieno* viola sections and cellos fill in the harmony with repeated quavers.

Certain string effects had become the stock-in-trade of opera composers and some of these were already being jeered at by contemporary critics – particularly *tremoli*, muted passages, and cellos doubling the voice. But although Vivaldi used operatic formulae, he added effects of his own such as a violin-line doubled in *pizzicato* and *arco*, or an unmuted solo violin against a muted string background: his originality as an orchestrator is comparable to that of Monteverdi.

The first form in which the orchestra became truly independent of the theatre was the *concerto grosso*, closely followed by the solo concerto. The *sinfonia*, from which the later title 'symphony' was derived, was at this period intended for performance in a theatre, usually as an overture – although titles were loosely applied and a *sinfonia* might in fact be a *concerto grosso*. Whereas the *concerto grosso* had clear derivations from the trio sonata, with many short movements using similar material throughout, we can see in one of Vivaldi's best-known solo concertos (opus 3, no. 6 in A minor) how the three-movement form was partly derived from the theatre. The fast–slow–fast arrangement of movements, string or wind fanfares, and brilliant tonal effects used by Vivaldi were all characteristic of the Italian *sinfonia*, and the A minor concerto shows

Concerto for 4 violins, op. 3 no. 10. Note the precise dynamic markings.

a form in which the orchestral *ritornello* is considerably extended in the opening of the movement and clearly concluded by a cadence in the tonic key. The solo violin restates, embellishes, and adds to this initial material, which is repeated in orchestral *tutti* sections throughout the movement, moving into one main closely-related key and returning to the tonic to give a loosely defined A B A key-structure. The *ritornello*, from its original place in the early operas when the same piece of orchestral music was repeated between vocal sections, thus moved into purely instrumental music and was gradually transformed into the orchestral *tutti* section of the Classical and Romantic concertos. The slow movement of opus 3, no. 6, differs from the outside movements in losing the *ritornelli* and the extra length derived from them; it resembles an operatic *arioso* and leaves the violin unaccompanied in the phrase before the cadence where a singer would add embellishments.

Vivaldi, remembered now as a composer, must have been one of the greatest violinists. His flair for dazzling and moving his audiences is felt particularly in the concertos which were probably intended for his own performance. The same performer's instinct is shown by Corelli in his last *concerto grosso*, which has a very soloistic part for the leader if one considers that it was written probably *c.* 1680. But the *bravura* and the touch of the theatre in Vivaldi's compositions gave them a new, direct appeal to the audience. A single personality standing in contrast to or in conflict with a group has been one of the most audience-drawing musical techniques ever since Vivaldi's rise to fame in the early 18th century.

A pupil of Vivaldi, Johann Georg Pisendel (1687–1755), carried the solo concerto to Germany, where the Italian *grosso* form had little influence although Muffat introduced it there in 1701. Pisendel knew Bach, who took over Vivaldi's concerto form almost exactly, transcribing some of the Italian's works for other instruments, and copying the form and key-structure of others. The technique used in Bach's violin concertos is not far in advance of that of Vivaldi, but the solo sonatas follow in the line of Biber and Pisendel and carry double-stopping techniques to the limit of contrapuntal ingenuity. Bach's Brandenburg Concertos follow no previous pattern but combine characteristics of the *concerto grosso*, solo concerto, and orchestral concerto. Here the *bravura* writing for violin equals that of Vivaldi, particularly in the Fourth Concerto, and the viola stands out as a soloist in the Third and Sixth Concertos as it never did with Vivaldi. Telemann also considered the viola worthy of a solo with string accompaniment, not sharing the lowly opinion of Quantz, a knowledgeable flautist-composer, who devoted his talents mainly to writing 300 flute concertos.

So great was the renown of Vivaldi that his talented contemporary Albinoni was unfairly neglected until recently. Composers who worked in countries less full of talent gained more repute – in England, for instance, where people liked to play new music as much as to listen to it, the *concerti grossi* of Francesco Geminiani, Charles Avison, and John Stanley were greatly appreciated. Hawkins[18] describes an occasion in

1724 when all twelve of Corelli's concertos were played through at a sitting, the parts having newly arrived from Amsterdam. Geminiani (1687–1762) was Corelli's pupil, and even some of his concertos in the Corelli tradition (with a viola added to the *concertino*) were considered by Burney to be 'so laboured, difficult and fantastical'[19] as to be unplayable. Vivaldi's concertos, although applauded when performed by visiting virtuosi, were not a standard part of English repertoire, as Handel's *concerti grossi*, with their limited technical requirements, soon became. A sonata for violin and strings with optional oboes, published in the Handel Society's collected edition, contains some virtuoso violin-writing more in the Vivaldi style, and Handel's organ concertos, which he wrote for himself to perform between the sections of his oratorios, are really soloistic, with obvious places where he would improvise cadenzas to the enormous admiration of his audiences.

Even the French succumbed at last to the influence of the Italian violinist, and Jean-Marie Leclair (1697–1764) published a distinctive set of twelve violin concertos, as well as some trio sonatas using a gamba as second instrument. Dance movements, now grouped together to form the orchestral suite, were still very popular in France. Bach and Telemann usually used French titles for the movements of their suites, as we see in Bach's partitas for unaccompanied violin. Jean-Joseph Cassanea de Mondonville (1711–72) used the solo sonata with figured bass to experiment with violin harmonics, explaining them in the preface. In other ways, as soon as the Italian style had been accepted in France, the French composers began to add their own facets of technical and formal ingenuity. Guillemain (1705–70) and Leclair used a wide range of double-stopping and bowing techniques, and an experimenter called Tremais, a pupil of Tartini, went as high as twelfth position, used multiple stops, alternate notes *arco* and *pizzicato*, and even octave trills.

In early 18th-century France appeared the sonata for harpsichord with violin accompaniment, in which the material was sometimes shared between the two instruments: this was the forerunner of the Classical sonata. In the latter part of the century French violinists were to become leaders of fashion, but during the early 1700s the conservative element was still strong and capable of causing inconvenience to the avant-garde violinists of their day. Van der Straeten[20] tells of the Musicians' Guild in France, who

> kept out all foreign artists, especially those who endangered their reputation, and even J. B. Anet, as pupil of Corelli, and the great J. M. Leclair, as a pupil of Somis, had to suffer from their maleficent influence.

The fame of French orchestral playing was on the wane, and by 1768 Rousseau[21] was complaining of the orchestra at the Paris Opera. 'It has been remarked that of all the orchestras of Europe, that of Paris, tho' one of the most numerous, caused the least effect.' He blames this partly on 'the bad choice of symphonists, the greatest number of which, receiv'd thro' favour, hardly understand music, and have no idea of concinnity', partly on neglected instruments left in the pit, on the bad training of cellists and contrabassists, and on the bad harmony of their compositions (which may have had middle parts added later). He also refers to the 'insupportable noise of the time-stick, which covers and stifles all effects of the symphony.' F. W. von Grimm[22] had comically described this time-beater in 1753:

> And I saw a man who was holding a stick, and I believed that he was going to castigate the bad violins, for I heard many of them, among the other, that were good and not many.
>
> And he made a noise as if he were splitting wood, and I was astonished that he did not dislocate his shoulder, and the vigour of his arm terrified me. . . . And I beheld that they called that 'beating the time', and although it was beaten most forcibly, the musicians were never together.

Rousseau[23] includes among the requirements of the first violin or leader of an orchestra a form of conducting, saying that he is the chief 'which gives the tone, guides all the symphonies, which rectifies them when in error, and on which they must all depend'.

Nettel[24] draws parallels between the early 18th-century orchestra and the 20th-century café orchestra (becoming a rarity today). The domination of the leading violin, the lack of balance between wind and strings, and the filling-in of missing instrumental lines at the keyboard are familiar to any group which has to provide occasional music within the available resources of a strictly limited economy. But no modern string-player has to contend with the unavoidable out-of-tune notes on all 18th-century wind instruments. When Hawkins[25] states of the flute in 1789 that it 'still retains some degree of estimation among gentlemen whose ears are not nice enough to inform them that it is never in tune', he might be speaking of any contemporary wind instrument. Probably the most skilled players learned to manipulate their imperfect instruments to produce good intonation, but the majority adapted their ears to accept the failings of their instruments, which caused Burney[26] to say 'I know it is natural for these instruments to be out of tune.'

Orchestral players, apart from the cellists, often played standing up;

a tradition which persisted in some countries until the beginning of the 20th century. Amateurs and professionals mixed freely in many 18th-century orchestras, which made the *concerto grosso* a most practical form, the difficult solo parts being left to the professionals. Sometimes the harpsichordist, sometimes the leader, and occasionally a non-performer would keep these varied forces together with a beat, often an audible one such as foot-stamping or knocking on a music stand. One of Sir Richard Steele's suggestions for improving contemporary musical performances is to

> order the Heels of the Performers to be muffled in Cotton, that the Artists in so polite an Age as ours, may not intermix with their Harmony a Custom, which so nearly resembles the stamping Dances of the Hottentots.   (*Tatler*, 2 May 1710)

and Pisendel was admired for preventing an orchestra of Italian musicians from rushing during difficult passages for the soloist, by loudly keeping time with his foot.

Pictures of 18th-century orchestras show other obvious differences from their modern counterparts. There are no chin-rests or cello-spikes, and bows vary considerably, as to both length and shape – the 'bipedalian [=2-ft-long] bow'[27] of Matteis, which so impressed Roger North, was still not universally accepted, although during the early part of the century bows were generally lengthening and straightening. The pike's head gradually gave way to a squarer type of head as the bow became straighter; and screw-mechanisms for tightening the hair began to replace the notched *crémaillère* bow (Fig. 6A).

Most 18th-century portraits of violinists show the instrument held on the shoulder close to the neck, although the chin is rarely touching the instrument (Plate 19). Orchestral musicians in pictures point their violins further downwards than is today's custom, but the recommendations in 18th-century treatises tend increasingly towards the modern practice. Leopold Mozart (1719–87) suggests in his treatise of 1756 gripping with the chin to the right of the tail-piece, Herrando (1756) with the chin on the tail-piece, L'Abbé le fils (1761) has the chin to the left of the tail-piece as we do today, and the German edition of Geminiani's treatise (1782) says definitely that the instrument is to be held between the jawbone and the collarbone.

The bow-arm was used freely as it is now: the practice of restricting the movement of the upper arm being an unfortunate 19th-century innovation. Corrette illustrates the difference between Italian and French bow-grips, still with the French holding the thumb on the hair close to the nut, but stating that the Italians hold the bow 'at three-quarters' (i.e., presumably a quarter of the stick-length away from the nut). Leopold Mozart's bow-hold in 1756 is far nearer to the modern practice than Geminiani's, which places the first joint of the index finger on the bow. Mozart[28] recommends 'the middle joint, . . . or a little behind it', which would indicate some pronation of the forearm and therefore more weight on the string. He points out that 'those who hold the bow with the first joint of the index finger and those who lift up their little finger' will find it far easier to produce 'an honest and virile tone'[29] if they change to his method.

The establishment of Stradivari's flatter, more powerful violin design and the winding of the G string with silver, together with the tonal requirements of the concerto forms, made this virile tone of the first importance to the leading professional players, particularly the Italians. The French still preferred a quieter sound, although with the beginning of public concerts in Paris on days when other entertainments were closed (the 'Concerts Spirituels' began in 1725) solo violin-concerto performances in a large hall must have begun to destroy the small-tone tradition. 'What can be more insipid than the playing of one who has not confidence to attack the violin boldly, but scarce touches the strings with the bow?' writes Leopold Mozart;[30] and Geminiani, who recommends a type of vibrato to be used 'as often as possible',[31] nevertheless points out that 'The Tone of the Violin principally Depends upon the right Management of the Bow.'[32]

The contrast between 18th-century and modern tone-production arises less from the differences between the old and modern bows (the former being heavier towards the nut, and having slightly more give in the hair) than from the basic conception of tonal aims. Today a first requirement is a stroke giving even tone from end to end of the bow, next a smooth *détaché*. Leopold Mozart mentions the possibility of a completely even stroke only as an afterthought, after naming the four normally employed types of stroke. 'Besides this, a very useful experiment may be made,' he writes. 'Namely, to endeavour to produce a perfectly even tone with a slow stroke.'[33]

He is very concerned to eliminate harshness at the beginning and end of a note, advocating 'a small, even if barely audible, softness'[34] at these points. His other main instructions are concerned with knowing 'how to divide the bow into weakness and strength, and therefore how by means of pressure and relaxation, to produce the notes beautifully and touchingly'.[34] Tartini's letter also calls for the 'small softness',[35] but in long notes it would occupy such a small fraction of the note as to amount to an almost normal modern bow-change: in the *détaché*, however, it would be more marked, causing clearer separation and articulation than today. Both smooth *détaché* and *martelé* are anachronisms in the performance of Baroque string music.

Sol Babitz[36] takes the first of Leopold Mozart's four dynamic divisions, the *messa di voce* ($\prec$ $\succ$), to be the basic 18th-century bow-stroke, on the grounds that it was most naturally produced by the old bow. But although this was a greatly admired effect, and Geminiani suggests that 'In playing all Long Notes the Sound should be begun soft, and gradually swelled till the Middle, and from thence gradually softened till the end',[37] the treatises describe this stroke as something to be practised and achieved, rather than something inevitable. Roger North gives a most picturesque description of the effect:

> The Italians have brought the bow to an high perfection, so that nothing of their playing is so difficult as the *arcata* or long bow, with which they will begin a long note, clear, without rubb, and draw it forth swelling lowder and lowder, and at the ackme take a slow waiver; not trill to break the sound or mix 2 notes, but as if the bird sat at the end of a spring [and] as she sang the spring waiver her up and downe, or as if the wind that brought the sound shaked, or a small bell were struck and the sound continuing waived to and againe . . . so would I express what is justly not to be shewn but to the ear by an exquisite hand.[38]

Leopold Mozart's second division is a diminuendo on down- or up-bow: he recommends its use 'more in cases of shortly sustained tone in quick tempo than in slow pieces'.[39] For his third division, a crescendo on up- or down-bow, he advocates increased speed as well as pressure – probably the first printed advice of this kind, although Geminiani points out that 'The best Performers are least sparing of their Bow'.[40] Mozart's fourth division has loud and soft twice within one bow ($\prec$ $\succ$ $\prec$ $\succ$), and he suggests that this loud-soft effect can be produced 'four, five and six times; yes, often even more in one stroke'.[41] Lastly he advocates mastery of the long even tone with a slow bow, but more as an exercise in bow control than for application in performance.

The heaviness of the heel of the 18th-century bow made it suitable for loud passages, and the bow's position in relation to the bridge was a recognised tonal factor. Additional weight at the heel caused the 'Rule of Down-Bow' to persist in some of Leopold Mozart's instructions:

indeed it is adhered to instinctively in some passages by most modern players. Not to the extent advocated by Mozart, however:

> If the first crotchet of a bar does not begin with rest, whether it be even or uneven time, one endeavours to take the first note of each bar with a down stroke, and this even if two down strokes should follow each other.[42]

The revolt against this tradition was already apparent in Geminiani's instruction for practising the scales in example VIII of his Tutor 'taking care not to follow that wretched Rule of drawing the Bow down at the first Note of every Bar',[43] and Quantz points out that

> Although certain notes must necessarily be taken with a down-stroke, an experienced violinist with the bow completely under control can also express them well with an up-stroke.[44]

Signs for down- and up-bows were still usually alphabetical (although Veracini used ↑ and ↓ in his opus 2).

Boyden[45] lists the following as the most common:

	Down	Up
England	d	u
France	t (*tiré*)	p (*poussé*)
Germany	*Herabstrich* or *Abstrich*	*Hinaufstrich* or *Aufstrich*
Italy	g (*giù*)	s (*su*)
Spain (Herrando)	O	A

Vivaldi unfortunately left no treatise or Tutor which would elucidate the styles of bowing required in his concertos, but he clearly possessed a remarkably brilliant and varied bow technique. Coupled with his ability to make passage-work lie comfortably under the left hand even when high positions were used, this gave his concertos the maximum effectiveness with the minimum of effort on the part of the performer – a very rare quality in music for the violin, and one which comes only from composer-performers. A glance through the four concertos comprising *The Seasons* shows wide leaps (bars 159/60 *l'Inverno*), rapid *bariolage* (94/95 *l'Estate*), and rushing scales indicating the various winds, wide-spread arpeggiation (*l'Estate* 237–40), and very rapid skips missing one or two strings (same 293–7). Rare indications, such as the violas *molto forte e strappato* in *la Primavera*, intended to represent the barking of a dog, may be dismissed as purely programmatic, but without these there exists within his music a range of bowing sonorities, alone or in combination, which outshines all his contemporaries. Even Locatelli, the great

experimenter from whom Vivaldi may have copied the use of the
brisure, a formula involving large skips, e.g.

Tartini

gains less effect from his bowings than Vivaldi, and certainly less
musical impact.

Vivaldi used *bariolage* on the two lower strings: Locatelli used a
slurred *bariolage*, and Bach was also aware of its effectiveness, as we see
in the last movements of his concerto in A minor, in the Fourth Brandenburg Concerto, and in the very unusual three-string *bariolage* in the
first movement of the E major partita for violin alone.

J.S.Bach

Not all 18th-century musicians admired Vivaldi's technical feats:
Roger North names him as one of those who strove to represent subjects
resembling 'ye hurry of football play, ye madfolks at bedlam or mortall
Battels at Bear Garden'[46] and Hawkins regretted Vivaldi's backsliding
from the 'chaste, sober and elegant' manner of his Corelli-style writing
to 'a style which had little but novelty to recommend it'.[47] But certain
18th-century English composers show signs of Vivaldi's influence, and
it is noticeable in some of Handel's writing, although not nearly to such
an extent as in the compositions of J. S. Bach.

The published treatises do not cover bow or left-hand technique to
the virtuoso standard of Vivaldi, but they do give valuable (if sometimes
conflicting) evidence concerning the interpretation of printed and written
notational signs. The most difficult question for the modern interpreter
is the *staccato*, a term now associated with a series of *martelé* strokes
within one bow-stroke, or more generally with the shortening of notes
to separate each from the next by a rest. Degrees of shortness and ways
in which they are to be produced are rarely stipulated even today: the
decision has to be taken by soloist, leader, or conductor.

The modern 'up-bow *staccato*' had no exact counterpart in the 18th
century, as the bow had less bite, but a series of *staccato* notes under a

slur was known before 1700. The different effect of the modern and old bows makes a literal application of, for instance, Geminiani's and Tartini's instructions about bowing fast semiquavers inappropriate today, for with their bow the stick could bounce when playing at the point, allowing the sound to ring on while giving a bouncy separation. This can be achieved with the modern bow by using a long *spiccato* (sometimes called rebounding *détaché*) close to the point of balance of the bow, actually allowing it to leave the string between the notes so that the string continues to vibrate, but beginning each note without a hard attack. A modern bow changing direction on the string dampens it and stops the sound, whereas the lesser hair tension of the old bow would not entirely stop the sound if the pressure was reduced by bouncing the stick. The word 'bounce' never occurs in 18th-century treatises, however; only degrees of lifting the bow are mentioned. All these instructions must be interpreted with the knowledge that there were three manners of bowing as opposed to our two: (1) on the string; (2) with the stick lifted but the hairs remaining on the string; (3) with the hairs lifted. This is why Mozart takes pains to emphasise that notes beneath a slur are 'bound together in one stroke, without lifting the bow or making any accent with it'.[48] Geminiani approves of lifting the bow off the string only in *allegro* quavers, which according to Quantz should be played

> with a very short bow-stroke, but the bow must never be detached or removed from the strings. If it were always raised as high as is required when we say that it is detached, there would not be enough time to return it to the string at the proper time, and notes of this kind would sound as if they were chopped or whipped.[49]

Geminiani possibly had a better bow-technique than Quantz's acquaintances. Quantz claims that a stroke (❘) over the note meant a lifted bow when the tempo permitted, whereas a dot (·) signified a detached stroke on the string, but this cannot be taken as a general 18th-century rule as all *three* staccato signs – ❘ , ' , and · – appear interchangeably.

Among lifted *staccato* strokes illustrated by Leopold Mozart are the following:[50]

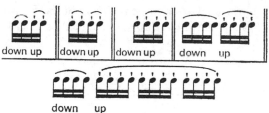

In the quaver passage [51]

which he bows in thirty-four different ways, he does not always indicate whether an up-bow or a down-bow should be taken at the beginning: above is shown the last and most complicated bowing. Modern violinists would start numbers 30 and 31 with an up-bow, but as this would be contrary to the 'Rule of Down-Bow', Mozart probably intended a down-bow *staccato* as in ♩♩♩♩ . This and the fact of the twelve semiquavers within one bow-stroke shown in the earlier example indicate that his 'lifting' of the bow may have been merely a release of pressure on the stick, without the hairs leaving the string, but it is impossible to know whether or not a kind of flying *staccato* was intended by Leopold Mozart, Vivaldi, and their contemporaries in similar passages, in spite of Mozart's very detailed description of the technique required.

> A certain relaxing of the right hand is necessary for it, and a retarding of the bow. . . . The weight of a violin bow contributes much, as does also in no less degree its length or shortness. A heavier and longer bow must be used more lightly and retarded somewhat less; whereas a lighter and shorter bow must be pressed down more and retarded more. Above all, the right hand must here be made a little stiff, but the contracting and relaxing of the same must be regulated according to the weight and length, or the lightness and shortness of the bow. The notes must be played in an even tempo, with even strength, and not over-hurried or, so to speak, swallowed. But in particular you must know how to hold back and guide the bow. . . .[52]

A thrown bow would seem to be indicated in the following passage from Veracini's opus 2 (in which he placed the dots *above* the slurs).

Allegro assai

But we can only guess at the degree of throw, just as we can only guess at the amount of lift required by Mozart at the dot in this example.[53]

down   up

At the dot the bow is lifted

Lifting the bow after dotted notes and delaying the following short note was a characteristic form of double-dotting advocated by Quantz and others, especially in music of French style or influence.

Dots beneath a slur over repeated notes are found far more frequently in early 18th-century string parts than any since that time, even at quite rapid tempi. Handel often used them on his accompanying figures, and remembering that the old bow was less likely to damp the string between notes, it is probably advisable to use slightly lifted separate bows with the modern bow, or a *portato* rather than a *staccato* stroke at slower tempi.

It will be seen that no definite rules can be laid down about the representation of 18th-century *staccato* bowings, except that *martelé*, dry sounds, and any hard attacks should be avoided, and the string allowed to resonate more freely than when the modern bow rests on it. The instructions of contemporary pedagogues must be interpreted within the concept of a bow heavy at the nut, which bounces most successfully close to the point.

A glance through the facsimile of J. S. Bach's unaccompanied violin solos reveals no *staccato* marks whatsoever. This does not mean that he expected all the sounds to be smooth and long. On the contrary, the rapid unslurred semiquavers would sound detached, as described earlier, and he would expect the traditional practice of shortening or separating the longer notes in lively movements. Quantz gives some examples in the Entrée, Loure, and Courante, remarking that 'the bow is detached at each crotchet whether it is dotted or not'.[54] It will be noticed that there are movements of the French suite which, following the traditions of the dance musicians with their shorter bows and 'Rule of Down-Bow', contained considerably more articulation than Italian-style music. All of Bach's solo partitas follow the French tradition, but Quantz has some advice to offer which would apply to the solo sonatas as well:

> If in an Allegro assai semiquavers are the quickest notes, the quavers must be tipped briefly for the most part, while the crotchets

must be played in a singing and sustained manner. But in an Allegretto where demi-semiquaver triplets occur, the semiquavers must be tipped briefly, and the quavers played in a singing fashion.[55]

Presumably if these note-values were all doubled in length, the same would apply, but perhaps then it would be too obvious to be worth mentioning.

Not all intended slurs and staccatos were marked, as Quantz instructs the performer

> Note here in passing that if many figures of the same sort follow one another, and the bowing of only the first is indicated, the others must be played in the same manner as long as no other species of note appears. The same is true of notes with strokes above them.[56]

Probably the orchestra's leader would often decide the bowing to be used, as he does today, but orchestral discipline was not yet so widely accepted. Quantz again has good advice to impart.

> Should there be some among the ripienists whose execution differs from that of the others, the leader must undertake to re-hearse them separately, lest one, for example, add a shake where others play without it, or slur notes that are attacked by others . . . for the greatest beauty of performance stems from the uniformity with which all the members of the orchestra play.[57]

Perhaps these uninitiated ripienists tended to ignore slurs altogether, as Leopold Mozart complains. 'Among the musical signs the slur is of no little importance, although many pay but little attention to it.' [58]

Looking at the solo violin parts of Bach's Fourth or Fifth Brandenburg Concerto, one may apply Quantz's advice that

> Long notes must be sustained in an elevated manner by swelling and diminishing the strength of the tone, but the succeeding quick notes must be set off from them by a gay execution.[59]

C. P. E. Bach also indicates that a detached style was more prevalent than today: in his *Essay* (1753) he writes:

> In general the briskness of allegros is expressed by detached notes and the tenderness of adagios by broad, slurred notes. . . . I use the expression 'in general' advisedly, for I am well aware that all kinds of execution may appear in any tempo . . .

and later:

> Tones which are neither detached, connected, nor fully held are sounded for half their value. . . . Quarters and eighths in moderate and slow tempos are usually performed in this semi-detached manner.[60]

Since 1800, editors have added so many of their own dots and slurs to 18th-century music that it is often almost impossible to sort out what is original, although *urtext* editions of the great works are becoming increasingly available. Where there is no chance of seeing the composer's original markings, the performer might be well advised to eliminate all indications, including nuances, and insert his own, in the light of contemporary advice and of his own interpretation of the music. References to personal expression are frequent in the 18th century, and Quantz points out:

> The good effect of a piece of music depends almost as much upon the performer as upon the composer himself. . . . Almost everyone has an individual style of execution. The reason for this is found not only in musical training, but in the particular temperament that distinguishes one person from another.[61]

An editor who stamps his own temperament and character clearly on the music may seriously interfere with the performer's natural and stylistically correct interpretation.

Personal expression was by now recognised as a vital aspect of the performer's art, as C. P. E. Bach indicates.

> A musician cannot move others unless he too is moved. He must of necessity feel all of the affects that he hopes to arouse in his audience, for the revealing of his own humor will stimulate a like humor in the listener. . . . Constantly varying the passions, he will barely quiet one before he rouses another.[62]

Geminiani opens the preface to his *Art of Playing on the Violin* with the words

> The Intention of Musick is not only to please the Ear, but to express Sentiments, strike the Imagination, affect the Mind and command the Passions,[63]

and Vivaldi in particular used *cantabile* writing after the style of the operatic aria to allow the full range of expressiveness on the violin. The slow movements of his concertos are often *cantabile* arias with accompaniment, and this lyricism occasionally appears in his quicker movements. It may be inferred from Galliard's comment (in the introduction to his translation of Tosi's *Observations* [1743]) 'a little less *Fiddling* with the *Voice*, and a little more *Singing* with the *Instrument*, would be of great service to Both',[64] that this practice was not really widespread.

The treatises of Leopold Mozart, Geminiani, Quantz, C. P. E. Bach are all available today in English translations, and a further valuable source of information is the letter from Giuseppe Tartini (1692–1770) to Signora Maddalena Lombardini (1760), which was translated by Burney (London, 1771). Tartini and Francesco Maria Veracini (1690–1750) were the leading violinists contemporary with Vivaldi, and although Tartini was the more notable composer and teacher of the two, he is said to have been so impressed by Veracini's playing that he went into retirement for a year to polish his own technique. Trained for the Church and for the law, Tartini was a romantic figure whose history is clothed in legends – the most famous being that of the Devil's Trill sonata, which he claimed had been played to him by the Devil in a dream. He secretly married the fifteen-year old niece of a cardinal and fled to Assisi under an assumed name to escape the cardinal's wrath: only the prelate's forgiveness allowing him to resume musical activities in Padua and gain international repute as composer, performer, and teacher. His 'School of the Nations' included such famous students as Pietro Nardini, and besides the letter referred to above he published a treatise on ornamentation.[65] Many of his violin compositions remain unpublished: they include a large number of solo sonatas and concertos, standing in style somewhere between the Baroque and the Classical periods. Vivaldi's solo sonatas are very restrained by comparison; Tartini did not reserve the use of complicated double stops and high positions for the solo concerto, but, like Pietro Locatelli (1695–1764) and Jean-Marie Leclair 'l'aîné', brought technical feats within the realm of chamber music.

Tartini's *Art of Bowing*, a set of fifty variations on a gavotte by Corelli, contains no written instructions, but it is interesting for its ornamentation as well as the styles of bowing used. His 'letter' is rather like an isolated violin lesson given by a visiting virtuoso; it covers many basic aspects but leaves one wishing that a longer series was available. Commonly attributed to him also are certain alterations in the bow, which were almost undoubtedly taking place in various places at the same time, and the discovery of resultant tones (the third note which becomes audible when two notes of a chord are firmly stopped with good intonation – see below, Chapter 11). It is probably true that Tartini was one of the first to draw attention to this phenomenon, which serves as an aid to intonation in double stops, and which was referred to by Leopold Mozart in his Violin School.

The late Baroque was an age for formulating rules and publishing dissertations on the scientific and natural laws of music, harmony, keys, and vibrating bodies: one of these (*Les Sons harmoniques* by Mondon-ville, opus 4, c. 1738) expounds in the preface all the natural string harmonics which are theoretically possible. Later in the century L'Abbé le fils was to add the range of artificial harmonics, permitting the writing of a piece entirely in harmonics. Leopold Mozart rather disapproved of this extension of the violin's technique: 'When . . . the perpetual inter-mingling of the so-called flageolet is added, there ensues a really laugh-able kind of music. . . .'[66] But it is worth noting that here the French were taking a lead, as in cello music, where Cervetto was emulating on the cello Tartini's feats of double-stopping and high positions. During the latter half of the 18th century, the majority of technical developments came from France.

Since 1750, string-playing has become louder and more highly pitched: vibrato has become an integral part of the sound instead of an ornament, and the basic bow-stroke has become smooth rather than nuanced. These are perhaps the main details to be kept in mind if the modern performer wishes to approach the true intentions of a Baroque composer. Bach's solo sonatas have given rise to various modern attempts to fashion bows which could sustain the chords as written, but these have been proved to be based on a fallacy: the 18th-century violinist could not sustain four-note chords, nor did the 18th-century composer expect him to. Schering, who invented the 'Bach bow' in which Schweitzer took a great interest, renounced before 1920 his theory of a convex bow with hair tension adjusted by the thumb. The more recent Vega Bach bow used by Telmányi appears to have no pretensions to imitate the 18th-century equipment: it aims to make Bach's sonorities more pleasing to the modern ear schooled in a different tradition.

Rapid arpeggiation of triple and quadruple stops as described above in Chapter 3 continued to be the rule during the 18th century, although Quantz indicates that the more percussive practice sometimes used today of striking three or four strings at once was at least approached by 18th-century players. He refers to their 'unexpected vehemence', advocates repeated down-bows with the heaviest part of the bow, but qualifies the description 'where three or four strings are struck at once' by instructing that the strings 'must be struck quickly one after the other'.[67] Mozart's instructions on bowing chords refer only to triple stops, which 'must be taken together at the same time and in one stroke'.[68] Breaking chords two-and-two, the preferred method today, is not mentioned during the 18th century, but downwards arpeggiation as demonstrated in Leclair's *Tombeau* was used to bring out a melody in a lower part.

Chordal progressions would frequently be broken into elaborate arpeggiations, sometimes indicated by the composer as in Bach's solo chaconne, sometimes left to the performer. The chaconne arpeggiation at first requires quite a complicated slurred *bariolage*, and Bach's indicated pattern cannot be sustained throughout the 32-bar chordal section: the violinist would be expected to adapt his arpeggiation to fit the four-part chords, and probably to increase the number of notes per beat as the climax of the section was reached. We have the harpsichord cadenza of the Fifth Brandenburg Concerto as an example of this building-up effect written out by Bach. Geminiani devotes the whole of his example XII in *The Art of Playing the Violin* to showing eighteen ways of breaking up a three- and four-note chord-passage. These are not simply arpeggiations, they are rhythmic variations rather in a chaconne style, and the page bears a certain resemblance to Ševčik's much later bowing exercises on three-note chords. François Duval gave examples of arpeggiation starting on and returning to the top note of a chord, and Tartini's *Fifty Variations* show some ingenious combinations of rhythm and bowings to vary a basic three-note chord-progression. Fingering extensions and even an occasional bottom note stopped with the thumb were used in complicated chord-passages.

Bach's works for unaccompanied violin stand alone in the modern repertoire by reason of the way in which musical completeness is achieved within the very strict limitations of the instrument, and the lack of an accompanying bass-line is never felt. None of his contemporaries could conceive unaccompanied works on such a vast scale, but following Biber, Pisendel in Germany, Guillemain in France, and Roman in Sweden all produced unaccompanied works for violin. Telemann's twelve solo sonatas are easily available and make an attractive addition to the repertoire, but their movements are short and the required technique very limited.

Double stops in later Baroque music present the same problems as were discussed with reference to Corelli's music (above, Chapter 3), especially with regard to chains of suspensions; but certain fingerings advocated by Geminiani and Leopold Mozart indicate that as left-hand technique developed, more of an effort was made to sustain both lines,

even if this necessitated a change of finger on one note. Mozart used
stretches of up to a tenth in order to sustain a lower line, but this is not
to be taken as an indication that a sustained-looking lower part must
always be played that way. There are several instances in Bach's solo
sonatas where this is physically impossible, or at the least very unlikely,
owing to the fact that the same finger would be used on non-adjacent
strings, or trilling on one string but not the next, or that complicated
stretches and shifts unknown in the 18th century would be required.
Sol Babitz lists twelve of these occasions, from which the following
are taken.[69]

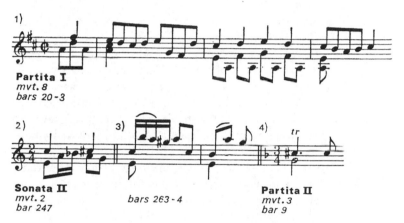

Partita I
mvt. 8
bars 20-3

Sonata II
mvt. 2
bar 247

bars 263-4

Partita II
mvt. 3
bar 9

Double trills, unisons on two strings, trills against a sustained note,
and even trills in sixths were used by early 18th-century composers,
especially Leclair. Most modern editions indicate a top-note trill for the
sixths at the end of the first movement in Bach's A minor partita, but a
double trill is clearly shown in the manuscript and it is possible that a
very close hand-contraction was expected.

The performer who manages to see an original 18th-century manuscript or first edition has first to sort out certain notational conventions
which have altered since then. Accidentals applied only to the immediate
note, not throughout the bar, and the natural (♮) sign was only slowly
becoming customary; often a sharp was used instead to cancel a flat.
The double sharp sign (✗) was becoming known, but two sharps might
be used, or a sharp before a note sharpened in the key-signature.
Similarly two flats, or a flat before an already flattened note.

Exceptions to the G-clef second line for violin music were found in
France, where the G-clef first line was used in the early part of the
century, and occasionally composers would write violin or viola parts in

the bass F-clef and expect the players to transpose them up at sight, if they were the lowest line of the ensemble, called 'bassetschen' by Quantz. A wavy line *below* and a sign (8ª) above the stave in Locatelli indicates that the notes are to be played an octave higher – the line would today be dotted and above the stave.

The rhythmic conventions discussed above in Chapter 3 continued during the first half of the 18th century, and Boyden [70] adds ♩. ♫ standing for ♩ ♫. With the development of the cadenza, the *fermata* sign (⌒) may have one of two meanings, a pause or a cadenza-point.

Beginning as an ornamentation of the final cadence, and at first often played over a sustained *tasto-solo* bass, the cadenza became during the 18th century a display-ground for the virtuoso's technical feats, which were often not used in the body of the work. As cadenzas were frequently improvised, we can only guess at their length. Early cadenzas for wind-players were limited to the amount of music which could be played in a single breath, but by the time of Locatelli's cadenzas for the 'Labyrinth' concerto, the cadenza was nearly as long as and far more complicated than the movement itself.

Vivaldi sometimes wrote out cadenzas, the longest being about thirty bars. Quantz's remarks on cadenzas were ahead of his time; he strongly advocated the use of themes from the movement, thus making the cadenza 'confirm the prevailing passion of the piece'. [71] This was not a common practice: scale and arpeggio figures mixed with special effects were most usual, probably in imitation of the vocal gymnastics which by now adorned each cadence-point of the operatic *da capo* aria.

Capriccio was sometimes used as a term for cadenza, often a long, written-out example (sometimes with its own cadenza-point at the final cadence). Tartini and Locatelli used this term, Tartini applying it only to final movements, while Locatelli's opus 3 has two caprices for each of twelve concertos, each caprice equalling or even exceeding the actual movement in length. These would seem more practical as works in their own right than as part of a concerto, and they may have initiated the form of the virtuoso solo caprice used by Paganini, who admired Locatelli's compositions. J. S. Bach's written-out cadenzas tended in precisely the opposite direction to Locatelli's, as they were carefully integrated into the total structure so effectively that the impression of a separate cadenza is sometimes lost. Not until the late 18th century do we find the familiar cadential pause on a $\frac{6}{4}$ chord introducing an unaccompanied cadenza which contains virtuoso elements yet serves to weave together the main themes and provide a climax to the movement.

Among the special effects found in cadenzas and occasionally in solo works were harmonics (only natural harmonics before 1750, and mainly in French music, as Mondonville's opus 4 of 1738 first introduced them into violin literature); *scordatura* (one concerto of Vivaldi uses the G string tuned to B flat); *con sordino* (with a mute); *sul tastiera* (bowing over the finger-board); and *pizzicato*. Leopold Mozart gives clear instructions for playing *pizzicato* but ignores other special effects, and he treats vibrato as an effect to be used sparingly, referring to performers 'who tremble consistently on every note as if they had the palsy'.[72] Geminiani, on the other hand, differentiates between the ornamental vibrato of the flute, used only on long notes, and a quicker vibrato on the violin which 'should be made use of as often as possible'.[73] Roger North was doubtful as to the advisability of this perpetual vibrato among English players. He wrote:

> I must take notice of a wrist shake, as they call it, upon the violin, which without doubt is a great art, but as I think injured by overdoing; for those who use it well never let a note rest without it, whereas it ought to be used as the swelling wavee, coming and going, which would have a much better effect.[74]

Only wrist and finger are included in contemporary instructions for vibrato, use of the arm being a later development, and although Tartini and Leopold Mozart describe a measured vibrato with additional pressure to pulse the beat divisions of a long note, this could be a pedagogic measure.

Vibrato was for a long time connected with a swelling of sound towards the middle of a long note (*messa di voce*), and the actual name 'vibrato' appeared somewhat later. 18th-century terms were *tremolo, Bebung, tremblement, balancement*, and close shake (Geminiani). Vivaldi's opening to the solo part of the 'Spring' concerto from the *Four Seasons* shows *m* over each note, a sign used by Geminiani, Leopold Mozart, and Tartini to indicate vibrato, but which might mean a mordent: it is shown as a trill in some modern editions.

The notation of ornaments varied from country to country at different periods. A glance at the summary-chart of 125 different notations in Donington's *The Interpretation of Early Music*[75] will show the impracticability of attempting any kind of survey here; but the performing violinist needs some knowledge of Baroque traditions of ornamentation. A good deal was written on the subject but, as Roger North pointed out, 'The spirit of that art is incommunicable by wrighting',[76] and some of the writings have increased instead of decreasing confusion. Quantz and C. P. E. Bach agree on several points, however, such as that ornaments must not be used excessively, and that they must be consistent in fugal movements. The cadential trill, with its upper-note preparation on the beat or long appoggiatura, was so generally accepted that it was often not indicated at all, and the musician was expected automatically to add the necessary accidentals to an ornament. C. P. E. Bach points out that 'the small notes rather than the principal tone are struck with the bass and other parts',[77] indicating that ornaments invariably fell on the beat rather than before it; and Geminiani explains with care the expressive intention of each type of ornament, the 'Superior Apogiatura' expressing 'Love, Affection, Pleasure &c.', while 'The Beat' (or mordent) can show 'Fury, Anger, Resolution &c. . . . Horror, Fear, Grief, Lamentation &c.' or 'Affection and Pleasure'[78] according to its mode of performance. It is interesting that he lists 'holding a note' as one of his 'Ornaments of Expression' with the remark: 'It is necessary to use this often; for were we to make Beats and Shakes continually without sometimes suffering the pure Note to be heard, the Melody would be too much diversified.'[79]

Leopold Mozart devotes a whole chapter to various kinds of appoggiatura, divided principally into the long kind, which is played on the beat and more loudly than the note on to which it resolves, taking at least half of the time-value of that note, and the short kind, which falls on the beat but allows the resolution-note to bear the main stress. The reason for writing long appoggiaturas as small notes is that insensitive musicians might add an appoggiatura to a note which is in itself an appoggiatura, thus spoiling the harmony, he explains. The appoggiatura of medium or indeterminate length, popular in the 17th century and associated especially with Purcell, is not mentioned by Leopold Mozart, but it was undoubtedly still used by 18th-century performers. The violinist was expected to know that these small notes must be slurred to and played on the same string as the succeeding note, but the main writers differ on details of nuance, and both Quantz and Mozart contradict C. P. E. Bach's statement that all ornaments fall on the beat.

The mordent normally used the note one semitone below the main note: inverted mordents using the note above were rare, the note above being connected with the trill. Leopold Mozart[80] gives

under the title mordent: only no. 1 corresponds with the single and double mordent of today. Geminiani's sign for a mordent (//) was rare, like Veracini's 'Mr': more common was ⋏⋏. Mozart mentions an elongated mordent,

calling it *Zusammenschlag*.[81] The trill (referred to as trill, *tremblement*, cadence, tr, t.) normally began on the note of the scale above the printed note: this could be lengthened and accented as a long appoggiatura, or the main note could be held as a prefix. Cadential trills usually employed the long appoggiatura and stopped on the chord-note to establish it clearly before the turn or anticipation of the final note which was used as a termination of the trill, e.g.[82]

♩♪ at a cadence almost invariably became ♩.♪♪. Different speeds of trill were considered suitable to different movements, and crescendo and diminuendo would often occur during the longer trills. Leopold Mozart disliked trills using open strings, and he gives instructions for consecutive and double trills which are far in advance of 17th-century technique.

Combinations of trills, turns, and mordents each gained their own signs during the 18th century, resulting in a plethora of squiggles which tended more and more to represent pictorially the direction in which the notes should move. A cross ($+$) was still used to indicate that this was a suitable place for an ornament, but the ornament was not obligatory: a good deal was left to the discrimination of the performer.

Nuances were indicated more frequently after 1700, when the signs ◄▬ and ▬► , predecessors of our $\prec$ and $\succ$ began to appear, but they were incompletely dictated and again a great deal more was left to the performer's taste than in modern scores. Vivaldi employed as many as thirteen dynamic markings, from *pianissimo* to *fortissimo*, but *crescendi* and *diminuendi* indicated before 1750 are generally of very short duration – rarely more than one bar. Veracini[83] uses ◢ over a note, meaning to start loud and decrease; ◣ meaning the opposite; Geminiani uses similar but not identical signs (◤ ◢) in the same context.

Leopold Mozart gives detailed instructions on nuancing, condemning the player who goes on 'playing always in one tone like a hurdy-gurdy';[84] referring to Light and Shade, he emphasises chromaticisms and the natural nuances of the bow. C. P. E. Bach points out that 'in general it can be said that dissonances are played loudly and consonances softly, since the former rouse our emotions and the latter quiet them', and claims that on the clavichord 'all varieties of loud and soft can be expressed with an almost unrivaled clarity and purity'.[85]

The lack of crescendo and diminuendo signs over long passages has caused many performers to believe that only terraced dynamics were used, but the spacing of dynamic signs frequently implies crescendo or diminuendo. Roger North, after referring to the violin as 'the nightingale of instruments', goes on to say 'but organs and espinetts doe not so well soften by degrees; but with a skillfull hand and variety of stops, performes it tolerably'[86] and in his autobiography he gives a most picturesque description of nuancing.

> Learn to fill, and soften a sound, as shades in needlework, in sensation, so as to be like also a gust of wind, which begins with a soft air, and fills by degrees to a strength as makes all bend, and then softens away again into a temper and so vanish.[87]

Rousseau's *Dictionary*, in the 1782 English edition, devotes nearly five pages to the article on 'expression': it would be remarkable if the 'transport of violent passions' to which he refers were achieved without the aid of *crescendi* and *diminuendi*. And although he commends the expressive qualities of wind instruments, he adds

> But there is no instrument from which there can be drawn a more varied and universal expression, than the violin. This admirable instrument forms the foundation of every orchestra, and suffices, to a great composer, to draw from it all the effects which a bad musician seeks in vain in the alliance of different instruments.[88]

Here we see the violin's position as the basis of the orchestra confirmed, and Leopold Mozart applies to the violin the expressive qualities of 'tempo rubato', usually associated with keyboard-writing, where the melody 'steals time' by slowing up some notes but 'restores it' by hurrying others, allowing the accompaniment to proceed undisturbed.

Tempi in general during the 18th century may have been quicker than has become traditional today: certainly Quantz's list of tempi, based on an estimated heart-beat of 80 to the minute, are very rapid if applied to Bach's music. But the only clear ruling about tempo that we can follow today is that of Leopold Mozart and Rameau, both of whom point out that every movement contains a passage which dictates quite clearly the speed of the whole. Nationality, as well as the exact period of origin of a work, can strongly affect its correct tempo, and the style of rhythmic interpretation of the written notes. French music in particular still used *notes inégales* and double dots (see above, Chapter 2). Quantz, Mozart, and Rousseau all refer to the slight holding of the first of a slurred pair of quavers or semiquavers, Rousseau making a ♩♪ rhythm of this habit, while Quantz says that 'this lengthening must not be as much as if the notes were dotted'.[89] Mozart considers that the practice prevents hurrying on notes slurred in pairs, although in general he prefers even notes. Today, it is as well to restrict the practice of *notes inégales* in 18th-century music to French compositions, or music in French style; to running passages of mainly conjunct notes in time-values of half or a quarter of the main beat; and to the long-short rather than the short-long type found more commonly during the 17th century. Repeated notes or *staccati* automatically make equal notes.

The French style of playing, particularly the French overture, frequently required double- and triple-dotting in place of the written single dot. Speaking of 'bourrées, entrées, rigaudons, gavottes, rondeaux, etc.', Quantz says:

> In this metre, [alla breve] as well as in three-four time, the quavers that follow the dotted crotchets in the loure, sarabande,

courante and chaconne must not be played with their literal value, but must be executed in a very short and sharp manner. The dotted note is played with emphasis, and the bow is detached during the dot. All dotted notes are treated in this same manner if time allows; and if three or more demisemiquavers follow a dot or a rest, they are not always played with their literal value, especially in slow pieces, but are executed at the extreme end of the time allotted to them, and with the greatest possible speed, as is frequently the case in overtures, entrées, and furies. Each of these quick notes must receive its separate bow-stroke, and slurring is rarely used.[90]

Leopold Mozart agrees that 'the note following the dot be played somewhat late'[91] to prevent hurrying, or to prevent the performance sounding too sleepy. C. P. E. Bach considered that having established the double-dotting pattern, it should not be so rigidly adhered to as to spoil a 'suave effect' indicated in other parts, but should be flexible as to the length of the dot; this is particularly relevant to some of the French-style movements of J. S. Bach. Harmonic factors will usually indicate the length of the dot in ♩. ♪ when written beneath ♩♪♩♪ or ♩. ♪♫, but there are sometimes places where it is difficult to decide the composer's intention. On the whole, the note or notes after a dot were played emphatically and late, with separate bows for short runs of notes, in slow French-overture-style movements. Rests were inserted before the short notes, when the bow might be lifted and returned to the heel or left on the string. The exact length of the dot depended on the tempo and mood of the piece, the interpretation of the performer, and the movement of the inner parts. All this means that a number of decisions must be made by the conductor or leader before the double-dotting tradition can be applied to the overture to *Messiah* or other Handel oratorios, for instance, or the opening movements of Bach's suites.

The question of assimilating dotted ♩♪ patterns to the basic triplet rhythm of a movement (discussed above in Chapter 3) occurs frequently in early 18th-century music. Leopold Mozart agrees with Quantz when he speaks of lengthening the dot in the following passage:[92]

but as C. P. E. Bach says that 𝅘𝅥𝅮𝅘𝅥𝅮 should equal 𝅘𝅥𝅮𝅘𝅥𝅮 in this type of case, the decision today is left to the performer, who may prefer Quantz's livelier version or C. P. E. Bach's smoother one. The last movement of the Fifth Brandenburg Concerto would seem automatically to assimilate to a 6/8 rhythm throughout, but the final movement of Handel's Concerto Grosso opus 6, no. 12, where the dotted rhythm is established first, is more suited to Quantz's method. A debatable movement is the Corrente from Bach's D minor partita for violin alone. Recent research[93] has added yet more room for conjecture by indicating that at times triplet rhythms were assimilated to duple rhythms: 𝄽 ; possibly this was the case in Geminiani's version of Corelli's gavotte in A major, printed in Hawkins's *History*.

There is little doubt that the formula [musical notation] found so frequently in Handel's works was played [musical notation], but a glance at the first movement of his D major violin sonata shows this pattern written out after a tie instead of a rest [musical notation] when the dot could easily have been inserted. From this we may conclude that he was writing in the Italian style and using accurate notation, but the opening to Concerto Grosso opus 12, no. 11, implies the opposite interpretation from the fact that [musical notation] is repeatedly placed against [musical notation]. From these instances it will be seen that each movement has its own problems and sometimes several possible solutions within the 18th-century tradition.

An additional aspect for consideration in performing 18th-century string-music is the different fingerings in common use. Although Locatelli used up to the eleventh position and Vivaldi's fingers occasionally 'almost touched the bridge',[94] according to a contemporary writer, most 18th-century music stopped at seventh position on the E string and third or fourth on the lower three strings. Orchestral instances of seventh position are rare (there is one in Bach's Mass in B minor), and the violist was almost invariably confined to the first three positions. Leopold Mozart, however, was aware of the advantages of playing a melody entirely on one string for the sake of the tone-colour, and although Geminiani does not allow *portamenti*, Mozart shows fingerings which would produce them, and by 1776 Burney is advocating them. Mozart justifies the use of positions by reason of their 'Necessity, convenience and elegance'.[95] A frequent modern cause for shifting is to give a continuous vibrato and avoid a fourth-finger vibrato, neither of which would be considered necessary in the 18th century, but shifts to avoid fourth-finger trills were recommended by Quantz.

Geminiani uses large shifts, thus reducing their number, but making it advisable for the violinist to grip the instrument with his chin on downward shifts. Both he and Mozart advocate the use of second position (called the half-shift; third position was the whole shift, sixth position the double shift, and seventh the last shift).

Finger extensions were particularly common in double-stopping passages involving downward suspensions, when the hand would creep down through the positions, shifting a finger at a time.[96]

Mozart

Sometimes a finger would change during a tied note, e.g.[97]

Geminiani

During the present century the performance of Baroque music has taken a great swing away from the over-lush interpretations of the 19th century to what is sometimes an over-dry, rigid, interpretation, eliminating vibrato, slides, lifted bowings, and subtle nuances. The latter approach would seem as mistaken as the former; late Baroque string-playing possessed most of the attributes of modern performance but carried none of them to excess. Over-exaggerated tempo variations, especially *ritardandi* within movements, and an over-pervasive vibrato are most likely to give away a performer's lack of familiarity with 18th-century style. But there is a great deal of freedom within that style, so that, as Rousseau requests,

the expression will be sweet, agreeable and strong; the ear will be delighted, and the heart moved; the physical and the moral will jointly concur to the pleasure of the audience.[98]

NOTES

[1] 51 Elkin, p. 85.
[2] 76 Hawkins.
[3] 135 Pincherle, p. 28.
[4] 42 Demuth, p. 126.
[5] ibid. p. 108.
[6] 60 Gal, p. 34.
[7] 49 Donington, pp. 522–4.
[8] 115 Mattheson.
[9] 144 Quantz, p. 237.
[10] 26 Burney.
[11] 129 North, p. xx.
[12] 130 North, p. 37.
[13] 157 Sandys, p. 162.
[14] 135 Pincherle, p. 84.
[15] 144 Quantz, p. 214.
[16] ibid. p. 213.
[17] 135 Pincherle.
[18] 76 Hawkins.
[19] 26 Burney.
[20] 174 van der Straeten, vol. 1, p. 79.
[21] 152 Rousseau, article on 'Orchestra'.
[22] 175 Strunk, p. 623.
[23] 152 Rousseau, article on 'Violin'.
[24] 126 Nettcl.
[25] 76 Hawkins.
[26] 26 Burney.
[27] 129 North, p. 168.
[28] 123 Mozart, p. 58.
[29] ibid. p. 58.
[30] ibid. p. 96.
[31] 65 Geminiani, p. 8.
[32] ibid. p. 2.
[33] 123 Mozart, p. 99.
[34] ibid. p. 97.
[35] 179 Tartini.
[36] 7 Babitz.
[37] 65 Geminiani, p. 2.
[38] 129 North, p. 164.
[39] 123 Mozart, p. 98.
[40] 65 Geminiani, p. 2.
[41] 123 Mozart, p. 99.
[42] ibid. p 74.
[43] 65 Geminiani, p. 4.

[44] 144 Quantz, p. 223.
[45] 21 Boyden, p. 403.
[46] 129 North, p. 293.
[47] 76 Hawkins.
[48] 123 Mozart, p. 45.
[49] 144 Quantz, p. 232.
[50] 123 Mozart, chapter 7.
[51] ibid.
[52] ibid. p. 119.
[53] ibid. p. 125, example 8d.
[54] 144 Quantz, p. 291.
[55] ibid. p. 133.
[56] ibid. p. 210.
[57] ibid. p. 210.
[58] 123 Mozart, p. 45.
[59] 144 Quantz, p. 132.
[60] 8 Bach, p. 149.
[61] 144 Quantz, p. 121.
[62] 8 Bach, p. 152.
[63] 65 Geminiani, p. 1.
[64] 21 Boyden, p. 341.
[65] 180 Tartini.
[66] 123 Mozart, p. 101.
[67] 144 Quantz, p. 227.
[68] 123 Mozart, p. 160.
[69] 7 Babitz.
[70] 21 Boyden, p. 367.
[71] 144 Quantz, p. 182.
[72] 123 Mozart, p. 203.
[73] 65 Geminiani, p. 8.
[74] 129 North, p. 165 note.
[75] 49 Donington, p. 573.
[76] 129 North, p. 149.
[77] 8 Bach, p. 84.
[78] 65 Geminiani, pp. 7–8.
[79] ibid. p. 7.
[80] 123 Mozart, p. 202.
[81] ibid. p. 209.
[82] 49 Donington, pp. 184–5.
[83] 21 Boyden, p. 486.
[84] 123 Mozart, p. 219.
[85] 8 Bach, pp. 163–4.
[86] 129 North, p. 218.
[87] 128 North, section 106.
[88] 152 Rousseau, article on 'Expression'.
[89] 144 Quantz, p. 123.
[90] ibid. p. 290.
[91] 123 Mozart, p. 130.
[92] ibid.

[93] 49 Donington, pp. 402–3.
[94] 21 Boyden, p. 377.
[95] 123 Mozart, p. 132.
[96] ibid. p. 157.
[97] 65 Geminiani, example XXIII.
[98] 152 Rousseau, article on 'Expression'.

CHAPTER 6

The Rise of the String Quartet: 1750–1800

THE DECADE ENCOMPASSING the deaths of Bach in 1750 and Handel in 1759 marks the end of the Baroque period in music as it is generally understood today, but in fact Bach's genius was a late flowering of the contrapuntal school of writing, and well before 1750 a new intermediary stage of development was establishing itself particularly in Austria and France. Typical of this movement was its emphasis on grace, melody, and embellishment, on lightness and gaiety. It had its exact counterpart in painting and architecture, where the term 'Rococo' was first applied to the French school of Watteau, Boucher, Fragonard. In reaction against the intellectual paintings of the Baroque, Rococo artists aimed at providing pleasure – through the delicately curving ornamentation of buildings or through paintings with lighthearted subjects, 'fêtes galantes' or pastorals, showing lovers reclining in a landscape or similar scenes of light and leisure.

In the same way the term Rococo or *style galant* has come to refer to the purely melodic style brought about by the swing of the pendulum away from the more intellectual, contrapuntal school of composition which culminated with J. S. Bach. François Couperin's delicate miniatures for harpsichord are as typical of the Rococo as Watteau's pastorals, and the influence of this school was passed on to Haydn and Mozart through the works of C. P. E. Bach, Schobert, the early Viennese symphonists, and the Mannheim school.

A casualty of the Rococo style was the viola. Never a very high-ranking instrument in the Baroque period, owing to its lack of importance in forms based on a *basso continuo*, it nevertheless clung to some degree of self-respect as composers were often forced to give it an independent line in strictly contrapuntal orchestral music. But in the *style galant* all parts became subservient to the upper melody, and often no viola part was written at all. In the earliest symphonies the viola mostly doubled the bass-line an octave above, or occasionally played a third below the melody: sometimes it would supply a missing harmony note. Quantz[1] gives a depressing picture of the violist's role, especially in arias, where 'he has the easiest time . . . since in them he usually only has to play a plain middle part, or perhaps double the bass'.

A faint ray of light appears 'In concertos . . . occasionally the viola must even play a singing ritornello in unison with the violins . . .', but on the whole the instrument is considered to be hardly worth the attention of a good musician except as a stepping-stone to higher things, and any players worth their salt would seek to '. . . advance their position, instead of remaining chained to the viola to the end of their lives. . . .'

By the end of the 18th century, however, this picture has radically altered. In symphonic and chamber music the viola has achieved an equal status with the other strings, and in Mozart's Sinfonia Concertante the violist has to cope with technical problems equal to those of the violin – an enormous stride for an instrument which had considered the third position to be its upper limit for one hundred years.

It is probably no coincidence that the greatest composers of the late 18th century chose to play the viola. They were likely to apply their abilities wherever there was the least available talent. Under the patronage-system all musicians were servants, but playing the viola was not considered a sufficient occupation in itself. The violist might double on another instrument, or like Specht, who played the viola in Haydn's Esterházy orchestra, have other responsibilities such as tuning the harpsichords, winding up the special clocks, and singing in the choir. Haydn was especially aware of the unrecognised potential of the viola; by 1768 he was sending instructions for the performance of one of his cantatas and asking for two viola-players, owing to the importance of the part, adding, 'You will find in all my compositions that the viola rarely doubles the bass.'[2] But the composers were probably well ahead of their contemporaries in recognising the importance of the viola to the string family: to most people it was still very much the last and the least of the strings Kelly names the viola-player last in his account[3] of a quartet party given by Storace in Vienna, c. 1785.

The players were tolerable; not one of them excelled on the instrument he played, but there was a little science among them, which I dare say will be acknowledged when I name them:

The First Violin	Haydn
The Second Violin	Baron Dittersdorf
The Violoncello	Vanhall
The Tenor	Mozart

But by this time the instrument was competing on equal terms with the other members of the string quartet in Mozart's and Haydn's works, and was gradually assuming an individual role in symphonic writing as a distinctive orchestral tone-colour.

At Storace's party, about thirty-five years after Bach's death, it is quite likely that one of Mozart's latest quartets, dedicated to Haydn, was played. The second of the set, in D minor (K.421), provides an excellent example of the changes which had taken place in writing for strings in general and the viola in particular since the middle of the century.

A first glance reveals that the keyboard continuo has disappeared, that there are four movements of which the first and longest contains contrasted elements of key and mood, that dynamics, note values, and ornaments are clearly marked, and that no single instrument has a monopoly of the thematic material. The trio sonata, the most popular Baroque chamber form, used one main theme, mood, and key per movement and often started with a slow movement. Quantz, in his instructions for writing trio sonatas, advises that 'the trio must be so created that it is impossible to divine which of the two [upper] parts is foremost'.[4] In Mozart's quartet this continual crossing and paralleling of the violins is absent: any one of the four instruments may predominate for a time.

In fact, the quartet did not really develop from the trio sonata, except possibly in the social aspect of four people meeting together to play music for pleasure. The rudiments of Mozart's and Haydn's sonata form were present in Pergolesi's trio sonatas, as he began to introduce new material when modulating to the dominant before the first double bar, and to reintroduce this material in the tonic key at the end. But the movements were very short and insubstantial: a long way from the well-rounded structure of K.421.

Oddly enough, the most important element in the early development of the string quartet and symphony was an 18th-century fashion for serenading one's friends by engaging a band of musicians to play beneath their windows. From a purely practical point of view this music genre had to dispense with the non-portable continuo instrument, and in works such as Starzer's *divertimenti* (D.T.O., vol. 31)[5] the viola joins the two violins and bass. *Divertimento, cassation, serenade,* and *nocturne* were all titles for this type of outdoor music, which was usually written with the dominating top part of the *style galant*. Serenades were often commissioned around the middle of the century and usually patterned on the quick–slow–quick scheme of the Italian *sinfonia*. To this scheme the south German and Austrian composers added one or more movements from the suite, usually minuets, and here we have the *allegro–andante–menuetto–finale* pattern found in Mozart's K.421.

The second violin, viola, and cello in Starzer's *divertimenti* all have a share in the musical matter, although the first violin is allowed to dominate; the viola even has a leading part in one minuet. Other serenades of the period reveal a more elaborate first-violin part and mere supporting harmonies in the lower parts, and it is possible that Starzer's violist might have been doubled by a wind instrument (oboe or horn), although there is no written indication of this. Horn parts have been discovered for some of Haydn's earliest 'quartets' – which points to the origin of quartet-writing in the serenade.

The use of two violins with viola and cello had occurred occasionally during the previous fifty years, but in works with a definite Baroque, contrapuntal flavour. In this class we must include Alessandro Scarlatti's *sonata a quattro* and similar works by Tartini and Allegri. A comparison of the earliest quartets by Haydn with the later ones will show that his style of writing derived from the Galant composers rather than the contrapuntists: at first the first violin is *prima donna* and only gradually do the viola and cello become real individuals in the ensemble, worthy of presenting thematic material. Probably all of his earliest quartets were conceived as *divertimenti*; in opus 1 we find two minuets after the Austrian tradition, and it is interesting to note that as late as 1782 Haydn may have been thinking in terms of a cello-line doubled an octave below when he wrote the crossing parts in the first bar of the rondo of opus 33, no. 3. Forster's English edition of these quartets and Kerpen's edition printed in Soho have 'with a thorough bass' on the title-page.

With regard to variety and detail of dynamic markings, both Haydn and Mozart derived a good deal from the Mannheim school of composers, led by the Stamitz family.

The Elector Palatine in Mannheim, Duke Carl Theodore (described in Burney's *Travels*[6] as a very good performer on the German flute), was one of the principal 18th-century patrons of the arts, spending over 35 million florins during his reign. To the Mannheim tradition of performing all the newest operas, J. Stamitz added a remarkable standard of stylish orchestral playing after his appointment in 1745. His own fiery performance on the violin had caught the attention of Carl Theodore and led to the appointment, and he drilled the orchestral musicians individually and in ensembles until their uniformity of attack, phrasing, and nuance were internationally famous.

Burney's only criticism of this orchestra was that the wind, as was usual, played out of tune: he could find no fault with the strings, and he was greatly impressed with their dynamic effects, for here

> . . . every effect has been tried which such an aggregate of sound can produce; it was here that the *Crescendo* and *Diminuendo* had birth; and the *Piano*, which was before chiefly used as an echo, with which it was generally synonimous, as well as the *Forte*, were found to be musical *colours* which had their *shades*, as much as red or blue in painting.[7]

We saw in the last chapter that graduated dynamics were being recognised in solo performance, but their application orchestrally provided a startling effect which all Europe tried to imitate, naming certain striking mannerisms the 'Mannheimer sigh' and 'Mannheimer rocket'. Reichardt, another 18th-century traveller, finds it necessary to point out why he is *not* going to speak of the Mannheim dynamics:

> Of the increasing and diminishing of a long note or of many notes following one on another, which, if I may so express myself, passes through the whole shading of a light or dark color and which in Mannheim is executed in so masterly a fashion – of this I shall not speak here at all, for neither Hasse nor Graun ever employed it.[8]

Mozart visited Mannheim at the age of twenty-two, hoping to secure a position there, but musical politics served to keep him out. He became acquainted with this effective orchestral style, however, and his next symphonies (especially the 'Paris' Symphony of 1778) show a possibly tongue-in-cheek reproduction of Mannheim effects.

Turning back to the D minor quartet, we can see how the contrasting dynamics have become integrated into a style which contains sufficient variety of mood, rhythm, and key to sustain the interest throughout a movement almost three times as long as an average trio-sonata *allegro*. Stamitz in his orchestral trio-sonata-type compositions (sometimes labelled 'for trio or orchestra') used abrupt changes of style and texture to differentiate between the fairly short sections of his $\frac{A\,B}{I\,V} . \frac{A\,B}{V\,I}$ form. Mozart's sections are longer, and less abrupt in their changes, but nevertheless the amiable second subject in the relative major (bar 25) has a quite different mood from the more intense and dramatic opening theme. The reference to a 'second subject' shows how Stamitz's short contrasting section has grown in stature: the modulation to dominant now occurring half-way through the first section of the piece, allowing a whole new mood and theme or themes to be established in the new key. Vivaldi had used different themes for his soloist and orchestra in his concertos, C. P. E. Bach used two themes (the second often derived from the first, giving overall unity) with different keys in the opening of his keyboard sonatas, repeating both in the tonic in the final section, and bridging the two main sections with material from the first subject used in the second key. One of Haydn's letters to his publisher ends with the request: 'Please also send me C. P. Emanuel Bach's last two pianoforte works',[9] and although Mozart was more influenced by the graceful compositions of the younger brother, J. C. Bach, his sonata form must owe something to C. P. E. Bach's structural explorations.

After the double bar in the D minor quartet we find twenty-seven bars of thematic development ranging through various keys, starting with what promises to be a restatement of the opening in a fairly distant key (E-flat major) but soon merges into an imitative fantasy based on the trill in the second bar. A series of fugal entries of the first two bars of the opening theme lead to a complete contrast of mood as the violins alternately sing a theme derived from bar 3 over an accompaniment using fragments of the triplet figure which appeared before the double bar. The triplets are thrown from one instrument to the other in a purely rhythmic–harmonic section before the first and second subjects are reintroduced (recapitulated) in the original tonic key.

This music has come a very long way since Pergolesi's timid attempts to bridge the two main sections of the work by using the opening theme in a different key. Mozart and Haydn were themselves mainly responsible for building up the development section until it became a vital centre to the movement. Both of them used a brief statement of the opening theme in the dominant key before plunging straight into the recapitulation in their early works, but gradually a wider range of key coupled with the introduction of contrapuntal techniques made the development section, especially for Mozart, the place where harmonic, contrapuntal, and chromatic ingenuity could abound without interfering with the classical symmetry of the whole. Haydn's D minor quartet opus 76, no. 2, shows how completely the old strict contrapuntal techniques could be submerged into a harmonic effect: he uses his basic motive in inversion and in canon, at various distances and intervals, all the time retaining a distinct if restless feeling of tonality, and most of the time using the persistent quaver harmonies of the opening (which makes an interesting comparison with Mozart's K.421).

The interaction between Haydn and Mozart is especially noticeable in their quartet-writing. To Haydn must be mainly attributed the steady development of the quartet form from serenade and early symphony forms of Starzer, Wagenseil, and other Galant composers. He, too, is responsible for presenting material on the lower instruments – after allowing the first violin to dominate throughout the early quartets he suddenly, in the opening of opus 20, no. 2, presents the first subject on the cello while the first violin's entry is delayed by six bars. Perhaps Haydn was influenced by Luigi Boccherini who had already written quintets using two cellos with a prominent and difficult part for the first cellist, as one might expect in the compositions of a virtuoso cellist. Haydn must have been acquainted with Boccherini's music, probably well before 1772: by 1782 he writes to his publisher, regretting that: 'I cannot at present write to Herr Boccherini in my own hand, but when occasion offers, please present my devoted respects to him.'[10]

In German music the introduction of material on any instrument other than the first violin was a new effect comparable to Mozart's opening of the E-flat major piano concerto (K.271), where the piano enters in the third bar instead of waiting until the orchestral *tutti* ends. In the same group of quartets (opus 20) Haydn appears to be considering how to achieve some equality in the sharing of the parts: the method with which he experiments is the introduction of contrapuntal techniques. Three of the finales are four-voice fugues.

For ten years after his opus 20 (1772–81) Haydn produced no more quartets. And for almost the same period (1773–82) Mozart also ceased quartet-writing. During this period we know that Mozart became deeply interested in the study of fugal composition, and he transcribed some of Bach's fugues for string trio, but even more important to the history of the quartet was the composition of his Sinfonia Concertante for violin and viola. Here at last the viola was raised to the status of soloist with the orchestra – even though Mozart did consider it necessary to tune the instrument a semitone higher and transpose to make the tone sound brighter. The whole work introduces the principle that anything the violin can do, the viola can do too, and as Boccherini had already established this principle with regard to the cello, which frequently outshone even the violins in virtuosity in his many string quintets, the way was prepared for Haydn's six 'Russian' quartets, opus 33.

> I am issuing . . . a work consisting of six Quartets for two violins, viola and violoncello *concertante*, correctly copied and WRITTEN IN A NEW AND SPECIAL WAY (FOR I HAVEN'T COMPOSED ANY FOR TEN YEARS)[11]

wrote Haydn to his publisher Artaria in 1781. The word *concertante* may have some significance in referring to all four instruments; a letter describing three symphonies pointed out that they were 'all very easy, and without too much concertante. . . .'[12] Presumably the quartets were not considered easy.

From opus 33 onwards Haydn allows the lower parts an increased share in the texture even when the contrapuntal writing is so disguised as to sound homophonic. As he begins to feel unfettered by the technical limitations of the viola and cello, their parts become more independent of each other, more interesting to play, and infinitely more subtle as fragments of melody are tossed from one instrument to the other. Not that this is a suddenly apparent development: the cello especially has already had to tackle a high *concertante* part in the variations of opus 20, no. 4, but nothing like the opening of the slow movement of opus 33, no. 2 (viola and cello alone) had been heard before.

The single quarter of opus 42 dated 1785 may have been conceived earlier, for although it contains a long singing melody in the slow movement more typical of the later works, the overall style of writing lacks the freedom seen from opus 33 onwards. The following set, opus 50, published in 1787, shows a particularly brilliant use of the cello: Mozart's last three quartets do likewise, and for the same reason; they were dedicated to the cello-playing Frederick William II, King of Prussia (1786–97). In opus 50, no. 2, the second violin is entrusted with a long singing melody – an idea not favoured by Mozart unless the first violin was busy adding embellishments above – and we find the principle of thematic development through fragmentation in the recapitulation section as well as the development section. Mozart adhered more strictly to the Classical pattern, but we must remember that these opus 50 quartets were written after the set which included K.421.

The interaction between the two composers, and the incredible speed with which Mozart could accept Haydn's developments and make them his own, make a fascinating study for quartet-players. An evening exploring Haydn's opus 20 and Mozart's K.168–173, written a year later, reveals all kinds of minor similarities apart from the obvious one of the use of fugal writing. Haydn's opus 33 also provided a model for Mozart's six quartets of 1782 which were dedicated to him, and here we see how the mature Mozart could learn from and surpass his master: no one will deny that these quartets, 'the fruit of long and laborious toil', as Mozart wrote in the dedication, are superior to opus 33. Some of the ideas may have sprung from actual themes in opus 33 – it is worth playing the finale of opus 33, no. 5, immediately followed by the finale of K.421 to see how subtle and inventive Mozart's treatment was. In each of Mozart's variations the main character of the variation is presented by a different instrument: the viola has an especially beautiful line to sing in the third variation, and although the cellist is not allowed to dominate alone, his high entries give the fourth variation its particular flavour.

That Haydn in his turn learned from these quartets is evident from his own words, spoken to Leopold Mozart in 1785:

> I tell before God and as an honest man, that your son is the greatest composer I know, personally or by reputation, he has taste and apart from that the greatest possible knowledge of composition.[13]

The influence of the younger composer could also be recognised from the increased use of chromaticism in Haydn's quartets after 1785. Haydn continued to develop, vary, and imbue the quartet form with his own cheerful, lovable character for the remainder of his life: Dittersdorf may have written earlier quartets, and Mozart masterpieces of form and deep expressiveness, but Haydn made the medium into a personal expression of himself. Every quartet-player knows the feeling that the Haydn quartet one has most recently discovered is the greatest of them all.

For the newly appreciated viola a further opportunity came in the later years of Mozart's life: the quintets for string quartet with an additional viola. Einstein believed that Boccherini's quintets, with an 'alto violoncello' part written in alto clef, were intended for two violas rather than two cellos, but as Boccherini was a virtuoso cellist this seems unlikely. Mozart knew Boccherini's and Michael Haydn's works for quintet, and wrote an early homophonic one himself (in B flat, K.174, 1773). Fourteen years then elapsed before the great quintets in C, G minor, D, and E flat, appearing 1787-91. The dark and sometimes plaintive colouring given by the violas is especially exploited in the G minor quintet: one is reminded of the opening of Symphony no. 40 in G minor. Handel had experimented earlier with *divisi* violas in his operas and oratorios as a special effect, and Mozart, an admirer of Handel, may have been aware of this. He employed *divisi* violas in several of the Salzburg symphonies and used them consistently in the Sinfonia Concertante, without ever producing a thick or bottom-heavy texture.

In symphonic music the string parts were slower to achieve equality than in the string quartet: where it might be possible to find one viola-player capable of performing a quartet, it was still almost impossible to find enough viola-players to form an efficient orchestral section, with rare exceptions such as Mannheim. Perhaps the two violists at Salzburg were both capable players, as Mozart wrote a line for each of them in some early symphonies, but there was probably some deterioration when one of the viola-players played the oboe instead, and one of the ten trumpeters filled in on his second instrument, the viola. About the middle of the century we find Geminiani, champion of the viola in England by adding it to the *concertino* group, rearranging the works so that a violinist could take the viola part. But England must have possessed some fairly able viola-players: the chamber music of William Shield (1748–1829), mainly written before 1800, contains interesting viola parts, and Haydn entrusts the violas with some exposed passages in the symphonies written for performance in London. Often, however, he doubles them with a wind instrument, and this could be for practical rather than aesthetic reasons.

The technique required of the viola up to 1800, except in the occasional concerto (Mozart, Dittersdorf, Stamitz), still did not extend above the third position apart from very rare excursions, although the bow technique and agility within this limited compass became as varied as that of the other strings. Probably, the rarity of high positions was due to the awkward dimensions of the instrument: without a chin-rest it must have been very difficult to surmount the viola's broad shoulders and to slide back again into first position. Large and small violas were played: Mozart's Sinfonia Concertante was almost undoubtedly intended for the smaller type which would tune up a semitone more easily. The final viola-run presents problems to the players of large instruments even with the modern aids of chin- and shoulder-rests: that it did the same to Mozart's contemporaries we can gather from his rendering of the passage in the 'Musical Joke', K.522, where the violist ends up in quite the wrong key.

Stradivari is known to have made very few large violas: the fashion for the smaller instrument (referred to by Stradivari as *contralto viola* as against *tenore*) came in before 1700, and he apparently worked mainly on the smaller pattern, which the Hill brothers consider to have an inferior tone on the lower two strings. It is significant that the making of violas ceased almost entirely during the first part of the 18th century, but began again with the revival of interest due to the string trio and quartet. Italy, still the main home of instrument-making, was no longer in the forefront of musical fashion, and the viola was slower to assume its rightful place in the string ensemble there than in Germany, Austria,

France, or even England, although attention was lavished on the cello. Dr Burney was very disappointed on his travels to find the state of music in the country which had for so long dominated musical fashion: most of the Italians who still had influence over musical development now lived abroad, like Viotti and Jommelli. Opera, dominated by the virtuoso singer to an extent that musical values were almost unconsidered, was the only fashionable kind of music, and the only real instrumental composer, Boccherini, was too devoted to melody with delicate accompaniment to outgrow the Rococo style. Gluck's attempts to make opera more dramatic and less subservient to the coloratura met with little support in Italy, and although the Italian *opera buffa* was an early influence on Mozart, Vienna rather than Rome had become the Mecca of student composers.

In France, several Italian expatriates enjoyed a certain vogue: Cherubini (1760–1842), Spontini (1774–1851), Piccini (1728–1800), and Viotti (1755–1824) among them. Although they were well aware of the developments taking place in Mannheim and Vienna, the old school of Italian violin-writing persisted and the viola remained in obscurity. Mozart, on visiting Paris in 1778, was shocked by the lack of good taste he found there. Viotti, who introduced the violins of Stradivari to Paris about 1775, also possessed a fine Tourte bow: his equipment and technique were pointing ahead to the 19th century, but it was the influence of L'Abbé le fils (J.-B. Saint-Sévin; 1727–1803) and his most advanced treatise on violin-playing, plus the presence of a great violin-maker, Nicolas Lupot, and the perfecting of the bow by Tourte, which gave Viotti's school of playing the lead towards the end of the century. Viotti's compositions are not very interesting thematically or structurally, although they give a certain satisfaction to the performer by obtaining brilliant resonances from the instrument by the use of double-stopping sequences and chord-patterns: these tend to sound more difficult than they are, as they invariably lie well under the hand. Louis-Gabriel Guillemain (1705–70), a relatively unknown composer today, three of whose pieces were published in J.-B. Cartier's *L'Art du Violon*, may have led more directly to Viotti than Leclair, particularly in advanced bowing requirements. La Laurencie describes Guillemain as 'a past-master of arpeggiation and bariolage', and labels him 'notre premier violoniste à panache';[14] but Viotti was a pupil of Pugnani, himself a pupil of Tartini, and not until Viotti's pupils (Rode and Baillot) were established as leaders of a school of violin-playing can it really claim to be a French rather than an Italian school.

It is remarkable that any technical developments should be taking place amid the upheavals of the French Revolution and events leading up to it, although maybe the French turned to music as a relief from strain: as Madame Cherubini remarked, 'In the morning the guillotine was kept busy, and in the evening one could not get a seat in the theatre.'[15] Other countries were more gradually feeling the pressure from the poorer classes: under the 'benevolent despotism' of the nobility, music flourished with certain patrons, while random reforms were made in different European states to indicate a new recognition of the rights of man. None of these reforms was consistent enough to pay more than lip-service to the philosophers of the 'Age of Reason', however, and musicians were still eager to don the livery of servants and petition for leave of absence in letters phrased in such terms as

> Your Serene Highness
> Most Worthy High-born Prince of the
> Holy Roman Empire,
> Most Gracious Prince and Lord!
> Your Serene Highness was recently most graciously pleased benevolently to permit me to remain some months longer . . . etc.
> (Leopold Mozart to Prince-Archbishop of
> Salzburg, 1769)[16]

Only in later life was Haydn able to insist on being addressed as Herr von Haydn.

In England, where patronage was less an accepted part of the musicians' lot, a flourishing concert life brought music to a comparatively wide section of the community, but it was often not the best music. Concert-rooms such as Hickford's, where Mozart played at the age of eight, and the Tottenham Street Rooms, where for a time the *Concerts of Antient Music* were held, were only for the aristocracy. A writer described one of these concerts, at which Handel's music normally provided the basis of the programme, in these words:

> . . . the 'King's Concert Rooms' were crowded to suffocation, chiefly with the 'nobs' and their ladies, rich in gorgeous attire, sparkling with jewels, and graced with feathers and flaunting fans. Rapturous applause greeted the performers from first to last, and many a dainty bouquet was flung from the boxes on to the stage.[17]

He goes on to describe the numbers of pickpockets waiting outside for the audience to emerge.

Rival concerts were put on by J. C. Bach with Carl Friedrich Abel (backed to the extent of £1,600 by Lord Abingdon), and Johann Peter Salomon, who arrived in London in 1781, and won the competition for the privilege of presenting Haydn to London audiences. These concerts were often referred to as 'Gentlemen's concerts'; they were for the educated, cultured, discriminating gentry. For a comparatively small sum of money, however (one shilling at Marylebone and Vauxhall, two shillings and sixpence at Ranelagh), anybody could gain entrance to the pleasure-gardens where concerts of widely varying music were given regularly, to say nothing of the illuminations, refreshments, and fireworks for the less seriously-minded. At Vauxhall, where Handel's statue was a centrepiece, serious programmes gradually gave way to the light airs and ballads, Scottish reels and popular overtures, produced in profusion by Charles Dibdin, William Shield, James Hook, and William Smethergell. Marylebone rarely attempted to present anything but the most popular music, but Ranelagh, where Mozart played as a child, saw some more intellectually stimulating programmes. One function of these pleasure-garden concerts was to give employment to English musicians and encouragement to English composers, for at the 'Professional' and 'Bach–Abel Concerts' only continental composers were considered estimable. English musicians could make a living by hiring themselves out through agents for balls and private functions. For one ball at Bedford House in 1759 an agent was paid 14 guineas, and for this supplied 3 'violas', 1 hautboy, a pipe and tabor, and 2 basses. A single performer on the French horn received three guineas.[18]

England had its first well-known viola-player in Benjamin Blake (1761–1827) who played the viola in the Italian Opera and taught it as well. His three volumes of duets for violin and viola were entitled 'A Musical Dialogue between master and scholar' and he also produced three solos for viola with cello accompaniment. Educational literature for the violin was produced by Smethergell, who wrote solos 'for the Improvement of Juvenile Performers' (c. 1795), and John Valentine's easy symphonies for junior orchestra were used by at least one junior musical society in Leicester.[19] In England the social rank of the professional musician was advancing faster than on the continent. The often-quoted Dr Charles Burney, whose General History of Music (vol. 1) was published in the same year as that of John Hawkins, and who travelled abroad to study the 'present state of music in Italy, France, Germany and the United Provinces', provided careful and valuable first-hand accounts of contemporary music and musicians. He was probably the first professional musician to gain acceptance as a 'gentleman'; moving with ease in polite society, and raising the status of the profession by doing so. Among his friends were Dr Johnson and Joshua Reynolds, and although he tends to be remembered now as the father of Fanny Burney, he was a man of very considerable importance in the musical world.

Burney was a sincere admirer of C. P. E. Bach both as a performer, who 'possesses every style, though he chiefly confines himself to the expressive' and on occasion 'contrived to produce from his instrument a cry of sorrow and complaint',[20] and as a composer. Haydn and Mozart acknowledged their indebtedness to Carl Philipp Emanuel, but Mozart reveals more of the 'English Bach', Johann Christian, in his early works. J. C. Bach was a Galant composer who wrote purely to please, but his works are stylish and show a clear sonata form which Mozart imitated in his earliest concertos. It is unlikely that the young Mozart would have achieved the five remarkable violin concertos of his nineteenth year without experiencing and imitating J. C. Bach's works during adolescence: as a child prodigy he met Bach in London. Johann Schobert (d. 1767) was the other strong influence on Mozart's keyboard composition. Schobert's originality in chamber music with a dominating harpsichord part and in the harpsichord concerto apparently greatly impressed the young Mozart on his visit to Paris in 1763. The earliest piano concertos contain close copies or even arrangements of movements by both Schobert and J. C. Bach.

Mozart wrote concertos in every stage of his creative life, and the complete concertos give a more gradual and comprehensive picture of his development than do the string quartets. The main concertos of the early part of the century had been for the violin: J. S. Bach began to substitute the harpsichord as soloist and Mozart made the pianoforte the principal concerto instrument, completing the changeover initiated by J. C. Bach. The importance to the violin-historian, however, lies in the emergence of a new relationship between soloist and orchestra, the cohesion of a structure built on sonata form which was to be the basis of concerto-writing for more than a hundred years, and a subtle ability to balance the soloist's virtuosity against the orchestra's greater power which was to open the way for the virtuoso violin concerto of the following century. By the time of the C minor piano concerto (K.491) of 1786, Mozart was using the full 19th-century orchestra of strings, 1 flute, 2 oboes, 2 clarinets, 2 bassoons, 2 horns, 2 trumpets, and timpani, interweaving the wind- and piano-writing instead of alternating *tutti* sections with solo and mere accompaniment figures, and introducing emotions even more passionate than in his symphonies.

All the string concertos except the Sinfonia Concertante (K.364) were written before Mozart was twenty: the *concertone* for two violins dates from 1773, two years before the five violin concertos. Mozart played his violin concertos himself, describing one of his performances (23 October 1777) of the D major concerto (no. 4, K.218) in the words 'it went like oil' and 'everyone praised my beautiful pure tone'.[21] A valuable description of the qualities Mozart admired in a violinist (Fränzl) is contained in one of his letters from Mannheim, dated 22 November 1777.

> I like his playing much. You know that I am no great amateur of difficulties. He, indeed, plays difficulties, but in such a manner that nobody is aware of them; it seems as if one could immediately do the same thing, which is the highest merit of execution. He possesses a very beautiful round tone, and not a note is missed in his performance; you hear everything, and nicely marked too. He has also a beautiful staccato in a bow both up and down, and such double shakes as his I never before heard. In a word, if no absolute sorcerer, he is certainly a very solid fiddler.[22]

The Sinfonia Concertante (K.364) for violin and viola was one of a group of concertos written for more than one solo instrument, and undoubtedly influenced by the Mannheim orchestra, the Sinfonia Concertante for four wind instruments and orchestra being written for four Mannheim players who visited Paris at the same time as Mozart. K.364 is remarkable for its length, all the material being treated by the orchestra and each solo instrument in turn (in contrast to the D major violin concerto whose first theme is never recapitulated at all), and for the sheer technical difficulty of the viola part. The beauty of the counterpoint and the effectiveness of the written-out cadenzas make this one of Mozart's greatest works, and violinists must always regret that he did not return to the violin as a concerto instrument during the later years of his life. The slow movement of the Concertante has similarities of mood, key, and thematic content to the *andantino* of the earlier E flat piano concerto (K.271), another work on which Mozart lavished especial care and originality.

Technically, Mozart rarely exceeded the demands catered for in his father's Violin School, although a violin concerto containing very advanced high-position work and double stops is considered by some authorities to be the work of Mozart and written in 1777. Habeneck is said to have owned the original manuscript, from which a copy was made for Baillot, who may have added the consecutive tenths which seem unlikely to be Mozart's. Haydn's violin parts, especially in the string quartets, were often higher and more difficult, perhaps because he was not forced to neglect the violin in order to earn his living as a piano virtuoso. In 1761 L'Abbé le fils had included compositions going into the tenth position in his treatise on violin-playing, although Geminiani's use of seven positions even on the lower strings for double-stopping passages was not followed up until the very end of the century.

Besides the very important work of L'Abbé le fils, which put France in advance of the rest of Europe with regard to violin technique, treatises were produced in Germany by G. S. Löhlein (1774) and J. A. Hiller (1795). The changes advocated from Leopold Mozart's and Geminiani's methods were not extreme; probably L'Abbé le fils's application of false harmonics to the violin, and Rust's sonata on one string, were the most startling innovations of the second half of the century, but Löhlein is particularly interesting in his instructions for the deportment of the whole body while playing. He and Hiller considered the great pedagogic treatises too complex for beginners, especially young beginners, Hiller being especially conscious of this in his position as Cantor of St Thomas's at Leipzig. Several of his very practical instructions savour of the choir-school. He advises violinists not to use saliva on an obstinate peg, for instance, and suggests tuning by singing the opening notes of a well-known hymn.

Löhlein's postural instructions are very much in accordance with modern practice except in that he recommends a slight leaning forward of the upper part of the trunk. He notices that the body remains most free if the chin is not pressed down on the violin all the time, but suggests that chin-pressure should be applied to the right of the tail-piece during technically difficult passages and frequent shifts. L'Abbé le fils was the first to suggest the modern practice of the chin to the left of the tail-piece, in 1761. Löhlein points out that the left elbow must always remain free and relaxed, otherwise fatigue will occur, and he varies the position of the feet according to the way the face is turned, aiming at stability through the centre of gravity falling between the feet. Like Leopold Mozart, he warns against any unnecessary twisting movements. The violin must not be too high, to avoid fatigue of the bow-arm, and every joint must be flexible.

Much of this is in accordance with the best modern teaching, like L'Abbé le fils's bowing instructions which include *imperceptible* movements of flexible fingers on the bow, adding considerably to the beauty of the tone. Teaching methods involving considerable *active* movement of the bow-fingers, making a large, visible movement at the bow-change, are today usually considered old-fashioned and unnecessary, but they

are not as old as the 18th century. It is quite possible that some of the
odd teaching practices of the 19th century were derived from watching
Paganini, who had a most unusual physique and used it in a way which
would be impossible for the more normally equipped learner. He
appears from pictures to have held the right arm very close to his side,
for instance: Löhlein and L'Abbé le fils present a much more natural
physical picture by suggesting that it should be away from the body.

Both of these writers consider that the bow should be held at the nut
and not further up the stick, but Viotti's Tourte bow used much later
in the century has wrappings covering almost half the stick, and
Pincherle considers that the early Tourtes were intended to be grasped
a considerable distance from the nut. Both F. Tourte and John Dodd are
considered to have arrived at similar solutions to the problem of bow-
design before the end of the 18th century, although Tourte is usually
named as the originator of the modern bow, with possible advice from
Viotti. He standardised the length of playing-hair at approximately $25\frac{1}{2}$
inches, slightly less for viola and cello. He combined a concave curve of
the stick (achieved by heating and bending a straight stick) with
a delicate hatchet-shaped head, using Brazilian Pernambuco wood for
strength and elasticity, and tapering the stick towards the point. To
balance the heavier hatchet-shaped head, Tourte added metal inlays to
the nut, but even so the 'point of balance' or centre of gravity now lies
further from the nut than in the old bow. Tourte widened the ribbon of
hair and added the ferrule to hold the hairs flat, concealing the hair-
fastening with a slide of mother-of-pearl. Frogs were generally made of
ebony with silver, occasionally tortoise-shell or ivory and gold. Earlier
bows had shown most of these characteristics separately and in a more
rudimentary form: it was their combination and balance which made
Tourte's bows the model for the years to come (Plate 20). Although he
designed his bows by eye and by instinct, it was later discovered by
Vuillaume that the taper of the stick corresponded to a logarithmic curve.
The underslide for the frog was added by Lupot.

The modern bow tapers evenly from about 0·32 inch (8 mm) at the
heel to about 0·21 inch (5 mm) just below the head. All bows are
octagonal at the nut end; some continue this shape throughout the
length of the stick, others become round after approximately $4\frac{1}{2}$ inches
(11 cm). A hole for the screw is bored in the stick for about $1\frac{1}{2}$ inches
(38 mm) at the nut end, and a slot or trench $\frac{3}{4}$ inch (19 mm) by about
$\frac{1}{8}$ inch (3 mm) is cut starting about $\frac{3}{4}$ inch from the end: in this slot the
eyelet moves back and forth as the screw is turned to regulate the hair
tension (Fig. 6B, 7B).

The head of the bow (Fig. 7A) is cut in one piece with the stick, and is the feature which demonstrates most clearly the qualities of the individual craftsman. The flat part of the head away from the stick is called the face, and may be reinforced by ivory or metal backed with ebony. This facing turns up at a right-angle to form the extreme point or peak of the bow. A small box, the mortice, is hollowed out of the

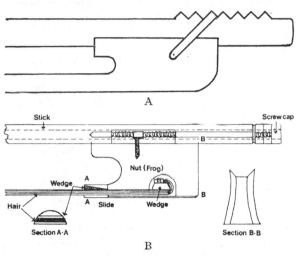

Fig. 6A   Mechanism of the 'cremaillère' bow
6B   Mechanism of the modern bow

head to hold the knotted end of horsehair and a wooden plug to keep the hair in place, the ivory or metal face protecting the head around this box.

A similar mortice with plug holds the knotted end of horsehair in the nut (frog, heel) of the bow, covered by a slide, usually of mother-of-pearl, which fits into a groove at either side. The hair is kept flat and the slide kept in place by a band of metal called the ferrule, and additional pieces of metal cover the back or heel of the frog, a small section behind the slide, and the underside (stick side) of the entire frog. These give protection against wear and ensure the smooth functioning of the screw-tensioning system. The eyelet or screw-eye is itself screwed into the underside of the nut – a frog which fits either too tightly or too loosely may occasionally be adjusted by giving this eyelet a turn in the right direction.

The end of the adjusting screw is fitted with a tip or button which is usually a combination of ebony and metal, continuing the shape and dimensions of the end of the stick. Decoration is occasionally found on the button or face, frequently on the sides of the frog; it may range from the simple 'eye' of mother-of-pearl found on most bows, to elaborate inlays of gold or silver. Silver or whalebone lapping protects the stick from excessive wear beneath the first and second fingers: cheaper substances are sometimes used, but it is important for the balance of the bow that the weight of the lapping is sufficient. A band of leather secures the lapping at the nut end.

The exact dimensions of Tourte's bows were:

Length:[23]	violin bow including the button	74 or 75 cm
	viola	74 cm
	cello	72 or 73 cm

(Early Tourte bows were often shorter, and J. Dodd only produced full-length bows late in life.)

Length of hair (violin)	65 cm[23]
Centre of gravity (point of balance)	19 cm from the nut[23]
Weight: [24] violin	$1\frac{1}{2}$–$2\frac{1}{4}$ oz
viola	2–$2\frac{3}{4}$ oz
Width of hair[25] at nut	*c.* 10 mm
Width of hair at point	*c.* 8 mm

John Dodd was less consistent than Tourte: he experimented widely with various weights, shapes of head, lengths and forms of stick, and mountings on the nut (Plate 20). His best bows, particularly those for cello, are considered to be among the finest early examples of the modern style, and some of these were almost undoubtedly made before he saw Tourte's bows (probably in 1792, when Viotti settled in London) for the first time. Occasionally Dodd would cut the curved bow from a solid block of wood instead of bending it, but these bows feel rather stiff to the player. It was probably an infrequent experiment on Dodd's part, as the wood would cost more, and he was known to be very miserly. Roda describes Dodd as 'eccentric, illiterate and secretive',[26] addicted to strong drink, and stubbornly opposed to taking pupils. John Dodd was the first maker who regularly signed his bows, although his father's bows are occasionally branded 'E. Dodd'. Lupot, Thomassin, Lamy, Sartory, and Tubbs bows are usually branded; Peccatte's bows, which were rarely signed, can be confused with those of Tourte. Among the other leading French bowmakers must be included Vuillaume (who also designed a 'fixed-frog' bow, easily rehaired by the violinist), Henry, Simon, Eury, Pageot, Lafleur, Maire, and Voirin, while in Germany the Nürnberger and Pfretschner families provided leading bowmakers.

The later 18th-century treatises are naturally concerned with technique for the older types of bow: not until the Paris methods of Baillot, Rode, and Kreutzer can we clearly expect a Tourte-model bow, although Campagnoli's instructions in 1797 seem surprisingly advanced. L'Abbé le fils's instructions on bowing correspond very closely to Leopold

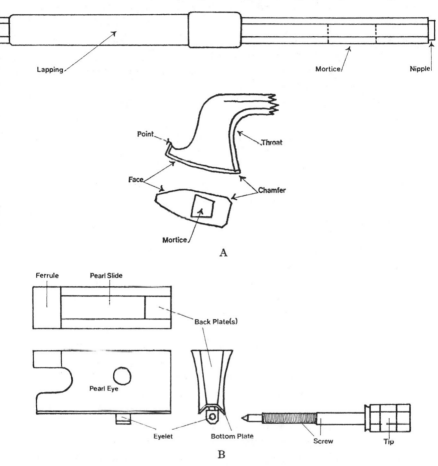

Fig. 7A The Stick and its component parts
    7B The Nut and its component parts

Mozart's, but he gives separate crescendo and diminuendo signs (⊲ ▷), an example of the gradual move towards clearly marked dynamics around the middle of the century. Löhlein suggests for the learner an aid to straight bowing, obtained by bending a piece of whalebone in an arch over the strings and tucking the ends into the f-holes. He also suggests clean hands and short finger-nails for the violinist: perhaps he taught in a boys' school!

The Mannheim school's influence on dynamic markings could possibly have reached France by 1761, or L'Abbé le fils may have been an innovator in marking a crescendo beneath fourteen ascending demisemiquavers, whether bowed separately or slurred. His inclusion of as many as thirty-six notes under one slur had been anticipated by Biber and Walther, but it was more generally acceptable now that bows were longer. His bowings across the strings were not more advanced than those of J. S. Bach or Tartini.

L'Abbé le fils's instructions on performing *staccato* are limited to a long series of demi-semiquavers within one bow-stroke, where he advocates a very free wrist; he also implies the use of *notes inégales*, which were already becoming obsolete. By 1765 there were already so many composers writing rhythms exactly as they were intended to sound, instead of in the Baroque tradition, that F. W. Marpurg (*Anleitung*, 2nd edition, Berlin, 1765) was demanding a list of composers who intended 'two against three' when triplets were used, and those who did not.[27]

A similarly rapid decline in the use of improvised embellishment and frequent cadenzas was seen as the Classical style overtook the Rococo, and Löhlein had some harsh words to say about the 'extensive display of musical nonsense'[28] inserted too frequently and at too great a length into solos and arias. With the disappearance of the keyboard continuo (whose part was always improvised from a figured bass) from all music save opera, and the restriction of improvised embellishments, improvisation was on the way to becoming the lost art it is today. Mozart would improvise for half an hour or more at the piano to please his audience after a concerto, and pianists continued this tradition in the salons of the early 19th century, but it would be a rare experience today to hear a virtuoso improvise the cadenza to a concerto.

Certain details of ornamentation, such as the turned ending to a trill, were intended to be added by the performer even when not indicated in the works of Mozart, Haydn, and Beethoven, but the position and basic type of ornament were clearly indicated. L'Abbé le fils gives all the dynamic signs used by the Classical composers, but makes no mention of vibrato either as an ornament or as an aspect of tone-production, and even in the 1830s it was still being suggested that vibrato should not be used in 'improper places'.[29]

In Classical works, appoggiaturas were still written as small notes; this was either to prevent the insertion of yet another embellishment or, as Thomas Busby suggests (*Complete Dictionary of Music* [1786]), 'to avoid a *visible* breach of the laws of harmony'.[30] Probably the practice was a legacy of the dying Rococo tradition, of whose passing many, like Dr Burney, did not approve: on visiting the Court of Frederick the Great he wrote:

> . . . if any of his Italian troops dare to deviate from strict discipline, by adding, altering or diminishing a single passage in the parts they have to perform, an order is sent, *de par le Roi*, for them to adhere strictly to the notes written by the composer, at their peril. This, when compositions are good, and a singer is licentious, may be an excellent method; but certainly shuts out all taste and refinement.[31]

C. P. E. Bach considered varied repeats 'essential' still in 1760, and even in the 19th century we hear of quartet parts being embellished by violin virtuosi, but the modern violinist would be well advised to limit his ornamentation to works of the Baroque and Rococo. Dr Burney's views were clearly not shared by Haydn, Mozart, or Beethoven.

> An adagio in a song or solo is, generally, little more than an outline left to the performers abilities to colour . . . if not highly embellished, [slow notes] soon excite languor and disgust in the hearers.[32]
>
> (Burney in Rees's *Cyclopaedia* [1819])

and in his *History of Music* (1776):

> Purcell, who composed for ignorant and clumsy performers, was obliged to write down all the fashionable graces and embellishments of the times, on which account, his Music soon became obsolete and old fashioned; whereas the plainness and simplicity of Corelli have given longevity to his works, which can always be modernised by a judicious performer, with very few changes or embellishments.[33]

The double trill which Mozart so admired in Fränzl's playing is mentioned by L'Abbé le fils, as well as a trill in harmonics, but the most interesting application of trills with double stops and extensions is to be found in Tartini's 'Devil's Trill' sonata. L'Abbé le fils kept the fingers on the string, and held the violin between thumb and first finger, 'without effort': he used the fourth finger frequently and sought to avoid open strings. A whole piece in harmonics by him is recorded by Alan Loveday on the disc accompanying David Boyden's *History of Violin Playing*.

Few of these extensions of violin technique were utilised until the alterations of neck and bass-bar taking place around 1800, and the perfection of the modern bow, brought new power and resonance to the violin. These suggested its potentialities as a solo instrument, to be placed alongside the piano in its ability to stand out as soloist against the newly enlarged symphony orchestra. Viotti's exploitation of the particularly powerful resonances of Stradivari's violins (Löhlein like many of his contemporaries preferred Stainer's instruments), especially in high passage-work, octaves, and double stops, points the way to the first of the great virtuoso concertos, to be written by Beethoven in 1806.

J.-B. Cartier's *L'Art du Violon*, published in 1798, contains hundreds of examples of violin music up to the end of the 18th century and is a mine of information for students of the history of violin technique. Donington (in *The Interpretation of Early Music*) reprints a page of this work showing different methods of varying an *adagio* by Tartini. The written-out ornaments are frightening in their complexity, but to learn to play the theme followed by even one of the variants shown would give a clearer picture of Rococo embellishment than could ever be gained by reading books on the subject.

One of the main reasons for the decline of embellishment during Mozart's lifetime was the replacement of the harpsichord, with its light touch and comparatively ethereal sound, by the *fortepiano* or pianoforte – at first an instrument without a sustaining pedal, and with leather-covered hammers giving a lighter, more brittle sound than we expect today. The keyboard instruments seemed to take their revenge for the decline of *basso continuo* writing by relegating the strings to a position of subservience in sonatas and trios for strings and keyboard. The earliest violin-keyboard sonatas were for clavier with optional violin, as in Schobert's works which were imitated by the young Mozart, and for many years piano solos *accompanied* by violin or violin and cello were written. Some of Haydn's trios could dispense with the string parts without great loss: the earliest are called 'Sonatas for the Harpsichord, with Accompaniment of a Violin (and Violoncello)';[34] later ones become 'sonatas with accompaniment of a violin & violoncello';[35] and Haydn's correspondence refers to sonatas rather than trios. In Mozart's works, this domination of the keyboard instrument was to die much sooner and the term 'with obbligato violin' was replaced by 'with violin' as material was shared more equally between the instruments. The new duality of violin and cello versus pianoforte was an aspect of Mozart's trio-writing which was more fully exploited by Beethoven: Mozart's piano quartets provide a more satisfactory balance than the trios, although the trio for clarinet, viola, and piano (K.490) and the two big piano trios (K.502 and K.542) are written with particular interest in the balance of parts and colouring of the instruments.

This chapter began with the lighthearted outdoor *divertimento* of the Galant Viennese composers: it ends with a *divertimento* of a quite different nature, the trio in E flat (K.563; 1788) by Mozart. The only clear similarity between the compositions is in the number of movements, and the reader who really wishes to appreciate the changes in string-writing over the second half of the 18th century should settle down to play this work, or at least to listen to it while following a score. The first violin has a virtuoso part, and the others hardly less so; all material is shared between the players; and all the favourite forms of the Classical era (including sonata, variation, and rondo) are present. The variety of colour from the three instruments is remarkable, and in Mozart's mind, if not in the eyes of the world at large, the principle of equality of opportunity for the viola-player is clearly already established.

NOTES

[1] 144 Quantz, pp. 237–8.
[2] 77 Haydn, p. 9.
[3] 46 Deutsch, p. 532.
[4] 144 Quantz, p. 318.
[5] 45 D.T.O., vol. 31.
[6] 27 Burney.
[7] ibid. vol. 2, p. 35.
[8] 175 Strunk, p. 702.
[9] 77 Haydn, p. 75.
[10] ibid. p. 37.
[11] ibid. p. 33.
[12] ibid. p. 43.
[13] ibid. p. 50 note 2.
[14] 104 La Laurencie, p. 22.
[15] 105 Lang, p. 788.
[16] 46 Deutsch, p. 88.
[17] 51 Elkin, p. 89.
[18] 186 Thomson, p. 284.
[19] 198 Young, p. 371.
[20] 26 Burney.
[21] 122 Mozart.
[22] ibid.
[23] 55 Fétis, pp. 114–15.
[24] 150 Roda, p. 59.
[25] ibid. p. 65.
[26] ibid. p. 152.

[27] 49 Donington, p. 402.
[28] 173 van der Straeten, p. 247.
[29] 170 Spohr, p. 161.
[30] 49 Donington, p. 149.
[31] 27 Burney, vol. 2, p. 207.
[32] 49 Donington, p. 94.
[33] 26 Burney.
[34] 77 Haydn, p. 77.
[35] ibid. p. 123.

CHAPTER 7

The Unrivalled Virtuoso: 1800–50

THE YEARS WHICH saw an incredible extension of violin technique by a man of physical genius and mental ingenuity, Niccolò Paganini (1782–1840), saw also many of those alterations in the balance of power and class distinction which have led to our modern way of life. Economic changes resulting from advances in industrial machinery and transport, and revolutionary movements as the poorer classes began to make use of their superior numbers in demanding their rights, caused on the one hand a new kind of slavery on the factory floor, on the other a conviction of the individual's right to freedom. Beethoven, who saw in Napoleon the personification of mankind's right to be free from the trammels of aristocratic rule, dedicated the Eroica Symphony to him, only to strike out the dedication when Napoleon named himself Emperor. The violinist Spohr, who as a young man was too preoccupied with music to notice the upheavals which surrounded him (his comment on the battle of Jena was that shortly after it he found a loading-piece giving the note B, which served as a tuning-fork for the harp), became in later life an ardent democrat. Aristocratic Courts gave way to parliaments and trade unions, mass audiences were housed in new, great opera-houses and concert-halls, and the form and style of music expanded to encompass the wider range of emotion and dynamic demanded by the atmosphere of the time.

Structural alterations to the violin *c.* 1800 to give it more power have already been noted: these form just one tiny aspect of a great expansion of instrumental and orchestral volume. Beethoven, who extended the Classical symphony to twice its former length, introduced trombones and the double bassoon to the symphony orchestra, and was the first to use the modern grand piano to real effect in his concertos and sonatas, was very much a child of his time. Although he took the Classical forms of Haydn and Mozart, he used them without the aristocratic reserve and politeness which was typical of Mozart and breached only rarely by Haydn. Beethoven could on occasion display boorish bad manners in high society, and his conception of music could not conform to the

135

self-imposed restraints described by Mozart in a letter to his father, dated 26 September 1781.

> For just as a man in such a towering rage (as Osmin in Die Entführung aus dem Serail) oversteps all the bounds of order, moderation and propriety, and completely forgets himself, so must the music too forget itself. But as passions, whether violent or not, must never be expressed in such a way as to excite disgust, so music, even in the most terrible situations, must never offend the ear, but must please the hearer, or in other words must never cease to be *music*.[1]

The era of the aristocratic portrait (Reynolds and Gainsborough) was past: only Goya looked over his shoulder by portraying a fading Spanish aristocracy, while identifying himself with the modern thinkers by refusing to flatter his subjects, thus providing a study of aristocratic dissolution which, amazingly, did not lose him his job as court painter. David linked Classical and Romantic thought by illustrating both ancient classics and revolution scenes, while Delacroix, who strongly influenced Liszt, was a real Romantic in the dramatic intensity of his paintings.

Literature, more than art, turned its attention to the life and emotions of the middle and lower classes. Dickens and Balzac used their talent for portraying sympathetic characters to highlight serious wrongs in the social system, while Wordsworth commented on the philosophic relationship between man and nature, using (in contrast to his predecessors) simple everyday language.

Although the end of the Classical era is usually given as *c.* 1830, the beginning of romanticism dates from the last years of the 18th century, and many individual works show Classical restraint in their construction with an unmistakably Romantic feeling for tone-colour. The violinist might think of some of Mendelssohn's early works in this context, the string octet (1825), for instance, the *Midsummer Night's Dream* overture, and even the violin concerto. Technically, it is the combination of rapid *spiccato* and high positions which gives the strings a colouring unknown or unwanted in the 18th century: Tourte's bow was fully appreciated and its qualities displayed by Mendelssohn. The appeal of fairy-tale themes in opera and incidental music brought to Romantic composers a new range of illustrative tone-colours – especially those requiring *spiccato*, *tremolo*, harmonics, and high positions – and a newly revived interest in programme music stimulated by Beethoven's Pastoral Symphony played its part in calling new effects from the orchestra.

With the expansion in size and in variety of tonal effect from the orchestra, partly due to improvements in the construction of orchestral instruments, came an extension of instrumental virtuosity. This was most apparent in the solo concerto, where in order to compete with the larger orchestra on equal terms the soloist had to answer in an increasingly brilliant style. But possibly the most rapid advancement of technique was that required from the rank-and-file orchestral string-players: suddenly second violins, violas, and even basses are expected to find their way into high positions and cope with difficult, rapid bowing, *tremoli*, and big leaps. Beethoven's symphonies allow none of the traditional simplifications adopted by 18th-century bass-players, and Rossini's *divisi* cello parts made demands on each member of the section. Berlioz wrote in his treatise on orchestration of 1844,

> Many double-bass players permit themselves – from idleness, or from a dread of being unable to achieve certain difficulties – to simplify their part. This race of simplifiers, be it said, has existed for forty years; but it cannot endure any longer.[2]

Weber seems to have been particularly conscious of the viola's tone-colour: he writes a viola obbligato in *Der Freischütz*, and his orchestral viola parts are not easy. Mendelssohn played the viola, and even at the age of sixteen, when he wrote the string octet, he expected considerable technique from his first violist. Schumann also gave the viola prominence both in chamber music and symphonic writing: he used the treble clef for its higher register, and exploited its slightly mournful sound in *cantabile* melodies. The status of the orchestral violist must have improved immeasurably over the previous fifty years for Schumann to entrust the section with some of the rapid passage-work in his Second Symphony, and Wagner forced an even more rapid development when the seemingly impossible string parts of his early operas were first placed on the stands during the 1840s. The violas found themselves sometimes soprano soloists, and sometimes the bass-line: often *divisi* and *tremolo* with broken-chord and arpeggiated figures which were not only difficult but very tiring to play.

Many orchestras, it should be remembered, still played standing up or perched on high stools at this time; marathon performances must have been hard on the players' legs as well as their arms. A present-day orchestra asked to rehearse Schubert's last symphony (the Great C major) without sitting down would undoubtedly refuse, even if chairs were for some reason not available. This should make us feel more sympathetic towards those English string-players who first rehearsed

the piece, a rehearsal which broke down amid laughter at the unprecedented length and difficulty of the parts, causing the conductor,
Mendelssohn, to abandon the performance. The symphony contains
very few rests for the strings, and without the stability given by modern
chin-rests and shoulder-pads the repeated triplet figures in various
positions must have been extremely exhausting.

The extension of technique required by the orchestral first violins in
the early 19th century was less startling than that of the lower parts, as
it was approached more gradually, but it is surprising how rapidly the
demands of the violin-concerto composers, Viotti, Rode, and Kreutzer,
were applied to orchestral violinists. Apart from the multiple-stopping
passages, the technique required for some of Viotti's concertos is not
much greater than that for Weber's overtures. Possibly the more widespread interest in teaching caused a general improvement in playing
standards. France, England, and Germany established conservatories for
training musicians, a habit mainly confined to Italy in previous years.
England's Royal Academy of Music was at first a fee-paying institution,
for boys and girls aged ten to fifteen who wore respectively blue swallow-
tail coats and white high-waisted dresses. At the first 'exhibition' of this
institution, held in the Hanover Square Rooms in 1823, the orchestra
consisted of 2 pianos, 1 oboe, 4 violins, 1 viola, 1 cello, and 1 double-
bass.[3] Financial and other problems prevented the R.A.M. from playing
a vital role in the country's musical education until much later in the
century. The Paris Conservatoire, on the other hand, developed a renowned school of violin-playing and teaching, with Rode, Baillot, and
Kreutzer as the three principal violin professors in the early part of the
19th century.

Pierre Rode (1774–1830) and Pierre Baillot (1771–1842) were pupils
of Viotti, and Rodolphe Kreutzer (1766–1831) had some lessons with
Anton Stamitz, brother of Carl. Both Rode and Baillot wrote Violin
Methods, while Rode's twenty-six caprices and Kreutzer's studies are
considered essential to the student's technical development today. This
group of composer-violinists, beginning with Viotti who was himself a
pupil of Gaetano Pugnani (1731–98; and thus a grand-pupil of Tartini
and Somis, great-grand-pupil of Corelli!), established the technical style
exploited by Beethoven in his violin concerto. Broken octaves, double
stops, an absolutely free use of eight or more positions, combined with
a bow technique not far removed from that of the Mozart concertos,
make this work stand midway between the true virtuoso and Classical
concerto. The English found its technique startling enough, however,
for one critic to write 'it is a "fiddling" affair, and might have been

written by any third or fourth rate composer' (*Harmonicon*, May 1832). He was clearly misled by the violin's virtuoso passages into confusing the style with that of the contemporary violinist-composers, who accompanied a melodic and virtuoso violin part with a series of pedestrian repeated chords in the orchestra. Samuel Butler did not think much of Beethoven's violin concerto either: he wrote of it as 'longer and more tedious still. I have not a single good word for it',[4] comparing the second subject of the last movement to a music-hall tune.

Ludwig (or Louis) Spohr (1784-1859), who developed his instrumental technique along similar lines to the French school in that he preferred a warm sound and noble posture to technical gymnastics, was also a prolific composer, much appreciated during his lifetime, and a great admirer of Viotti and Rode as well as Beethoven, Mozart, and later Wagner. Among his many claims to remembrance are the invention of the chin-rest and the fact that he was the first man to conduct with a baton in England. He admired English string-playing, and was disgusted at the derogatory treatment expected by an English musician. His influence was felt throughout Europe, and although his compositions have failed to remain in the repertory, mainly because of their tendency to cloying chromaticisms, the concertos are still used as a valuable stepping-stone for the student approaching the great virtuoso concertos. Spohr pointed out that the link between his playing and composing was so close that the qualities of the violin he was using at the time became apparent in his compositions.

> One endeavours to hide the weaknesses of the violin, and bring out its beauties, and since one prefers to play that which shows off the violin, gradually the method of playing adapts itself to the idiosyncracies of the instrument. So one can recognise from the compositions of a virtuoso, the character not only of his playing but also of his instrument.[5]

It is this quality of identification with the instrument that a student needs to acquire before he can become freely expressive in the instrument's terms, and works by the great violin virtuosi of every age are the most likely to provide for its development.

Exploration of chromatic harmonies was a feature of Romantic music which has been carried beyond saturation point in 20th-century film and popular music, causing a reaction not only against chromaticism but often against romanticism in general. The pendulum inevitably begins to swing the other way, however, and Berlioz, a truly Romantic figure in his versatility (writer, composer, conductor), has again become popular a hundred years after his death. A similar resurgence of interest in Spohr's compositions seems unlikely, although he was a broadminded man and conducted early performances of Wagner's operas at the Court Theatre of Cassel to which he was attached as *Hofkapellmeister*, and his music cannot be condemned as merely a vehicle for his own virtuoso violin-playing. In England his oratorios and his conducting were as enthusiastically received as his violin-playing: *Calvary* remained in the English oratorio repertoire long after the string-works had vanished. But perhaps Spohr's most important contribution to musical development lay in his experiments with the solo violin concerto: he sought to interrelate the concerto and the Romantic elements he so admired in opera by writing a *scena* for violin and orchestra divided into recitative, aria, and *bravura*, an attempt which foreshadowed Liszt's programmatic orchestral works.

Admired features of Spohr's performance on the violin were his wide vibrato and warm, singing tone: he played on a Guarneri del Gesù violin given to him by his friend Remi, until this beautiful instrument was stolen during a coach journey. After this he probably used a Guadagnini, purchased with money sent by his patron the Duke of Brunswick, but he exchanged this instrument for a Lupot played by the leader of the merchants' orchestra in Munich. Spohr's last violin was a Stradivari, which was repaired by Vauchel after an accident: the actual whereabouts of the instrument today is not known.

Spohr's comments on contemporary violinists were sometimes unflattering: he was very conscious of his own superiority. Of F. W. Pixis, who became a famous virtuoso, he wrote:

> Pixis held the bow a hand's breadth from the handle and raised his arm far too high. Thus his playing is completely lacking in strength, and he is incapable of differentiating between forte and piano.[6]

This dictum is interesting in that it shows the persistence of the old custom of holding the bow away from the nut, even with the Tourte bow, and that it illustrates the dogmatic adherence to physical methods of performance, regardless of the performer's physique, which has been such a damaging tradition of 19th- and 20th-century teaching.

As might be expected, Spohr's reaction to Paganini's playing was not as wholehearted as the spellbound thousands who flocked to hear him in opera-houses and theatres all over Europe. The German admired Paganini's intonation, his use of the G string, and his left-hand technique in general, but spoke of 'a strange mixture of consummate genius, childishness, and lack of taste'.[7] The genius is incontrovertible, the other two attributes probably correct, but it is Paganini's predilection for showmanship and violinistic 'tricks' that we have to thank for the full exploration of the technical potentialities of the violin. A legendary figure during his lifetime, surrounded by myths of imprisonment and communication with the devil, he led a life dogged by ill-health and unfortunate love-affairs. So many romanticised biographies have been published that it is almost impossible to sort out the truth, but there is ample evidence that a Paganini cult swept Europe, comparable to the Beatles cult during the 1960s, but encompassing a wider age-group and lasting a good deal longer. Paganini portraits flooded the shops of the towns he visited; cakes and sweetmeats, handkerchiefs, tie-pins, snuff-boxes, anything which could possibly be ornamented received a violin, bow, or picture of Paganini. In Vienna he even rivalled the vogue of the giraffe, an animal recently introduced to that city, which had given rise to a fashion for spotted gloves and regular outings to the zoo.

The virtuoso's emaciated appearance added to his fascination for the public, but it was not only his ability to achieve technical impossibilities which hypnotised his audiences. He must, in addition, have possessed an uncanny flair for playing upon their emotions, until their reaction approached hysteria. Technical expertise alone would never have gained him the following he experienced wherever he played: personal and musical magnetism must have been paramount. Even in England, where for his first concert he had to reduce the prices before people would come, he was later able to earn £5,000 in twelve nights – a formidable sum in those days, when Stradivari's violins changed hands for around £200. Paganini played on a famous Guarneri del Gesù violin nick-named 'The Cannon'; he left it to the town of his birth, Genoa, where it may still be seen.

Enforced practising during childhood, under the watchful eye of his father, gave Paganini a sound basic technique: the extraordinary flexibility of his joints allowed him to achieve unprecedented feats when, having fled from his father's house, he was given the Guarneri violin by a wealthy Frenchman and devoted himself to exploring the potential of this marvellous instrument. The twenty-four Caprices, written before he left home, show a decided talent for composition, which Paganini studied with Rolla and Paër. Later works allow his zest for showmanship to outweigh this musical purpose, but the early caprices were written for private study and employ their very considerable technical require-ments in a manner which is not so ostentatious as to hide their true musical value. The Caprices of Locatelli were known to Paganini, and were probably the inspiration for his own set of twenty-four, written at the age of nineteen.

Paganini's fame as a performer was derived almost entirely from his performance of his own works; he was unable to resist inserting *tours de force* into the works of other composers, even into Beethoven and Mozart quartets. (This practice was far removed from Spohr's instruction to quartet leaders in his Violin School of 1831: 'In passages *decidedly solo*, the usual embellishments may be allowed.')[8] On a very rare excursion into the realms of chamber music as a viola-player, Paganini appears to have been more restrained, as we read in the *Morning Post* of 15 May 1833:

> It has been frequently said that Paganini could not take part in a quartet with any effect. This is far from being correct. At a soiree given by Dr. Billing the other evening, Paganini, Mendelssohn, and Lindley performed a trio for viola, guitar, and violoncello (composed by Paganini), Mendelssohn playing the guitar part on the pianoforte, adding a bass in the most ingenious manner. Paganini's performance on the tenor was of the true school; there were no tricks, no jumping and skipping, but all the passages were legitimately and beautifully played, as were those given to the violoncello by Lindley. As a composition it reflected credit on the Signor; it was well conceived, scientifically written, and remarkably pleasing and effective.[9]

Karl Guhr, a violinist who followed Paganini on his journeys wherever possible and studied his playing technique, pointed out that through his creative ability Paganini made a new instrument of the violin, different from anything heard in the world before. The main differences of Paganini's technique from other violinists Guhr methodically listed in a treatise dedicated to 'the great masters, Rode, Kreutzer, Baillot, Spohr'.[10]

First was the tuning of the instrument: occasionally Paganini would tune his violin a semitone sharp, to make it sound extra brilliant, he would thus be playing in D major and sounding in E-flat major. Mozart, as mentioned earlier, had used this effect in his Sinfonia Concertante in E-flat major for violin and viola: the viola was tuned a semitone higher and played in D major. Probably a dual purpose was intended by Mozart, making the tone brighter and more piercing, and the passage-work easier.

Guhr's next example of Paganini's singularity was in his method of bowing, but here one cannot believe the description given, which claims that the maestro held his right arm tightly against his body and only the wrist was allowed free mobility. A complete bow-stroke would be impossible under these conditions, and the numerous (often contradictory) paintings and statuettes of the violinist in action show a low right elbow but never one pressed to the trunk. A high arch to the wrist is a natural result of this low elbow, and the arm is hardly pronated at all: the bow is generally held at some distance from the nut in pictures.

Fétis pointed out that Paganini tightened his bow so much that the stick was less curved than usual, and Guhr, while admiring the subtle and tender nuances of Paganini's melodic playing, chose his varieties of *staccato* and ricochet as the main point of difference from other performers. Although it is untrue that Paganini was the first to use flying-*staccato* and ricochet bowings (in principle at least they were understood by 18th-century string-players), certainly with an extra-tight modern bow and at the extraordinary speeds Paganini was able to accomplish, they would sound quite different from anything heard before.

Combining *arco* and left-hand *pizzicato* produced another dazzling effect new to 19th-century ears: Guhr states that it had been used earlier but allowed to lapse, and that extra-fine strings were needed to produce a satisfactory bowed melody with plucked accompaniment. Paganini's habit of playing with the left elbow held close to the trunk and well in front of the body (described by Guhr and Ole Bull, and portrayed thus by innumerable artists with the notable exception of the Romantic Delacroix) may have given an extra stability to his instrument, allowing the left hand to abandon responsibility for supporting the violin when engaged in such gymnastics. Certainly Paganini's violin sloped downwards, in contrast to the 'noble posture' advocated by Spohr and Baillot, and it may have been partly supported by the upper arm. He used no chin-rest, and pictures show his chin on either side of or above the tailpiece. The varnish on his violin is heavily worn to the left of the tailpiece, but this could be for a variety of reasons. He moved his violin about very considerably when playing, but he may not have changed the relationship between chin, instrument, and left shoulder: his contemporary Schottley reports that Paganini's bowing movements were 'accompanied by such strange body movements that one could expect at any moment that the upper body part would detach itself from the lower'.[11]

Guhr cites Paganini's use of harmonics as another revelation to the listener, while acknowledging that their existence had been previously recognised. Later writers mistakenly credited him with the 'discovery' or 'invention' of false and double harmonics, but the novelty lay in

Paganini's application of them – chromatic slides, single and double trills, and double-stopping passages all executed in harmonics. Performances on the G string only, a device much admired by Paganini's audiences, used harmonics to extend the range of a string already tuned up high, a major or minor third above the normal. It is also reported that Paganini placed his G string next to the E in the *Prayer of Moses*, and Fétis mentions that he used his left thumb on occasion, even reaching it across the finger-board to stop a note on the E string. This extraordinary elasticity confirmed by Paganini's doctor made multiple-stopping passages already a routine requirement of the earliest compositions, and finally enabled Paganini to gain as much variety of effect from his single instrument as had previously been obtained from a whole orchestra. Each string was used in nine or more positions as a different tone-colour, runs were executed in combined *pizzicato* and *arco*, and effect piled upon effect until his audiences were roused to frenzied admiration. The variations on *God Save the King*, enthusiastically received in England, include a melody accompanied by a drum-roll on the bottom two strings; then the melody is transferred to the G string while *pizzicato* demi-semiquavers accompany it on the E string.

Today Paganini's compositions, even the most difficult of them, are included in the repertoire of the virtuosi, but the more fantastic show-pieces arouse amusement rather than awe from modern audiences. Not because the technical feats have been surpassed by later violinist-composers, but possibly because the ability to accomplish these tricks is more widespread, and audiences look for more than technical glitter in their music. 20th-century violinists have in general (there are specific exceptions) achieved a greater virtuosity by avoiding muscular contortion in order to gain the maximum efficiency from each part of the body: Paganini, with his long, emaciated, black-clad body and muscular contortions which had to be compensated by extraordinary suppleness in other joints, created a visual impression which was almost as powerful as the impact of his uncanny technique. Modern performers can only bring off his works with a large admixture of 19th-century *bravura* or with a tongue-in-cheek reserve which entertains the modern audience but is far removed from the original atmosphere and intention of the works.

Paganini was probably the most famous of the 19th-century travelling virtuosi, a species which came more and more into favour as music 'for the people' became increasingly widespread. Musical festivals, especially in Britain where the Three Choirs Festival and the Handel Commemoration concerts had drawn large audiences in the 18th century, became annual events in many large towns, and audiences of up to 12,000 attended Jullien's concerts in the Royal Zoological Gardens. Not all of the music presented was noteworthy for musical reasons. (Percy M. Young[12] refers to Bellini's *Suona la Tromba* arranged for 20 cornets, 20 trumpets, 20 trombones, 20 ophicleides, and 20 serpents.) But Jullien conducted Haydn, Mozart, Beethoven, and Mendelssohn. Audiences have always tended to support personalities, and the conductor in his new position standing before the orchestra holding a baton became the new idol of the musical public. Offering a satisfying illusion of power over the orchestra, the long-haired conductor could count on attention from audiences and cartoonists if not from the players, and with this rosy delusion (the acclaim of a virtuoso, without the practising) another genre came into being: the professional conductor.

By the time of his treatise on orchestration (1844) Berlioz, as a choral singer, had already suffered enough at the hands of inefficient conductors to voice the orchestral players' eternal complaint:

> If they [the public] clearly perceive certain defects of execution, not he [the inefficient conductor] but his victims are in such cases made responsible. If he have caused the chorus-singers to fail in taking up a point in the finale, if he have allowed a discordant wavering to take place between the choir and the orchestra, or have absurdly hurried a movement, if he have allowed it to linger unduly, if he have interrupted a singer before the end of a phrase, they exclaim: 'The singers are detestable! The orchestra has no firmness; the violins have disfigured the principal design; everybody has been wanting in vigour and animation; the tenor was quite out, he did not know his part; the harmony is confused; the author is no accompanist; the voices are – etc., etc., etc.'[13]

Jullien was one of the first professional conductors and in spite of (or perhaps because of) his excess of showmanship (he only conducted Beethoven in white gloves, handed to him in a silver salver) he considerably benefited English music and musicians by giving concerts for large numbers at low prices. His Promenade Concerts drew large crowds, and as the musical public widened, the orchestral musician's prospect of a comparatively stable income improved. Freelance players, then as now, were mainly centred in London and would visit provincial cities for musical festivals. Sir George Smart, who conducted from the pianoforte, was most sought after for festivals in the early part of the century: his fee for the Newcastle Festival of 1824 was £157 10s., as compared with three to seven guineas for a rank-and-file string-player. String-players were generally treated as second-class citizens, except for the leader of the orchestra: they were expected to give their services for the first Philharmonic Concerts, while the wind-players were paid. Not unnaturally, they rebelled against this practice, and many withdrew from the orchestra to found their own group known as *The Professional*. The Philharmonic directors were thus forced to pay substitutes, and the original members returned with pay. For the first time the English string professional had improved his lot by bargaining on a supply-and-demand basis, which has been the uneasy foundation of negotiation ever since. His only security lies in the comparative rarity of the ability to fill that particular position, and against this minimal security he has to accept the fact that his employers may have very little knowledge of who is doing a job well or badly within an orchestral section. Only the players themselves really know, and they may have different views on what is ideal.

Berlioz, with experience as conductor, choral singer, composer, and critic, had a low opinion of orchestral violinists. He recommends sectional rehearsals for all parts of the orchestra and choir, and devotes a whole paragraph to the sins of the violins in particular.

> It happens everywhere (I do not say in some orchestras only) – it happens everywhere, I repeat, that violinists, who have, as is well known, to play – ten, fifteen, twenty of them – the same part in unison, do not count their bars' rest; each, always from idleness, relying on the others doing it. Whence it follows that scarcely the half of them come in again at the right moment; while the rest still hold their instrument under their left arm, and look about them. Thus the point is greatly weakened, if not entirely missed. I invoke the attention and rigour of conductors to this insufferable habit. It is, however, so rooted that they will only ensure its extirpation by making a large number of violinists amenable for the fault of a single player; by inflicting a fine, for example, upon a whole row, if one of them misses coming in. Even were this fine no more than half-a-crown, I will answer for it that each of the violinists would count his rests, and keep watch that his neighbours did the same, since it might be inflicted five or six times upon the same individuals in the course of one performance.[14]

He does not castigate violas in the same way, possibly because he was more aware of a missing high entry than a missing middle part: that his observation was not one hundred per cent reliable may be deduced from the fact that violinists tuck their instruments under their right arm, not the left, during rests! The first violin section, as opposed to the idle violinists who make it up, he considers to be among the most subtle and moving of musical instruments:

> Nothing can equal the touching sweetness of a score of first strings made to sing by twenty well-skilled bows. . . . Violins are faithful, intelligent, active and indefatigable servants. . . .[15]

On the other hand,

> Of all the instruments in the orchestra, the one whose excellent qualities have been longest misunderstood is the viola. It is no less agile than the violin, the sound of its low strings is particularly telling, its upper notes are distinguished by their mournfully passionate accent, and its quality of tone altogether, profoundly melancholy, differs from that of other instruments played with the bow.[16]

He goes on to enumerate the reasons for the 'unjust treatment of this noble instrument', pointing out that 'viola players were always taken from among the refuse of violinists', but optimistically predicting that 'little by little, the viola will, like other instruments, be confided only to clever hands'. Although he champions the instrument, he warns against using it too much, as the tone 'soon palls; it is too unvaried, and too much imbued with mournfulness for any other result'.[16] His *Harold in Italy*, however, written for Paganini but never performed by the virtuoso, was the first big Romantic solo for viola and orchestra, and Berlioz must have been influential in raising the viola (the full-size instrument – not the small one he deplores in French orchestras) to a position of general esteem. The technique required for *Harold*, including double stops and rapid runs, was well in advance of the few earlier works for viola with orchestra – Telemann's concerto, Mozart's Sinfonia Concertante, Stamitz's concertos, and Dittersdorf's concerto with double-bass, for instance.

Berlioz suggests that 18 violas should be used with 21 first and 20 second violins, 15 cellos, and 10 double-basses, in a full Romantic orchestra including full woodwind with piccolos, cor anglais, bass clarinet, and 4 bassoons, 4 horns, and substantial brass and percussion sections; the proportion of violas being rather higher than in the accepted symphony orchestra today. By contrast with Quantz's opinion that 'one viola, if a good and strong instrument, is sufficient against four or even six violins'[17] we must conclude either that the power of the

violin was increased more than that of the viola by the structural alterations applied to both instruments *c.* 1800, or that 19th-century composers were more eager to hear the violas within the orchestra. The
former may be true, the latter is easily proved by studying 19th-century
scores, especially those of Weber, Mendelssohn, and Wagner before
1850; R. Strauss, Mahler, and Debussy in the later part of the century.

String-writing in chamber music tended to be less adventurous than
orchestral music during the early Romantic period. The reasons for this
conservatism are not difficult to find: there was no call to match the
brilliance of an enlarged orchestral wind-group or to depict imaginative
Romantic programmes and operatic fantasies, and the virtuoso effects of
a concerto soloist had no place in a conversation on equal terms, which
had become the essence of Classical chamber music. Spohr attempted to
mix virtuosity (on the part of the first violin alone) and quartet-writing,
but succeeded only in writing a concerto with a particularly feeble-
sounding accompaniment. His later experiments in double-quartet
sonorities and mixing strings with wind were more valuable; his nonet
may be his most lasting work.

The immense variety of sonority obtainable from a small group of
single strings stirred the imagination of both Classical and early
Romantic composers: while the string quartet proved itself the most
satisfactory form of expression on a deep intellectual and emotional
plane, the addition of one or more viola or cello called forth some of the
most beautiful sounds ever produced – or so it seems to the string-player,
at least – in Mozart's two-viola quintets, Schubert's quintet with two
cellos, Mendelssohn's octet, and Brahms's string sextets.

When Beethoven introduced a dominating violin part into his septet
opus 20 for strings and wind, even giving the violinist a cadenza, he
seems to be looking backwards towards the serenade with violin soloist
(Mozart's *Haffner* Serenade, for instance) rather than to the coming era
of the virtuoso instrumentalist. In the string quartets, which cover all
three periods of his composing life and contain some of his greatest and
most serious music, he increasingly subordinates the natural tendencies
of instrumental technique to the requirements of his musical thought.
This is one reason why the late quartets are so difficult to perform:
Beethoven in his deafness had probably not handled a stringed instrument for many years, and the music no longer grew out of the natural
virtuoso elements of the instruments, as did the middle-period works
such as the violin concerto and the Kreutzer Sonata. Instead, he trans-
cended the limitations of the group, dismissed the instrumental clichés
which lie so easily under the hand, and wrote pure music, often very

awkward to play. A glance at the rapid leaps and six-flat section of the *Grosse Fuge* will rapidly convince a string-player that Beethoven was not writing with the player's comfort in mind, but the unity of structure, the cyclic cohesion of opus 130–133, and the depth of personal expression in these works make them stand alone, aside from the mainstream of development of the medium. No one could take up where Beethoven's late quartets left off.

Beethoven was closely associated with chamber-music players throughout his lifetime, and he gained invaluable experience as a viola-player in the instrumental ensemble at the Elector of Cologne's Chapel and Court Musical Establishment at Bonn. Rovantini was his childhood teacher, and we learn from Ries that

> Beethoven still took violin lessons in Vienna, with Krumpholz [a violinist at the Court Opera], and when I was first there we sometimes played his violin sonatas together. It was really dreadful music, though, because in his enthusiasm he did not hear when he began a passage with wrong fingering.[18]

It seems probable that Beethoven also studied quartet composition with Emanuel Alois Förster, whose house was a regular meeting-place for chamber-music players, as was the residence of Count Rasumovsky. Foremost among the musicians was the corpulent violinist Schuppanzigh, who must have led most of the first performances of Beethoven's string quartets. The standard of playing was probably high, as Count Rasumovsky was not only a very wealthy but a very musical man who had gained practical experience of quartet-playing as a second violin, reputedly under the direction of Joseph Haydn himself.

Other string works may have been less fortunate in their initial presentation; Beethoven felt that he had to restrict himself technically in composing the last violin sonata on account of the limitations of the violinist Rode, whose powers were declining. 'In our Finales we like to have fairly noisy passages, but R does not care for them and so I have been rather hampered.'[19] The first performance of the Kreutzer Sonata was given at 8 o'clock in the morning, by the talented coloured British violinist George Bridgetower (*c*. 1780–1860) and Beethoven himself. Bridgetower later recounted how he inserted an imitative cadence at bar 18 of the *presto*, which pleased Beethoven so much that he jumped up and requested the violinist to repeat it while he held down the sustaining pedal of the piano. The sonata was finally dedicated to Kreutzer because Beethoven had a dispute with Bridgetower. Its finale was written originally for the earlier sonata in A major, opus 30, no. 1, but Beethoven substituted the variations in this work because he considered the finale too brilliant.

The violin concerto in D major was first performed by Franz Clement, leader of the orchestra in the Theater an der Wien, who gave a graceful performance and was particularly applauded for his improvised cadenzas. Beethoven's notebooks indicate that Clement assisted in making the *bravura* passages lie well for the violin, a precedent of co-operation followed by many 19th- and 20th-century composers. The famous pianist Clementi persuaded Beethoven to rewrite the violin concerto for piano, and in doing so the composer added a new cadenza including solo timpani.

Compared with the lifelong association with Schuppanzigh, these works for other violinists were the fruits of passing phases: of the works for strings only the quartets cover all periods of Beethoven's life. They increasingly reveal his gradually diminishing regard for the immediate approval of his audiences. The first of the Rasumovsky quartets, opus 59, seems to have been particularly badly received; the great cellist Romberg trampling his part underfoot and declaring the work to be an undignified joke, while the first performance by Schuppanzigh's quartet was laughed at. Each quartet as soon as it was ready received a performance, often for a small group of Beethoven's admirers: this very important benefit of the patronage-system must be envied by many of today's composers. Sir George Smart describes one of these occasions in his Journals:

> There was a numerous assembly of professors to hear Beethoven's second new manuscript quartette, bought by Mr. Schlesinger. This quartette is three-quarters of an hour long. They played it twice. The four performers were Schuppanzigh, Holz, Weiss, and Lincke. It is most chromatic and there is a slow movement entitled 'Praise for the recovery of an invalid'. Beethoven intended to allude to himself I suppose for he was very ill during the early part of this year. He directed the performers, and took off his coat the room being warm and crowded. A staccato passage not being expressed to the satisfaction of his eye, for alas, he could not hear, he seized Holz's violin and played the passage a quarter of a tone too flat. I looked over the score during the performance. All paid him the greatest attention. About fourteen were present, those I knew were Boehm (violin), Marx ('cello), Carl Czerny, also Beethoven's nephew. . . .[20]

Although some of his later works were not immediately accepted by critics or audiences, Beethoven always had admirers who realised that first hearings were not sufficient for passing judgement; and he is reported to have replied to the news of a poor reception for one of his quartets with the words: 'They will like it one of these days.'[21] Performers and audiences have found the *Grosse Fuge* 'as incomprehensible as Chinese',[22] but the core of listeners who were prepared to recognise a genius with ideas whose magnitude was beyond their present comprehension has expanded until even the late quartets are universally appreciated.

Somewhat surprisingly, the chamber music of Schubert seems to have been considerably slower than that of Beethoven in achieving recognition and acceptance during the 19th century. Schubert's string-writing is pervaded with his feeling for song, just as Mozart's is often most easily understood in the terms of opera. The Schubertian *Lied* is a Romantic rather than a Classical genre, and in his chamber music one meets the Romantic ability to create a mood or atmosphere within a few bars of accompaniment, and the songwriter's gift of pure melody. Both of these are apparent in the opening phrases of the A minor string quartet, opus 29, the only one of his quartets to be printed during his lifetime. Lively accompanying figurations (a good *spiccato* is a first requisite for the quartet playing Schubert's works), colourful modulation, and unforgettable melodies (the second subject of the C major quintet) within a fairly strict Classical framework make all except his earliest attempts at chamber-music composition delightful both to play and to listen to. The string-player is neither under- nor over-taxed, and the balance, even in groups with unusual scoring such as the octet and the Trout Quintet, appears to remain effortlessly ideal.

Mendelssohn's string octet, a very early work, contains a comparable felicity of exploitation of *spiccato* bowing-techniques, but causes considerable problems of balance in performance; the first violin is easily swamped even in the opening bars. Formally, Mendelssohn remained a Classicist in his chamber works, while Schumann, who was at his best when abandoning the Classical forms in his piano music and songs, found formal restrictions uncomfortable and appeared to produce his best chamber-music movements in spite of rather than because of the medium. Individual movements are successful, but only the piano quintet is regularly heard on the modern concert platform. Schumann's quartets and quintet occasionally make original use of the viola's individual tone-colouring, and the *Märchenerzählungen* for the unusual combination (once used very successfully by Mozart) of clarinet, viola, and piano, have a fairly difficult viola part using rapid *spiccato* and double stops, but although Schumann was the first to write high viola parts in the treble clef, no viola-player would think of him as one of the great emancipators of the instrument. A little-known sonata for viola and piano, left unfinished by Glinka (1828) but recently published, gives the violist a more advanced and integrated part than Schumann's *Märchenbilder*, where the piano is allowed to dominate.

The Romantic virtuoso concerto really flowered after the middle of the 19th century. Following Beethoven's concertos came a period occupied by the assimilation of still greater virtuoso techniques (Spohr, Paganini, Hummel) into the realm of concerto-writing; then during the 1840s Schumann's piano concerto and Mendelssohn's violin concerto introduced a new era of concerto-writing. Just as the reader identifies himself with the hero of a Dickensian novel, the listener identifies with the soloist of a Romantic concerto, and in the conflict between size and range of power on the orchestra's part, and subtlety with range of brilliance on the soloist's part, the soloist always wins. The battle for supremacy must be on fairly equal terms to hold the audience's interest, however, which is the reason for the failure of Spohr's and Paganini's concertos. In these the orchestra is so subjugated as to make them display-pieces for the violin: on these grounds they achieve a rare hearing today.

Spohr's interest in other forms of music (he played Beethoven and Mozart quartets, conducted Wagner's operas) might have led him to a more balanced sense of form and part-writing. In fact he did in his later string quartets share some of the interest with the lower strings, but he wrote for an immediate, admiring public, and had little reason for self-appraisal while he was fêted wherever he went, as violinist, composer, or conductor. His Violin School, published in 1831, is a valuable guide to the teaching methods of that period, but Campagnoli's Method, published earlier in Italy, is closer to the modern approach. Bartolommeo Campagnoli (1751–1827) was the first to point out what Percival Hodgson proved in his *Motion Study and Violin Bowing*,[23] that consecutive bow-strokes are made by curved patterns, circles, or figures of eight, and that to teach bowing in straight lines is therefore an anomaly. Spohr, and most of his successors, managed quite well without recognising this fact, but one can only speculate on the troubles caused by certain of the demands in his Violin Method.

Spohr recommends, for the first time, holding the violin with a chin-rest, firmly between chin and collar-bone. The stance should be 'noble and free, facing the desk, the eye looking over the bridge, the left hand being opposite to the music page'.[24]

The bow-hold, with fingers almost touching and slightly curved, looks comfortable and natural, but would probably produce a small tone by modern standards, and the injunction 'the wrist must be held high, the elbow, however, low, and as close to the body as possible'[25] does not give a picture of free or natural physical movement. Still less does the statement that 'The following exercise is to be played throughout with a stiff back-arm'.[26] This 'stiff back-arm' is referred to several times, and is probably an attempt to make the student use a free forearm movement without involving much upper-arm; it is an excellent example of the way physical movement can be misrepresented in words, if only by a translator. Undoubtedly such a naturally gifted player as Spohr did not need to stiffen or even consciously to hold his upper-arm muscles to produce a forearm *détaché*, but because he saw his pupils confusing the movement, he instructed them to hold still the one part to force the movement into the other. No wonder he warns his prospective students that 'the violin is a most difficult instrument',[27] requiring an hour's tuition per day (as well as practising) for the beginner, and at least two hours' practising per day for the amateur.

Spohr makes no mention of the position of the body and feet with relation to the violin, although he warns against altering the instrument's position when playing on the lower strings. Baillot, on the other hand, whose Violin Method came out in 1834, gives detailed instructions regarding the vertical line of trunk and head and the position of the feet. A sitting position with the left foot raised on a step is recommended in order to allow the trunk to maintain an erect position. Both Spohr and Baillot show rather plump young men (Plate 22) with short necks and upright posture to demonstrate their ideals of violin stance: this is the build which seems to adapt itself most easily to violin-playing. Baillot's bow-hold has straighter fingers and thumb, and therefore more acutely arched knuckles than Spohr's, but the right arm is similarly low: the standing violinist rests most of his weight on the left foot. Spohr regards the extra pressure for loud bowing as coming from the first finger of the right hand: Baillot mentions thumb, index-finger, and wrist-joint pressure. Baillot's young man in the illustrations invariably has at least one finger of the left hand pointing vaguely towards the ceiling, and this was borne out in the instruction to drop the fingers from a high initial position to achieve a degree of momentum. This practice was accepted by the Franco-Belgian school, and is still occasionally taught today, although most teachers find that the less active method of holding the fingers down or closely curved over the strings, as recommended by Leopold Mozart, gives more reliable intonation.

Spohr names the positions as we do today (see above, p. xii), giving studies for the first six and going much higher in the concerto studies at the end of the Method: one of the criticisms levelled at this violin school was the rapidity with which the student is expected to progress. He still writes *tiré* and *poussé* out in full to indicate down- and up-bows, and suggests adherence to the old 'Rule of Down-Bow' in the remarks prefacing one of the studies. The section on ornaments is a useful guide to a changing practice: trills, for instance, now begin on the note (Spohr quotes Hummel's *Pianoforte School* as his authority): they may be quick and even, or (in *adagii*) begin slowly and accelerate, but they must never begin quickly and slow down, and they are never performed on open strings. On the other hand, Cramer, Clementi, Rode, Baillot, and Kreutzer all retained the upper-note start to the trill. The majority of writings on trill-endings seem to accept a turned ending to trills whether or not it was indicated: this would settle the old argument about the opening phrase of Beethoven's last violin sonata, opus 96. Spohr gives no ruling about whether ornaments should be played on or before the beat, but the impression given is that more ornaments were played before the beat than in earlier practice.

The appoggiatura tradition of the 18th century persisted well into the 19th, and Donington considers[28] that the appoggiaturas in the slow movement of Beethoven's opus 127 quartet should, in accord with this tradition, be played long, as dotted crotchets. In deciding how to perform Beethoven's ornaments, it is safer to look back to 18th-century tradition than to the more advanced of his contemporaries, as deafness must have cut him off from the changes in performing traditions during the latter part of his life. In the opening of his very last quartet we find the traditional Baroque slide, which is played on the beat and receives the accent.

Vibrato, called *tremolo* by Spohr, is still listed by him as an ornament: he recommends varying speeds and intensities, but points out that 'The motion must however be slight, and the deviation from the perfect intonation of the tone should hardly be perceptible to the ear. . . . Avoid its frequent use, or in improper places'.[29]

The practice of ornamenting *adagii* died a slower death than one might imagine; in spite of the fact that they were clearly not expected in the works of the great Classical composers, A. E. Müller and Spohr gave instructions for ornamenting in their respective Methods, the former restricting the opportunity to those trained in composition, the latter to passages *decidedly solo* in string quartets. But in Italy (*c.* 1840) N. Vaccai even denounced the habit of free ornamentation for singers, in the words:

'All the ornaments or so-called embellishments which singers are so apt to add to the original melody and accent, are out of place and bad.'[30] Spohr includes in his Violin Method some advice on the style of playing concertos, which may have become distorted in the English translation. To the warning 'It is not enough to conquer difficulties, they must also apparently be done with elegance and without exertion' he adds a plea for 'a sentimental delivery'[31] in order to gain the intimate participation of his audience. His notes on Rode's A minor concerto give some detailed instructions on how this is technically to be achieved, including the use of *portamento*, bowing repeatedly confined by the limits of that 'stiff' or 'fixed' back-arm, and emotion increased by 'a grander tone and increasing tremulous passion'.[32] In the last movement he indicates 'tempo rubato' with the words 'At the 3 slurred notes of bars 40 and 41, and particularly on the first, retard a little, and play the three following notes so much the faster',[33] but of his own works he writes: 'The compositions of the Author seldom require the time to be increased, or decreased, to heighten the expression.'[34]

Spohr, even more than Paganini, was a violinist who represented the Romantic period: his versatility and breadth of outlook, admiring the Classical composers on the one hand and the Romantic opera-composers on the other, his willingness to turn his hand to any type of composition, conducting, or musical performance, and in later life his democratic views, made him the complete Romantic musician. Unfortunately, his musical ideas were not valuable enough to last, and he has come to be regarded as one of the composers of whom E. T. A. Hoffman was thinking when he wrote: 'Romantic taste is rare, romantic talent still rarer, and this is doubtless why there are so few to strike that lyre whose sound discloses the wondrous realm of the romantic.'[35] Some of the greatest manifestations of the 'wondrous realm of the romantic' were to follow; in their compositions for solo violin and orchestra Spohr, Paganini, and their contemporary virtuosi had prepared the ground.

NOTES

[1] 122 Mozart.
[2] 19 Berlioz, p. 256.
[3] 51 Elkin, p. 101.
[4] 42 Demuth, p. 158.
[5] 116 Mayer, p. 196.
[6] ibid. p. 22.
[7] ibid. p. 137.
[8] 170 Spohr, p. 231.

[9] 36 de Courcy, vol. 2, p. 136.
[10] ibid. vol. 1, p. 374.
[11] 138 Polnauer, p. 53.
[12] 199 Young, p. 187.
[13] 19 Berlioz, p. 245.
[14] ibid. p. 256.
[15] ibid. p. 25.
[16] ibid. p. 25.
[17] 144 Quantz, p. 237.
[18] 159 Schmidt-Görg, p. 50.
[19] 16 Beethoven, p. 391.
[20] 167 Smart, p. 108.
[21] 149 Robbins Landon, p. 335.
[22] 159 Schmidt-Görg, p. 105.
[23] 89 Hodgson.
[24] 170 Spohr, p. 12.
[25] ibid. p. 12.
[26] ibid. p. 32.
[27] ibid. p. 1.
[28] 49 Donington, p. 150.
[29] 170 Spohr, p. 161.
[30] 49 Donington, p. 118.
[31] 170 Spohr, p. 180.
[32] ibid. p. 193.
[33] ibid. p. 198.
[34] ibid. p. 202.
[35] 175 Strunk, p. 777.

CHAPTER 8

The Orchestral Virtuoso: 1850–1900

'I AM HEARTILY sick of the word "Romanticist" ',[1] wrote Schumann in 1837. Yet the Romantic movement was still young; in different forms it was to persist well into the second half of the century. Champions of the different aspects of Romanticism refused to allow themselves to be considered in the same category as rival groups, and while today the loose heading 'Romantic composer' is used to include Schumann, Liszt, Wagner, Berlioz, and Richard Strauss, Schumann's supporters decried the works and personal attributes of Liszt, so that two distinct schools of thought grew up; pro-Schumann and Brahms or pro-Wagner and Liszt.

The history of the violin and viola is directly concerned with each of these schools: as orchestral instruments their range was extended beyond all recognition by Wagner and Liszt, while the violinist Joseph Joachim (1831–1907), an ardent supporter of the Schumann faction, made the violin concerto, the violin recital, and even the string quartet popular with large audiences throughout Germany, France, and England.

The technical capabilities of the violin were so thoroughly explored by Paganini that the history of the instrument changes its aspect after 1850, and becomes increasingly concerned with the social role of players and teachers. Technical progress has been concerned less with extending the limits of virtuosity than with making it attainable by a wider range of performers, so that considerable technical feats might be expected from the orchestral string section. No longer do we meet the hen-or-egg problem as to whether instrumental technique preceded the demands of the composer: since Beethoven the instrumentalist has been involved in a continual struggle to fulfil the composer's demands.

Wagner in particular, both as composer and conductor, asked more from the orchestra than it was at first able to give. He was quick to point out the weaknesses of the 19th-century orchestra in his book on conducting; first of all in the lack of balance in German orchestras, particularly the weakness of the viola section.

The viola is commonly (with rare exceptions indeed) played by infirm violinists, or by decrepit players of wind instruments who

157

happen to have been acquainted with a stringed instrument once upon a time; at best a competent viola player occupies a first desk, so that he may play the occasional solos for that instrument; but I have even seen this function performed by the leader of the first violins. It was pointed out to me that in a large orchestra which contained eight violas, there was only one player who could deal with the rather difficult passages in one of my later scores![2]

Later, failure to produce sustained tone (probably a result of the ⊂ ⊃ bow-stroke of the previous century) comes under attack.

Suppose the conductor was to attempt to hold the fermata as here directed, what would be the result? A miserable failure. After the initial power of the bow of the stringed instruments had been wasted, their tone would become thin and thinner, ending in a weak and timid *piano*; for (and here is one of the results of indifferent conducting) our orchestras nowadays hardly know what is meant by *equally sustained tone*. Let any conductor ask any orchestral instrument, no matter which, for a full and prolonged *forte*, and he will find the player puzzled, and will be astonished at the trouble it takes to get what he asks for.[3]

Wagner finds the string-players of German and English orchestras far inferior, in details such as string-crossing and bow-change, to the Paris Conservatoire Orchestra.

His book contains an admiring reference to a composition by Brahms, but ends with a mocking comment about Joachim which is typical of the verbal warfare between the rival Romanticists. Joachim, after a youthful friendship with Liszt, joined the Schumann supporters, reviling in a letter to Clara Schumann (10 December 1855) Liszt's 'vulgar misuse of sacred forms' and 'repulsive coquetting with the noblest feelings for the sake of effect'.[4] The violinist was, by all reports, a serious musician, with a formidable technique which was never given more prominence than the musical content of the works he performed. The glitter and show-manship of Liszt's compositions were so much the antithesis of Joachim's own nature that the violinist was blinded to his true values as a musician, so much so that he belittled on many occasions the work of the 'New Germans', as Wagner, Liszt, and their school were sometimes called. In later life, however, some of Joachim's friends became warm sup-porters of Wagner, pointing out that the two names should never have been arbitrarily linked by rival factions. In 1879 one of them, Levi, wrote:

I have never been able to understand how anyone could be a Wagnerian and a Lisztian at the same time. During the seven years I have been at Munich I have only had Liszt's name on my concert programmes twice; on both occasions the public met my wish that the items should be omitted. . . .[5]

and Joachim himself was upset by the news of Wagner's death.[6]

Joachim serves as a single example of the steadfast antagonism between the opposing factions. He regarded Schumann and Brahms as the great figures of the age, but Schumann died in a mental hospital in 1856, and Brahms was not so much a Romantic composer as a late offshoot of the Classicists; his forms were Classical, and unlike Mendelssohn he did not disguise them under a froth of Romantic coloration. Brahms recognised the incompatibility of Classical sonata form and Romantic lyricism; he wrote that 'the great Romanticists continued the sonata form in a lyric spirit which contradicts the inner dramatic nature of the sonata'.[7] And although the modern violinist is more likely to take part in the works of Brahms than of Liszt, and to recognise in the grandeur of concept and the intricacy of rhythmic detail a style which is neither Classical nor Romantic but entirely original, probably the New Germans had more effect on the instrumental music of the next hundred years.

Joachim, like Liszt, was a Hungarian, and his passionate denunciation of his fellow-countryman was so marked that one feels a moralistic approach: it is as though by decrying the 'bad', 'fantastic', 'shallow' virtuoso effects of the pianist-composer, he was trying to deny the national flair for *bravura* which he discovered in himself, and attempted to express in acceptable terms in his most successful composition, the Hungarian Concerto. 'Liszt makes a parade of the moods of despair and the stirrings of contrition with which the really pious man turns in solitude to God' he wrote in 1855.

I shall never be able to meet Liszt again, because I should want to tell him that instead of taking him for a mighty erring spirit striving to return to God, I have suddenly realised that he is a cunning contriver of effects, who has miscalculated.[8]

Even Joachim's pupil and biographer, Andreas Moser (1859–1925), was drawn into this fanatical opposition: he gives the impression of wholehearted concurrence with Joachim's opinion in the words

he would probably have overlooked Liszt's musical impotence, his poverty of conception, and the total lack of the creative faculty, for these qualities are innate, but he was repelled by Liszt's attempt to conceal the absence of these necessary gifts by the cunning expenditure of dazzling orchestral effects.[9]

These dazzling effects, with an original conception of form expressed in the symphonic poem and one-movement concerto, an almost Paganini-like control over the modern grand piano which earned him the title of 'father of modern piano technique', and a truly Romantic conception of programme in music which interpreted the spirit rather than the literal sense, made Liszt, if not one of the greatest composers, one of the most influential musicians ever to have lived. Joachim saw only the immoral life, exotic display, and Romantic posing of this legendary figure; he was unable to admit that the spread of good music – Beethoven, Schubert, Brahms, Berlioz, Schumann, even Bach – which Liszt achieved (having enticed the crowds to attend by the brilliance of his piano fantasias or the fascination of his myth-surrounded life) was of value or even existed. He would have been surprised and shocked to know that Liszt's one-movement symphonic poems and concertos are today considered a natural step in formal evolution after Mendelssohn's attempt to eliminate the pauses between movements in his symphonies, paralleled by Schumann's cello concerto and Wagner's rejection of the set aria in opera.

The violin concerto has not (apart from Chausson's *Poème*) adopted Liszt's one-movement form, but it has made use of his brilliant orchestral colourings to counterbalance the new virtuosity derived from Paganini's techniques. Paganini himself wrote concertos in Classical style, formally speaking, and he failed to lavish on the orchestra the attention given to the solo part. Chopin's piano concertos, played for the extreme beauty of their piano figuration, similarly fail to evoke the tension of two equal forces in opposition, which is the essence of the 19th-century concerto. Liszt, on the other hand, whose early works had to be orchestrated for him by Raff, became such an expert in orchestration that his remarkable virtuoso writing for the piano was matched by a virtuoso orchestra, with effects that contemporary critics found too modern to accept. Hanslick nicknamed the E flat concerto 'The Triangle Concerto' because of a conspicuous appearance of that instrument (used by Beethoven in the 9th Symphony but still considered vulgar if noticed). Liszt himself cited a previous contraction of the three-movement concerto form into one movement in Moscheles's *Concerto Fantastique*, and although his concerto in A major has no programme, it is in effect a symphonic poem with the added contrast of solo piano with orchestra: in its unity of thematic material it probably descends from Schubert's 'Wanderer' Fantasia and Berlioz's *Harold in Italy*.

The later violin concertos have accepted Liszt's abandonment of alternating solo and orchestral statements, but Schumann and Mendelssohn had already done this. Brahms's violin concerto is exceptional among the 19th-century violin repertoire in its use of an opening *tutti* to state the main themes: Tchaikovsky, Lalo, Bruch, and Dvořák, even Brahms himself in the double concerto, introduce the soloists at an earlier stage in the proceedings. Brahms and Tchaikovsky wrote their concertos in the same year, 1878: that of Brahms, called a 'concerto against the violin' by some, was favoured by Hanslick, who came down heavily against Tchaikovsky. 'The violin is no longer played,' he wrote, 'it is yanked about, it is torn asunder, it is beaten black and blue.'[10] Leopold Auer, for whom the piece was written, found certain passages too difficult: he produced a revised edition which was used for many years, but today the tendency is to return to the original, and the concerto is a standard part of the professional violinist's training. Tchaikovsky had a clear idea of the concerto's aims: of his B-flat minor piano concerto he wrote:

> Here we are dealing with two equal opponents; the orchestra with its power and inexhaustible variety of colour, opposed by the small but high-mettled piano, which often comes off victorious in the hands of a gifted executant.[11]

The concertos of the violinist-composers de Bériot, Wieniawski, Vieuxtemps, David, Ernst, Joachim, and Ysaÿe, usually overbalance in favour of the soloist and in spite of many promising ideas, they have failed (except for a rare hearing of the Wieniawski D minor) to remain in the repertoire. Great concertos are usually the work of symphonists, even if the composer failed fully to come to terms with symphonic writing.

Lalo's *Symphonie Espagnole* is a successful concerto in five movements which belies most generalisations about the concerto: written for Sarasate by a professional viola-player, its brilliant violin-writing (the soloist rarely stops playing except during the introduction to each movement), colourful orchestration, and Spanish rhythms make it an excellent musical entertainment. Lalo was associated with the French rather than the Spanish schools of composition, so this concerto is not really a representative of the nationalist schools which grew up in the latter part of the 19th century: Grieg, Dvořák, and Tchaikovsky reveal more nationalist characteristics with less stated intention. Joachim, dedicatee of the concertos by Brahms and Dvořák (although he never performed the latter, after revising the manuscript), wrote a Hungarian Concerto which was popular for a time. Brahms had Joachim and his quartet cellist Hausmann in mind when he composed the double concerto in A minor, a work which audiences found puzzling for many years – not surprisingly, as the more traditional violin concerto was hissed at its first performance. Brahms himself had doubts about the double concerto: he wrote to Clara Schumann: 'I might have left the idea to someone else who understands fiddles better than I do',[12] and the violin-writing is not so well suited to the instrument as that of the violin concerto, but the work is now a widely appreciated part of the concerto repertoire.

'I am anxious about Johannes' Concerto because of the orchestra',[31] wrote Clara Schumann of the D minor piano concerto in 1858. She was referring not to the orchestra's technical capabilities, but to their possible unwillingness to co-operate in the performance of a new work. The growth in size of the Romantic orchestra, coupled with its increased relative importance in the concerto, put the soloist at the mercy not only of the conductor but also of those temperamental virtuosi who were now found within the orchestra. Essentials of a great concerto performance are a soloist whose interpretation sufficiently convinces and moves the orchestra to stimulate their personal co-operation, and a conductor who is able actively to participate in the interpretation. Negative efficiency with an accompanying atmosphere is the best one can expect from the modern practice of limiting rehearsal to a run-through on the day of the concert. 'Like everywhere else, there are not enough rehearsals here . . .',[14] wrote Joachim from Vienna in 1867, and the phrase has echoed through musical life ever since.

In England, rehearsing for concerts was largely a 19th-century concept, linked with the growth of concert-giving for large audiences: in the early part of the 18th century, concerts had frequently consisted of a performance at sight by mixed amateurs and professionals. Previous rehearsals were rare enough to be specially announced in advertisements. Later in the century, rehearsals for special concerts were held, but often before an audience. In the rest of Europe, however, court musicians had ample rehearsal time and sometimes very high standards: Stamitz with the Mannheim orchestra, Lully, and Graun were all admired and feared for their standards. Musicians rehearsing under Gluck had to be given double pay, so rigorously did he enforce attention to dynamics and ensemble. Twenty or thirty rehearsals might be held for an opera in Paris, and Kussner, conductor of the Hamburg Opera, would go over the parts with unsatisfactory performers in his own house.

As the harpsichord became dispensable, the leading violinists took over the role of conductor, partly playing, partly waving their bows as the orchestral forces became larger and more difficult to control. The practice of standing for orchestral concerts was replaced by the Viennese custom of sitting on benches or chairs: if the leader stood to direct, he looked more like the modern conception of a conductor. A period of orchestral indiscipline appears to have accompanied the rapid growth in orchestral numbers and techniques at the beginning of the 19th century, combated by a few eminent concert-masters who conducted from the leader's chair, and by the gradual ascendancy of the conductor with baton after Spohr's popularisation of this method. Schuppanzigh, David, and Habeneck were of the former school; Weber replaced his roll of music with a baton in the theatre, and instituted separate rehearsals for soloists, chorus, and orchestra (a system still applying in some continental opera-houses, often to the detriment of the final result when the forces are not united until the dress rehearsal or first night). Spontini earned his very high income in Berlin by drilling his players into frightened but accurate submission, using a large ebony baton in contrast to Spohr's small ivory stick.

Berlioz, whose fairly low opinion of the average orchestral player was quoted in the previous chapter, learned from the precision of Habeneck's performances and transmitted some of his zeal as a conductor to Liszt. He did not always run down the players, as did some conductors; from Dresden he wrote to Joachim: 'The orchestra, chorus and soloists show an ardour, a devotion, a patience, and intelligence, an enthusiasm, which would delight you. And what musicians!'[15] Liszt, whose conducting was as individual as his piano-playing, had a high regard for the musicians: his intention was to overcome technical details at rehearsal, leaving the individual artists free to express themselves at the performance. This principle, abandoned by various autocratic conductors since, has been retained by those for whom the players give of their best: for the orchestral player, the greatest conductor is the one who can produce a unified performance while allowing the performers the sense (or illusion) of untrammelled personal expression. To do this he must, as Wagner once pointed out, choose and sustain the right speed: 'The whole duty of a conductor is comprised in his ability always to indicate the right *tempo*.'[16] Wagner visited the Albert Hall in London in 1877 to conduct the orchestra of 170 players assembled for the Wagner Festival. George Bernard Shaw wrote of his 'tense, neuralgic glare', his stamping, and the way in which he 'looked daggers – spoke them too, sometimes – at innocent instrumentalists'.[17] In reaction, the more peaceful Herr

Richter, who 'did not pose and gesticulate like a savage at a war dance',[17] was applauded by the orchestra.

Shaw credits Richter with authorising approximations of difficult Wagner parts.

> 'How' exclaimed the average violinist in anger and despair 'is a man to be expected to play this reiterated motive . . . in demi-semiquavers at the rate of sixteen in a second? What can he do but go a-swishing up and down as best he can?' 'What indeed?' replied Herr Richter encouragingly. 'That is precisely what is intended by the composer.'[18]

Hans von Bülow (1830–94), talented pianist, conductor, and writer, was among the first to take a symphony orchestra (the Meiningen Court Orchestra) on tour with him – Eduard Hanslick (1884) referred to this phenomenon as 'a novelty reserved for our railway epoch'.[19] This critic was vastly impressed by the same orchestra's performance of the Brahms D minor piano concerto with no conductor other than von Bülow at the piano, and by their 'flawless performance'[20] of the *Grosse Fuge*. At a time when Joachim was writing from England to say that 'unfortunately the second violin and the viola are not capable of playing Beethoven's last Quartette',[21] this was quite a feat. Hanslick's praise was qualified by the words 'A stunt, to be sure, and thoroughly unenjoyable at that',[22] but his admiration for the playing under Bülow was marked. He refers to the addition of unusual instruments, a five-string bass doubling the whole range of the cello, and chromatic timpani, both used today, plus Ritter's *viola alta*, devised for Wagner and pitched lower than the normal viola. Bülow's orchestra stood while playing, a custom by then out of fashion, and according to Hanslick they were under a discipline to which larger orchestras would not submit.

The question of orchestral discipline was a touchy one in an age of dispute over the rights of man. Hans Richter, having called out 'Ass!' after an incorrect entry by a second violin in Vienna, was given the choice of either apologising to the player or resigning. French and English orchestras were rarely in a position of such power, however: they were often only semi-permanent, disbanded at the end of a season, and dependent on the conductor or promoter for employment. Lamoureux's orchestra caused quite a stir when it visited England, but Carl Flesch (1873–1944) had the experience of playing in it as a young man, and emerged with no great opinion of the conductor. 'His lack of technical talent was the first thing to strike one. His beat was awkward, his memory quite inadequate.'[23] The principal memories of Lamoureux's rehearsals were of cold stools without backs, and the conductor's churlishness. 'French conductors do not extend the Proclamation of the Rights of Man of 1789 to orchestral musicians',[24] claims Flesch, but he withdraws this statement when speaking of Pierre Monteux, who was a violinist, then a viola-player, before becoming a conductor. Lamoureux heard each violinist play alone different parts in Strauss and Wagner, a practice which would not be appreciated by modern orchestral players, and he personally checked the tuning of each instrument.

A highly respected but less autocratic school of conductors followed in the direct tradition of Liszt, using gesture and facial expression to coax expressive playing from the orchestra, instead of the domineering tactics which produced dry accuracy from the Lamoureux orchestra. Among Liszt's successors were Richter, Seidl, Mottl, Strauss, Muck, Nikisch, Mahler, and Weingartner. Of Nikisch, Flesch wrote:

> The orchestra went with him through thick and thin. . . . As a former violinist he understood the practical side of orchestral playing . . . his rehearsals were of a comforting brevity . . . there is nothing to which the orchestral musician is more responsive.[25']

Verdi complained that no sooner was music freed from the privileged *prima donna* than it began to suffer from the high-handed conductor, and many of the great 19th-century and early 20th-century conductors were guilty of tampering with the works they conducted. Not only by making transcriptions, rendering small-orchestra works with large assorted bands, or reducing the big works for small numbers, but by arranging Beethoven's piano sonatas for orchestra (Weingartner, Habeneck) and making cuts and alterations in opera scores. Shaw complained[26] of Costa adding trombones to Beethoven's scoring, and describes a performance at a Promenade Concert, held in Covent Garden in 1877, of Mozart's 39th Symphony, which was followed by

> a transcription for orchestra and military band of Handel's See the Conquering Hero Comes, in which the delighted listeners had the pleasure of hearing the simultaneous explosions of six cornets, six horns, four euphoniums, one ophicleide, and seven trombones, in addition to the full orchestra of reeds and strings.[27]

Mendelssohn and Schumann added to Bach's solo violin sonatas piano accompaniments which frequently alter the intended harmonies, and Wagner, Reger, and Mahler not only reorchestrated works of Beethoven, Gluck, and Weber, but altered their content. Today this seems parallel to brightening up a painting by an old master. Certain editions with blatant deviations from the original have been reprinted over and over again by the more conservative publishing houses: only now are they beginning to make *urtext* editions available to a text-conscious public. In a recent television documentary, a member of an American youth orchestra complained about the cuts imposed on the music by their conductor, a world-famous figure. Musical education has spread to the point where audiences will insist on hearing exactly what the composer wrote.

In contrast to the freedom with texts indulged in by leading conductors, composers, and violinists (especially Wilhelmj), we have instances of what even today might be considered musicological pedantry. Joachim found 'ten or twelve *oboi d'amore* and other obsolete wind instruments'[28] for a performance in Berlin of Bach's St Matthew Passion, probably including the natural trumpet which so impressed G. B. Shaw in the hands of a musician from Berlin in 1885. For an 1894 performance of Bach's St John Passion, Berlin musicians learned to play the viola d'amore and the viola da gamba. The era of the musicologist was beginning, with monumental biographies of great musicians: Chrysander's *Handel* (1858), Spitta's *Bach* (1889–90), and an important work (1866–79) on Beethoven by an American, A. W. Thayer.

During the 19th century, with the improvement in communications, the United States ceased to be cut off from Europe's musical life, and became accepted as a field for the touring virtuoso. The pianoforte's metal frame came from America, and besides visiting pianists like Thalberg, the United States began to produce her own virtuosi, Gottschalk being among the first to reach international fame. Jenny Lind and Ole Bull made frequent recital tours in the United States, the New York Philharmonic Orchestra was founded in 1842, and the Metropolitan Opera in 1883. With the influx of Italians, Frenchmen, and Germans (including Graupner, the oboist who settled in Boston and founded the Philharmonic Society in 1810) towards the turn of the century, European influence became widespread, and concert life ran parallel to that in England until a genuine national culture began to make itself felt later in the century.

Edward Holmes, writing in the *Musical Times* (May 1852), pointed out that England too had become the home of many foreign musicians, with the dissolution of so many royal Courts. 'Establishments broken up, salaries suspended, and old grey-headed artists within armchair days, revolving speculations of flight to America. . . .' Musicians in Germany left suddenly without security; and sought refuge wherever some concert life was established. Not, as Holmes regretted, like the musical life in Dresden, where concerts of Beethoven, Mozart, and Haydn took place in 'a kind of open summer-house' in the gardens, and 'the players do not scruple, during the pauses, to avail themselves of certain ham sandwiches and sundry bottles of wine, thus repairing dilapidations of their spirits, and keeping up excitement'. Concert life in England was on the whole more formal, although there were concerts of light music in the public gardens at Vauxhall, Marylebone, and Ranelagh, and of course Jullien's *concerts monstres* at the Royal Zoological Gardens, which began in 1845.

The early part of the 19th century showed a bias towards choral music in England, where because there were no small royal Courts there was a dearth of well-trained instrumentalists. Musicians mainly earned their living by playing at the big choral festivals. The second part of the century showed a growing preference for instrumental music throughout Europe, however: Edward Fitzgerald was writing to Tennyson in 1848 'I think the day of Oratorios is gone, like the day for painting Holy Families etc.'[29] The day of symphony orchestras was just arriving, and the years 1850–1900 saw the Hallé, Bournemouth Municipal, Scottish, and Liverpool Philharmonic orchestras working in the British provinces, usually on a semi-permanent basis at first.

Concerts require a promoter, a hall, and an audience, as well as performers. Apart from the local music societies, who were inclined to be conservative in their concert promotions, a few wealthy men made themselves responsible for the initial outlay on instrumental concerts and turned the tide in favour of the instrumental rather than the choral concert. Among these we meet the names of Gustav Behrens and James Forsyth, who with another big manufacturer, Henry Simon, prevented the Hallé orchestra from dispersing after the death of its founder Sir Charles Hallé in 1895. Another Behrens, Adolph, was responsible for guaranteeing the financial side of the first performance in England of Brahms's clarinet quintet, with Richard Mühlfeld specially brought over to play the clarinet part.[30] Chappell, England's leading promoter, would not take the risk, but in fact the hall was packed and the work warmly received. Joachim mentions in a letter to Brahms[31] that Adolph Behrens had once offered to have the *German Requiem* copied and performed at his own expense, and the composer was very touched to receive a legacy of £1,000 from this practical supporter whom he had never met.

Packed halls for chamber music became fairly common towards the end of the century, but the medium was only slowly appreciated by a wide public. Even today the words 'chamber music' carry an implication of snobbery or exclusive intellectualism to many English-speaking people. The first of the touring quartets, the Müller Brothers String Quartet, left the service of the Duke of Brunswick in 1831, but it was probably the famous name of Joachim which drew popular attention to the medium. Joachim's quartet soirées in Weimar, however, were very expensive: as Bülow pointed out, 'In consequence of this only the best society will be present, but in sufficient number; the entire court and the grand ducal household will be present.'[32] The trend of concert-giving was towards larger audiences and lower prices, however, and at the other end of the scale John Willy in London was attempting to establish low-price quartet concerts in London – an attempt repeated some thirty years later when Shaw reported that the People's Concert Society only charged one penny and 3d. for admission to their pro-grammes of chamber and vocal music. Concert prices for a series in Birmingham that year averaged only 4d. a head, but London concerts were very expensive. The 'cheaper' concerts cost from one shilling to 7 shillings a seat; the cheapest seats for Richter were 2s. 6d.; and the Philharmonic concerts cost 4 guineas for eight concerts, or one guinea for a single concert. Numbered seats were introduced in 1830, at first only in theatres, where they met with some resentment, but as Hanslick points out,[33] London preceded Vienna by a hundred years in requesting ladies not to wear hats at performances.

Concerts were normally expected to make a profit: Hanslick gives some details about Richter's series.

> While other concert institutions in London are content with a single rehearsal, and that rather inhibited by the presence of a half-price audience, Richter has two and sometimes, when especially difficult novelties are involved, even three, with the public excluded from all of them. Richter is extraordinarily strict, and exacting at rehearsal, but he is generous in his acknowledgment and recog-nition of the exemplary discipline and industry of the English musicians. Each concert costs £400, including one rehearsal, box-office receipts with a full house run to £600.[34]

He goes on to describe Richter's provincial tours with his orchestra, where the financial risk was undertaken by local music-lovers.

In 1886, Hanslick was making the point that the musical season in Vienna or Paris was small compared to London,

> a mecca for everyone in England who plays, fiddles or sings and for everyone on the continent who has achieved musical fame.[35]

He refers to 'ten or twelve concerts announced every day of the week';[35] yet in 1891 Shaw was to write 'London is as badly off as ever for orchestral concerts'.[36] The Crystal Palace concerts conducted by Manns, who like Hallé was highly esteemed by the English, were too far away in Shaw's opinion; in any case the building was not acoustically ideal. Joachim wrote that 'as a place for making music it is monstrous'[37] and it was used most successfully for music with monstrous forces, like the choir of 3,000 and orchestra of 400 for Handel festivals. The Albert Hall was opened by Queen Victoria in 1871: it seated 12,000 and prices ranged from one to 15 shillings. All over Europe concert-halls were being built to house the new mass audiences. Joachim was moved by the sight of 'about 5,000 people, from academicians to labourers, sitting crowded together, listening, judging, believing and enjoying'[38] at Pasdeloup's concerts in Paris. He compared English audiences favourably with German ones with regard to enthusiasm and attention, and more than once refers in his letters to their increasing appreciation of chamber music: 'After all, it is not a small thing that 2,000 people should come reverently to hear Beethoven's last Quartette.'[39]

Schubert's chamber music was only gradually accepted during the 19th century, and the Bach revival, initiated by Mendelssohn and furthered by Joachim and Liszt, only slowly gained public approbation. Von Bülow was considered a brave man to include some of the forty-eight Preludes and Fugues in his programmes and Shaw, who thought Schubert's quintet decidedly too long, admitted that although with everyone he loudly applauded Bach's C major solo sonata played by Joachim, he really thought it a terrible noise. Joseph Szigeti (b. 1892) quotes his criticism of this concert:

> Joachim scraped away frantically, making a sound after which an attempt to grate a nutmeg effectively on a bootsole would have been as the strain of an Aeolian harp. The notes which were musical enough to have any discernible pitch at all were mostly out of tune. It was horrible – damnable![40]

Concert programmes tended to be extremely long: two of Shaw's favourite topics were the advisability of reducing the average programme length, and the extreme expensiveness of printed programmes (one shilling).

Advertising on posters became advisable with the wide choice of concerts available to the public, and Vieuxtemps is said to be the first violinist to have had his name published in letters 2 feet high. August Wilhelmj, Eugène Ysaÿe, Ole Bull, and Pablo de Sarasate (1844–1908) joined the touring virtuosi, who following a precept initiated by Clara Schumann and Joachim gave solo recitals as well as concerto performances: the sonata with piano gained new importance in this type of concert. Playing from memory, a habit of Paganini's which so impressed his audiences, became customary in the solo concerto.

The custom early in the century of playing odd movements of symphonies, interspersed with *bravura* pieces or vocal ballads, gradually gave way to entire works with often two concertos, an overture, a symphony, and a number of *bravura* pieces included in one evening. Rehearsing for such long concerts must often have been inadequate. To a certain extent the Promenade Concerts, which began in their modern form in 1895, have sustained the long-programme tradition into the 20th century. One tradition that has almost lapsed with 20th-century virtuosi is the practice of leading quartets: nowadays a violinist usually becomes either a soloist or a chamber music player, but Ysaÿe, Wieniawski, and Joachim all led chamber-music groups at Chappell's concerts besides sustaining international reputations as concerto soloists.

Joachim considered concert performance to be often underpaid and was pleased to take up an appointment as head of Berlin's *Hochschule* with a life income of 2,000 thalers. 'Think how long it would have taken me to make a capital of 40,000 thalers by playing at concerts!',[41] he wrote to his wife. For many years he had enjoyed or endured the benefits of the patronage-system, which only finally disappeared during the 1860s. He became *Konzertmeister* to the Court of Hanover in 1853, leaving a similar post in Weimar, where Liszt was Capellmeister. Moser lists his duties:

> To act as principal violin at the more important operatic performances, to pay special attention to an uniformity of bowing and equality of tone in the strings, to raise the standards of the orchestral performances by co-operation as soloist, to lead the Symphony Soirées and to act either as conductor or soloist at State Concerts.[42]

Five months' leave of absence was allowed during the summer, and permission for concert tours readily given at other times. In spite of these admirable terms of employment, Joachim never really felt comfortable in the position: his letters are punctuated by complaints, disputes, and resignations. In a long, impassioned letter to Gisela von Arnem (1854) he writes

> I am still in the service of the King of Hanover after all – not without the wish, certainly, to attain as soon as possible (but with

no demonstrations!) to a quiet independence, even if it means sacrificing something. I hate serving even the gentlest master.[43]

A few months later he was petitioning the King for two years' leave – beginning the letter with the words 'I humbly request your Majesty to grant me leave . . .',[44] but allowing no further flavour of servitude to creep into the wording. A marked change from 18th-century practice. King George appears to have been very patient and long-suffering, while unwilling to accept Joachim's resignations on various counts. In 1856 the violinist is still at the Court, although his immediate superior by 'continued double-dealing and other intrigues once more made my position here so unbearable that I was obliged to send in my resignation twice!'[45] There was trouble at orchestra rehearsals taken by Joachim, too, but he tells Clara Schumann that 'at last my position is what I wished it to be'.[45] Three weeks later he discovers that the members of the orchestra have 'the souls of tradesmen instead of artists . . . no hearts at all, but at the most a pair of scales filled to the brim with stupidity and vanity . . .'[46] and some of them refuse to play for him. Moser appears to have been unaware of these storms, tea-cup-sized or otherwise; they are not mentioned in his biography of Joachim.

The letters continue to be more explicit: while rebelling against the indignities of the patronage-system, Joachim is reluctant to abandon its security. On the one occasion when the King will not fit in with his plans for a tour, because of the visit of a Grand Duchess, he finds the refusal 'most galling'. He also complains about the long, badly-organised court concerts, the first half of one of them lasting from 9.15 p.m. to 1.30 a.m. The frustrations were not, however, sufficient to prevent him from sending a warm invitation to Clara Schumann to join him in the King's service: she refused. Joachim's fame as a violinist was now inter-national: he was welcomed especially in England, and he could well have afforded to leave his position at Hanover. Once again the King prevented this move, by appointing him *Konzert-director*, a new post, and offering him two years' leave on full pay in return for directing six concerts a year.

In 1862 he was nevertheless talking of resigning once again, with the brave statement

> The royal enthusiasm for art is not rooted nearly so deeply in Georg of Hanover as is republicanism in Georg Joseph Joachim. As a courtier I have put up long enough with graciousness and patronage, thus sinning against my nature.[47]

Again the King's graciousness triumphed and a new contract for four months' stay at Hanover each year was signed on 1 March 1862.

The later resignations may have been caused by an upsurge of republican spirit in Joachim, typical of the age he was living in, or they could have been an example of the musician's one way of improving his contract – by threatening to withdraw his services. Certainly better and better contracts were forthcoming. But finally trouble arose over a quite different matter of principle: Joachim proposed the violinist Jakob Grün for promotion to the post of chamber musician, and the promotion was refused because Grün was a Jew. Joachim, a Jew converted to Christianity, would not accept this reason, and matters were not helped when it was pointed out that Grün would never have been employed by the Court at all if his race had been known to them. Joachim tendered yet another resignation, and was the subject of bitter dispute in the local press. Grün was appointed *Kammervirtuos* (an evasion of the title *Kammermusikus* which was the position in dispute) for life, and Joachim's decision wavered again. Finally in 1866 the break with patronage was made, as with many other musicians, by the onset of war and dispersal of the Court, never to be reassembled as the small states became part of Prussia. Joachim was freed from a yoke which cannot have been very restricting, or he would have abandoned it many years earlier: as a family man he was glad to replace it with a different kind of bondage in return for security in Berlin, where he became principal of the new school of music, responsible to the town's ministers.

Grün reappears in the memoirs of Carl Flesch, in Vienna, where he became leader of the Vienna Court Opera, and the unfortunate butt of his predecessor Hellmesberger's wit. The Hellmesberger dynasty dominated Viennese musical life during most of the 19th century, and introduced late Beethoven and Schubert quartets which were previously unknown to a wide public. Flesch and Moser give directly opposed pictures of the Joachim quartet, which did similar pioneer work in Europe with late Beethoven and Brahms quartets.

Moser, the hero-worshipper, says that 'Joachim does not play "First Fiddle" and relegate his partners to a subordinate position',[48] but Flesch (who tends to be over-critical) considers that

> the quartet consisted of a solo violin with three instruments accompanying. . . . But then, the regulars at these concerts only wanted to hear Joachim anyway; willy nilly, the other players had to be accepted as part of the bargain.[49]

The unwillingness of the concert-going public to accept Schubert's instrumental works seems strange today: Joachim thought it was because he had been labelled a songwriter and minds were closed to any other opinion. He wrote of an English audience's dismissal of a Schubert quartet in 1852, and in 1897 the *Musical Times* carried an account of a rehearsal of the 'Great' symphony in C major which shows little relaxation of prejudice.

> . . . at the close of the first movement, the principal horn called out to one of the first violins, 'Tom, have you been able to discover a tune yet?' 'I have not', was Tom's reply.[50]

The Trout Quintet, which is fairly bursting with tunes, was the first of the chamber works to achieve some sort of popularity: now the piano trios, quartets, string quintet, and octet are all best-sellers in the chamber-music repertoire. Some of the later 19th-century chamber music follows Schubert in mood rather than Beethoven: the nationalist composers, especially Dvořák and Smetana, introduced folk-song influence and national dance forms and rhythm in the way that Schubert drew on his song-writing for melodies and accompanying textures.

Smetana gave the viola new prominence in his first quartet, *From My Life*, given an autobiographical programme with the viola's first theme representing Fate. Programme music for chamber ensembles is rare: Haydn's *Seven Last Words on the Cross*, Smetana's quartet, and Schönberg's *Verklärte Nacht* are spaced across more than a century. The second movement of Smetana's quartet is a national dance, a polka, and Dvořák makes considerable use of another dance, the *dumka*. Dvořák is said to have used American as well as Czech themes after visiting the New World during 1892–94, hence the nicknamed 'American' Quartet, opus 96, but it is probably only an increased use of the pentatonic scale from hearing American folk music which makes these works sound slightly less Czech. In opus 96 the viola introduces the principal theme, as in Smetana's first quartet, and in his *Terzetto* for two violins and viola (possibly a descendant of Beethoven's serenade for violin, flute, and viola), Dvořák treats all the instruments with complete freedom and obtains some delightful sonorities. Dvořák, like Brahms, played the viola himself.

Brahms appreciated the viola's special role in chamber music, especially towards the end of his life when he wrote the songs with viola obbligato and arranged his two clarinet sonatas for viola and piano. His quartets and quintets often give more prominence to the viola than the second violin: one particularly beautiful instance being the third move-ment of opus 67, where the unmuted viola sings above its three muted colleagues. The second quintet using two violas (opus 111 in G) makes the first viola prominent throughout, as it had been for an occasional movement in Mozart's quintets.

Perhaps Brahms's regard for the viola was increased by Joachim, who occasionally played the instrument and wrote 'Hebrew Melodies' and a set of variations for it. Moser's comment that the viola 'unfortunately has been almost discarded as a solo instrument' [51] makes no reference to low playing standards: by 1900 the viola's status had risen to the point where a viola class could be held alongside the violin classes at the Paris Conservatoire, and where the most romantic tunes (e.g. in Tchaikovsky's *Romeo and Juliet*) were given to the orchestra's violas instead of the long-favoured cellos.

Debussy, whose quartet was published in 1893, obtained new sounds from the medium which were quite unlike the orchestral effects intro-duced by Tchaikovsky into his quartet-writing. The names of Debussy and Ravel are usually linked with the Impressionist group, whose aim in painting, or in music, was to depict moods, suggestions, impressions, leaving a great deal of detail to be filled in by the imagination. The play of light upon an object became more important than the object itself, as can be seen in the paintings of Monet, Renoir, Pissarro. Debussy's Nocturnes, *La Mer*, and *L'Après-midi d'un faune* are effective examples of orchestral impressionism. The string quartet, which appeared in 1893, one year before *L'Après-midi*, successfully carries this new repertoire of tonal effects into a most unlikely medium; the public and critics were baffled by its strangeness at first. One basic theme is transformed by various harmonies and tonal colours, seen, as it were, in different lighting. Backgrounds are as important as the main melodies, often more so, and each instrumentalist needs to be a concerto soloist one moment, providing an ethereal background effect the next. All four instruments play chords together, and octaves, trills, tremolos, har-monics, high positions, and rapid *pizzicati* appear in each part in both Debussy's quartet and Ravel's, which was written in 1902. For the performer these two works meant not so much an increase in virtuosity, however, as a challenge to produce a more varied palette of sound than was hitherto associated with chamber-music playing: bow technique in particular needed to explore the realms of *flautando* and *ponticello* effects not formerly expected from the string quartet, save for a rare instance such as the *ponticello* in Beethoven's opus 131.

Schönberg is generally considered neither a Romantic nor an

Impressionist, but his string sextet *Verklärte Nacht* ('Transfigured Night'), composed in 1899, shows traces of both schools. It was refused performance in Vienna because the composer had used a chord of the ninth with the dissonant ninth in the bass part, which was against the rules of harmony! Today the harmonies remind us of Wagner or Richard Strauss rather than Schönberg's later compositions, but this full-length tone poem inspired by Richard Dehmel's poem was at first rejected as cacophonous. Schönberg himself played the violin, and he is not afraid of giving each instrumentalist a part abounding in technical problems, particularly harmonics: the detailed interweaving of parts and frequent tempo-changes may also have caused early performances of the work to be less than ideal.

A viola-player capable of performing these chamber works written at the close of the century, Strauss's tone poems, and Wagner's operatic orchestral parts must have a technique which is equal to concerto-playing: with Strauss the viola was still playing Sancho Panza to the cello's Don Quixote, but 20th-century composers were to lavish on this instrument the attention deserved by a new school of virtuosi.

Italy, the home of the violin and viola, while still providing many of the world's best instruments during the 19th century, made practically no contribution to the development of instrumental music outside the opera pit, even becoming famous for her resistance to Classical instrumental music. Spohr found touring there unrewarding – he complained that audiences would clap after every *bravura* passage, and that an Italian orchestra made no difference between *forte* and *piano*. At the Palazzo Ruspoli in Rome he found 'ignorance, stupidity and lack of taste'[52] in the orchestra, who clung to Baroque free ornamentation in Classical and post-Classical works.

In 1857, Joachim was refusing to visit Rome because 'There is no music there; I should be homesick for the strains of an orchestra'[53] and he states that even church music is neglected. But Scholz, who was in Rome in 1863, wrote: 'I am surprised to find that good music is beginning to gain a footing here in Rome. There are some very good Chamber music concerts being given.'[54]

The *Società del Quartetto* of Milan was founded in 1864 by Verdi's publisher, Ricordi; up to that time, according to its historian Confalonieri, 'A sonata, a quartet or a septet had never been heard in its entirety in a concert or at a musical entertainment'[55] in Milan. Joachim and Sarasate gave concerts for the society, odd mixtures of quartets (possibly with local players), concertos, unaccompanied Bach, and virtuoso solos – even single movements such as the variations from the Kreutzer Sonata played by Sarasate. After Paganini Italy took the lead in no aspect of instrumental music save violin-making, until the 20th century when the *Virtuosi di Roma* and Italian string quartets became internationally important.

Wilhelmj was the first major violinist to appreciate the qualities of the 19th-century Italian violin-makers Rocca and Pressenda, whose instruments have so rapidly increased in value during the last twenty years. In spite of the enormous reputation of Vuillaume as a copyist, most violinists by now were choosing to play on old Italian instruments, particularly those of Stradivari and del Gesù, which were discovered to stand out against the large-sized concerto orchestra most successfully. Joachim's quartet all played on Stradivarius instruments, as did Sarasate (who left two to a museum), Sauzay (whose violin became Thibaud's), Grün, Ernst, Wilhelmj, Ysaÿe, and Vieuxtemps (who also had a Storioni and a del Gesù). Ole Bull played on violins by Amati and del Gesù, finally preferring one by Gasparo da Salò and using, according to Shaw, a bow 2 inches longer than the normal. De Bériot used a violin by Maggini, and Sivori a Vuillaume, although the latter received a violin by A. and H. Amati as a legacy from Dragonetti. Phipson, in *Famous Violinists and Fine Violins* (1896), describes the increase in value of Vuillaumes during his lifetime. 'When I came to London, about 1861, the violins of Vuillaume, with box and bow included, were being sold here for £14. Many of them now fetch as much as £40 or £50, and even more.'[56] Flesch reports that in Vienna c. 1890 the lesser Italian makers' violins, such as those by a Grancino or Gagliano, cost far less than those made by Lupot or Vuillaume.

These prices sound low but were often beyond the means of the orchestral player – Phipson complains at length about the disparity between solo and orchestral fees.

> Why do we pay a prima donna or a primo tenore – often of rather limited musical education – by some hundreds of guineas a night, when the leading violin – often a highly educated musician – is obliged to content himself with a guinea or, under special circumstances, say, two guineas?[57]

This undervalued musical education has been the subject of dissension for the past one and a half centuries, both from the angle of efficiency of orchestral training and of the status and rewards of the orchestral player. No one seems to deny that an orchestral player needs to be well-trained, but European institutions of musical education have always shown a reluctance to deal with the problem.

Berlioz enumerated shortcomings of the Paris Conservatoire towards the middle of the 19th century:

> the study of the Violin in Paris is very incomplete, the pupils are not taught the *pizzicato*. . . . Neither is the use of harmonics properly studied in a business-like manner. . . .
> It is to be regretted that there is no special class for the Viola. This instrument, notwithstanding its relation to the violin, needs individual study and constant practice if it is to be properly played. Whenever a violinist is mediocre, it is said 'he will make a capital tenor'.[58]

After pointing out the lack of available tuition in various instruments, including percussion, he adds: '*There is no class for rhythm*, devoted to initiating all pupils without exception, whether singers or instrumentalists, into the various difficulties of the division of time.'[59] Flesch was complaining that students of the Paris Conservatoire picked up their orchestral training in the café orchestras at the end of the last century, and although most institutions have their own orchestras today, Szigeti is making an almost identical complaint about lack of orchestral training in his book *Szigeti on the Violin*, published in 1969.

Institutions for musical instruction multiplied rapidly during the latter half of the 19th century; in England the Guildhall School, Trinity College, and the Royal College, all in London, were followed by the Royal Manchester College in 1893. Joachim's *Hochschule*, which began with nineteen pupils in 1869, had 250 by 1890, and with the expansion in musical education came the appointment of music-masters at schools such as Harrow and Uppingham, opening a new form of musical career.

The violin was by 1890 'the most fashionable instrument', according to Phipson. 'Thousands of young girls have the violin thrust upon them by ambitious parents, because for the last twenty years it has become so much in vogue.'[60] Women joined the ranks of the virtuosi, in particular Wilma Neruda, who became Lady Hallé and thus set the seal of respectability on the violin as a woman's instrument in England. More violin instruction-books were published, most of them based on the system of Spohr and the French school. According to Flesch, however, standards of teaching were low. 'The usual method of teaching consisted of planless and purposeless primitive advice in interpretation',[61] he writes of his studies in Vienna, and he found 'complete ignorance of rational methods of study'.[62] He was to initiate a more scientific approach to teaching in the 20th century, but the methods handed down from generation to generation of violinists have proved remarkably resistant to the written word.

Joachim's influence as a player and teacher was very far-reaching, and he must to a certain extent have been responsible for the persistence of a physically unnatural method of restraining the bow-arm, so that the elbow was not allowed to rise and a right-angle was formed by wrist and forearm when the bow-stroke reached the nut. The few remaining advocates of this system point out that Joachim's bow-arm was admired by all, but it should be remembered that (a) Joachim's style was not entirely natural, as a boy he was troubled by a stiff bow-arm, and he learned his bow technique entirely from Böhm; (b) although he used this method with success, few of his pupils had anything like a similar success, and most of them became teachers – sometimes encouraging the low bow-arm by tying it to the player's side with string, or making the pupil hold heavy books with the right elbow while playing!; (c) Joachim was himself troubled with pains and inflammation of the arm if he did too much playing.

Flesch describes Joachim's bowing in detail:

> the bow was held by the fingertips, the index finger touched the stick at the line of the top joint, while the little finger remained on the stick even at the point. The change of bow at the nut was accomplished with stiff fingers by means of a combined movement, very difficult to describe, consisting of a horizontal jerk of the wrist and a slightly rotating movement of the forearm. [63]

It should be remembered that Flesch only encountered a rather elderly Joachim, and he blames the violinist's followers and imitators for perpetuating a very individual style which caused 'the majority of the students thus maltreated' to contract arm troubles, and, as violinists, to become 'cripples for life'. [63]

Neither the illustrations in the Joachim–Moser Violin School nor the written text appear to emphasise the 'right-angle style' caused by a combination of low elbow and high wrist, although Flesch's personal observations are endorsed by Menzel's drawing of the violinist playing a sonata with Clara Schumann (Plate 23). The Violin School actually denounces as old-fashioned Leopold Mozart's statement that the bow-arm should be held low all the time: it advocates free movement of the upper arm at the shoulder-joint. The high arm of the Franco-Belgian school (de Bériot) and the low arm of the German School (David) were both to be avoided – although when playing on the E string, the upper arm was expected lightly to touch the trunk, which is low by modern standards.

Courvoisier, who published *The Technics of Violin Playing on Joachim's Method* in 1899 (no. 1 of 'The Strad Library'), speaks strongly against restricting upper-arm mobility.

> Nor need the elbow be pressed down in the course of a stroke on a lower (more distant) string, as some players will have it. What is the good of caricaturing a swan's beak with one's arm, in an affected attempt at elegance, if thereby we render an already complex action more complex still, and at the same time take all strength out of the middle portion of the stroke? [64]

Spohr's central chin-rest was rejected, as by now (1905) the violin was held to the left of the tail-piece; indeed Courvoisier balanced the whole body to the left.

> Place the weight of your body entirely on the left foot, resting the right foot loosely on the floor, a little forward and outward. [65]
> You secure thereby a quiet attitude for the left side of your body, on which the instrument rests, and at the same time freedom of action for the right side, which handles the moving bow.

David's Violin School (1863) depicts a bowing style apparently closer to Joachim's own than the Joachim–Moser Method: it is possible that Joachim's only contribution towards the perpetuation of this damaging tradition was in appearing to make it work. David mainly followed Spohr, adding a few details such as the use of a small pad under the violin to prevent the left shoulder being too much raised. Ole Bull, largely a self-taught violinist, produced no Violin School of his own, but contemporary reports mention his high position of the violin, supported by the left hand rather than the chin, and the oblique finger-action and erect posture resulting from this.

Leopold Auer (1845–1930), himself a pupil of Dont and Joachim, became the founder of the Russian school of violin-playing, whose bow-hold was advocated by Flesch and whose exponents included Elman and Heifetz. Another Joachim pupil, Jenö Hubay (1858–1937), founded the Hungarian school, and taught Vecsey, Telmányi, and Szigeti. In fact, the evidence seems to contradict Flesch's denunciation of the part played by Joachim in spreading 'wrist mania', as he calls it: Joachim's followers in Berlin were drawing on the traditions of the old German school, which was visually vindicated by Joachim's own playing, while the virtuoso himself was teaching a less cramped method of bowing.

Joachim's early studies were concentrated on the Rode–Baillot–
Kreutzer Violin Method, and Kreutzer's *Études*; later Rode's Caprices
and Mayseder's works were used. His practising was often supervised,
and duets were used to encourage a sense of ensemble. This was in the
best tradition recommended by Spohr, who would, however, have been
shocked by the statement that the boy needed to practise only one hour
daily in his early teens.

The Paris Conservatoire, which gained an early lead in establishing
teaching-methods, rested on its Rode–Baillot–Kreutzer laurels for most
of the 19th century: bad pay for the teachers, the exclusion of any foreign
teachers, and an extreme conservatism prevented any really dynamic
developments in teaching. Dancla, in 1890, was still holding his bow
5 inches above the nut, and the test pieces for the top violin prize were
still concertos by Viotti or Kreutzer.

Dont, Schradieck, Sauret, and Ševčik are credited by Flesch with the
principal development of technique and teaching in the later years of the
19th century. Dont's studies and caprices are still widely used, while
Ševčik's thousands of mechanical exercises, reducing technique to its
smallest components, have gradually found their place in modern teaching as an occasional remedy for unfocused practising: used as a Violin
Method they can be dangerous owing to their profusion and the lack of
detailed information on how to practise them. Ševčik was the teacher
of Kubelik, whose technical virtuosity revived memories of Paganini.
César Thomson (1857–1931), a pupil of Wieniawski and Vieuxtemps,
had already contributed to the revival of pure virtuoso playing which
declined for a time after Paganini's death; Thomson had a particular
facility in fingered octaves. Szigeti can recall how the first movement of
Bach's E major partita was dashed off at top speed by virtuoso violinists
of the Sarasate–Kubelik period: smooth tone (Sarasate's bow remained
almost invariably the same distance from the bridge) and virtuosity were
prized very highly for a time after Joachim's intensely musical but not
very pure-toned performances. Flesch considered that a large part of
Sarasate's popular appeal was due to his avoidance of the bridge area
with the bow, making him stand out from the 'scraping fiddlers' [66] of
his day.

Sarasate may have been the first to present the modern ideal of violin
technique: to quote Flesch's description

> With the precise and effortless function of both his arms, he
> represented a completely new kind of violinist. The fingertips of
> his left hand were quite smooth and ungrooved; they hit the

fingerboard in a normal fashion, without excessive raising or hammering. His vibrato was rather broader than had been customary.[67]

Vibrato was changing both in breadth and continuity: Flesch writes of Ysaÿe

> His vibrato was the spontaneous expression of his feeling, and a whole world away from what had been customary until then: the incidental, thin-flowing quiver only on *espressivo* notes.[68]

Kreisler was to carry the broad, continuous but varied vibrato still further as a means of intense personal expression, before recording techniques made a faster, slightly narrower vibrato more fashionable.

To Fritz Kreisler (1875–1962), Flesch attributes the modern technique of bow-spacing. Although the writer's view of pre-1890 technique could be somewhat over-pessimistic (after all, Leopold Mozart had introduced principles of bow-spacing and Geminiani mentioned continuous vibrato a century and a half earlier), he may have been noting a tendency which grew up with the need to dominate the large Romantic concerto orchestra when he says: 'Before him [Kreisler], we had the apparently unshakeable principle that the whole bow must be used whenever possible and at all costs.' [69] Courvoisier includes a chapter on bow-distribution in his book on Joachim's method of violin-playing (1899), but leaves out vibrato altogether. Economy of bow combined with varied bow-pressure and vibrato gave Kreisler's playing its expressiveness: to this technical model, later 20th-century virtuosi added more variety of point of contact of the bow with the string.

Fingering techniques were gradually liberated from the one-to-four octave hand-pattern by the use of fingered octaves, and the trend during the 20th century was gradually towards flexibility and extension of the basic patterns, especially in avoiding *portamenti*. But Joachim-Moser (1905) still considered an augmented fourth too great a distance for the young violinist to attempt to stretch, and the slide from position to position on one finger within a slur was sought after rather than avoided, to judge from 19th-century editions.

Violin-playing fashions may change fairly rapidly with the rise to popularity of great individuals, but teaching techniques lag far behind: it is rare for even the best books on teaching to be abreast or ahead of their time (although the 20th century has provided one or two examples); it is possibly even rarer for a violin-teacher's methods to be altered by reading a book. For this reason, the shades of the less worthy spirits of

19th-century violin-teaching and editing are with us still, perpetuated by word of mouth and by conservative publishers. 19th-century styles of interpretation have fallen into disrepute in musical circles, but perhaps within the next hundred years we shall be struggling to reproduce Wilhelmj's *portamento*-laden fingerings as we are at present trying to recreate Baroque techniques of ornamentation.

NOTES

[1] 175 Strunk, p. 827.
[2] 191 Wagner, p. 4.
[3] ibid. pp. 31–2.
[4] 96 Joachim, p. 114.
[5] ibid. p. 416.
[6] ibid. p. 422.
[7] 105 Lang, p. 817.
[8] 96 Joachim, p. 114.
[9] 121 Moser, p. 106.
[10] 83 Hill, p. 219.
[11] ibid. p. 219.
[12] 190 Veinus, p. 233.
[13] 96 Joachim, p. 162.
[14] ibid. p. 370.
[15] ibid. p. 68.
[16] 191 Wagner, p. 20.
[17] 163 Shaw, p. 52.
[18] ibid. p. 53.
[19] 72 Hanslick, p. 231.
[20] ibid. p. 233.
[21] 96 Joachim, p. 378.
[22] 72 Hanslick, p. 233.
[23] 56 Flesch, p. 73.
[24] ibid. p. 73.
[25] ibid. p. 149.
[26] 163 Shaw, p. 36.
[27] ibid. p. 38.
[28] 121 Moser, p. 230.
[29] 42 Demuth, p. 211.
[30] 96 Joachim, p. 447.
[31] ibid. p. 451.
[32] 121 Moser, p. 88.
[33] 72 Hanslick, p. 249.
[34] ibid. p. 265.
[35] ibid. p. 260.
[36] 163 Shaw, p. 194.
[37] 96 Joachim, p. 170.
[38] ibid. p. 350.
[39] ibid. p. 379.

[40] 178 Szigeti, p. 126.
[41] 96 Joachim, p. 380.
[42] 121 Moser, pp. 116–17.
[43] 96 Joachim, p. 82.
[44] ibid. p. 96.
[45] ibid. p. 116.
[46] ibid. p. 121.
[47] ibid. p. 269.
[48] 121 Moser, p. 253.
[49] 56 Flesch, p. 31.
[50] 42 Demuth, p. 194.
[51] 121 Moser, p. 182.
[52] 116 Mayer, p. 96.
[53] 96 Joachim, p. 145.
[54] ibid. p. 301.
[55] 178 Szigeti, p. 9.
[56] 134 Phipson, p. 90.
[57] ibid. p. 170.
[58] 20 Berlioz, p. 232.
[59] ibid. p. 235.
[60] 134 Phipson, pp. 233–4.
[61] 56 Flesch, p. 54.
[62] ibid. p. 53.
[63] ibid. p. 34.
[64] 37 Courvoisier, p. 87.
[65] ibid. p. 8.
[66] 56 Flesch, p. 39.
[67] ibid. p. 38.
[68] ibid. p. 79.
[69] ibid. p. 121.

CHAPTER 9

The Viola Virtuoso. Chances of Survival in the 20th Century

THE YEAR 1900 seems, perhaps because it is within living memory, to be a more arbitrary division of musical history than previous fifty-year periods. Because of the remarkable spread of popular music through radio and gramophone after the First World War, the first decade of the 20th century is often considered to be more a part of the 19th than of the 20th century. Alfred Fried, an Austrian pacifist and Nobel prizewinner, announced in the early years of the century that as the 19th century had been the century of nationalism, so the 20th would be that of internationalism. Radio, recording, and rapid travel have made this true of musical composition and performance: even the broad gap between Eastern and Western music with their different scales and concepts of rhythm is being bridged, but a new schism has appeared between the politically dominated compositions of the Soviet countries and the restless search for new, personal modes of expression in the West.

From the viewpoint of the string-player, several 20th-century trends prove disturbing. The exploration of new key-systems and the abandonment of key altogether have made the bowed strings, with their natural tonal systems reinforced by harmonics and left-hand positions spanning an octave, seem partly outdated, and the exploration of new sounds, electronics, machines, and computers as part of music makes string sound sometimes appear staunchly traditional if not actually old-fashioned.

On the other hand, new opportunities have opened up for the performer as radio, disc, and tape-recording have made music available to everyone, a process begun in the 19th century but completed with unforeseen suddenness with the arrival of these media. Recording studios providing music for films, radio, and discs have made improved conditions of employment available to large numbers of musicians, and brought with them a paradoxical situation whereby the fewer and easier the notes a musician plays, the more highly he is likely to be paid, unless he is a concert soloist. So there is born a new generation of string-players,

trained to play Paganini's caprices and the great concertos, who spend
their days in windowless studios, making backings for popular discs or
television advertisements. In Britain, they can receive up to twelve
times as much money per hour for this kind of work as for playing in
symphony concerts. Good players for symphony orchestras are therefore
in great demand: the London orchestras keep an uneasy balance between
concert and studio work by offering their players either additional
security or freelance contracts, so that they can escape periodically from
the boredom of 'pop' sessions, but are not permanently tied to the
lower income of the symphony-player.

The 20th century has come to accept a sharp division between so-
called 'Classical' and 'popular' styles of music. 'Classical' music,
although apparently winning an ever-widening audience, can never hope
to appeal to such a wide, money-spending audience as 'pop' – the very
permanence of a work of art detracts from its business potential in these
days of planned obsolescence. During the 20th century, however, more
and more symphony and chamber orchestras have sprung up, the latter
usually on a freelance basis, the size of an 18th-century orchestra, and
especially convenient for the performance of works written before and
since the Romantics. Boyd Neel was a pioneer in this field, and chamber
orchestras proliferate today owing to their relative cheapness of employment and compactness for touring purposes. The problem of finding
string-players for all these orchestras appears to be steadily increasing –
one of the chapter-headings in *Szigeti on the Violin* (1969) reads: 'An
over-ambitious attempt to compress into far too few pages alarming data
about the paucity of string players for orchestras in England, the United
States, Germany, and France.'[1] The recognition of this shortage has
led to a reconsideration of training methods, and considerable advances
have been made in the U.S.S.R., in Japan, and in the United States,
whose growth as a musical nation has been one of the most striking
aspects of 20th-century music.

On the one hand, therefore, we are seeking to train more and better
violin- and viola-players; on the other, music is tending to move away
from traditional techniques and instruments in search of more variety,
closer control, or even abandonment of control. Paul Henry Lang, author
of one of the most comprehensive histories of Western music, writes:
'One wonders . . . whether eventually we shall not be forced to turn to
the comfort and security of the machine. The way the difficulties of
execution are growing, no human hand or larynx will be able to cope
with them.' He offers T. W. Adorno's alternative solution: 'A silent
imaginative reading of music could make the sonorous performance

superfluous, just as reading the written word suppresses the spoken word.'[2]

Alongside the attempts to extend or even exceed the potentials of human performance (Charles Ives [1874–1954] pointed out in his volume of songs 'Some of the songs in this book . . . cannot be sung'), the 20th century has seen the replacement of human musicians with machine-made sounds, but so far there have always been leading composers who are content to express themselves within the limits of the traditional media. In 1920 Charles Ives was already complaining of the instrumentalist's tyranny over the composer: 'The Waiter brings the only fresh egg he has, but the man at breakfast sends it back because it doesn't fit his eggcup.'[3] This was how Ives saw the violinist who rejected a new piece of music because it did not lie well for the instrument. Yates also quotes Schönberg's comment on his own violin concerto: 'Heifetz cannot play it. Nobody can play it',[4] as an illustration of the composer-to-performer time-lag which seems to have become even more apparent during the 20th century.

The list of 20th-century composers writing for voices and instruments, including as it does many of the composers whose music seems likely to survive into the future, should give the string-player confidence in his role in musical evolution. But against this he must set the fact that the instruments of the violin family are basically tonal: their natural resonances favour certain keys and harmonic patterns. Thus Mozart, Beethoven, Brahms, Tchaikovsky, Sibelius, Stravinsky, and many other composers have chosen to write violin concertos in D major or minor. In their search for new sounds in music, 20th-century composers have abandoned diatonic scales and with them one of the strongest links with the string family, but such is the versatility of violin technique that it has proved equal to the whole-tone scale of Debussy and the twelve-tone compositions of the 'serialist' composers. Works such as Berg's violin concerto (on the twelve-note row shown below, each note normally being used in turn in the order shown) retain a link with the instrument's natural resonances by using the open-string sounds.

The fact that these notes are 1, 3, 5, and 7 of the row make this particular work more tonal, more Romantic, and more violinistic in effect than most serial works: it is therefore more accessible to the listening string-player, but still extremely difficult for the performer. One of the conflicts arising from the performance of serial music on the violin or viola is that only tempered intonation should be used: the other intonation-systems emphasising the keys which 'atonal' composers are seeking to avoid. Schönberg considered the tempered scale to be the musical one: '. . . to be musical means to have an ear in the musical sense, not in the natural sense. A musical ear must have assimilated the tempered scale. And a singer who produces natural pitches is unmusical. . . .' [5] Many people would disagree with this statement; in fact certain 20th-century composers have taken precisely the opposite view and reacted against the 'dullness' of equal temperament by writing works for which just intonation is specified. An American composer, Harry Partch (b. 1901), used a 43-tone scale to emphasise just intonation and had to create instruments, including an elongated viola, to play his works. Just intonation emphasises dissonance, and the use of dissonance without resolution is one of the most noticeable differences between music of the 20th century and that of previous centuries.

Seeking freedom from traditions of tonality, rhythm, timbre, and harmony, *avant-garde* composers have experimented with non-musical sounds, noise machines, animal sounds, and various tributes to the machine age. Edgar Varèse (b. 1885) used traditional instruments with noise-makers such as car-hooters and barge-sirens in his search for new combinations of timbre: Henry Cowell (1897–1965), preceded by Ives, made up chords or tone-clusters from intervals of a second, whereas Alexander Scriabin (1872–1915) used intervals of a fourth. Quarter-tones, obtainable on stringed instruments, were used by Ives and occasionally by Bartók, but electronic machines produce this kind of effect far more easily and efficiently than bowed strings. Luciano Berio (b. 1925), Karl Heinz Stockhausen (b. 1928), and Milton Babbitt (b. 1916) have produced electronic music of great complexity, and the synthesiser, with its enormous range of precisely controllable sounds, appeals to many young composers.

An almost directly opposed school of composition to this is the 'aleatory music' or music of chance, one of whose principal exponents is John Cage (b. 1912). Improvisation and composition are mixed in varying degrees in these works, and the performer may be left to choose the point at which he starts a work or have the point dictated to him by a dice or similar instrument of chance. Timing, pitch, loudness, or all three may be left to chance or choice.

This kind of music leaves the string-player feeling almost as super-fluous as he is in electronic music. For soloists and small groups it could be a matter of personal expression; for orchestras the feeling is rather that a computer plus an electronic synthesiser could produce similar effects more cheaply. The requirements of 20th-century *avant-garde* scores tend to be increasingly intellectual and divorced from the tradi-tional potentialities of an orchestral group: the new importance of silence and of individual timbres has led to a position where a day's work sorting out a modern orchestral score can leave the instrumentalist with the feeling that he has not played his instrument at all, although he has counted innumerable rests. Anton Webern (1883–1945), in particular, due to his habit of selecting a different instrument for each note accord-ing to its particular timbre, leaves the player with this impression, although the audience may receive a cohesive effect. Players who laugh at the fact that Tchaikovsky's concerto was described as a 'concerto against the violin' make similar complaints when required to play most of a movement with the wood of the bow (Berg's *Lyric Suite*), or to bow behind the bridge (Villa Lobos's *Amazonas*): nor are they very willing to accept the opposite extremes of freedom to play what they like, within certain time and dynamic limits.

In these instances, scores no longer contain traditional notation: various combinations of lines, straight or wriggling, dots, splodges, and figures make up the scores of those who wish to avoid the arousal of traditional reactions to traditional signs, and to avoid performer-interpretation which might limit the listener's freedom to interpret subjectively. John Cage's *59½ seconds for a string player* is described in the catalogue as

> A graph in space where 2 centimetres horizontally equal metro-nome indication given. These indications change. Tone productions on the four strings are separately graphed, individual spaces being provided for each string, the range of each of which is determined by the player. Noises on the box, vibrati and bowing pressure are also graphed. Only indications for direction and place of bowing and changes from hair to wood employ conventional symbols. The piece may be played on any four-stringed instrument [6].

The performer must carry out an intellectual exercise to assimilate this kind of explanation before attempting to play from the score. He is unlikely to achieve any kind of conviction in performance unless he understands something of the philosophy and aims of the composer, and although this is claimed to be true of Beethoven or Mozart, the fact remains that we have all heard convincing performances of Classical violin music given by the instinctive, non-intellectual player. Possibly string-players of future centuries will appear to have the same kind of instinct for performance of what seem to be intellectual conundrums of the 20th century.

In countries like Russia where politics have been allowed to dictate to the arts, no such break from traditional patterns is permitted. Since the first Soviet Five-Year Plan in 1929, the composer's function has been regulated by the requirements of the society of which he is a member: his personal emotions (except where, as in the case of fervent patriotism, they happen to coincide with a group ideal) are not recognised as material for musical expression. The yardstick for judging musical worth has become universal acceptability – thus ruling out the chance of the 'class distinction' within music which has become such a feature in the Western world.

In place of subjective feelings such as melancholy, 'progressive feelings of the broad masses'[7] should be portrayed. Folk-song idiom, with a wide variety of available material owing to the many races within the Soviet Union, has been strongly cultivated and has provided inspiration for some of the most widely accepted compositions under the régime, particularly those of Khachaturian. Rachmaninov and Tchaikovsky, at first banned as exponents of subjective feeling in music, are now held up as ideals. Shostakovich's opera *The Lady Macbeth of Ntensk* (1934), a kind of satire on the bourgeoisie, was officially acclaimed as a model of Soviet musical aims: two years later it was condemned as containing music incompatible with Soviet ideals.

Sergei Prokoviev (1891–1953) returned to Russia in the mid-thirties, choosing this kind of musical restriction in place of the political freedom of the Western musician. His writing for strings, while based on traditional tonality and techniques, has a distinctly personal flavour. Many find that the second violin concerto, written in Russia in 1935, is a more personally sincere work than the more brilliant and witty first concerto written outside the Soviet Union. Both are difficult for the soloist, but in a way which fits the instrument and makes them satisfying to perform. Shostakovich and Khachaturian have also produced music which is admirably written for the string-player, even when its musical content leaves Western musicians puzzled or unmoved. Dmitri Shostakovich (b. 1906), a remarkably prolific composer especially in the fields of chamber music, film music, and the symphony, has contributed many string quartets to the repertoire, but his piano quintet appears most regularly on Western concert programmes. He has achieved nothing like the acceptance accorded to Bartók's six quartets as an extension of the standard repertoire.

While Russian musical education has reached a peak of organisation and achievement by providing musically gifted children with a comprehensive but musically biased education from an early age, producing an astonishing number of string-players who achieve international recognition, no young Soviet composers seem to be making a mark outside their own country.

The role of the string-player in Soviet music remains clear and traditional, but the impact of the music itself appears gradually to diminish. In Western music, on the other hand, the importance of the string-player may be seen as very gradually diminishing in music which has international impact. While not remaining an exponent of *musique concrète* (a form evolved by Pierre Schaeffer, in which sounds of all kinds are arranged on tape, mixed, speeded up, and slowed down, to form an organised composition) Pierre Boulez (b. 1925) considers that musicians are amateurs in matters of timbre, compared with acousticians.[8] The difference between a musical sound and a noise has long been considered that a musical sound, owing to its regularity of vibrations, may be repeated. But today any sound may be electronically repeated, and now that laboratory technicians are producing sounds in which the intensity of each partial (and therefore the timbre) may be regulated and repeated, notes played by live musicians begin to seem by contrast a series of happy or unhappy accidents.

Interpretation on a personal level is often discouraged in modern compositions: both Schönberg and Stravinsky opposed expressive interpretation. Cage and others of his school aim to make the listener into the interpreter, rather than the performer: a peak of non-activity on the performer's part being achieved in Cage's *4' 33"*, or *Silent Sonata*, during which the performer or performers sit with their instruments and make no sound at all. Music which expressively suits the violin, such as some of Messiaen's chamber and orchestral music, is bound to tempt the performer into personal expression beyond what is indicated in print: only machines can perform in an entirely impersonal way. And music continues to be written in which the stringed instruments play an important and satisfying part: new organisations of pitch, rhythm, and space do not necessarily make a work unsuitable or unattractive for the string-player. Stravinsky, Messiaen, Britten, and many others continue to produce music in which the violin and viola play a vital part and the player can enjoy the sonorities of his instrument.

The recognition of the viola's potential as a solo instrument could never have taken place in a musical climate where personal expression and instrumental timbre were rapidly declining in importance, for its establishment as a concert instrument was largely achieved by two distinct personalities, Lionel Tertis (b. 1876) in England and Paul Hindemith (1895–1963) in Germany. Hindemith had the advantage of being a composer as well as a first-class executant on the viola, Tertis that of producing such emotionally moving sonorities from his instrument that his contemporaries were eager to produce works for him to perform. William Primrose (b. 1903) in America used his outstanding technique to convince musicians and audiences that the viola is a virtuoso instrument. The viola concertos by Bartók (finished by Serly) and Walton, Bloch's suite, and Stravinsky's Elegy are a few of the best-known additions to viola repertoire which indicate the widespread interest in the instrument. Tertis, an indefatigable arranger of standard string-works for viola (including an arrangement of Elgar's cello concerto, sanctioned by the composer), gave first performances of works by Bax, Vaughan Williams, Holst, Dunhill, and York Bowen, leaving to Hindemith the first performance of Sir William Walton's viola concerto. In his book *Cinderella No More*, Tertis tells of a lifetime devoted to gaining recognition for the viola.

The instrument's reputation towards the end of the 19th century was even worse than one would imagine from tracing its previous history; possibly it was treated worst of all in England. In 1933 Flesch[9] asserted that the world's finest viola-players came from the viola class founded by Laforge at the Paris Conservatoire: certainly when Tertis went to the Royal Academy of Music in 1896 there was nobody teaching or learning the instrument there, and a single professional player was brought in for orchestral rehearsals. 'The viola is commonly regarded as of little importance in the musical establishment',[10] wrote Quantz in 1752, and in spite of the fact that composers gradually recognised the instrument's potential, Tertis found almost the same state of affairs in a musical establishment 150 years later.

'The viola was generally played by violinists too inferior to gain a position in orchestras as such', writes Tertis in a now familiar refrain. 'A wretchedly low standard of viola playing was, in fact, accepted.'[11] His own training was received from violinists and from listening, particularly to Fritz Kreisler, whose beauty of tone and personal expressiveness made him one of the most admired and best-loved violinists of the early 20th century. Once Tertis had applied his very considerable talents to the viola, he rapidly became outstanding, jumping from last violinist to principal viola overnight in Henry Wood's

Queen's Hall orchestra. He became full professor of the viola at the R.A.M. in 1901, and at last the instrument had an exponent of sufficient talent and musicianship to break the vicious circle of no players – no compositions – no pupils, which had existed for so long.

Viola methods, which began to appear during the 19th century, were at first designed mainly for violinists. Klingenfeld's (1897) was actually entitled *Viola School for Violin-Players*, and presented reasons for studying both instruments simultaneously. He considered that the viola should be studied because it is indispensable to the string quartet and the orchestra, and because viola-playing for the violinist strengthens the arm and finger muscles, gives stronger bowing and a wider left-hand stretch, and increases the capacity for rapid calculation. Brähmig's earlier *Practische Bratschenschule* made no attempt to deal with elementary technique because the student was expected to have acquired it already on the violin, and A. B. Bruni (1751–1821) expected complicated multiple stops on the third page of his very early *Tenor Method*. After 1900, the change in attitude towards the viola gradually made it seem feasible that a beginner might choose the instrument, and Hans Sitt (viola-player in the Brodsky quartet), and Berthold Tours were among those who catered for real beginners in their Viola Methods. Owing to the size of the instrument, it is still usual for children to start on the violin and later transfer to the viola; even the more recent Methods such as Mackay's *Modern Viola Method* appear to presuppose a knowledge of basic violin technique, and Primrose parallels the two instruments in *Technique is Memory*, a Method for violin- and viola-players. A modern English Viola Method designed for absolute beginners in their teens,[12] leaves consideration of bow technique to the first-year Violin Method in the same series.

Tertis himself has given us no Viola Method, but by adding an upper octave to the accepted range of the instrument and proving it capable of soloistic sonorities particularly in the region of multiple stops and harmonics, he has brought the viola technically in line with the violin and cello. The modern viola-player, still rather short of technical literature written specially for him, tends to pride himself on the 'capacity for rapid calculation' pointed out by Klingenfeld, and to work at advanced technique directly from violin copies, transposing down a fifth at sight. The Tertis Model viola, 16¾ inches in length and designed in collaboration with Arthur Richardson with the aim of establishing dimensions which would give satisfactory tone on the lower strings but allow reasonably easy manipulation of the high positions, has proved too large for general acceptance; violas of various shapes, sizes, and sonorities will be found within any modern orchestral viola section.

Paul Hindemith's interest in the viola may have been originally a practical one, for viola-players were rare, viola player-composers rarer still in the first half of the 20th century, and he was an intensely practical man, besides possessing a powerful intellect, as one may discover from his writings on music and musical education. Described as 'the most energetic, most cheerful, and most nearly successful advocate and architect of a new common order between the wars',[13] Hindemith's name became linked with the term *Gebrauchsmusik* (utility music, written to suit a particular medium or occasion), a short-lived movement in Germany which was partly a reaction against the numerical excesses of the late Romantics, Mahler and Richard Strauss. Weill even went so far as to state that 'if music cannot serve the interests of all, its existence cannot be justified',[14] thus approaching the Soviet philosophy without trying to lay down exactly how these interests must be served. But Hindemith resented his label as an exponent of *Gebrauchsmusik*, complaining in *A Composer's World* that 'it has been impossible to kill this silly term and the unscrupulous classification that goes with it'.[15]

Hindemith was intensely concerned with the performing amateur:

> Once you join an amateur group, you are a member of a great fraternity, whose purpose is the most dignified one you can imagine; to inspire one another and unite in building up a creation that is greater than one individual's needs. Amateurs of this kind, when listening to music, will not be the stupid receivers, the targets of virtuosity, the idle gourmands of which our audiences predominantly consist. . . . They know what they want, and they intend to get it! It is here that the composer comes in. He would have to provide the music needed and appreciated by the amateur . . . he would have to search for a new technical and stylistic approach – a new human approach too![16]

It is possibly this human approach which makes certain of Hindemith's chamber works particularly interesting and rewarding for the string-player: although they limit the required technique, they are usually well suited to the instruments and make no concessions by way of avoiding dissonance. Hindemith's immense output invites comparison with Telemann, and only a few works seem to receive regular performances: for the string-player it could be that his educational writings and his part in achieving recognition for the viola as a solo instrument will have a more lasting effect than his actual compositions.

Stringed instruments have not lost any of their popularity with serious composers who have accepted the mass media as a challenge to make their music acceptable to a far wider audience. Aaron Copland, the American composer born in 1900, tells in his lectures on 'Music and Imagination' how this problem has concerned him. 'How,' he asks, 'are we to make contact with this enormously enlarged potential audience, without sacrificing in any way the highest musical standards?'[17] 20th-century composers have shown concern in very different ways about the various roles of composer, performer, and audience, and in Copland's opinion, 'Whether or not contemporary composers think about this matter of communication with their audience, they haven't been signally successful at it.'[18] Perhaps Schönberg's attitude prevails with many composers; he wrote in 1918:

> The second preliminary question is that of consideration for the listener. I have exactly as little of this as he has for me. All I know is that he exists, and in so far as he isn't 'indispensable' for acoustic reasons (since music doesn't sound well in an empty hall), he's only a nuisance.[19]

Schönberg regarded as a fortunate escape his pricing himself out of the mass media: 'I almost agreed to write music for a film, but fortunately asked $50,000 which, likewise fortunately, was too much, for it would have been the end of me.'[20] But Copland claims that 'Every artist, whatever his convictions, must sooner or later face the problem of communication with an audience',[21] and even more important to the modern string-player, he considers that 'The principal concern of the composer is to seek out the expressive nature of any particular instrument and write with that in mind.'[22] He writes sometimes for a limited, cultivated audience, sometimes aiming at a broader appeal, but always for audiences and for instruments: in this kind of musical philosophy the strings have a clear role in the future.

Copland with several other composers was influenced at one stage by the popularity of jazz, and made an attempt to fuse popular and 'classical' idioms. Some of these attempts have served merely to emphasise the gap between the two: on the other hand, the gap has been bridged merely by adding a rhythm section to a sung version of Bach. In the 1920s jazz was hailed as the true music of the masses: improvisation and derivation from the folk-music of the American Negro being its basis. Serious contemporary composers were seeking to break away from the restrictions of tonality by experimenting with polytonality, atonality, and serial techniques: jazz at its best broke down metric restrictions while retaining an unmistakable rhythmic drive. As soon as it became an international financial success, however, jazz lost its roots in spontaneity; it became organised around certain chord progressions; and acquired clichés comparable to the cadential endings of the 18th century. Scores were often written out, the harmonies being largely derived from the impressionist composers at the turn of the century, and the time rapidly arrived when (as Constant Lambert pointed out): 'Most jazz is written and performed by cosmopolitan Jews.'[23]

One of the few popularly successful attempts to introduce jazz idiom into symphonic music is Gershwin's *Rhapsody in Blue*, which has certainly on occasions served to induce a wider than usual audience into a concert-hall. But it is neither jazz nor serious music, and its popularity wanes as jazz becomes history. Stravinsky's *L'Histoire du Soldat*, Ravel's piano concerto and violin sonata, and Milhaud's *La Création du Monde* have successfully introduced jazz and blues elements into the 'classical' repertoire.

The string-player, apart from *pizzicato* bass, has never really been a part of the jazz scene, music which originated for voices and percussion and became almost exclusively the realm of a few wind instruments with percussion. But in music for the cinema, a standard symphony orchestra was for a long time the basic requirement: in America, where the film industry first flourished, a new source of income was opened to the string-player. The French were the first to commission a film score from one of their leading composers (Saint-Saëns) in 1907; since which few composers have completely avoided the field. Old films seem to have far too much music to modern ears: the tendency has been to reduce the amount of music and use it to bring out moments or sequences of particular emotional impact. With the growing importance of television and subsequent slump in cinema profits, the orchestration has become reduced in scale, often with a corresponding increase in piquancy and ingenuity. Sometimes strings are cut out altogether. An extreme example of this tendency is the British film *Genevieve* (1953), for which Larry Adler wrote the music and performed it himself on the harmonica, with a little orchestral or piano backing.

Although the importance of string-tone is no longer pre-eminent in cinema or theatre, and radio and television experiment increasingly with electronic background music, *legato* string sound has a seemingly inseparable bond with a certain type of sentimental singing which never seems to lose its popularity. If the present status of the string-player rests solely on the fact that a 'pop' star singing 'Baby, I'm in love with you' to an electronic backing is inconceivable, however, there could be some justification for thinking that the decline of the violin family has already started. Instruments are unlikely to survive if contemporary composers do not write for them: it is conceivable that the violins could go the way of the viols after a century of the cult of the mass media. Financial reasonings make more and more inroads on the preservation of musical standards.

Against this rather depressing picture we have to set one of increasing interest in and availability of string tuition to children and students in various parts of the world. We hear of thousands of tiny children performing Bach's double concerto together in Japan, of 1,966 children's musical schools, and twenty-two schools for specially talented children in Russia; of the widespread availability of free violin classes which have mushroomed in England since the introduction of penny classes at Birmingham in the 19th century. But in 1964 a symposium was held in the United States 'dedicated to the problem of a diminishing interest in string instruments'.[24] And the reiterated complaint of Western orchestras is lack of adequate string-players.

The stress, however, is on the word *adequate*, and the education of string-players as well as string-teachers has been investigated in several countries and found to contain a frightening lack of consistency or even practical relevance to future careers as orchestral players or teachers. In an education-conscious century, music has been left far behind: probably no other profession insists on training its students for one career (that of a concert soloist) while knowing that a quite different life's work is in store for them. In matters of qualifications, private music-teaching in particular lags far behind the rest of the teaching profession: music is dogged by the fact that anyone who can play reasonably efficiently is therefore considered trained to teach.

The failure of musical education to keep up with the changing demands of the profession may be one cause of a decline in interest in string-tone on the part of *avant-garde* composers. There are those who consider that only music using traditional resources falls within the mainstream of musical history, and that experimental sounds are just an irresponsible striving for effect: a great confidence trick on the part of the composer. England, where contemporary music of all kinds was enthusiastically welcomed for a period in the early 1960s, provided a contradiction to this theory in the Zak Incident of 1961. Stockhausen's *Zyklus* had recently won great acclaim in London. Hans Keller and Susan Bradshaw at the B.B.C. decided to test the genuineness of such approval, and they made up a spoof composition on tape, using sounds from *Zyklus* and other electronic devices. The tape was broadcast in a contemporary music programme as Piotr Zak's *Mobile* for electronic tape and two partially improvising percussion-players, and received a unanimously bad press. Although the critics were taken in to the extent that they treated it as a serious composition, none of them considered it to have any musical merit at all.[25]

Electronic music may have come to stay, but it is unlikely that mixtures of live and recorded sounds will become an accepted part of concert-giving. Milton Babbitt's *Correspondences* for string orchestra and synthesised tape, for instance, shows electronic thinking in the impossible demands made of the string-players: no human being could play the notes at the indicated speed and volume (a dynamic range of ten gradations from *fffff* to *ppppp*, with a new dynamic for practically every note), quite apart from the practical problems of time-lag in hearing the sound from a tape and trying to synchronise a beat with it.

Composers who have in the past written most effectively for strings have usually themselves played a stringed instrument, but the reputed difficulty of violin-playing and the necessity of long hours of practising emphasised over the centuries by violin-teachers and the authors of Violin Schools (Spohr requests a minimum of two hours a day for amateurs) discourages potential string-players, while wind instruments become increasingly popular. An additional attraction towards wind instruments is the higher pay and more soloistic position of the orchestral wind-player. This movement away from strings can only slowly be combated by isolated teachers who secure good results with young people on stringed instruments without excessive duress, and can introduce them to the unique social opportunities of string chamber music which may benefit them for a lifetime. Methods of fulfilling such aims will be discussed below in Chapter 10, but before considering ways of training future violinists, it is important to estimate what role – if any – the violin family is destined to play in the future.

Increasing leisure-time will give the adult of the future more opportunity for cultural pursuits: if a young person has engaged in social music-making before leaving school, this is likely to become one of his hobbies. The Tanglewood Symposium report (1964) quotes a West German report on automated factories, pointing to a 'very noticeable increase in nervousness, depression and slowdown of comprehension'[26] among the workers. Gradually, recreational forms of stimulus will be needed to combat the increasing de-personalisation of working hours, and live rather than electronic music is likely to prove a most efficient antidote.

Unfortunately, although youth orchestras now flourish in most countries, chamber music (more complicated to organise, less financially viable) which gives the ideal combination of individuality and self-reliance within a social group, is introduced to only a tiny élite of modern schoolchildren. Yet not one of the great teachers of our time fails to point out its value, and complaints about the inability of aspiring orchestral players to listen, to count, to sight-read would be highly unlikely had those students been accustomed to reading chamber music throughout their student days. As Max Kaplan pointed out (Tanglewood, 1964),

> We will obtain better string players by raising standards in the school, not by involving more students. And string quartet or ensemble coaching ... will demand better musicians, for then they cannot hide behind the baton or in a dilution of tunes from *South Pacific*.[27]

Szigeti quotes a pessimistic letter[28] from a New York musicologist who was formerly an orchestral player, prophesying that in less than twenty years symphony orchestras will go out of existence because of lack of replacement string-players. Meagre rewards for long training and unwillingness to submit to orchestral discipline are among the reasons often quoted; yet there are often dozens of unsuitable applicants for orchestral posts, and the music colleges turn out numbers of instrumentalists in Britain alone who fail to gain orchestral posts and therefore turn to the job for which they are least equipped: teaching a future generation of musicians. Probably the more intelligent students are going to university courses and better-paid jobs in other professions: they are often the good readers and keen chamber-music players. For the less self-sufficient student, training is frequently not good enough to allow him to cope with the essentials of an orchestral career. There just is not time for him to learn every piece in the orchestral repertoire as though it were a concerto: only an early start in group-reading, in addition to the later opportunity for orchestral training under an experienced orchestral leader now obtainable at some music colleges, can equip the less intellectually gifted player (who may achieve good technical results on his instrument) for an orchestral career. Szigeti adds that 'Women violinists have to be considerably better than men in order to be engaged'[29] – a fact recognised by most professional musicians. As orchestras approach extinction for lack of suitable candidates, however, their attitude towards women tends to meliorate, and this prejudice may disappear within the foreseeable future.

  There has been no decline in the amount of literature published on violin- and viola-playing, rather the reverse. A monument in the history of the violin treatise appeared with Carl Flesch's *The Art of Violin Playing* in two volumes – the first, on technique in general, appearing in 1923, the second, on artistic realisation, following in 1930. For the first time, a violinist who was both a great performer and who possessed the analytical qualities of a great teacher made an exhaustive inquiry into contemporary methods of playing and teaching; the result was to become the standard reference work on violin-playing for the 20th century. Flesch expected individual aspects to be treated by other people in still greater detail, but the awe-inspiring thoroughness and assurance with which almost every aspect is dealt with have prevented any successor from usurping his position of eminence.

Flesch's combination of performing and teaching abilities was very rare, as he himself pointed out in the chapter on violin-teaching. The fact of his finding time to collate and present his experience and knowledge at such length made him unique, and although modern schools may not agree with everything he writes, all of them owe a great deal to his systematic and logical presentation of a very complex subject.

The Art of Violin Playing differs from previous treatises in that, as Flesch states in the foreword, it is

> not meant to be a 'School of Violin-Playing' in the current meaning of the term. It is broadly conceived, from the pedagogic standpoint, its intention is not only to advise the teacher how to train his pupils most advantageously, on the basis of the most modern acquisitions in the domain of violin technique, but also – by leading him to think logically, and by cultivating analytical investigation of the problems of violin technique – to bring the violinist to a plane of development which, in time, will enable him to be his own teacher. Hence this work is not addressed to violin beginners, nor to advanced students; but to reasoning violinists, or those who wish to become reasoning violinists.[30]

He goes on to justify his selection of method as having been tested and found successful in the concert-hall – a convincing argument to the aspiring performer, but one which fails to take into account the fact that a violinist of different physique and mentality from Flesch might encounter a different set of problems in concert performance. He rejects much of Steinhausen's work on the physiology of bowing on the grounds that the physiologist is not a concert performer and that

> in consequence of his imperfect preparatory violinistic training . . . he has been misled into an announcement of certain principles

(theory of rolling elbow-joint movements, etc.) the use of which not only does not stand any serious test, but would absolutely ruin a bowing, good in itself.[31]

Later research has proved this statement to be incorrect, and a muscular condition of which Flesch writes: 'My experience is that it is hardly possible absolutely to cure this evil'[32] may be cured by the correct use of those 'rolling elbow-joint movements.'

Flesch gives detailed instructions not only for acquiring all aspects of left-hand and bowing technique, but for analysing impediments to progress and showing how to cure them. He covers posture, movements of the left hand from string to string, shifting with the aid of intermediary notes, and arm, wrist, and finger vibrato. His theory of intonation is that the note is adjusted immediately after it is sounded: that bad intonation is 'an aural, not a manual deficiency'.[33] Advanced multiple-stopping and harmonics are covered in detail before bow technique is touched upon.

Flesch considers that

> the technique of bowing is more complex than the mechanism of the left arm, because in the latter the finger is in direct contact with the string; while the right arm comes into contact with the string only through the medium of the bow-stick and bow-hair.[34]

He describes the three main bow-holds prevalent at the time: German, Franco-Belgian, and Russian, which is the one he recommends to the reader. In his *Memoirs* he describes how he adopted this bow-hold after hearing Auer's pupils.

> It was the tone of Auer's good pupils which interested me above all; it seemed to possess a roundness and mellowness not easily to be found elsewhere. From the outset, I was convinced that the cause of the phenomenon must rest in some inconspicuous peculiarity of bowing or of the actual holding of the bow, and shortly before the First World War I did in fact succeed in establishing by exact observation that Russian violinists place the index finger about one centimetre higher on the stick (wrist-wards) than is customary in the Franco-Belgian school.[35]

With this hold he recommends the more pronated arm which most naturally accompanies it, and the method is the most widely used today.

Such detailed instructions are given concerning wrist- and finger-movements with the bow that these have sometimes been mistakenly used out of context and caused unforeseen troubles; occasionally Flesch appears to fall into the dangerous habit of trying to induce natural passive movements by practising unnatural active ones. But there can be little doubt that, had every violin-teacher since 1930 been thoroughly versed in the contents of *The Art of Violin Playing*, Szigeti would not be discussing today 'alarming data about the paucity of string players'. Flesch was particularly concerned about teachers, and one of his pupils, Max Rostal, became a world-famous teacher of the next generation. He was not prepared to advise teachers of beginners, for 'the instruction of beginners is a science in itself, and the most intimate knowledge of the sum total of the result to be obtained is a preliminary necessity'.[36] But his plea for better teaching was intended to raise the standard of the whole profession.

In consequence of my intentional division of my career into solo playing and pedagogic activities I have had opportunities which, perhaps, have been accorded none other, to observe the results of contemporary violin teaching close at hand. The impressions thus received have in large part been cheerless. In spite of improved technical methods the average among present-day violinists stand on a startlingly low level. Nor is lack of talent responsible for the fact, but rather the lack of a *teaching body* whose members possess sufficient technical and musical schooling as well as the faculty of transmitting their own attainments. In addition, they should know enough about psychology to be able to recognize and satisfy the technical, musical and psychic *needs* of the pupils entrusted to them. I am convinced that progress in our art does not depend on the ennobling of the *individual* student, but on the elevation of the whole student body. Hence the *training of a new type of teacher* is also the purpose of this work.[37]

Flesch also has a suggestion for providing these teachers, but fifty years later it is far from being generally carried out, although alarm about falling standards is widespread.

The young violinist who has just completed his studies, be he never so qualified and who devotes himself to teaching without special preparation, is already unfitted to do so because he is inclined, without regard for the manifold kinds of individual talent, to apply in every case the method according to which he himself was taught, hence to *schematicize*. Not until many hapless victims have thus been bagged will he begin to realize (if he possesses any pedagogic gifts at all) that the foundation of all superior teaching activity must be based on *individualization*. This transitional stage might be elided by a course in pedagogy paralleling the violin instruction. . . . *Learning how to teach* should be a major subject in the curriculum of musical educational institutions.[38]

Although Flesch can be said to have made a minor revolution in 20th-century approaches to string-playing, it could be that the writings of F. A. Steinhausen and W. Trendelenburg, physiologists who studied the physical basis of string-playing during the early part of the 20th century, may ultimately be seen to provide a more practical approach to teaching than any one school of performance or tuition, obscured by tradition as these tend to be. A further largely unrecognised attempt at a general approach to bow technique appeared in England in 1934, with Percival Hodgson's *Motion Study and Violin Bowing*. (It is perhaps significant that the reissue in 1958 was by the *American* String Teachers' Association.) Hodgson, whose book follows Steinhausen's physiological principles and applies them to the standard bowing-patterns which provide the basis of all bow technique, illustrates his thesis with cyclegraphs, tracing the movement of a first-class violinist's hand as he performed various bowings. They were taken with several synchronised cameras in a darkened room with (usually) a single light-source at the heel of the bow. (Occasionally elbow movements were cyclegraphed as well.) In his emphasis on the difference between active and passive muscles, and curved rather than straight bowing movements, Hodgson was well ahead of his time: not only was he a violinist and teacher ready to accept the findings of the physiologists, but he avoided the 'do it my way' approach of Violin-School writers and concentrated on principles.

The very gradual move towards seeking basic principles of good performance which may be adapted to varying physiques and types of intelligence is indicated in the titles of two books by famous teachers of the 20th century: *Violin Playing as I Teach It* by Leopold Auer (1921) and *Principles of Violin Playing and Teaching* by Ivan Galamian (1962). The latter deals broadly with physical and psychological aspects of playing, as one would expect from one of the leading teachers in one of the most advanced teaching institutions of the world (The Juilliard School of Music in New York), but it nevertheless lays down one method of violin-playing, which the author describes as 'the one that I believe to be the most practical, but I do not contend that it is the only right or only possible one'.[39]

Galamian lists deficiencies of some of the present-day teaching systems, but he does not attempt to tackle the problem of how these deficiencies might gradually be eliminated on a large scale. The approach which implies that by adopting this particular method one may avoid certain deficiencies has been tried so often and failed to reach more than a narrow school of adherents, that an approach from the opposite viewpoint – 'what to avoid and how to avoid it' – may be the only chance of producing an entire generation of violinists and teachers capable of preventing their pupils from tying themselves into physical and psychological knots in the attempt to learn to play this reputedly difficult instrument.

If the violin family is to survive, teachers who are capable of making string education a painless and sociable occupation are vital. To achieve this, the social status and rewards of teacher and orchestral player will need to be raised to bear a reasonable relationship to the talent and training required. Alternatives seem to be the complete disappearance of the violin family, or the discovery that string-players who are competently trained to teach become inevitably better string-players, and begin to fill those vacant seats in the orchestra. This would at least be substituting a benign circle for the present vicious one, and orchestras organised on the assumption that members will teach on one or two days of the week could become a more closely integrated part of the community. Joseph Szigeti (in *Szigeti on the Violin*) takes as his motto 'There Is No Substitute For Perfect Intonation': the motto of this book seems to be emerging as 'There Is No Substitute For Good Teachers'. The elements of good violin-teaching should surely be emerging from two centuries of treatises on the subject: the following chapter attempts to draw conclusions from the material covered in writing this book and from personal experience in the fields of playing and teaching.

NOTES

[1] 178 Szigeti, p. 21.
[2] 106 Lang, pp. 9–10.
[3] 197 Yates, p. 78.
[4] ibid. p. 44.
[5] ibid. p. 8.
[6] 29 Cage, p. 26.
[7] 39 Culshaw, p. 166.
[8] 106 Lang, p. 153.
[9] 56 Flesch, p. 66.
[10] 144 Quantz, p. 237.
[11] 183 Tertis, p. 24.
[12] 35 Copperwheat.

[13] 6 Austin, p. 396.
[14] 43 Demuth, p. 193.
[15] 6 Austin, p. 401.
[16] 86 Hindemith, p. 217.
[17] 34 Copland, p. 107.
[18] ibid. p. 47.
[19] 60 Gal, p. 441.
[20] ibid. p. 443.
[21] 34 Copland, pp. 75–6.
[22] ibid. p. 29.
[23] 39 Culshaw, p. 150.
[24] 101 Krasner.
[25] 106 Lang, p. 14.
[26] 101 Krasner, p. 32.
[27] ibid. p. 22.
[28] 178 Szigeti, p. 24.
[29] ibid. p. 22.
[30] 57 Flesch, Foreword, vol. 1.
[31] ibid. note to Foreword, vol. 1.
[32] ibid. vol. 1, p. 67.
[33] ibid. vol. 1, p. 20.
[34] ibid. vol. 1, p. 50.
[35] 56 Flesch, p. 253.
[36] 57 Flesch, vol. 1, p. 5.
[37] ibid. vol. 2, p. 125.
[38] ibid. vol. 2, p. 129.
[39] 61 Galamian, p. vii.

CHAPTER 10

Education for Survival

While artistic demands are greater than ever before, there is a national, if not world-wide, shortage of string players of the required quality. Concern for the future is directed more to the need to produce string players than to the supply of wind instrumentalists, though the importance of the latter is acknowledged. There are today more children learning to play orchestral instruments than ever before; but there seems to be a serious shortage of instrumental teachers, and the tuition offered at school age needs to be considerably better as a basis for later advanced studies at a college of music. This is the stage when the more fortunate children who are able to benefit from the tuition of good specialist teachers will be embarking upon a lifetime of musical enjoyment. The relatively advanced age at which serious training now normally starts robs a student of that period which is the most fruitful for physical development – the early formative years: as in all physical development (ballet is an example), muscular adaptations become more difficult as we climb into the 'teens. The initial stages of training are vital to the instrumentalist; basic training has to be sound, because ingrained faults are difficult to eradicate. The young musician needs a thorough foundation of musical knowledge, instrumental technique and interpretation, so that he can take the fullest advantage of studies in a music college. At present, it is only in exceptional cases that the standards of musical and instrumental attainment are high enough when such advanced studies begin.[1]

THESE PARAGRAPHS FROM the Report on Orchestral Resources in Great Britain 1970 (generally referred to as the Peacock Report) underline the problem of finding adequate string-players, without placing all the blame on the music colleges, as writers on the subject have tended to do since Berlioz started the fashion by pointing out that 'the study of the Violin in Paris is very incomplete'.[2] Szigeti's brief chapter summing up reasons for the present shortage of adequate violinists, criticises tuition at all stages; 'present-day violin tuition suffers from various musical and instrumental shortcomings and neglects'.[3] He quotes from a letter written by George Szell, who for years auditioned talented string-players for greatly sought-after positions in the Cleveland Orchestra.

Everything in their tuition seems to have been concentrated on producing as big a sound as possible and having as swift a left hand as possible. Any subtle function of wrist and fingers of the right hand is practically unknown to them. Therefore while they are able to go through some of the concerti, particularly the cantabile passages, with some semblance of brilliance, they are completely helpless when confronted with, say a second violin part of a Mozart symphony, with its problems.

They have never been told that the bow has to articulate the music. Very few of them know how to play near the frog. Many of them, because of the stiffness of wrist and fingers, have no smooth bow change on either end. Generally speaking, these students are trained and coached solely with a view to the soloist's career, which of course only a very small percentage of them can make anyway, whereas all preparation that would enable them to be relatively happy and not disgruntled members of orchestras or chamber ensembles is completely neglected.

They are not taught, or not sufficiently taught, chamber music and ensemble techniques and, moreover, they are not stimulated to love music as such, instead of loving only themselves and their careers.[4]

The complaint that too many institutions train their string-players for a soloist's career is frequently met with in Western countries, yet a soloist's technique is necessary today in order to become a first-rate orchestral player, and both time and money are often somewhat limited at the stage of full-time study. In contrast to the players described by Szell, musicians in Europe and America have been startled by the easy, flexible bow-arms of Japanese children demonstrating the Suzuki method. These children, before they reach the age of twelve, do know how to play near the frog, they do have a smooth bow-change, and the second-violin part of a Mozart symphony would not present them with any special technical challenge. One obvious conclusion to draw from this is that Western countries are not making sufficient use of the formative years, as the Peacock Report suggests. Another might be that the music colleges would be well advised to concentrate more of their time and budget in the immediate future on providing well-trained string-teachers, so that the development of technique might be efficiently spread over a longer pre-college period. Gradually the colleges themselves would benefit by the rise in standard of their intake.

In Britain, an increasing number of local education authorities are setting up centres for the education of the more promising young musicians, usually providing private lessons on one or two instruments, orchestra, choirs, written music, and aural training, with occasionally chamber music for advanced students. The major colleges have accepted young people into their junior departments for many years, tuition being paid for by education authorities; now more local authorities are organising their own centres and very young students are occasionally accepted if the parents will bear the cost. But as an attempt to raise standards nationally, these encouraging signs seem foredoomed to failure. Owing to the improbability of professional players being regularly free to give lessons on Saturday mornings, and to the acute shortage of able string-teachers, it is difficult to staff even the highest-paid musical centres. In London, home of four major musical institutions and five major symphony orchestras, knowledgeable parents may have to send young children on an hour's journey to receive an efficient half-hour's tuition on the violin. If school and private instrumental teaching were of a generally efficient standard, musical centres would be able to devote their time to all kinds of group music-making: orchestral training, rehearsing and reading in chamber ensemble, singing, rhythm groups, jazz bands – anything which stimulates enjoyment and efficiency simultaneously. Instead, the Saturday music schools are bound by room shortages, timetable restrictions: their teachers fight a constant battle to remedy ingrained habits due to faulty early training.

One of the newest of these centres in England suggests as a guide to candidates that a child nearing the age of twelve should have reached Grade III of the Associated Board examinations (major and minor scales and arpeggios – two octaves in first and third positions, pieces using third position, exercises for *spiccato*, *martelé*, and shifting, no vibrato). In Japan, by the Suzuki method, thousands of children reach this stage by the age of six. A frequent complaint in English schools is that a child has not time to cope with the heavy school syllabus as well as practising. But from the age of six to twelve children do not have a heavy school syllabus. Professional musicians know that Grade III at twelve is too late: even if the technical ground is covered later with the help of excellent teaching and exceptional application on the string-player's part, he is likely to have to work harder all his life to attain and retain high standards than his more fortunate colleagues who covered the ground at an earlier age. He is also more likely to be susceptible to physical problems, like Joachim, whose early training was bad.

If a national attempt were made to provide a generation of string-players whose technique was well founded (to include, say, three-octave scales and arpeggios up to D major and minor; basic bow techniques including *spiccato*, *sautillé*, and *martelé*; the ability to sustain a string quartet part at sight, and to perform Baroque concertos or a Schubert sonatina with fluent vibrato) by the age of twelve or thirteen, pressure during the scholastically full years would be considerably reduced. The musical institutions would be left with the task of completing a musical education instead of providing it from an elementary level as so often happens at present, and the full-time student would have time to devote to the finer points of musical training instead of concentrating solely on acquiring instrumental technique.

But for such a revolution to take place, the institutions themselves would have to take the first step, by turning out a generation of teachers equipped to provide the right kind of string-teaching for children. In England, where teachers of any class subject must now take a teachers' training course in addition to a degree or diploma, individual music lags lamentably behind. Many amateur musicians have gained teaching diplomas: their diploma is of equivalent status to that achieved by full-time students. Talented and intelligent amateurs may take teaching diplomas between their final school examinations and their first university examinations in a quite different subject, 'and may, after examination, append the letters of a famous institution to their names, without having undergone any systematic institutional training',[5] as the Gulbenkian Report points out.

Why individual tuition should be considered so much less important than class tuition is difficult to understand, although it is not so difficult to find reasons for the lack of attention to teacher-training in the tradition-bound institutions. The professorial staff are likely to raise objections on the grounds that the students have enough to do already and that their own authority as teachers may be questioned. The colleges, aware of the deficiencies of the system, are perpetually short of money. Other objections frequently heard are that you cannot teach people to teach, and that occasional excellent teachers emerge from the present system. But occasional teachers are not sufficient. What is needed is a whole army of string-teachers ready and able to stimulate musical development among five- to twelve-year olds in Britain, and a national policy on the part of education authorities and parents to bring the children to the teachers.

Primary-school music is leaping ahead, but when a county has to advertise for a string-teacher 'with at least Grade 8 of the Royal Schools of Music',[6] even when diploma requirements are so low, a vicious circle of lack of teachers – lack of able string-players is obviously being perpetuated. Shortage of money, to provide special training courses with examining boards and special diplomas recognising the completion of full-time study, is a basic problem in Britain. In 1965 a report for the Gulbenkian Foundation on the training of musicians pointed out the 'avoidable confusion' of letters awarded by English musical institutions, adding, 'There is some justification for the belief that the variegated array of letters is perpetuated partly because of the colleges' dependence on the income derived from examination fees.'[7] The report calls for a diploma obtainable only after a specified course of internal study, and suggests that music colleges should be given similar status to universities. But at no point does it suggest what would appear to be the ideal target for musicians leaving the colleges: the ability to turn from solo performance to orchestral playing and teaching with both knowledge and enjoyment.

Segregation of teachers from performers is rejected in the report, as 'teachers must be performers too, and the basic musical training of both is identical in many respects'. This statement, which few would deny, brings us back to the aims of the musical institutions with regard to string-playing. Should they be training soloists? Or orchestral players? Or teachers? Given the present minimal funds there is still a very strong case for reallotment of the student's timetable to allow two hours group work per week on all aspects of string-teaching during the first full-time year of study.

Already London's Guildhall School of Music has included a compulsory year of teacher-training in its professional diploma course: in this case, the second and third years are used, but the first year could be particularly suitable. This year is rarely used to best advantage by students, as the Gulbenkian Report points out.

> The Normal Curriculum . . . appears to many of our witnesses to impose too heavy a responsibility on the individual students. . . . The single weekly lesson with his teacher in his principal instrument does not provide enough time for the general guidance which a student needs in addition to detailed technical instruction.[8]

A tutorial system is recommended and is now in force at some music colleges, but a group in which teaching and playing methods could be demonstrated and discussed could provide not only a stimulus to interest in teaching but a conference ground for problems encountered in practising, and a social group in which students can exchange viewpoints. The aim of such a group should not be to lay down rights and wrongs in teaching methods, but to increase awareness and openmindedness in the students.

The professor who fears that his methods may be questioned by a student attending such a group is right: they will be questioned in an attempt to establish reasons for various didactic statements. In looking for basic problems and how to avoid them, the string-player is bound to consider himself, his own problems, and their relation to past and present teaching. But the advantages to the professor should considerably outweigh this fear of criticism, because while a student learns to teach, he learns to teach himself. New students rarely know how to practise: they practise their faults. Making a study of how to help the string-player, from beginner to performer, to practise without reinforcing faults, must increase awareness and direction in the student's own practising.

One has only to watch championship tennis to become aware that similar ends can be achieved by amazingly varied physical means. Yet certain aspects of approach can be discovered which are common to all great players, and players with widely varying styles are often coached or trained by the same person, who is alert to prevent habits of balance, muscle-tone, or thought which might interfere with the player's ability to react instantly in any direction. The same kind of basic training is needed for a practical musician as for an athlete, but the musician is far less likely to be aware of the need for readiness and co-ordination of his mind and his whole body. Efforts to sort out basic similarities as opposed to differences in schools of violin-playing have so far been minimal.

Nearly all string-players are going to play in an orchestra and to teach at some period of their lives, although some of them may be unwilling to recognise the fact on arrival at one of the colleges. Untutored in these skills, they can be not only useless but dangerous should they fall into the wrong job, and as peripatetic teaching posts in particular are difficult to fill, a string player may take such a position because he has failed to obtain any other. A single inept peripatetic teacher can stifle enthusiasm and misguide talent over a whole area; a good one, on the other hand, can rapidly make music a flourishing social activity. One education authority in north-east England purchased ninety violins and installed its first peripatetic teacher in 1968. After two terms a short holiday string course was held, with one hundred per cent attendance and a concert for parents. By then a cello-teacher was available. The children were eight to nine years old. By the end of the second holiday course, with sectional, orchestral, and chamber-music coaching, after one year's tuition, groups of children were able to perform simple chamber music without a conductor. Christmas saw the same children going from school to school in the area to play for carol concerts; Easter of the second year saw their first residential course of one week, and a resulting concert of considerable variety now that third position and a number of keys were technically available. All of these children were taught in groups of three; only a very tiny percentage failed to continue with the lessons after starting.

This particular town was fortunate in its music adviser and its peripatetic teacher: isolated examples can be found of excellent work with young people. But where high standards are achieved, they serve to show up the gulf between what could happen and what usually does happen. 'We are saddled with inefficiencies',[9] says the Tanglewood Symposium report on the shortage of string-players in the United States; this will also remain true in Britain until string-teaching becomes a recognised career with adequate preparation and remuneration.

It might be useful at this stage to summarise some of the ground which could be covered by a teaching course without insistence upon any particular school of violin-playing. A good starting-point, because of its relevance to the student's immediate curriculum, is practising: its organisation into technical and musical work, the value of scales and studies at various stages, and of repetition. Habits of thinking as well as of moving will need consideration, methods of persuading children to practise at all, and of teaching them to practise well. This must lead on to the danger of practising one's faults, perpetuating weaknesses, and to the necessity of isolating problems and finding their cause. Shortcomings of reading, creating a musical image, and projecting it on the instrument can be discussed separately. Many children are still taught to read music by learning the lines and spaces on the stave by letter-names: is this necessary, or would musical phrases be quicker, like the word-recognition method of learning to read? Suzuki method (below, p. 217) children learn by rote at first. Singing and tapping are quicker and easier than learning to read straight on to an instrument: the student teacher should at least be aware of the existence of the Suzuki, Orff, Kodály, and Hindemith educational systems.

From a consideration of his own ability to imagine an ideal

performance which can be aimed at in practising and performance, the student can go on to consider methods of stimulating musical imagination in pupils. Under this heading comes consideration of tone-production, when to teach vibrato, the use of tapes and recordings, the influence of pupils on each other in chamber groups, etc., stimulating repertoire, listening to concerts, and the pupil's self-image. The student-teacher can gain a new insight into the relevance of musical history, form, and harmony to style in performance.

The third heading, and the one about which so much has already been written, is the physical aspect of performance: a great deal of damaging teaching could be prevented if students were introduced to basic concepts of natural physical posture and movement; the differences between active and passive muscular states; and the possible mental causes of muscular problems. Recognition that different physiques need to find different styles of performance should prevent dictatorial insistence on one school of violin-playing; recognition of natural posture should make it easier for the student to spot physical contortion. Under this heading students should be made aware of the possibilities of muscular education away from the instrument, and of the existence of methods of training such as Alexander technique (see below, p. 228). Conflicting opinions about muscular practices should be welcomed: this is the stage where a student will benefit most by considering whether 'the left shoulder muscle and chin must be developed in order to hold the violin with ease'[10] (Jacobsen) or 'The weight on the chin-rest from the back of the head creates not only a natural position, but also serves as a perfect counter-balance to the jutting forward position of the violin'[11] (Havas). Or with regard to tone-production, whether relatively small pressure with considerable bow velocity is preferable to the converse as a basic premise, and whether arm weight or wrist, thumb, or finger pressures are the principal sources of volume: all of these have been suggested by various pedagogues.

It may be some years before any training of muscular movements away from the emotional context of playing is given in most colleges of music; although the Juilliard School in New York has two teachers of Alexander technique, it is available to British ballet and drama students, and already to a privileged minority of music students. But a step forward would be the mere recognition that the physical basis for ease of performance is the same for all instruments as for ballet, drama, or any physical occupation: that of complete body mobility. Training a student to recognise interfering bodily tensions which may have become completely habitual is really a job for the professional in this field, but a part of efficient string-training should be an ever-increasing awareness of the body as a whole, posture and breathing, as a basis for free muscular movement.

The single teacher–pupil relationship system is fraught with danger in a subject which is so much a matter of personal experience and so difficult to express in words. Many violinists have one teacher until they enter a college, a further teacher who then carries them as far as their entry into the profession, at which stage they become teachers themselves. Even the most intelligent of students feels disinclined to question the theories and doctrines of a player so much more proficient and established than himself, especially when the pupil lacks any kind of yardstick on which to base his conclusions. Group discussion on teaching methods could reduce the danger of this perpetuation, which is usually caused in the single teacher-pupil relationship, not so much through observation as through incorrect verbalisation. An example is Spohr's instruction: 'The following exercise is to be played throughout with a stiff back-arm.'[12] The habit of immobilising the right upper-arm with the intention of acquiring an active wrist or forearm movement for rapid bow-strokes is one of the more frequently met instances of a damaging and illogical tradition perpetuated from teacher to pupil since the time of Spohr: teachers today are still recommending pupils to hold cushions or telephone directories under their arm to practise the so-called 'wrist-stroke', without realising that although they may have themselves been taught by this peculiar method it is only by *losing* the upper-arm restriction that they have managed to make the stroke work in performance. Some pupils will succeed in overcoming this hurdle in the same way as their teacher: the natural will supersede the unnatural as soon as the telephone directory is removed: others, more analytic in approach, will remember that the upper-arm was immobilised and will attempt to immobilise it by tightening the muscles at the sight of a rapid passage. In this way a teacher can destroy a pupil's natural ability to tackle technical problems.

Often the apparently most successful teachers are those who do not verbalise their sensations but who are able to demonstrate successfully. Here we meet with a double problem: that of inadequate financial reward in teaching compared to playing, so that the person best able to demonstrate is least likely to be doing so, and the fact that physiques differ to such an extent that a physical movement exactly copied by a pupil may be entirely unsuited to him. Again the pupil suffers from the lack of any yardstick to judge by: he may try to *feel* the way his teacher *looks*, or he may spend hours in front of the mirror trying to look the way his teacher looks, without ever succeeding in his real aim, which is to *feel* the way the successful performer *feels*.

Serious damage may be done by starting a child very young with a second-rate teacher: on the other hand, the early starter who is well taught, even though early progress may be (and usually should be) very slow, has a definite advantage over the child whose violin-playing habits are gained after postural tensions have become habitual. This can be as early as seven years old in the tense child, but usually in the West only the children of professional musicians are fortunate enough to be sent to a first-class teacher at the age of four or five. A first-class teacher for this age-group being one who can instil enthusiasm, and introduce basically correct muscle-patterns through games, singing, and tapping rhythms, until the bow-movement is clearly enough developed to be used rhythmically on the strings. Often pairs of very young children work well together, as the space of concentration is short: they learn from each other and develop different faculties by, for instance, one pointing to the notes while the other plays.

It is vital at any age that the emotional atmosphere of the lesson should be a pleasant one: fear of the teacher might give rise to more regular practising, but it is likely to be work of the least constructive kind if the pupil cannot feel free to express his own problems. The first impediment between a student and a satisfactory performance is often fear; the more eager the child, it seems, to do well, the more likely he is to allow fear or panic to creep in and prevent himself. A calm person has maximum available control of his own nervous system; panic may block off all or part of this. Fears of one kind or another dictate wrong physical habits in the violinist: fear of the teacher's wrath, of playing the wrong note, of not playing as well as a friend or the man at the desk behind, of dropping the fiddle while shifting or the bow while playing *spiccato* – these and many others can be at the conscious or unconscious root of mental and physical playing problems.

Part of Dr Suzuki's success must be attributable to his special concentration on eliminating certain of these fears – of dropping the violin or bow, for instance – at a very early age, by encouraging small children to play fiddle- and bow-holding games, and to march around or play 'follow-my-leader' while playing the instrument. Dr Suzuki has proved that almost any child started at an early age and given sufficient encouragement can learn to play the violin to quite a high standard, which should make Western countries think again about their search for 'talent' at the age of eleven or twelve. What they may in fact be discovering, except in the rare case of outstanding ability, is either good teaching or a good background, where music is enjoyed by the family.

A letter from a British music-teacher studying Suzuki method points out that

> This is just a country town area, where the children have no particular musical backgrounds, and yet at the Graduation Ceremony this year, there were seven children playing a Mozart Concerto, 27 Bach A minor, 30 Fiocco Allegro, etc.
>
> The emphasis is undoubtedly on the enjoyment of music for its own sake, and although obviously some children do not always want to practise at home they are 'made eager', to use Suzuki's expression, by continually hearing other children better than themselves, and having the opportunity from the very early age of three of joining in with the others.[13]

Of course, not all of these children are likely to possess talent in the fullest sense of the word, but should a thousand Suzuki-trained eleven-year-olds suddenly become London residents, the selectors for talent education-schemes would at the very least have to revise their standards.

Musical talent (for the performer) consists of several different kinds of ability: (1) that of recognising and differentiating musical sounds; (2) of reproducing them in the imagination; (3) of being aroused by them emotionally; (4) of being capable of sustained thinking in musical terms; and (5) of co-ordinating the physique in order to reproduce the mental image. The talent which is the easiest to train is the one where all these qualities are present in a reasonably comparable degree, and all develop at the same rate. The teacher needs only to find the natural rate of development of the pupil, and his various abilities will mature together, given a similar amount of attention. Where certain of these qualities are considerably more marked than others, however, or where training has developed one aspect of talent while neglecting the others, problems are bound to arise.

For the musician who is going to make the fullest use of his talent, the ability to recognise musical sounds must at a reasonably early stage become accurately associated with music as a written language. With exceptionally young or dyslexic students this stage may be by-passed in the early years, as it is with Suzuki method, but for the older student it should be the *first* step in musical performance. Unfortunately, it is so much quicker to teach a beginner the mechanical action of placing one finger on the A string in order to produce the sound indicated by the middle line of the stave, that only rarely is the student taught to pitch that note mentally or vocally before he plays it. Thus the note which he plays becomes the one he believes to be correct, and the seeds of bad intonation are firmly sown from the start. Those with a well-developed sense of pitch will gradually reverse this process and expect the correct sound from seeing it in print, especially if they frequently read tunes they already know. It is on this kind of hardiness that too many teachers depend: the adaptability of the pupil in reversing, avoiding, or ignoring errors in tuition.

Hindemith, in the preface to his *Elementary Training for Musicians*, points out that 'save in a few exceptional cases, the methods by which those basic principles are taught are deplorable'.[14] He gives a comprehensive set of exercises designed to develop the student's ability to sustain a basic pulse while reading varied rhythmic patterns; to pitch one note after another within or without a tonal framework; and finally to combine these abilities. Most of this work is achieved away from the performer's instrument, making clear the difference between the physical processes of playing, and the mental processes which must precede them.

Violin lessons are often short and crowded, and to spend a period of time working away from the instrument seems wasteful, especially as, once these problems are tackled, they seem to require an inordinate amount of time before muddled thinking is sorted out, unless the pupil has been steadily trained to think first, play later. It is undoubtedly quicker to say to him 'No, no – it goes like this' and let him copy – hoping that the combination of aural and visual stimuli will somehow 'click' and make him play a similar passage in the same way next time. But in fact this is the slowest way of achieving the aimed-for result – which is a violinist who knows how he wants a piece of music to sound, and can produce the sounds from his instrument. Most teachers recognise the fact that children who sing from music and learn percussion instruments in school are far easier to teach than those who merely receive a weekly violin lesson: few are prepared to devote a section of this weekly lesson to singing or tapping out rhythms. Thus all too often the confusion in the pupil's head is transferred straight on to the instrument, and we have one of the origins of the 'nervous' violinist who associates his difficulties with the instrument and does not dare to use his muscles naturally in case he is wrong – because he is not sure how to check right from wrong. Even at an advanced stage of performance the student should sing any passage which causes difficulty, until pitch and pulse and natural phrasing are clear, before seeking technical reasons for the difficulty.

The order given above: read; imagine; play is accepted by most 20th-century musical education systems. Belgium and France lay great stress on *solfège*, so that the student learns to sing pitch and rhythms at sight, often before he is allowed to touch an instrument at all. The Hungarian Kodály method, which introduces harmonic structure through singing as well as interval pitching, has produced excellent results in schools. The Carl Orff method, which has spread from Germany into primary schools throughout the Western world, lays initial stress on rhythm and adds a harmonic sense by using percussion instruments with different pitches but only a few keys. Improvisation is particularly successful with the Orff instruments.

One 20th-century method which must be considered very carefully from the viewpoint of providing violinists for the future reverses these processes in the early stages. This is the Suzuki Teaching Method, devised by Dr Shinichi Suzuki, and the order he uses at first is: listen, remember, play. Later it becomes listen, remember, play, read; then reading and playing are reversed, and the imagination is substituted for the gramophone record.

Suzuki initially considered the way in which children learn to speak their mother-tongue and decided to find out whether children could absorb a skill like violin-playing at an early age by similar methods. Vital points are that the child must from babyhood hear repeatedly on records the sounds he is going to reproduce. The mother is involved in the teaching; she sets the example (and must therefore learn the violin herself first) which the child copies, daily, for short periods throughout the day. Starting at about the age of three, the child learns by ear until he reaches book four of the Suzuki method, which contains the first and last movements of the Vivaldi A minor concerto and therefore uses first, second, and third positions. Thus a symbol is immediately connected with a sound, not a finger, avoiding one of the problems mentioned earlier. By continuing to play by ear but watching the music, reading appears to come quickly and naturally to these children.

All of the children play the same pieces, which means that once a month they can join together in a group of all ages, and play items from the easiest to the most difficult, the less advanced players gradually dropping out to listen. Basically, however, the Suzuki method is not for group teaching; a certain amount of individual tuition for mother and child is considered vital. Three private lessons and one group lesson a month is the pattern often followed, but sometimes small groups of three or four will come together for a lesson, each child receiving some individual attention. A child who cannot yet play the first piece ('Twinkle Twinkle Little Star' with variations) will come to the group lesson and just bow (as in bough, not beau!) with the others, then listen: thus he becomes involved in the social aspects of the method and realises what he can look forward to.

For very small children, violin-playing has to be made as simple and enjoyable as possible. Dr Suzuki has allowed for this by marking the finger-board with tapes which can be felt, to aid intonation, by using the upper part only of the bow and by adopting a bow-hold with the thumb outside the frog at first. He has devised games which aid posture, security of bow and instrument, and freedom of bodily movement. Tiny instruments for beginners are made in the Suzuki factory.

This method has been broached with considerable success in Canada and the United States, but it seems evident to an observer that there will be new problems outside Japan, owing to the emphasis on individuality and the comparative lack of discipline among Western children. Japanese mothers learn the violin for three months before their children start. Western mothers often refuse to do this. Japanese children have the patience to spend up to a whole year learning one piece of music, Western children and mothers would be very likely to give up before this, unless the social aspects were very rewarding. Japanese children sit quietly and listen to each other: Western children, at best, wriggle; at worst, raise a clamour to draw attention to themselves. Dr Suzuki points out that his problems are more with the mothers than the children: a nagging or over-ambitious mother can spoil the enjoyment for the child.

Critics of the Suzuki method point out that the children are copying an old-fashioned style of playing, that individuality and creativity are being stifled, that bad postural habits may be emphasised so early that they cannot be eliminated later. But it is impossible to write off the method on these grounds when one considers that thousands of seven- and eight-year-old children in Japan are achieving a technical standard which only a comparatively small number of fifteen- to eighteen-year-olds achieve in Western countries. The method is now applied to other instruments besides the violin, and it could be that with a certain amount of adaptation to suit other cultures, and with constant revision to keep in touch with modern playing requirements, the Suzuki method may become the basis for training future generations of young instrumentalists who will acquire technical fluency plus a realisation of the social values of instrumental playing, before they reach the age where schoolwork begins to crowd out other pursuits. The value of continuing to follow the method strictly after the age of seven or eight can be questioned: certainly as soon as a child can read music he should be encouraged to explore and create, and there seems to be no argument against running the Suzuki, Orff, and/or Kodály methods simultaneously: the result should be a more rounded musician.

With young children teaching is often carried out by rote because it is feared that the eye cannot follow a line regularly before they learn to read. But most young children love to sing and to bang things, and training in reading can be carried out by the pupil pointing to the notes while the teacher or parent plays, then by reversing this process. The violin is in some ways ideal for the smallest learners, as the four strings are so clearly spaced apart on the stave. The names of the lines and spaces on the staves may be absorbed much later, provided the pupil correctly imagines the sound connected with the note he is seeing – which is much simpler than learning to read, especially when parents and teachers are prepared to sing words to the elementary violin tunes with the pupil. This game can in fact be very helpful in the acquiring of word-reading skills. At all stages of learning, activities away from the instrument but connected with rhythm and pitch help to clarify the mental images derived from the printed page.

'The aim of this book ought to be clear: it is *activity*', says Hindemith, in the preface to *Elementary Training*; 'Activity for the teacher as well as the student.'[15] Most violin-teachers are justified in feeling that they have too much to do in too little time, but unjustified in considering that elementary training is not part of their job. They are responsible for the violinist's total development, and it is possible that a lack of synchronisation of the various aspects of a student's development may bring him to a complete standstill if one side is over-stressed while another is neglected. Intellectually lazy minds, which are sometimes found with well-co-ordinated physiques and a strong response to musical sounds, respond initially with apparent success to the spoon-feeding approach in which the teacher demonstrates and the pupil copies. But although it is possible to reach the stage of professional, full-time training without growing out of this method, each year makes it more difficult for the student to acquire the reading facility required by the professional musician. And should the student not be of the soloist class, able to rely on his knowledge of a limited repertoire, he will be unlikely to cope with the demands of the profession as an orchestral or chamber-music player.

The metronome is a common substitute for activity on the performer's part, the activity which is the most vital to performance and the first to be abandoned once muddle sets in, that of keeping a constant pulse.

A metronome has its uses, but never as a substitute for the player's activity: it can reveal lapses in this activity, provide subdivisions of the basic pulse marked by the player, or mark bigger divisions in conjunction with the player; but if it becomes an external substitute for an internal sense of pulse, it may become a potential danger instead of an asset. Groups and classes have an advantage in that different members can be employed by turn to mark the pulse and its subdivisions; the gradual spread of the Carl Orff method in primary and junior schools should make the job of the violin-teacher simpler. Children who use records as an aid to practising soon lose the childish habit of disturbing the rhythm in order to cope with a technical difficulty, and gain the desirable habit of tackling the technical point out of context until it ceases to interfere, but records, if over-used, may themselves become a substitute for activity and initiative.

The second stage in musical performance, that of imagining the music in terms of violin sound, is the least conscious of the processes, the least easy to teach, and the most frequently by-passed. The good teacher demonstrates the sound and the physical movements producing the right kind of sound by playing scales and pieces to the pupil. Some pupils seem slow to recognise tonal differences: most teachers have followed up a pupil's scratchy performance on a factory-made fiddle by a resonant, beautiful rendering on their old Italian, only to be told, on asking the pupil to point out differences, 'You didn't play the third note quite in tune' or 'You played it slower than me.' This is because a pupil rapidly associates a certain string-sound with himself, and a quite different sound with the teacher. Sometimes the gap is too wide to be bridged in the imagination; the pupil just cannot imagine himself making a sound like the teacher. This is another weakness in the system of single private lessons with each pupil sent away as the next arrives: the pupil may be at a standstill in some respects because he is unable to imagine playing like his teacher, but just as soon as he hears his friend, who is only a little more advanced than himself, he realises he could easily play like that, and the next step in the imagination leads to progress on the instrument.

Commercially recorded music is probably the least valuable stimulus to the imagination; its disembodied quality provides an over-perfect end (gained by many repeats and much tape-splicing) without showing the physical means, and a student will quite often tie himself into physical knots trying to imitate the speed and slickness of a recorded performance. Tapes or records made with the learner violinist in mind, however, can bring good standards of rhythm and pitch into homes where only the child is interested in making music, and make practising a pleasure instead of a chore, ensuring harmonic completeness to back good intonation, and guarding against pauses in rhythm which break up the melody.

Live concerts are a vital stimulus, and any opportunity of mixing with other players of different standards, whether it is by lessons overlapping for a few minutes or in classes, orchestras, chamber groups (these are ideal), students' concerts, or summer schools, may help the pupil to take the necessary steps in imagining himself producing a better result. The proviso must be added that supervision and discussion by the teacher are necessary, as the student will be as quick to imitate the bad habits of his colleagues as the good ones.

Preoccupation with accuracy of intonation and note-values often prevents the intellectual pupil from developing his tonal imagery, and the teacher may be so grateful to have a pupil who is accurate as regards time and pitch that he feeds him more and more difficult music to keep the intellectual mind interested. This can be damaging to the physique, which will put up with all kinds of physical contortions in order to achieve the demands of the intellect, and it will reinforce a lack of synchronisation between the various aspects of his talent; it is always the weakest aspect which must be most developed, not the strongest. Emotional satisfaction in playing comes from producing sounds of a quality and sequence which are pleasing or moving to the listener, and the instrumentalist who does not think or hear in terms of the sound of his instrument is unlikely to achieve any emotional satisfaction beyond that of solving an intricate mathematical problem.

Into this stage of musical imagination the performer gradually feeds his knowledge of musical architecture, form, style, history. Many students consider these subjects irrelevant to the main task in hand, which is learning to play their instruments, certainly they are often made irrelevant by the method of their presentation. It would take an exceptionally intelligent and industrious student to relate the performance of the Handel sonata which he is learning this week to the couple of lectures in which he 'did Handel' a year or more ago. The isolation of different aspects of musical education has led to a lack of appreciation of their value to the performer, although a wave of 'style-consciousness' has considerably changed some aspects of modern concert performance. The teacher who is qualified and able to acquaint his pupils with even the realisation of the importance to performance of history, harmony, form, and style is a rare but much needed figure in musical education.

In Great Britain, this brings one back to the very lowly position which instrumental tuition holds on the income-scale. A professor of the less practical aspects of music may command a reasonably high income for taking charge of a small department within a university. A man of equal ability who chooses to devote his talents to the more directly communicative branch of musical performance has no equivalent post to aim for; no matter how broad his knowledge and teaching abilities, he will be expected to confine himself to teaching one aspect, usually to one pupil at a time, for an hourly wage which ceases during vacations. There are some advantages in this system, which, if it were paid on a rate comparable to professional playing, would maintain the maximum contact with the profession by allowing performers to teach for a limited number of hours per week while continuing a freelance professional career. But the enthusiasm of professional string-players for this kind of work in teaching institutions must be considerably dampened by the fact that they could often earn twice as much money by playing for a comparable number of hours. And although the system tries to avoid the risk of a full-time professor who may become increasingly out of touch with live performance, it has two inherent dangers. The first is that the remuneration may be insufficient to attract teachers of the right kind of ability, the second that integration of the students' courses cannot be achieved without some figure akin to the university professor in charge of an entire department, with the knowledge, time, and opportunity to ensure the development of all aspects of the students' abilities. The Juilliard School of New York has pioneered a successfully integrated course for performers at a cost which would be prohibitive for British institutions, but it is debatable whether the present allocation of money which is available for musical training in England is satisfactorily organised.

Soon the English musical profession will be feeling the first effects of a move made some years ago to give talented children a musical training while still at school age, first with the Central Tutorial School for Young Musicians in London, later the Menuhin School. Manchester, Wells, and London now have schools where musically talented children may receive subsidised special courses at school, Wells concentrating on violinists. All of these schools aim to give the opportunity for a musical education which is complete in all the basic aspects before the student enters a full-time school of music. The pupils are exceptionally fortunate in being enabled to assimilate the right things in the right order, not just instrumental technique but all aspects of the musical language. Some consider them exceptionally *un*fortunate in being dedicated to a life of such questionable security before they are really old enough to decide for themselves, but, as in the cathedral choir schools, it has been found that with smaller classes and more personal tuition, the child who decides to prepare himself scholastically for a different career can do so while receiving intensive musical training. At present, however, the cost of such training is so high as to limit it to the few who show the most outstanding talent at an early age, and it is therefore not likely to alter very greatly the general standard of string-playing. It may be that a specialised course within a large school, as started recently by Wells Cathedral School and by the Inner London Education Authority, will prove more satisfactory than isolating talented children from an early age; a musician needs to be able to mix with a varied society.

The spread of class teaching has enabled many children to start learning the violin who would not otherwise have had the chance, but the enthusiasm generated by the Rural Music Schools Association and class-teaching experts like Gertrude Collins does not seem to have been carried through into the later stages. Class teaching in capable hands has certain advantages in the early stages besides offering the widest possible range of children the chance to try the instrument; they learn from as well as with each other; soon lose the fear of playing before others; and gain a feeling for ensemble; while rivalry tends to encourage practising. But the system inevitably ignores the fact that all children are different and will have different problems and rates of progress; the child who shows talent should be given individual lessons as soon as this is recognised, and after the initial impetus has been lost, usually during the second year in a class, the child of average musical ability will need individual tuition to extend his personal musical horizons and make rapid progress. Up to three years in a class is possible, but the student receiving individual tuition usually progresses considerably faster after the early stages.

Reasons for practising the violin before the age of ten are sometimes difficult to explain to the child, and the actual sounds produced from a tiny instrument often bear a minimum of resemblance to real violin sound. Parental supervision is unavoidable with very young beginners, and here the teacher has an additional problem because 'bossy' supervision is worse than none at all, and an overhelpful parent can so cushion the pupil's progress that he never learns to think for himself. Really practical supervision can be given by parents who attend the lessons. The aim should always be to develop the student's independence, and as soon as possible his should be the initiative with regard to what to practise and how to practise it; the teacher must make this as clear as possible. Reasons for practising at all as opposed to the rival attractions of television and games vary from family to family. Even a really talented child is often reluctant to practise, and bribery, the choice between household chores or practising, the hope of a gold star from the teacher or of learning a piece quicker than the boy next door have often played a part in the early development of a real musical talent. A more consistent habit is sometimes achieved when the child finds in the practising time an opportunity to have one of the parents to himself, away from brothers or sisters: at a later stage, chamber-music sessions with family or friends provide an invaluable stimulus and education. This atmosphere of a pleasure shared is the most conducive to progress in a young child, and cannot be achieved by a disciplinarian approach. Only a few Western parents seem willing to spend the time and patience every day to give their children an early start in music: professional musicians, recognising that the lack of an early start is rarely made up for later, often attempt to start their children at an early age, but the irregularity of a performing musician's life tends to prevent the formation of the right kind of practising habits, and the child loses interest. Running battles may ensue between parents and child, in which the teacher needs to act as referee (rather than as a third parent, which ranges everybody against the pupil, increasing his resentment). Unless the teacher can stimulate the pupil's desire to practise, by using attractive pieces, tapes, records, contact with other pupils, or any other method, the pupil would be best advised to give up the instrument in these circumstances.

An interesting experiment would be to compare the rate of progress of five children who practised together with a teacher for half an hour each day (and alone at weekends), and five children who had weekly half-hour lessons. There would be more variation in the individual pupils, according to the amount of parental support, but the group of five with professional supervision would be less likely to allow bad habits to creep in, and the consistent supervision would probably produce superior results in the early stages. At least part of the success of the Suzuki method must be attributed to regular, *supervised* practising.

Unsupervised young people tend to practise those things they are best at and ignore their own weaknesses, which can be very frustrating for the teacher. The use of practising time, even its exact allotment in minutes, should be constantly advised, discussed, and revised: after all, the pupil does most of his instrumental learning away from the teacher. Innumerable hours can be wasted in practising bad habits which must be unlearned by further practising; like Alice and the Red Queen, some of the most fervent practisers keep running in order to remain in the same place. The teacher who can persuade his pupils to seek out their weaknesses and remedy them in practising will achieve the quickest and most far-reaching results, even if the methods seem slow and devious to the pupils.

Lessons can be made into a pattern on which practising habits are based: it is easy to spot where the student is practising bad habits if the practising routine is checked in the lesson, but the teacher must restrain his desire to interfere, until a clear picture is obtained. Violin-teachers tend to check audible faults regularly, visible faults sometimes, faulty thinking habits not at all. Yet musical performances in all their aspects originate in the brain, and if the mind is not properly prepared before playing, then the body is not in a state to carry out its messages. Flesch points out that bad intonation is the result of faulty thinking rather than incorrect muscular movement. A most valuable habit of thinking, which is a necessary part of Alexander technique and has been advocated by some of the greatest instrumental teachers, is a moment of poise, of calm readiness of the whole body and mind before going into action. The player whose synchronisation of body and mind is exact can regain this state of poise at any moment in a performance: panic, muddled thinking, and excess physical tension are incompatible with it. The student whose mind is quick and clear tends to begin playing before he is physically prepared, and irregular breathing and muscular contortion may accompany the efforts of his physique to keep pace with his mind. The slow-minded pupil will be less liable to muscular contortion, but his playing may be inaccurate as regards note-values and pitch: his aim before playing is to acquire a clear mental picture covering such details as key, intervals and time-signatures, mood and nuance. The moment of poise before playing allows a rapid mental and physical check-up: posture, breathing, clarity of image can be checked briefly if the habit has once been acquired. It serves as an antidote to 'nerves' before an audience: panic is unlikely while such a routine is carried through. Playing from memory is both aided by and an aid to the sensation of poised preparedness.

This brings us at last to the third stage of performance, the stage on which most books on violin-playing concentrate. Given the ideal student, whose mind can assimilate the printed music before him, and visualise the sounds he is striving to achieve, what is likely to come between him and a musical performance as satisfying as the one he imagines? Great stress has been laid on the difficulties of learning the violin, and innumerable exercises have been devised for training sections of the anatomy most obviously involved with playing it, the fingers, the wrists, the forearms, etc. This splitting-up of the problem, which disregards the fact of the body as a whole organism, has set up barriers which only the most physically gifted can surmount. To give an instance: a student is attempting to play the gigue from Bach's D minor solo partita. He has been told that the bow-stroke is a forearm movement, so he moves the forearm conscientiously, unconsciously tightening the muscles of the upper-arm to isolate the forearm movement. He may have spent hours of preparatory practising on Ševčik's exercises, which recommend that semiquaver patterns of this type should be played from the wrist. The held upper-arm interferes with his string-crossing, and the unevenness worries him. The fact that he is concerned about the string-crossings makes him catch his breath at these movements and his basic sense of rhythm is disturbed. Tension breeds tension: as the mind runs ahead to foresee possible problems or back to explain problems, synchronisation between mind and physique is temporarily lost, and with it the sense of balance and rhythmic poise vital to a good performance. Had the teacher been less analytical in approach, this sequence of events might possibly have been avoided by the student copying the correct physical movement. With good basic teaching resulting from correct analysis, the problem would never have arisen.

The practice of dividing up the body into various parts which receive individual attention deflects the student's attention from the awareness of his whole self: it ignores the fact that an arm or finger can only work to its fullest ability by the co-operation of the entire body. Violin-teaching should therefore be directed towards awareness of the whole – rather than exclusive concentration on a single part. Our hypothetical student playing the D minor gigue should ideally be aware of feeling physically free, easily breathing and balanced on his feet before playing; his picture of a 'forearm movement' should include mobility of the rest of the arm, and he should feel free to punctuate the music with moments of poise which reinforce the feeling of physical balance and mind–body synchronisation, thus giving his audience the impression of music with breathing-space and time for phrasing. If he has been trained in this type of awareness, he will notice when his breathing is interfered with, or when his trunk-muscles tighten and pull him off-balance, interfering with the rhythm. Rhythmic and physical poise are usually very closely related, although occasionally one meets a performer who sustains a very vital sense of rhythm in spite of a physique contorted by tension.

Finding the origin of playing problems can be fairly complex once the fault has become a habit. The student practising the gigue might, if unchecked, begin to tighten the muscles of his upper-arm whenever he sees a similar semiquaver passage: in the effort to 'control' the evenness of the notes he may tighten the muscles of his right shoulder and neck, restricting his breathing and setting up a sympathetic tension in the left arm. He has come up against one of the basic problems of instrumental playing: that control is often gained by what feels like a release or abandonment of control. 'Control yourself' is used synonymously with 'Get a hold on yourself' or 'Get a grip on yourself', and one of the basic stages of physical learning must be that control comes through freedom, not restriction.

The teacher who notes interference through tension and advises the pupil to 'relax' may do more harm than good. This vague term must presumably be aimed at the limb which is the apparent source of trouble; if the student were to relax his whole body he would collapse on to the floor. But a relaxed arm would hang uselessly down at the student's side, and if he attempts to make the arm resemble as closely as possible this limp state, he is in danger of losing contact with the fingers on the bow-stick. The loss of feeling of contact between the right hand and the bow, even for a moment (as often happens at the bow-change), can throw into confusion the muscular organisation of the whole right arm in a nervous student. The student with the best chance of realising in performance the ideal image in his mind is the one who is most constantly in touch with his total physique: loss of sensation in a set of muscles can set up a physical impediment to performance. Unnecessary activity, such as overstressed active finger-movements on the bow, can also lead to confusion and tension in other muscles. The basic simplicity of Suzuki's bowing method (always a firm hold on the bow) seems to lead to an easy flexibility of the bow-arm in the early stages: more delicacy of contact is easily acquired later once confidence has been established.

Instead of considering violin-playing to consist of a series of acquired skills of mounting difficulty it is sometimes helpful to invert the process, considering the student as a person with the physique and mentality suitable for performance, but who manages to prevent himself from fulfilling this aim. Difficulties may be peeled away rather than surmounted by arduous toil: so much arduous toil is misdirected and harmful. The student needs to become acquainted with himself physically away from the instrument. It is no use attempting to feel a free right arm while holding a bow if he has never consciously experienced a free right arm without a bow. If he is not aware of how he feels when standing firmly and breathing easily without a violin he is unlikely to spot the moment when his easy stance breaks down and a barrier to free movement is set up.

One of the pioneers of training in self-awareness in the early part of the 20th century was F. M. Alexander: musicians at all stages of the profession have benefited from training in the Alexander technique.

F. M. Alexander was an English actor who developed throat and voice troubles through excessive muscular tension at times of nervous stress. He spent several years in exploring this problem, and made a series of far-reaching discoveries in the process: that feeling is often an inaccurate register of the way in which we are moving, that habits of movement which feel correct (through familiarity), but are in fact damaging, may be prevented by a moment's inhibition before movement, and that more natural physical behaviour-patterns may be substituted and reinforced by a conditioning technique associated with certain words of command.

This may sound a far cry from string-education, and the technique has so far found a place in re-education rather than in student training, but its value might be more apparent if we return to our hypothetical student with a bowing problem. We have noticed that practising makes this problem worse, and as he becomes more worried the problem spreads. Had he been trained in Alexander technique he would be able to inhibit this initial response to the sight of a page of semiquavers, check the tendency to tighten his upper-arm muscles and restrict his breathing through fear of losing control, and replace this physical state by one immediately ready for action of any kind by ordering his neck muscles to free themselves, allowing the balance of the head to direct the body into its most natural physical posture. In this way the student has replaced an unfavourable starting-state by a favourable one and broken the vicious circle between fear and physical tension. He is likely to be able to carry on the process while playing because successful training in Alexander technique leads to a constantly increasing accuracy of muscular sensation: soon he will recognise the holding of upper-arm muscles as the source of his problem as soon as it interferes.

Medical and psychological research confirmed various aspects of Alexander's work long after his initial discoveries, and it is now an accepted part of ballet- and drama-training, but it has only recently gained a foothold in the more go-ahead of the English schools of music, although for some years there have been Alexander teachers at the Juilliard School in New York. Opponents of Alexander's system object to the limited active participation of the student, and the apparent remoteness of the initial training (which normally deals with habit-ridden everyday actions such as standing, sitting, walking) from the problematic situation, i.e. playing an instrument. In fact, it takes a very able teacher of the technique and a far-sighted student to accept and successfully apply this training. The unthinking, passively accepting type of student may make more rapid progress than the one with some initiative and an inquiring mind, and certain schools of training have broken away from the traditional methods of the technique to seek similar results in terms of physical and mental awareness without such an apparently roundabout approach.

The approach to a physical awareness through relearning an everyday movement such as how to sit down, however, has the big initial advantage of being detached from any emotional situation. One is unlikely to be worried or afraid about sitting down: one can be very worried and afraid about a playing problem, particularly if it is likely to affect one's livelihood in the future.

The basis of the majority of playing problems *after* the preliminary stages of assimilation and imagination have been achieved is usually either habit or fear, which may be conscious but is more frequently unconscious. The teacher who can start a pupil on the violin at an early age may avoid one whole set of problems, as favourable violin-playing habits can be formed before unfavourable muscular tensions have become habitual through the everyday actions of writing or other acquired skills. The seriousness of these habitual tensions may be assessed in a new pupil by noting his posture and co-ordination while he attempts some unfamiliar physical action such as trying to tune one string of a violin. If this shows no excessive effort or contortion, then physical problems which ensue are probably being learned along with the instrumental skill, and the fact that they are appearing at all is frequently due to an unspoken or unrecognised fear.

Fear of dropping the violin or bow is perhaps the most basic and least perceived impediment to freedom of movement; it can lead to gripping of the neck muscles, the left shoulder, the right hand, and almost anything else, blocking off sensation in those parts. The violinist who achieves real physical freedom accepts the instrument as naturally as an extra limb; from the first it is vital to ensure that the natural posture is not pulled out of true by holding the violin, and that no part of the body is immobilised by the effort. This is difficult: it is possibly the most difficult thing to learn about violin-playing. Many violinists have been taught to hold the instrument firmly with the chin, and have rapidly become used to tight neck and shoulder muscles which may not trouble them in youth but can cause considerable pain and distress in later

professional life. On the other hand, the teacher who advocates supporting the violin entirely with the left hand instead of the chin, for fear of
destroying the total sense of balance which is most easily attained when
the head is unrestricted, often finds that certain muscles in the left arm
become immobilised, or that the left thumb is squeezing the neck of the
violin. Young pupils are naturally more interested in playing tunes than
achieving an easy sense of balance between head and left hand when
holding the violin, but avoidance of this basic problem can lead to a host
of later problems and a great deal of practising-time spent on 'un-
learning'.

Violin-teaching vocabulary is unfortunately full of words which have
a background of inappropriate connotations, and books about violin-
playing have frequently failed in their aims because of this. Teachers
can fall back on word-pictures when their normal vocabulary produces
the wrong results; a state of muscle-tone neither relaxed nor contracted,
for instance, can be described as floating or light: Kato Havas's simile
of a see-saw with the weight in the back is a useful example. These are
ways of acquiring a suitable starting-state: they are the exact opposite of
the type of instruction found in Spohr's Violin School, where he asks
for the elbow 'low and as close to the body as possible'[16] and short notes
played 'with a stiff back-arm'. 'The bow-grip', a common title for the
method of holding the bow, automatically suggests something tightly
held. One does not refer to one's 'pen-grip', because maximum sensitivity and flexibility are required in the pen-holding fingers: the
same sensitivity must be immediately available in the bow-hand.
The word 'relax' can set up muddled reactions in a student and cause
over-slackening of one set of muscles compensated by over-use of
another: real relaxation and physical activity are opposed to each other.
'Posture' often evokes a picture of a stiffly held stance, and the teacher
needs to verify the pupil's interpretation of such a word. Pianists suffer
less from vague terminology owing to the work of such far-sighted
teachers as Matthay: at present each violin-teacher has to verbalise his
muscular conceptions as clearly as he can with words used for quite
different processes. A few useful terms can be discussed with the pupil
and form a basis for physical advice: flexibility, stability, freedom, lightness, and their opposites need to be understood with reference to
muscle-tone and sensation apart from the violin before the student
associates them with playing.

Certain fears appear to be associated with the violin more by tradition
than anything else. One of these is the fear of the bouncing bow, another
is the fear of high positions. Either fear may be avoided by introducing

these phenomena at a very early stage, so that they become an accepted part of the violin's properties. The child who has learned his first scale on two strings is quite prepared to tackle the same thing on one string before anyone has explained that it is difficult, and if the shift causes a problem there is an ideal opportunity to sort out the fear of dropping the instrument. And the teacher who shudders at the thought of teaching *spiccato* in the first few lessons will find that ricochet is considered great fun and encourages flexibility in the right hand while diminishing the fear of the bouncing bow. Suzuki-trained children, who start with semi-quavers and later slow down to bow crotchets, are not liable to fear rapid bowings, as so many British children do.

Galamian lays great stress on the responsibilities of the teacher in his book on *Principles of Violin Playing and Teaching*, pointing out that

> The teacher must be a good psychologist. He must beware of discouraging the student, and he must know that there are times when it is advisable to correct certain things and times when it is not advisable to do so. . . . Above all, the teacher must not try to do too much at once. The ability to digest new things is limited with everybody, and an over-ambitious attempt on the part of the teacher to apply too many cures simultaneously will yield negative results.
>
> The decision of how and when to do . . . things . . . will have to be based on a considered judgment of the student's personality. This is why it is so important that the attitude of the teacher be a very personal one and, of concomitant importance, that he analyse the character of every student correctly.[17]

The instrumental teacher's job holds a particular challenge in that it embraces the physical as well as the mental, and is therefore so much more affected by personality and the teacher–pupil relationship than more scholastic subjects. Violin methods over the last two centuries have revealed an increasing awareness of the importance to the player of a good physical posture, and most of us recognise, unconsciously if not consciously, that posture, personality, and self-image are very closely linked. The over-anxious person with head thrust forward and shoulders hunched is not likely to prove the best instrumentalist, nor is the person who is too shy to stand up straight. Colloquialisms often use physical descriptions to indicate mental attitudes, such as 'stiffnecked' or 'keeping a stiff upper lip', and Galamian's suggestion that the character of each pupil be analysed implies that the teacher should not deal merely with physical problems but should be prepared to seek out their mental origins.

A startling illustration of the impact of personality on posture and appearance is contained in the classic case history of a multiple personality by Thigpen and Cleckley, entitled *Three Faces of Eve*. As the subject slipped from one personality into another, distinct alterations were noticed in her bearing: even her shape seemed to change.

> Like one awakened who has been sleeping in a cramped, uncomfortable position, her body shifted slightly its centre of gravity, carrying out by reflex, it seemed, numerous but scarcely discernible little readjustments. Almost instantaneously the figure had relaxed into the buoyant ease of Eve Black.
>
> Eve White regularly gave the impression of a taut fragile slenderness. Perhaps because of the easy laxness of this [E. Black's] girl's posture and her more vigorous movements, the lines of her body seemed somehow a little more voluptuously rounded.[18]

Eve Black would be less likely to encounter physical problems in violin-playing than Eve White!

The violin-teacher has to cope with postural habits developed in home- and school-situations over which he has little or no control. The better the teacher–pupil relationship, the more chance has the teacher of influencing his pupil's reaction to these situations by making him aware of the physical effects and broadening his perspective in considering the relationship of violin-playing to everyday living.

While the student learns the violin he is building an image of himself as a violinist. If his tuition is ideally arranged, the image will be of a person confident in his ability to cope with the instrument at this stage and aware of new horizons which he will be able to tackle as the time comes. Most of his learning and playing experience should reinforce this image. A student who tries to tackle too many problems at a time, or has all his shortcomings continually pointed out without being given time and method to work through them, may fail to cope with any of them and thus construct a self-image of a non-achieving violinist in certain directions. Failure to correct an obviously acquired fault may stem from laziness or lack of interest, or it may have deeper roots in that previous failure in this direction has caused the student to consider himself incapable of tackling it: he therefore accepts the fault as part of his self-image.

A surprisingly large number of violinists who reach the profession accept bow-tremor as part of their self-image. Although the inability to sustain soft long bows may cause considerable mental stress under certain conditions, it is frequently accepted as inevitable, something outside the player's control. Certainly it feels this way, but as we have already noticed, feelings are unreliable. The frightening thing about this and similar problems is that their origin is unconscious, and fear of the problem increases the likelihood of its occurrence. One way of reducing the fear is to make a problem more conscious, and a way to do this is to reproduce consciously the physical symptoms which occur spontaneously when they are least wanted. This alters the mental picture of the problem and makes it into something one does, instead of something that happens to one. Once the player becomes capable of thinking 'What precisely am I doing to make my bow shake?' during a performance, he is in charge: the fear of the unknown disappears and the way is open to solving his problem.

Physical problems tend to crowd in upon orchestral players approaching middle age. These may be caused by the strain of long hours of playing, mainly seated, when it is almost impossible to sustain the necessary physical support, or by legacies of bad teaching in early stages, or by personality problems which become expressed through one of the performer's main means of expression, his instrument. Osteopathy, traditional medicine, sedatives, massage, physiotherapy are resorted to, but in many cases of persistent back-pain or stiffness, physical and mental re-education provides the only lasting remedy. Certain types of physique are less liable to postural distortion than others: the person of broad-shouldered, short-necked build is least likely to spend his spare time on the osteopath's couch. Any busy professional player can encounter a period of physical discomfort, and part of his training for professional life should have been directed towards avoiding these problems and knowing how to cope with them when they arise. Learning how to sit in a chair in an orchestra may seem inessential to the young player, but by the time he has done it for six hours a day for twenty years, his body may be refusing to put up with the stresses of an incorrect sitting position any longer, and he cannot just change to a different method, because his habits are too strong. A system of re-education such as the Alexander technique is his best chance of re-adjustment: if he is not aware of such a system, or it is not available in the area where he works, there is a danger of the whole situation being worsened by worry about the ability to earn a living or support a family.

Should the pain or playing-problem have its roots in an unrecognised emotional problem, no system of physical re-education is likely to cure it, although the cause may become apparent as the player discovers more about his physical reactions to certain stimuli. The psychoanalyst would expect such a problem, even when apparently cured, to re-emerge in a different form, and the teacher of professional players as well as the player himself may need to recognise and accept this before he can begin to make the changes in outlook necessary to continued success in professional life.

Consideration of the violinist's emotional problems in adult life may seem far removed from the initial aims of this chapter, but it adds to the perspective of education. A violin-teacher or institution training a would-be professional is training him for life, and to restrict this education to any limited aspect such as technical efficiency is to fail to give him the necessary perspective and mental resources to cope with the problems which he may meet with in later life. Instrumental training should concern the mind, the whole body, and the outlook of the person on the situation in which he finds himself: until such training becomes available we are perpetuating the vicious circle which makes the music profession 'saddled with incompetencies'. The violin's chances of survival seem small unless we can increase enjoyment of string music by introducing a wider cross-section of the public to the pleasures of string-playing, while simultaneously reducing the problems and drawbacks of learning and continuing to play as an amateur or professional.

NOTES

1 3 Arts Council, p. 58.
2 20 Berlioz, p. 232.
3 178 Szigeti, p. 42.
4 ibid. p. 43.
5 70 Gulbenkian.
6 185 *TES*.
7 70 Gulbenkian.
8 ibid.
9 101 Krasner.
10 91 Jacobsen. Introduction.
11 75 Havas.
12 170 Spohr, p. 32.
13 118 Middlemiss.
14 87 Hindemith, p. vii.
15 ibid. p. ix.
16 170 Spohr, p. 12.
17 61 Galamian, p. 106.
18 184 Thigpen, p. 83.

CHAPTER 11

String Acoustics

THE ACOUSTICAL PROPERTIES of a vibrating string were used to make music long before they were explained by scientists, although theoretical conjecture about the nature of musical sound has been a favourite intellectual pastime since the time of the Greeks. Pythagoras used the simple divisions of a vibrating string which gave the octave, the fifth, and the fourth. The violinist tunes to Pythagoras' perfect fifths, but in fact Pythagoras' method of building up the Greek modes from the perfect fifth gave a major third which was high, and tuning is the only aspect in which the violinist now consciously follows his rule.

The most elementary violinist is making use of certain scientific phenomena as soon as he picks up the instrument and twangs a string. He is causing the string to vibrate: sound is caused by vibration and transmitted from point to point as compression waves in the air. The plucked string produces a sound which has a definite pitch: it is therefore recognisable as a musical tone and can be repeated. This is due to the regularity of the vibrations. In making musical instruments, man has explored ways of producing regular vibrations which may be varied in pitch and intensity and produced at will, successions of such sounds being known as music. Vibrating strings and vibrating columns of air provided the most easily controlled mechanical means, and different methods of setting the media in motion led to the different groups of instruments today, the plucked, bowed, struck, and blown groups.

Columns of air and vibrating strings are adjusted to provide notes of different pitch by altering the vibrating length: the shorter the length, the more frequent the vibrations, and the higher the pitch. A stringed instrument may have most of the essential string-lengths ready to be set in vibration, as in the harp or piano, and a wind instrument, the organ, may consist of columns of air of prepared length. Most wind instruments, however – flutes, oboes, trombones, etc. – adjust the length of the column of air as they go along, and the violinist adjusts the length of vibrating string by *stopping* it with his fingers. The *frequency* of any note is the rate of vibration which determines its pitch, an open string having a lower frequency than any stopped note on that string.

Returning to the beginner-violinist plucking the open strings; he may notice that there are four strings of equal length, each of which produces a sound of different pitch or frequency. Other factors besides length must therefore affect pitch, and if he turns the peg and alters the tuning he is demonstrating one of these; the pitch rises as the tension of the string increases. This is more accurately expressed in the *Law of Mersenne*: '*If all other factors remain constant, the frequency of a note from a stretched string varies as the square root of the tension.*' (Therefore the tension is quadrupled to double the frequency, providing an octave rise in pitch.) Thickness also affects pitch, the noticeably thinner E string showing that a thinner string will produce a higher note, and one further string property less evident to the eye affects pitch: the specific gravity. A heavy string made of metal will produce a considerably lower note than a lighter one (e.g. gut) should their thickness, length, and tension be equal. Progress in making the actual strings of the violin up to 1800 was mainly concerned with varying the thickness and specific gravity to produce better tone. Corelli's thick, slack gut G string would be tonally unsatisfactory; the metal-covered string giving a far superior sound. The actual length of viola-strings has always varied considerably, and in both violin and viola, the tension was increased with the new slanting angle of the neck around 1800.

As soon as the violinist learns to place his fingers on the string to produce a major diatonic scale, he is reproducing frequency ratios which are a basic property of any vibrating string, and demonstrating the *Law of Pythagoras*, which states that '*if other factors remain constant, the frequency of the note from a stretched string is inversely proportional to the length of the vibrating segment*' (e.g. a section of string half the length of the open string will give twice the frequency, raising the pitch by one octave). The string can vibrate not only over its whole length, but simultaneously in halves, thirds, quarters, fifths, sixths, etc., of the whole length – any sections which are evenly divisible into the whole. Each of these sections produces a sound or partial tone which is heard in addition to the whole length or fundamental tone, and the relative intensity of the partial tones causes the individual timbre of the note. The violinist may vary the strength or presence of partials by the method with which he sets the string in motion.

The frequencies of the partials always bear the same relationship to the fundamentals and are known as the harmonic series. The open C string of the cello might in theory produce the following sounds all at once although partials vary considerably in intensity; the frequencies shown result from a convenient tuning of C = 64 c.p.s.

Harmonic Series (bracketed harmonics out of tune)

	1	2	3	4	5	6	7	8	9	10	11	12	13	14	15	16
c.p.s.	64	128	192	256	320	384	448	512	576	640						

Each interval is successively smaller, and it will be noticed that the requisite intervals for building the major diatonic scale are present.

Frequencies of the notes of a pure scale may be worked out from the frequency of the tonic, as the *ratios* of these frequencies are constant: the mathematician will soon discover, for instance, that in the above example $G:C = 192:128 = 3:2$, and $G:E = 384:320 = 6:5$. Any pair of notes may thus be related to each other, using the harmonic sequence numbers 1–16 with 1 as the fundamental. The violinist places his fingers on the string at distances bearing approximately (because of the human element, and the influence of other scales to be discussed later) the same numerical ratios as the equivalent intervals in the harmonic series. We speak of him *stopping* the string when he presses it down on to the finger-board, his finger then becoming the equivalent of the nut of the finger-board. If he presses two, three, or four strings at once, it is known as double, triple, or quadruple stopping.

It has been pointed out that each interval of the harmonic series is slightly smaller than the previous one. This accounts for the 'out-of-tune' partials, no. 7 in the above example falling between B flat and B natural, giving a small minor third above G and a large tone below C. In the 'pure' scale (the one most nearly derived from the harmonic series and sometimes known as the natural scale) the different-sized whole tones with ratios $9:8$ and $10:9$ both have a place, the scale consisting of three major tones ($9:8$), two minor tones ($10:9$), and two approximate semitones ($16:15$). These appear in the following order:[1]

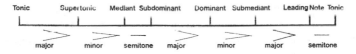

It will be noticed that if we now start a new scale on the dominant, the first tone will be a minor instead of a major one, and the same type of problem will occur at some stage of a scale starting from any other note. This means that the pure or natural scale is only suitable for use in one key, and although a violinist using only one string could use pure scale intonation all the time, the presence of certain fixed notes on any instrument rules out this possibility (unless open strings and natural harmonics are consistently avoided).

To gain freedom of modulation the fixed-note instruments adopted the tempered scale, with the octave divided into twelve equal semitones, one whole tone being the sum of two semitones. Few self-respecting solo string-players, however, consider that they play in tune according to the tempered scale, although Peter Yates quoted a critic's discussion of the Hungarian quartet:

> What was their secret, I asked, in achieving such perfect intonation . . .? They were quite agreed that the main point was their conscious decision to play in the evenly tempered scale. 'The size of a third has been a matter of argument in the Hungarian Quartet for thirty years', Székely said half in jest, but Koromzay put it more practically: 'We hate playing in the tempered scale, but we just have to.'[2]

The tuning of a stringed instrument by perfect fifths does not fit with the slightly small fifths of a tempered instrument. Conscious adjustments have to be made in duos with piano: if the viola-player tunes his A string accurately, his C string will sound flat to the piano. He must therefore tune the A a little high, or tune upwards from the C string. Whether string-players actually succeed in using pure scale intonation will be discussed later.

When the violinist stops the string with his finger, only the part of the string between the finger and the bridge is allowed to vibrate, and the string becomes in effect shorter, with a new fundamental tone and set of partials or overtones blending in to give the sound we recognise as violin tone. Each of these higher tones can theoretically be isolated by touching the string lightly at one of the points of rest (or nodes) between vibrating sections of the string. As we have remarked, the string vibrates in halves, quarters, fifths, etc. Touching the string lightly at a node allows vibration on either side of the finger, but only of sections which have a point of rest at that node. The sound produced is that note of the harmonic series which corresponds numerically with the number of vibrating sections of the string, e.g. to obtain the sixth note of a series (above, p. 237), the cellist would lightly touch the C string one-sixth of the total string-length away from the nut, causing it to vibrate along its whole length in sections one-sixth long.

The practical application of this property of a vibrating string may be heard in two forms, one clearly demonstrated in the violin and viola variations of the *Young Person's Guide to the Orchestra* by Benjamin Britten, the other in a famous instance about two-thirds of the way through the finale of Tchaikovsky's violin concerto. The first is the

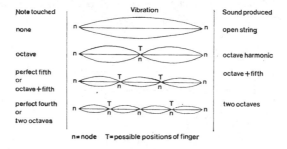

Note touched	Vibration	Sound produced
none		open string
octave		octave harmonic
perfect fifth or octave + fifth		octave + fifth
perfect fourth or two octaves		two octaves

n = node   T = possible positions of finger

'natural' harmonic – the one which is obtained by touching the *un-stopped* string lightly at one of its nodal points. The following natural harmonics are obtainable on the violin

sul G   sul D   sul A   sul E

while the viola loses the E string harmonics but adds harmonics of great clarity on its C string

sul C

Natural harmonics, like *pizzicato*, tend to sound better on the lower instruments. The other type of harmonic, known as 'false' or 'artificial', replaces the nut of the open string with a movable first finger; it is therefore more suitable for melodic writing.

Of the natural series, the octave harmonic occurs frequently in violin and viola literature since 1800: before then, harmonics were known but regarded with distrust. To indicate the octave harmonic, the composer places an 'o' over the note written at the pitch it will sound, the violinist being expected to deduce that as he has no open string at that pitch the octave harmonic is intended. For the other natural harmonics, indications vary: sometimes ordinary notes are written at the pitch they will sound but with 'o' above, as with the octave harmonic, in which case the composer relies on the performer to work out the position of the finger on the string. Other composers indicate by a hollow lozenge-shaped note the position where the finger must touch the string, sometimes omitting to show the pitch sounded altogether, sometimes indicating it with a bracketed note above. The last of these systems is the most satisfactory for the player.

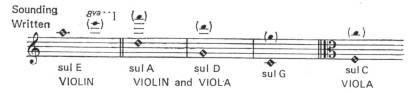

The node which divides the string into quarters is found in the same place as the perfect fourth stopped note above the fundamental (e.g. *c* on the *g* string): it produces the double octave harmonic. This one is fairly common, and might be indicated in the same way as the octave harmonic on the lowest string: on the other strings this would lead to confusion with the octave harmonic of the string below, which gives a different note, so lozenges are used. The other harmonics are more rare and require distinct notation: composers who require the particularly clear sound of a natural harmonic occasionally indicate the fact in words.

The node which is found at the same place as the stopped fifth above the open string divides the string into three vibrating sections, giving the third note of the harmonic series (a twelfth above the fundamental).

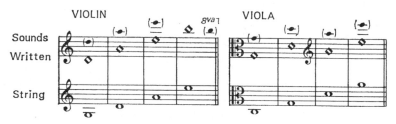

Britten uses this harmonic on the violin in *Les Illuminations* ('Phrase' bars 5–6) and on the viola later in the same work.

Touching the string instead of stopping it at the major third or major sixth position above the open string divides it into five vibrating sections: the area covered has to be very small indeed to gain a clear harmonic with these small string divisions.

A to T¹ = major third A to T² = major sixth T = possible positions of fingers

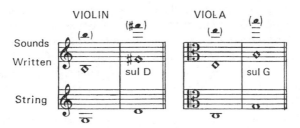

Both ways of writing can be found in Ibert's *Divertissement*, the major third position only in *Les Illuminations*. The end of the first movement of this work also shows how *glissandi* in harmonics can be written with accurate notation for the viola.

sul C

The harmonic a minor third distance from the nut is still more difficult to obtain on the lower strings: it divides the string into sixths, giving the sixth note of the harmonic series (two octaves plus a fifth above the fundamental), and is only normally used on the double-bass.

Other harmonics are theoretically possible, but not dependable enough for musical employment. Interesting experiments may be carried out using the edge of a stiff card to touch the nodes instead of a finger – this gives greater clarity and a wider range of harmonics.

The violinist does not only use the nodes closest to the nut: experienced players know how to find a fifth, quarter, or third of the string from the bridge end, and they will use these nodes if they are already playing in high positions – at the top of arpeggio passages, for instance, as in the second section of Wieniawski's *Scherzo Tarantelle*. Double harmonics may be produced by touching and bowing two strings at the same time: Paganini's 'Witches' Dance' mixes artificial and natural harmonics in double stops, one of the most difficult passages in violin literature to perform successfully.

Artificial harmonics are produced from a stopped string as opposed to an open one. As the finger stopping the string may be moved up and down to vary the string-length and therefore the pitch, they usually employ only one note of the harmonic series, no. 4, the double-octave harmonic. This lies easily under the hand, the fourth finger touching the string at its normal distance away from the stopped first, i.e. a perfect fourth. The length of string from first finger to bridge is caused to vibrate in quarters, and as the first finger moves up the string, shortening it, the fourth has gradually to close in towards the first, because the quarters become progressively smaller. Precisely the same process occurs when stopping octaves with the first and fourth fingers: violinists find that the precision required for selecting the node of a false harmonic provides useful muscular training for playing octaves. The stopped note is indicated normally, the touched node with a hollow lozenge.

Tchaikowsky

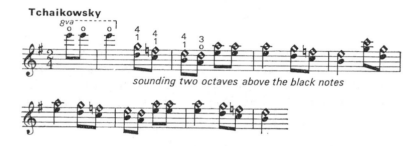

sounding two octaves above the black notes

As the lowest violin note obtainable from this type of artificial harmonic is *a″* flat above the treble stave, and the viola a fifth lower, the third note of the harmonic series is occasionally called for. The fourth finger is extended to touch the node found a fifth above the stopped first finger.

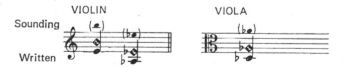

This provides five lower notes, but they are best used when the violinist has plenty of time to find his harmonic, as in the second violin part at the end of the Theme in Britten's Frank Bridge Variations: on the viola the stretch is too large to be convenient.

A narrow vibrato is sometimes used on artificial harmonics. Octaves and harmonics require a similar dexterity in shifting the first finger from note to note to play melodic passages, advanced players being able to produce in false harmonics a complete chromatic range of over $2\frac{1}{2}$ octaves.

Natural harmonics were known in the Middle Ages, when the *tromba marina*, a curious one-stringed instrument playing only harmonics (and fingered between the bow and the bridge), was popular. The bridge of this instrument left one foot free to drum against the table, an effect used by Paganini, who would use a single, over-tightened G string on the E string side of the bridge, leaving the bass foot comparatively free, and thus producing especially powerful harmonics. Mersenne discussed the theory of harmonics in 1636; Mondonville applied natural harmonics to the violin in his sonatas of *c.* 1738; L'Abbé le fils wrote a whole piece in harmonics (1761) and even used them for double stops and trills. Paganini extended the use of double harmonics to what seems the limit of their technical potential, and the French Impressionists, followed by Bartók, Stravinsky, and Britten, made exciting orchestral colours from *tremolo*, *glissando*, and even *pizzicato* harmonics.

The purity of sound of string harmonics makes them unsatisfying to the ear if used for an extended passage: they are mainly reserved as an extra, exotic colour in the composer's palette. Their tone is unvaried, as they lack the upper partials which by their relative intensity give individual timbre to stopped notes. A good violin strongly reinforces most partials, whereas the cylindrical bore of a clarinet, for instance, causes it to reinforce the odd-numbered partials, giving its characteristic tone colour. Timbre varies from note to note on any wind or stringed instrument; there is evidence to suggest that listeners recognise different instruments more by the way in which the sound is initiated than by its continuation. The bow itself can vitally affect the sound; it is not always recognised that each bow, like each violin, produces a different tone-quality.

Rosin, the residuary gum of turpentine after distillation, is used on the bow to provide maximum friction between horsehair and string. The friction causes the string to be pulled aside by the bow until its tension results in a restoring force; this increases as the string is displaced until it becomes greater than the frictional force. Then the string slips back against the pull of the bow until it is so far beyond its position of rest that the bow may grip it again, the friction on the return journey being considerably less (and therefore the speed greater) than when bow and string are moving in the same direction. This repetitive cycle may be varied by the player; if he wishes to produce greater volume, for instance, he increases the force of the bow on the string, causing greater friction and a wider displacement of the string.

The position of the bow on the string affects the strength of the partials and therefore the tone, the preferred point of contact being one-ninth or one-tenth of the vibrating string-length away from the bridge, a position in which dissonant partials are less obtrusive. Other bowing positions are used for special tonal effects, *sul ponticello* (very close to the bridge) emphasising the high harmonics and producing a metallic sound which becomes progressively gentler as the bow moves towards the finger-board and the high partials are made less obtrusive. The width of the bow-hair affects the sound: a wide band of hair tending to eliminate some of the highest harmonics, especially those with nodes lying under the hair. The violinist's fingers on the bow-hand are responsible for conveying to the stick messages regulating all these factors as well as the ratio of pressure and speed of bow which controls the intensity of the sound. The bow may be rotated in the fingers to give a wider or narrower area on the string, and between the extremes of maximum pressure with minimum bow-speed, and minimum pressure with maximum speed, lie an infinite variety of gradations in sound.

The body of a bowed instrument is designed to reinforce the partials, the larger structure of the viola strengthening a quite different set of partials from the violin, which accounts for their difference in tone when playing the same note. A good instrument reinforces the higher harmonics fairly evenly, while a poor one picks out certain lower harmonics, making them unduly strong while the higher ones are too weak. On the G string of the violin, the fundamental tone may actually be weaker than certain upper partials, or even hardly present at all, but the presence of a set of upper partials causes a psycho-physiological phenomenon in that the brain of the listener will supply the missing fundamental, which is 'heard' as having the rather nasal tone expected from half- or three-quarter-sized instruments. No satisfactory explanation has been found for this phenomenon, but it has been put to widespread use in the construction of, for instance, radios with tiny speakers.

The dimensions of the violin have received the closest attention from the old masters, and experimental shapes such as Savart's trapezoid violin (Fig. 8) have never gained acceptance. Taking the measurements of a standard violin to be ideal, therefore, a viola which sounds a fifth lower should have dimensions in the ratio 3:2 to those of the violin. But a 21-inch viola would be too large to hold beneath the chin, and various compromises have had to be made in the construction of both

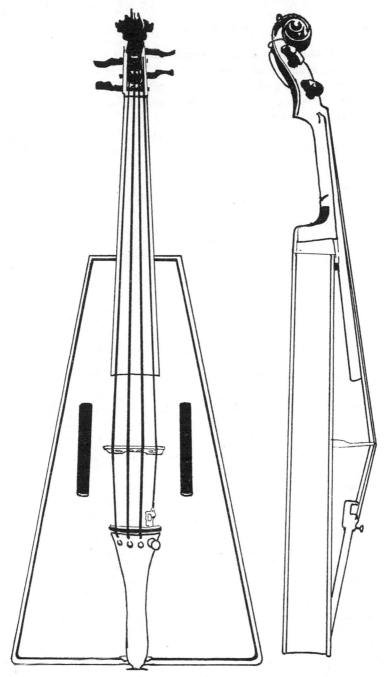

Fig. 8   Savart's trapezoidal violin, one of many unsuccessful attempts to simplify basic violin structure

violas and cellos to allow practical performance – sometimes employing
the phenomenon described above.

Bowed stringed instruments have in common a hollow box which
supports the strings to allow them to vibrate, and distributes these
vibrations to the air in such a way as to give them a satisfactory tone and
volume. Apart from the transverse vibrations of the string which the
player seeks to keep at a maximum by bowing parallel to the bridge,

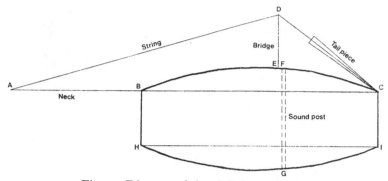

Fig. 9   Diagram of the violin's mechanism

other kinds of string vibration take place which affect the tone. Longitudinal vibrations (which may be isolated by bowing at an acute angle to
the string; they are the cause of the unpleasant sounds resulting from
what children call 'crooked bowing') give additional resonance when
they coincide with the frequencies of transverse harmonics. They are
not conveyed through the bridge to the body of the violin, but through
the joints at B, C, H, and I in Fig. 9).

Transverse vibrations are communicated to the belly by means of the
bridge D E, then to the back by the sound-post F G. The angle A D C
is especially important; a bridge which is too high will over-accentuate
the transverse vibrations, giving a sombre colouring, while one which is
too low can exaggerate the longitudinal vibrations giving a clear, bright
sound which lacks fullness.

The sound-post is situated about 5 mm behind the right foot of the
bridge (the E string side), and allows this foot slight freedom to vibrate;
the other foot, positioned above the bass bar, has far greater freedom.
The high strings depend mainly on the right foot, the low ones on the
left, which allows an even tone to be produced over the entire range of
the instrument. The pine of the belly is more flexible in the transverse
direction than in the direction of the grain. Both bass bar and sound-
post are vital to the tone; their position, dimensions, and rigidity can

dampen or exaggerate vibrations of belly and back. A mute, placed on the bridge, increases its mass, decreasing the transverse vibrations and reducing the amplitude of the upper partials. As certain high partials are affected more than others, a change of timbre as well as a decrease in volume results.

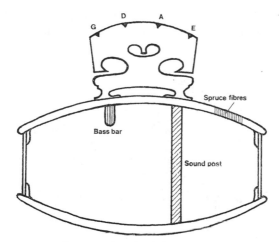

Fig. 10   Section of the violin

Each separate part of a violin – tail-piece, cavity, finger-board, bridge, back, belly, sides, and bass bar – has its own fundamental frequency, and will reinforce corresponding frequencies (Fig. 11). Most of the fundamental frequencies of the violin fall within the most sensitive zone of the human ear. The violin-maker's aim is to reinforce frequencies as evenly as possible, to avoid weak notes and 'wolf' notes (caused by a vibration of excessive amplitude in some part of the instrument coinciding with a stopped note). The firmness with which an instrument is glued together and the damping characteristics of the materials used affect the regularity of tone production; the quantity of air within the box should resonate at about 256 c.p.s. (just below c') but may be altered by an incorrectly fitted sound-post. 'Setting up' a violin requires attention to all these points, and is a job for the most expert craftsman.

Many tests have shown that listeners are unable to distinguish between valuable old instruments and modern ones. The difference seems to be more in the 'feel' of the instrument to the performer, how much direct response he can expect from it, and whether he feels that the contrast and carrying-power is sufficient to convey his musical emotion to the audience. A poor player makes the finest violin sound ordinary, a good one responds to the sensitivity of a fine old instrument and finds a new violin raw and unrewarding, but as Emile Leipp points out:

> The judgement of the player is different from that of the listener, because he hears the instrument from a distance of inches; his opinion only holds good for himself in his particular position.[3]

He concludes that 'sonority contests have shown that the instrumentalist should be eliminated'[4] and produces by means of scientific

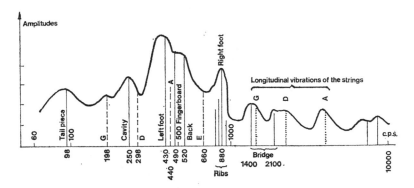

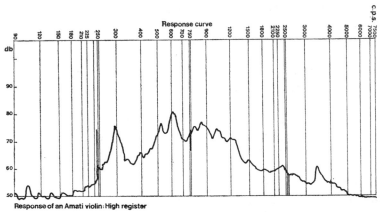

Fig. 11 *Above* The response curve of a violin, determined by the fundamental frequencies of each part of the instrument. Many of these frequencies fall within the sensitive zone of the ear (about 300–3,000 c.p.s.)

Below The response curve of an Amati violin, high register, taken by acoustical spectrograph measurements a method of calculating instrumental quality which may not only tell us which violins will be most sought after in future years for their tonal qualities, but may make instruments with a first-class sound available to the majority of players in future generations.

The strings themselves have undergone consistent revision during the present century. Gut strings, which stretch and are considerably affected by humidity, have sometimes been replaced by metal ones which will not stretch; these tend therefore to change in pitch if too much pressure is applied with the bow. The most modern metal strings have a flexible woven core which allows a certain amount of 'give'; they rival in popularity the strings made from gut or nylon wound with aluminium or silver, which extend like gut but are not much affected by humidity. These seem better suited to old violins, but the time taken for such a string to stabilise or to be 'played in', as the instrumentalist would say, varies from days to weeks. During this time the string stretches and gradually changes in timbre until it reaches its optimum, where it will stabilise; if left on for too long it will 'die' and sound false.

Besides the physical qualities of strings, instruments, and bows, the listener expects and actually enjoys the element of failure arising from the fact that humans, not machines, play stringed instruments. Today it is possible by electro-acoustical means to obtain a performance of, say, one of Mozart's string quartets, which is 'perfect' in the balance of overtones, in intonation, gradation of volume, and rhythmic values. As one might expect, the listener finds it very dull. Not only because the performance loses personal impact, perfection being too far divorced from human reality, but because the ear expects and welcomes slight inaccuracies of intonation as being characteristic of the instrument, and deviations from strict rhythm as being characteristic of the performer.

In fact, it is these deviations which make a 'live' performance, one with emotional impact. Arnold Small's survey (1937) of intonation in string-playing (quoted by Carl Seashore)[5] found a deviation from the tempered scale in over sixty per cent of the notes, preponderantly towards sharpening, and he lists possible reasons for this, including anatomical difficulties, accident, and the use of Pythagorean or natural-scale intonation. Nickerson (quoted by Winckel)[6] found in one experiment using six string quartets that neither the pure nor the tempered scale bore much relation to the performances, the Pythagorean tuning providing the nearest approximation. This tuning by perfect fifths would give a noticeable deviation over the seven octaves of the piano, as the range of frequencies covered by seven octaves is not the same as

that covered by twelve perfect fifths. But over the smaller range of a
violin or viola, where instant adjustments are possible, Pythagorean
tuning tends merely to make major thirds and leading notes high, sub-
dominants low, thus emphasising the tonality. The violinist checks his
intonation when practising by the open strings which are tuned to
Pythagorean fifths, and by double stops in which perfect fourths, fifths,
and octaves are given particular attention; beyond this he has no
absolute standard of pitch, and his sense of intonation becomes as personal as his accent when talking.

Small adjustments of pitch may be made within the vibrato, but a
violinist is almost as unlikely as a singer to be able to claim accurate
intonation according to the natural or tempered scales. 'Just intonation'
has been the subject of treatises over several centuries, and the term is
open to more than one interpretation. But the actual effect upon string-
players has been small: they play 'by ear', and the proposition in Smith's
Harmonics of 1749 will serve as well as any modern dictum for the
guidance of concerted string-players.

> Now the reason why the best performers acquire a habit of
> making perfect harmony is plainly this. When the harmony is made
> perfect they are pleased and satisfied, though the several parts do
> not move by perfect intervals. For the passing from one sound to
> the next, whether by a perfect or an imperfect interval, being nearly
> instantaneous, is almost imperceptible, and therefore is indifferent
> to the performer. But the succeeding consonance is long enough
> held out to give him pleasure or pain, according as he makes it
> perfect or imperfect.[7]

This could be one of the earliest statements of Carl Flesch's 20th-
century theory that the string-player adjusts his intonation directly *after*
the beginning of the note. Probably intonation, like other points of style,
is affected by the fashions of the period: there is some evidence that
during the 20th century, when dissonance has become such a vital part
of the musical language, singers and string-players are adjusting their
intonation to accentuate dissonance, instead of reducing it by tempered
tuning.

	2nd	3rd	4th	5th	6th	7th	8th
(a)	50·0	100·0	125·0	175·0	225·0	275·0	300·0
(b)	51·0	96·6	124·5	175·5	221·1	272·1	300·0
(c)	51·0	102·0	124·5	175·5	226·5	277·5	300·0

(a) is tempered, (b) natural, (c) Pythagorean.

It is possible to compare the intervals of the three principal versions of a major scale by dividing the octave into 300 *savarts*, as demonstrated by Alexander Wood in *The Physics of Music* (above).[8]

There are various indications that the ear hears what it wants to hear, and the question of intonation within groups can become a very vexed one as each instrument carries with it an inherited tradition of intonation which is part of the character of the instrument. An internationally famous orchestra was checked section by section with an oscilloscope after they tuned before a concert, and again after they had been playing for some time.[9] The first violins, cellos, and basses kept approximately to an accurate A throughout, the second violins tuned 2 c.p.s. sharp and stayed there, the oboe started 2 c.p.s. flat and ended in tune. Here we meet with the traditional contradictions of orchestral tuning: the middle parts find their lower open strings flat to the general pitch if their a' strings are in tune, so they tune sharp. The oboe expects the strings to tune sharp, and tends to insist on giving a slightly low a' at first, for them to tune to: this has become traditional too, and the violins tune sharper because they know that the oboe pitch will rise! People have a different interpretation of the pitch of a single note in terms of their own instrument, particularly of a harpsichord or piano a', and the electronic $a' = 440$ installed in some bandrooms is not generally considered a great help. Fortunately, good players possess adaptability of intonation, and in a group which listens to the total harmony the intonation becomes an acceptable compromise. A soloist who feels his tone drowned by the orchestra may sing or play a little sharper than the general pitch, consciously or unconsciously, to make himself heard: only if he over-exaggerates this effect will the audience notice. Flat pitch in a soloist causes discomfort to the listeners, however, although they will often put this down to poor tone rather than low pitch.

Pitch is again tending to rise, particularly on the continent. The standard pitch of $a' = 440$ c.p.s. was agreed by an international conference in 1939; today English orchestras are complaining about the problems of accompanying pianos tuned higher than $a' = 440$ on the continent (even as high as 450 in Germany), and London piano firms keep some instruments tuned to a higher a' for use with visiting continental orchestras. During the 19th and early 20th centuries, pitch became a very complicated problem, especially for wind-players. England seems for a time to have been sharpest of all: G. B. Shaw reported that Costa ordained for the London Philharmonic Society an a' of 452 c.p.s., more than a quarter-tone higher than the French were using. Then Steinway pianos began to be tuned to $a' = 458$ c.p.s. Shaw's imagination and irritation were simultaneously fired by these discrepancies: he asks his reader to

> conceive in your mind's ear a grand international concert in the Albert Hall, with the St. Paul's organ lent for the occasion to reinforce the permanent one, and the band assisted by contingents of players, civil and military, from America and the Continent. Imagine the process of tuning – the Albert Hall organ leading off with an A at concert pitch, the church organ responding, horribly flat, with an A at church pitch, the French and German oboists following a good ten vibrations flatter, the Philharmonic men asserting the dignity of England two-thirds of a semitone sharp, and the Americans and the military coming in with a crash, sharp even to the Philharmonic.[10]

Although pitch was probably equally variable or even more so before 1850, it seems to have varied around a generally lower a' to judge from Praetorius ($a' = 422\cdot5$ in 1751) and the London Philharmonic fork ($a' = 423\cdot3$ in 1820).

One reason for the orchestra's dislike of a pure-toned electronic a' for tuning is that the reiteration of any pure sound is irritating: sounded without a break it becomes positively maddening. This must be a factor encouraging the prevalence of vibrato in musical sounds: sustained notes are made acceptable to the ear by rapid fluctuations of pitch which are often only heard as part of a warm tone-colour. Carl Seashore[11] conducted a research programme into vocal and instrumental vibrato (1932), bringing some surprising facts to light. One of these was the width of pitch deviation (up to a semitone) which is acceptable to the listener as not distorting the basic pitch of the note, another the fact that quality of emotion and type of vibrato are apparently unconnected. The violinist will use the same kinds of vibrato for gay music as for sad music.

Today, vibrato is used on almost every note played by the violin or viola. The finger rocks regularly along the line of the string, causing an alternate sharpening and flattening of the pitch. The advanced performer does not stop the vibrato movement when he changes bow: the modern method of holding the violin with a chin-rest makes an almost continuous vibrato possible. Recording and broadcasting have probably affected speed and width of vibrato cycles in soloists, as a wide, slow vibrato which does not offend in a live performance becomes distractingly obvious through a loudspeaker. The average speed of violin vibrato as measured by Small[12] was $6\cdot5$ cycles per second, the average fluctuation in pitch $0\cdot25$ of a tone – half that of a singer. Extremes of speed were

4·5 and 9·5 cycles. Although writers on violin-playing tend to argue about whether one should vibrato upwards or downwards from the correct pitch, the scientists find that one hears the middle point between the two extremes as the pitch of the note, and it is only the start of the cycle which is affected by the player's determination to vibrato 'upwards' or 'downwards'. Leviste, in _The Rational Technique of Vibrato_,[13] recommends 8 cycles per second as a suitable speed, and it is possible that a more recent survey than Seashore's (1937) would reveal an increase in average speed.

Vibrato in relation to pace, pressure, and position of the bow on the string provides the basis of a performer's individual tone-quality, often significantly affected by personal characteristics. The gentle or shy person tends to use insufficient bow pressure to match the vibrato, the lazy person to have a wide slow movement and the over-intense person to use a narrow, rapid movement. Heifetz[14] recommends contact with players using the opposite type of vibrato to cure extremes of speed, and most teachers today would agree with Galamian[15] that a violinist should ideally be able to use and control both the pitch-range and speed of finger, hand, and arm vibrato.

Sustained sounds are not the sole source of a performer's characteristic tonal qualities, however: the way in which he uses the bow to begin each note is vital to the impression of timbre received by the audience. Indeed, it may be much more vital than we realise. Experiments in which the initial attack was removed from notes played on various instruments have caused considerable confusion among an audience which easily identified the instruments playing complete notes. The end of the note is less vital, although the quality of violin sound may be distinctly altered by lifting the bow (which allows the string to continue resonating, as in bounced bowing), as opposed to leaving it on the string and thus damping the sound immediately. The difference in attack is caused by the time taken for the note to reach its maximum (shortest in _pizzicato_, longest in very _legato_ bowing) and by the amount of audible percussive sound. On the violin, the first two partials develop more slowly than the upper partials.[16]

The alteration in tonal quality caused by placing a mute on the bridge of a stringed instrument is due to the reinforcement of a different set of overtones: the size and shape of the mute making a vast difference to the sound-quality produced. If the mute is too heavy, the bridge will vibrate with difficulty and volume will be considerably reduced: extra heavy mutes are made for practising in hotel rooms or other places where people may be disturbed.

Performing musicians are particularly conscious of the fact that the resonance of a concert-hall may make or mar a performance. Too little resonance is usually considered a worse fault by the performer than too much, although the audience might not agree. It has taken some time for musicians and acoustical experts to agree on this point. London's Royal Festival Hall, given an acoustic considered excellent by the scientists, proved too dry for performers and audiences. The reverberation time was increased by the use of resonators until it could rival the warm acoustic of the most popular concert-halls. Music sounds best with a longer reverberation time than speech, a fact which causes problems for the designers of multi-purpose halls. Some rooms favour the lower instruments, others the higher: a wise violin-buyer chooses a fairly dry acoustic rather than a resonant one in which to test various instruments. Carpets and curtains dampen resonance: so do audiences, so that a performance must often be adjusted to suit the change from rehearsal conditions.

Practising in over-resonant rooms can give the string-player an exaggerated impression of the volume and quality of his tone-production: many a violinist has had recourse to practising in a kitchen or bathroom to cheer himself up after struggling with tone-production problems in an over-furnished sitting-room. Loud practising can become quite over-powering in a resonant room, but the violinist who does not practise loudly loses one of the greatest aids to good intonation: an acoustical phenomenon discovered by Tartini (also by a German organist, Sorge) and sometimes called a 'Tartini note'. It may be heard if a double stop is played loudly, with little vibrato and well in tune. The ear supplies a third note some distance below the two sounded, and investigation of this note proves that its frequency is the difference between the frequencies of the two sounded notes. 'Tartini notes' are, therefore, referred to scientifically as 'difference tones', and the presence of 'summation tones' with frequencies the *sum* of the two sounded notes was noted later. Only the 'difference' or 'resultant' tones are of practical use to the violinist as a method of checking accurate intonation on double stops.

The reader will have noticed that this last 'scientific property of the violin' is in fact a phenomenon of the human ear, and that intonation, timbre, and vibrato cannot be satisfactorily described on a purely scientific level. Music was once considered one of the sciences rather than of the arts, but the performance of music is so highly personalised both from the performer's and the listener's angle, that no amount of research into acoustic and electro-acoustic phenomena is likely to explain or act as a substitute for the string-player's artistry: some 20th-century composers, however, profess to find string-playing too approximate, and have turned to electronics for the sake of the precise control which they can exercise. It remains to be seen whether these compositions, lacking the personal element in performance, will prove as durable as the great string-works in which an element of human failure is not only unavoidable, but welcome.

NOTES

[1] 110 Lloyd, p. 11.
[2] 197 Yates.
[3] 107 Leipp, p. 110.
[4] ibid. p. 111.
[5] 161 Seashore, p. 212.
[6] 192 Winckel, p. 128.
[7] 168 Smith.
[8] 196 Wood.
[9] 192 Winckel.
[10] 164 Shaw, vol. 1.
[11] 162 Seashore.
[12] 161 Seashore, p. 211.
[13] 109 Leviste, p. 3.
[14] 2 Appelbaum, p. 42.
[15] 61 Galamian, p. 37.
[16] 192 Winckel, p. 32.

Bibliography

1. Abele, H., trans. W. Alwyn. *The Violin and its Story.* London, 1905. The Strad Library no. 15.
2. Appelbaum, S. and S. *With the Artists.* New York, 1955. John Marbert & Co.
3. Arts Council of Great Britain. *Report on Orchestral Resources in Great Britain.* London, 1970.
4. Auer, L. *Violin Playing as I teach it* (1921). London, 1960. Duckworth, Hinrichsen.
5. Auer, L. *Graded Course of Violin Playing.* New York, 1925. Carl Fischer.
6. Austin, W. W. *Music in the Twentieth Century.* London, 1966. J. M. Dent & Sons Ltd.
7. Babitz, S. 'Differences between 18th century and modern violin bowing'. March 1957. *The Score.*
8. Bach, C. P. E., trans. W. J. Mitchell. *Essay on the True Art of Playing Keyboard Instruments* (1753). New York, 1949. W. W. Norton & Co. Inc.
9. Bachmann, A. *An Encyclopaedia of the Violin* (1925). New York, 1966. Da Capo Press.
10. Bachmann, W., trans. N. Deane. *The Origins of Bowing.* London, 1969. Oxford University Press.
11. Backus, J. *The Acoustical Foundations of Music.* London, 1970. John Murray.
12. Baines, A. (ed.). *Musical Instruments Through the Ages.* London, 1966. Faber & Faber.
13. Baines, A. *European and American Musical Instruments.* London, 1966. B. T. Batsford Ltd.
14. Barzun, J. *Berlioz and his Century.* London and New York, 1956. Thames & Hudson, Meridian Books.
15. Bazin, G., trans. F. Scarfe. *A Concise History of Art.* London, 1958. Thames & Hudson.
16. Beethoven, L. van, trans. E. Anderson *Letters.* London, 1961. Macmillan & Co. Ltd.
17. Benade, A. H. *Horns, Strings and Harmony.* New York, 1960. Anchor Books, Doubleday & Co.
18. Bériot, C. de, trans. Westbrook and Phipson. *Méthode de Violon* (opus 102, 1858). London, n.d. Schott & Co.
19. Berlioz, L. H., trans. M. C. Clarke. *A Treatise upon Modern Instrumentation and Orchestration.* London, 1858. Novello & Co.
20. Berlioz, L. H., trans. R and E. Holmes. *Autobiography.* London, 1884. Macmillan & Co.

257

21. Boyden, David D. *The History of Violin Playing from its origins to 1761.* London, 1965. O.U.P.

22. Brähmig, B. *Practische Bratschenschule.* Leipzig, before 1887. C. Merseburger.

23. Broadhouse, J. *How to make a Violin.* London, n.d. William Reeves.

24. Bruni, A. B. *Tenor Method.* London, n.d. Augener.

25. Bukofzer, M. F. *Music in the Baroque Era.* London, 1948. J. M. Dent & Sons Ltd.

26. Burney, Dr C. *A General History of Music.* London, 1776.

27. Burney, Dr C., ed. P. Scholes. *Dr Burney's Musical Tours in Europe.* London, 1959. O.U.P.

28. Burney, Dr C., ed. H. E. Poole. *Music, Men and Manners in France and Italy.* London, 1969. Folio Society.

29. Cage, J. *Catalogue of Works.* 1962. Peters Edition.

30. Campagnoli, B. *Metodo per violino* (opus 21, 1797). Milan, 1945. Ricordi.

31. Carse, A. *The Orchestra in the XVIIIth Century.* Cambridge, 1940. W. Heffer & Sons.

32. Carse, A. *The Orchestra from Beethoven to Berlioz.* Cambridge, 1948. W. Heffer & Sons.

33. Collins, G. *Violin teaching in Class.* London, 1962. O.U.P.

34. Copland, A. *Music and Imagination.* Cambridge, Mass., 1952. Harvard University Press.

35. Copperwheat, W. *First Year Viola Method.* London, n.d. Paxton.

36. Courcy, G. I. C. de. *Paganini the Genoese.* Norman, 1957. University of Oklahoma Press.

37. Courvoisier, C. *The Technics of Violin Playing.* London, 1899. The Strad Library no. 1.

38. Crickboom, M. *The Violin.* Brussels, n.d. Schott Frères.

39. Culshaw, J. *A Century of Music.* London, 1952. Dennis Dobson.

40. Dancla, C., trans. W. J. Westbrook. *Violin School.* Brussels, n.d. Schott Frères.

41. David, F. *Violin School 1863.* Leipzig. Breitkopf & Härtel.

42. Demuth, N. *An Anthology of Musical Criticism.* London, 1947. Eyre & Spottiswoode.

43. Demuth, N. *Musical Trends in the Twentieth Century.* London, 1952. Rockliff.

44. *Denkmäler Deutscher Tonkunst.* 65 vols. (D.D.T.) 1892–1931. Wiesbaden and Graz, 1958. Breitkopf & Härtel, Akademische Druck-u. Verlagsanstalt.

45. *Denkmäler der Tonkunst in Österreich,* ed. Adler. (D.T.Ö.). Graz, 1959. Akademische Druck- u. Verlagsanstalt.

46. Deutsch, O. E., trans. Blom, Branscombe, and Noble. *Mozart: a Documentary Biography.* London, 1966. A. & C. Black.

47. Doflein, E. and E., trans. P. Marler. *The Doflein Method.* Mainz, n.d. B. Schott's Söhne.

48. Donington, R. 'James Talbot's Manuscript (Christ Church Library Music 1187).' *Galpin Society Journal,* III. March 1950.

49. Donington, R. *The Interpretation of Early Music*. London, 1963. Faber & Faber.

50. Dounis, D. C. *The Artist's Technique of Violin Playing*. New York, 1921. Carl Fischer Inc.

51. Elkin, R. *Old Concert Rooms of London*. London, 1955. Edwin Arnold.

52. Evelyn, J., ed. E. S. de Beer. *Diary*. Oxford, 1955. O.U.P.

53. Ewen, D. *The World of Twentieth Century Music*. London, 1969. Robert Hale.

54. Farga, F., trans. E. Larsen. *Violins and Violinists*. London, 1950. Rockliff.

55. Fétis, F. J., trans. Bishop. *Notice of Anthony Stradivari*. London, 1864. William Reeves.

56. Flesch, C., trans. H. Keller. *Memoirs*. London, 1957. Rockliff.

57. Flesch, C., trans. F. H. Martens. *The Art of Violin Playing*. New York, n.d. Carl Fischer Inc.

58. Flesch, C., trans. B. Schwarz. *Violin Fingering, its theory and practice*. London, 1966. Barrie & Rockliff.

59. Forsyth, C. *Orchestration*. London, 1963. Macmillan & Co.

60. Gal, II. (ed.). *The Musician's World: Great Composers in their Letters*. London, 1965. Thames & Hudson.

61. Galamian, I. *Principles of Violin Playing and Teaching*. London, 1962. Faber & Faber.

62. Galamian, I. and Neumann, F. *Contemporary Violin Technique*. New York, 1963, 1966. Galaxy Music Corp.

63. *Galpin Society Journal*, see Donington, R.

64. Geiringer, K. *Musical Instruments: their history from the stone age to the present day*. London, 1949. George Allen & Unwin.

65. Geminiani, Facsimile ed. D. Boyden. *The Art of Playing on the Violin* (1731). London, 1952. O.U.P.

66. George, M. D. *London Life in the Eighteenth Century*. London, 1966. Penguin Books.

67. Goodban, T. *A New and Complete Guide to the Art of Playing on the Violin*. London, 1810. Preston in the Strand.

68. Guest, I. *The Dancer's Heritage: a Short History of Ballet*. London, 1962. Pelican Books.

69. Guhr, C., trans. S. Novello. *Paganini's Art of Playing the Violin*. London, n.d. Novello & Co.

70. Gulbenkian Foundation. *Making Musicians: a report to the Calouste Gulbenkian Foundation*. London, 1965.

71. Hamma, W. *Italian Violin Makers*. Stuttgart, 1964. Schuler Verlagsgesellschaft MBH.

72. Hanslick, E., trans. H. Pleasants. *Music Criticisms 1846–99*. London, 1963. Penguin Books.

73. Hart, G. *The Violin: its famous makers and their imitators*. London, 1875. Duhlau & Co., Schott & Co.

74. Havas, K. *The Violin and I*. London, 1968. Bosworth.

75. Havas, K. *The 12 Lesson Course in a New Approach to Violin Playing*. London, 1964. Bosworth.

76. Hawkins, Sir J. *A General History of the Science and Practice of Music*. London, 1776.
77. Haydn, F. J., ed. Robbins Landon. *Collected Correspondence and London Notebooks*. London, 1959. Barrie & Rockliff.
78. Hayes, G. *Musical Instruments and their Music 1500–1750*. 2 vols. London, 1928, 1930. O.U.P.
79. Helmholtz, H. L. F., trans. A. J. Ellis. *On the Sensations of Tone* (1875). New York, 1954. Longmans, Green & Co.
80. Henley, W. *Dictionary of Violin and Bow Makers*. Brighton, 1959. Amati Publishing Ltd.
81. Hermann, F. *The Study of the Viola*. London, n.d. Augener & Co.
82. Heron-Allen, E. *Violin Making as it was and is*. London, 1885. Ward Locke & Co.
83. Hill, R. (ed.). *The Concerto*. London, 1952. Pelican Books.
84. Hill, W. H., A. F., and A. E. *Antonio Stradivari* (1902). New York, 1963. Dover Publications.
85. Hill, W. H., A. F., and A. E. *The Violin-makers of the Guarneri Family*. London, 1965. Holland Press Ltd.
86. Hindemith, P. *A Composer's World*. Cambridge, Mass., 1952. Harvard University Press.
87. Hindemith, P. *Elementary Training for Musicians*. London, 1949. Schott & Co.
88. Hodgson, P. *A New Violin Method for Beginners*. London, n.d. Hawkes & Son.
89. Hodgson, P. *Motion Study and Violin Bowing* (1934). Urbana, Illinois, 1958. American String Teachers' Association.
90. Hutchings, A. J. B. *The Baroque Concerto*. London, 1961. Faber & Faber.
91. Jacobsen, M. *The Mastery of Violin Playing*. London, 1957. Hawkes & Son.
92. Jalovec, K., trans. G. Theiner. *German and Austrian Violin Makers*. London, 1967. Paul Hamlyn.
93. Jalovec, K. *Italian Violin Makers*. London, n.d. Anglo-Italian Publications Ltd.
94. Jalovec, K., trans. J. B. Kozák. *Beautiful Italian Violins*. London, 1963. Paul Hamlyn.
95. Jeans, Sir J. H. *Science and Music*. Cambridge, 1937. Cambridge University Press.
96. Joachim, J., trans. Bickley. *Letters to and from Joseph Joachim*. London, 1914. Macmillan & Co.
97. Joachim, J. and Moser, A. *Violin School*. Berlin, 1905. Simrock.
98. Kinsky, G. (ed.). *A History of Music in Pictures*. London, 1930. J. M. Dent & Sons Ltd.
99. Klingenfeld, H. *Viola School for Violin-Players*. [Leipzig], 1897. Breitkopf & Härtel.
100. Knocker. E. *Violinist's Vade Mecum*. London and New York, 1952. Curwen & Sons, G. Schirmer Inc.
101. Krasner, L. (Chairman) (Tanglewood Symposia). *String Problems: Players and Paucity*. Boston, 1964. Boston Symphony Orchestra.

102. L'Abbé le fils (J.-B. Saint-Sevin). Facsimile reprint. *Principles du violon* (Paris, 1761). Paris, 1961. Centre de Documentation Universitaire.
103. Lafontaine, H. C. De. *The King's Musick*. London, 1909. Novello & Co.
104. La Laurencie, L. de. *L'École Française de Violon*. Paris, 1922. Librairie Delagrave.
105. Lang, P. H. *Music in Western Civilisation*. London, 1942. J. M. Dent & Sons Ltd.
106. Lang, P. H. and Broder, N. *Contemporary Music in Europe*. London, 1966. J. M. Dent & Sons Ltd.
107. Leipp, E., trans. H. W. Parry. *The Violin*. London and Toronto, 1969, 1971. University of Toronto Press, O.U.P.
108. Leland. *The Dounis Principles of Violin Playing*. London, 1949. The Strad.
109. Leviste, R. *The Rational Technique of Vibrato*. London, 1951. Bosworth.
110. Lloyd, L. S. *Music and Sound*. London, 1937. O.U.P.
111. Lowery, H. *A Guide to Musica Acoustics*. London, 1956. Dennis Dobson.
112. Lütgendorff, W. L. F. v. *Die Geigen und Lautenmacher*. Frankfurt am Main, 1922. Frankfurter Verlags Anstalt A.G.
113. Mace, T. Facsimile reprint. *Musick's Monument* (1676). Paris, 1958. Editions du Centre Nationale de la Recherche Scientifique.
114. Mackay, N. *A Modern Viola Method*. London, n.d. O.U.P.
115. Mattheson, J. *Das Neu-eröffnete Orchestre*. Hamburg, 1713.
116. Mayer, D. M. *The Forgotten Master: the Life and Times of L. Spohr*. London, 1959. Weidenfeld & Nicolson.
117. Mersenne, M., trans. R. E. Chapman. *Harmonie Universelle* (1636), the books on instruments. The Hague, 1957. Martinus Nijhoff.
118. Middlemiss, J. Unpubl. Letter 'to all interested in Suzuki Method'. Talent Education Institute, Matsumoto-Shi, Japan.
119. Morley, T., ed. A. Harman. *A Plain and Easy Introduction to Practical Music* (1597). London, 1963. J. M. Dent & Sons Ltd.
120. Morris, Rev. W. M. *British Violin Makers*. London, 1904. Chatto & Windus.
121. Moser, A., trans. L. Durham. *Joseph Joachim – A Biography*. London, 1901. Philip Wellby.
122. Mozart, J. C. W. A., trans. E. Anderson. *Letters*. London, 1966. Macmillan & Co.
123. Mozart, L., trans. E. Knocker. *A Treatise on the Fundamental Principles of Violin Playing* (1756). London, 1948. O.U.P.
124. Myers, R. *Twentieth Century Music*. London, 1960. John Calder.
125. Nelson, S. M. *The Violin Family*. London, 1964. Dennis Dobson.
126. Nettel, R. *The Orchestra in England*. London, 1945. Jonathan Cape.
127. Newman, W. S. *The Sonata in the Baroque Era*. Chapel Hill, 1959. University of North Carolina Press.
128. North, R., ed. Jessopp. *Autobiography* (1695). London, 1887. D. Nutt.

129. North, R., ed. J. Wilson. *Roger North on Music*. London, 1959. Novello & Co.

130. North, R., ed. H. Andrews. *The Musicall Gramarian (c.* 1726). London, 1926. O.U.P.

131. Otto, J. A. *A Treatise on the Structure and Preservation of the Violin*. London, n.d. William Reeves.

132. Parke, W. T. *Musical Memoirs*. London, 1830. Colburn & Bentley. Peacock Report, *see* 'Arts Council of Great Britain'.

133. Pepys, S. *Diaries*.

134. Phipson, T. L. *Famous Violinists and Fine Violins*. London, 1896. Chatto & Windus.

135. Pincherle, M., trans. C. Hatch. *Vivaldi, Genius of the Baroque*. London, 1958. Gollancz.

136. Pincherle, M. *An Illustrated History of Music*. London, 1960. Macmillan & Co.

137. Playford, J. Facsimile. *An Introduction to the Skill of Music* (1674). Ridgewood, New Jersey, 1966. Gregg Press Inc.

138. Polnauer, Dr F. E. and Marks, Dr M. *Senso-Motor Study and its application to Violin Playing*. Urbana, Illinois, 1964. American String Teachers' Association.

139. Poznanski, I. B. *The Violin and Bow*. London, 1894. St Cecilia Music Publishing Co. Ltd.

140. Prelleur, P. Facsimile reprint. *The Modern Musick-Master* (1731). Cassel, 1965. Bärenreiter.

141. Primrose, W. *Technique is Memory: a Method for Violin and Viola Players*. London, 1960. O.U.P.

142. Pulver, J. *Paganini*. London, 1936. Herbert Joseph Ltd.

143. Purcell, H. *Note to 1st set of Trio Sonatas*. London, 1683.

144. Quantz, J. J., trans. Reilly. *On Playing the Flute* (1752). London, 1966. Faber & Faber.

145. Read, G. *Thesaurus of Orchestra Devices*. London, 1953. Sir Isaac Pitman & Sons Ltd.

146. Rees, C. B. *One Hundred Years of the Hallé*. London, 1957. MacGibbon & Kee.

147. Retford, W. C. *Bows and Bowmakers*. London, 1964. The Strad.

148. Richardson, E. G. *The Acoustics of Orchestral Instruments and of the Organ*. London, 1929. Edward Arnold & Co.

149. Robbins Landon, H. C. *Beethoven*. London, 1970. Thames & Hudson.

150. Roda, J. *Bows for Musical Instruments of the Violin Family*. Illinois, 1959. William Lewis & Sons.

151. Rode, Baillot, Kreutzer. *Method of Instruction for the Violin*. London, n.d. Boosey & Co.

152. Rousseau, J. J., trans. W. Waring. *Dictionary of Music*. London, 1782. J. French.

153. Rowen, R. H. *Early Chamber Music*. New York, 1949. King's Crown Press, Columbia University Press.

154. Saint-George, H. *The Bow, its history, manufacture and use*. London, 1896. The Strad Library, no. 111.

155. Saint-Sevin, J. B. *see* L'Abbé le fils.
156. Sammons, A. *The Secret of Technique in Violin Playing.* London, n.d. Hawkes & Son.
157. Sandys and Forster. *History of the Violin* (1864). London. William Reeves.
158. Schlesinger, K. *Instruments of the Orchestra and Precursors of the Violin Family.* London, 1910. William Reeves.
159. Schmidt-Görg, J. and Schmidt, H. (eds.). *Ludwig van Beethoven.* London, 1970. Pall Mall Press.
160. Scholes, P. *The Mirror of Music 1844–1944.* London, 1947. Novello & O.U.P.
161. Seashore, C. E. *The Psychology of Music* (1938). New York, 1967. Dover Publications.
162. Seashore, C. E. *The Vibrato.* Ames, 1932. Iowa State University Press.
163. Shaw, G. B., collected and ed. D. H. Laurence. *How to become a Music Critic.* London, 1960. Hart-Davis.
164. Shaw, G. B. *Music in London 1890–94.* London, 1931. Constable & Co. Ltd.
165. Simpson, C. Facsimile of 2nd ed. *The Division Viol* (1659). London, 1955. J. Curwen & Sons Ltd.
166. Sitt, H. *Practical Viola School.* Leipzig, n.d. C. F. Peters.
167. Smart, Sir G., ed. H. B. and C. L. E. Cox. *Leaves from the Journals of Sir George Smart.* London, 1907. Longmans, Green & Co.
168. Smith, R. *Harmonics.* London, 1749.
169. Spohr, L., trans. and ed. H. Pleasants. *The Musical Journeys of Louis Spohr.* Norman, 1961. University of Oklahoma Press.
170. Spohr, L., trans. C. Rudolphus. *Violin School* (1831). London. Edwin Ashdown.
171. Stainer, C. *A Dictionary of Violin Makers.* London, n.d. Novello & Co.
172. Steinhausen, F. A. *Die Physiologie der Bogenführung.* Leipzig, 1907. Breitkopf & Härtel.
173. Straeten, E. van der. *The Romance of the Fiddle.* London, 1911. Rebman Ltd.
174. Straeten, E. van der. *History of the Violin.* London, 1933. Cassell & Co. Ltd.
175. Strunk, O. *Source Readings in Musical History.* New York, 1950. W. W. Norton.
176. Suzuki, S. *Nurtured by Love.* New York, 1969. Exposition Press.
177. Szigeti, J. *With Strings Attached.* London, 1949. Cassell & Co. Ltd.
178. Szigeti, J. *Szigeti on the Violin.* London, 1969. Cassell & Co. Ltd. Tanglewood String Symposia 1963 and 1964, *see* Krasner.
179. Tartini, G., trans. Dr Burney (1771). *A Letter from the Late Signor Tartini (Padua, 5 March 1760) to Signora Maddalena Lombardini.* Reprint of 2nd ed. London, 1913.
180. Tartini, G., trans. S. Babitz. *Treatise on the Ornaments of Music.* Reprinted from *Journal of Research in Music Education*, IV, no. 2. Distrib. by Carl Fischer Inc.

181. Taylor, C. A. *The Physics of Musical Sounds*. London, 1965. English Universities Press.
182. Terry, C. S. *Bach's Orchestra*. London, 1932. O.U.P.
183. Tertis, L. *Cinderella No More*. London, 1953. Peter Nevill.
184. Thigpen, H. C. and Cleckley, H. *The Three Faces of Eve*. London, 1957. Secker & Warburg.
185. *The Times Educational Supplement*. 23 January 1970.
186. Thomson, G. S. *The Russells in Bloomsbury*. London, 1940. Jonathan Cape.
187. Tours, B., ed. B. Shore. *The Viola*. London, n.d. Novello & Co.
188. Trendelenburg, W. *Die natuerlichen Grundlagen der Kunst Streichinstrumentenspiels*. Berlin, 1925. Springer.
189. Ulrich, H. *Chamber Music: the Growth and Practice of an intimate art*. New York, 1948. Columbia University Press.
190. Veinus, A. *The Concerto*. New York, 1964. Dover Publications.
191. Wagner, R., trans. E. Dannreuther. *On Conducting*. London, 1919. William Reeves.
192. Winckel, F. trans. Binkley. *Music, Sound and Sensation*. New York, 1967. Dover Publications.
193. Winternitz, E. *Musical Instruments of the Western World*. London, 1966. Thames & Hudson.
194. Winternitz, E. *Gaudenzio Ferrari: his school and the early history of the violin*. 1967. Varallo Sesia.
195. Winternitz, E. *Musical Instruments and their Symbolism in Western Art*. London, 1967. Faber & Faber.
196. Wood, A. *The Physics of Music*. London, 1944. Methuen & Co.
197. Yates, P. *Twentieth Century Music*. London, 1967. George Allen & Unwin.
198. Young, P. M. *A History of British Music*. London, 1967. Ernest Benn Ltd.
199. Young, P. M. *The Concert Tradition*. London, 1965. Routledge & Kegan Paul.

Index

A CATALOG OF SELECTED
DOVER BOOKS
IN ALL FIELDS OF INTEREST

A CATALOG OF SELECTED DOVER
BOOKS IN ALL FIELDS OF INTEREST

CONCERNING THE SPIRITUAL IN ART, Wassily Kandinsky. Pioneering work by father of abstract art. Thoughts on color theory, nature of art. Analysis of earlier masters. 12 illustrations. 80pp. of text. 5⅜ x 8½. 23411-8

ANIMALS: 1,419 Copyright-Free Illustrations of Mammals, Birds, Fish, Insects, etc., Jim Harter (ed.). Clear wood engravings present, in extremely lifelike poses, over 1,000 species of animals. One of the most extensive pictorial sourcebooks of its kind. Captions. Index. 284pp. 9 x 12. 23766-4

CELTIC ART: The Methods of Construction, George Bain. Simple geometric techniques for making Celtic interlacements, spirals, Kells-type initials, animals, humans, etc. Over 500 illustrations. 160pp. 9 x 12. (Available in U.S. only.) 22923-8

AN ATLAS OF ANATOMY FOR ARTISTS, Fritz Schider. Most thorough reference work on art anatomy in the world. Hundreds of illustrations, including selections from works by Vesalius, Leonardo, Goya, Ingres, Michelangelo, others. 593 illustrations. 192pp. 7⅛ x 10¼. 20241-0

CELTIC HAND STROKE-BY-STROKE (Irish Half-Uncial from "The Book of Kells"): An Arthur Baker Calligraphy Manual, Arthur Baker. Complete guide to creating each letter of the alphabet in distinctive Celtic manner. Covers hand position, strokes, pens, inks, paper, more. Illustrated. 48pp. 8¼ x 11. 24336-2

EASY ORIGAMI, John Montroll. Charming collection of 32 projects (hat, cup, pelican, piano, swan, many more) specially designed for the novice origami hobbyist. Clearly illustrated easy-to-follow instructions insure that even beginning papercrafters will achieve successful results. 48pp. 8¼ x 11. 27298-2

THE COMPLETE BOOK OF BIRDHOUSE CONSTRUCTION FOR WOODWORKERS, Scott D. Campbell. Detailed instructions, illustrations, tables. Also data on bird habitat and instinct patterns. Bibliography. 3 tables. 63 illustrations in 15 figures. 48pp. 5¼ x 8½. 24407-5

BLOOMINGDALE'S ILLUSTRATED 1886 CATALOG: Fashions, Dry Goods and Housewares, Bloomingdale Brothers. Famed merchants' extremely rare catalog depicting about 1,700 products: clothing, housewares, firearms, dry goods, jewelry, more. Invaluable for dating, identifying vintage items. Also, copyright-free graphics for artists, designers. Co-published with Henry Ford Museum & Greenfield Village. 160pp. 8¼ x 11. 25780-0

HISTORIC COSTUME IN PICTURES, Braun & Schneider. Over 1,450 costumed figures in clearly detailed engravings–from dawn of civilization to end of 19th century. Captions. Many folk costumes. 256pp. 8⅜ x 11¾. 23150-X

STICKLEY CRAFTSMAN FURNITURE CATALOGS, Gustav Stickley and L. & J. G. Stickley. Beautiful, functional furniture in two authentic catalogs from 1910. 594 illustrations, including 277 photos, show settles, rockers, armchairs, reclining chairs, bookcases, desks, tables. 183pp. 6½ x 9¼. 23838-5

AMERICAN LOCOMOTIVES IN HISTORIC PHOTOGRAPHS: 1858 to 1949, Ron Ziel (ed.). A rare collection of 126 meticulously detailed official photographs, called "builder portraits," of American locomotives that majestically chronicle the rise of steam locomotive power in America. Introduction. Detailed captions. xi+ 129pp. 9 x 12. 27393-8

AMERICA'S LIGHTHOUSES: An Illustrated History, Francis Ross Holland, Jr. Delightfully written, profusely illustrated fact-filled survey of over 200 American lighthouses since 1716. History, anecdotes, technological advances, more. 240pp. 8 x 10¾. 25576-X

TOWARDS A NEW ARCHITECTURE, Le Corbusier. Pioneering manifesto by founder of "International School." Technical and aesthetic theories, views of industry, economics, relation of form to function, "mass-production split" and much more. Profusely illustrated. 320pp. 6⅛ x 9¼. (Available in U.S. only.) 25023-7

HOW THE OTHER HALF LIVES, Jacob Riis. Famous journalistic record, exposing poverty and degradation of New York slums around 1900, by major social reformer. 100 striking and influential photographs. 233pp. 10 x 7⅞. 22012-5

FRUIT KEY AND TWIG KEY TO TREES AND SHRUBS, William M. Harlow. One of the handiest and most widely used identification aids. Fruit key covers 120 deciduous and evergreen species; twig key 160 deciduous species. Easily used. Over 300 photographs. 126pp. 5⅜ x 8½. 20511-8

COMMON BIRD SONGS, Dr. Donald J. Borror. Songs of 60 most common U.S. birds: robins, sparrows, cardinals, bluejays, finches, more—arranged in order of increasing complexity. Up to 9 variations of songs of each species. Cassette and manual 99911-4

ORCHIDS AS HOUSE PLANTS, Rebecca Tyson Northen. Grow cattleyas and many other kinds of orchids—in a window, in a case, or under artificial light. 63 illustrations. 148pp. 5⅜ x 8½. 23261-1

MONSTER MAZES, Dave Phillips. Masterful mazes at four levels of difficulty. Avoid deadly perils and evil creatures to find magical treasures. Solutions for all 32 exciting illustrated puzzles. 48pp. 8¼ x 11. 26005-4

MOZART'S DON GIOVANNI (DOVER OPERA LIBRETTO SERIES), Wolfgang Amadeus Mozart. Introduced and translated by Ellen H. Bleiler. Standard Italian libretto, with complete English translation. Convenient and thoroughly portable—an ideal companion for reading along with a recording or the performance itself. Introduction. List of characters. Plot summary. 121pp. 5¼ x 8½. 24944-1

TECHNICAL MANUAL AND DICTIONARY OF CLASSICAL BALLET, Gail Grant. Defines, explains, comments on steps, movements, poses and concepts. 15-page pictorial section. Basic book for student, viewer. 127pp. 5⅜ x 8½. 21843-0

THE CLARINET AND CLARINET PLAYING, David Pino. Lively, comprehensive work features suggestions about technique, musicianship, and musical interpretation, as well as guidelines for teaching, making your own reeds, and preparing for public performance. Includes an intriguing look at clarinet history. "A godsend," *The Clarinet,* Journal of the International Clarinet Society. Appendixes. 7 illus. 320pp. 5⅜ x 8½. 40270-3

HOLLYWOOD GLAMOR PORTRAITS, John Kobal (ed.). 145 photos from 1926-49. Harlow, Gable, Bogart, Bacall; 94 stars in all. Full background on photographers, technical aspects. 160pp. 8⅜ x 11¼. 23352-9

THE ANNOTATED CASEY AT THE BAT: A Collection of Ballads about the Mighty Casey/Third, Revised Edition, Martin Gardner (ed.). Amusing sequels and parodies of one of America's best-loved poems: Casey's Revenge, Why Casey Whiffed, Casey's Sister at the Bat, others. 256pp. 5⅜ x 8½. 28598-7

THE RAVEN AND OTHER FAVORITE POEMS, Edgar Allan Poe. Over 40 of the author's most memorable poems: "The Bells," "Ulalume," "Israfel," "To Helen," "The Conqueror Worm," "Eldorado," "Annabel Lee," many more. Alphabetic lists of titles and first lines. 64pp. 5$\frac{3}{16}$ x 8¼. 26685-0

PERSONAL MEMOIRS OF U. S. GRANT, Ulysses Simpson Grant. Intelligent, deeply moving firsthand account of Civil War campaigns, considered by many the finest military memoirs ever written. Includes letters, historic photographs, maps and more. 528pp. 6⅛ x 9¼. 28587-1

ANCIENT EGYPTIAN MATERIALS AND INDUSTRIES, A. Lucas and J. Harris. Fascinating, comprehensive, thoroughly documented text describes this ancient civilization's vast resources and the processes that incorporated them in daily life, including the use of animal products, building materials, cosmetics, perfumes and incense, fibers, glazed ware, glass and its manufacture, materials used in the mummification process, and much more. 544pp. 6⅛ x 9¼. (Available in U.S. only.) 40446-3

RUSSIAN STORIES/RUSSKIE RASSKAZY: A Dual-Language Book, edited by Gleb Struve. Twelve tales by such masters as Chekhov, Tolstoy, Dostoevsky, Pushkin, others. Excellent word-for-word English translations on facing pages, plus teaching and study aids, Russian/English vocabulary, biographical/critical introductions, more. 416pp. 5⅜ x 8½. 26244-8

PHILADELPHIA THEN AND NOW: 60 Sites Photographed in the Past and Present, Kenneth Finkel and Susan Oyama. Rare photographs of City Hall, Logan Square, Independence Hall, Betsy Ross House, other landmarks juxtaposed with contemporary views. Captures changing face of historic city. Introduction. Captions. 128pp. 8¼ x 11. 25790-8

AIA ARCHITECTURAL GUIDE TO NASSAU AND SUFFOLK COUNTIES, LONG ISLAND, The American Institute of Architects, Long Island Chapter, and the Society for the Preservation of Long Island Antiquities. Comprehensive, well-researched and generously illustrated volume brings to life over three centuries of Long Island's great architectural heritage. More than 240 photographs with authoritative, extensively detailed captions. 176pp. 8¼ x 11. 26946-9

NORTH AMERICAN INDIAN LIFE: Customs and Traditions of 23 Tribes, Elsie Clews Parsons (ed.). 27 fictionalized essays by noted anthropologists examine religion, customs, government, additional facets of life among the Winnebago, Crow, Zuni, Eskimo, other tribes. 480pp. 6⅛ x 9¼. 27377-6

FRANK LLOYD WRIGHT'S DANA HOUSE, Donald Hoffmann. Pictorial essay of residential masterpiece with over 160 interior and exterior photos, plans, elevations, sketches and studies. 128pp. 9¼ x 10¾.   29120-0

THE MALE AND FEMALE FIGURE IN MOTION: 60 Classic Photographic Sequences, Eadweard Muybridge. 60 true-action photographs of men and women walking, running, climbing, bending, turning, etc., reproduced from rare 19th-century masterpiece. vi + 121pp. 9 x 12.   24745-7

1001 QUESTIONS ANSWERED ABOUT THE SEASHORE, N. J. Berrill and Jacquelyn Berrill. Queries answered about dolphins, sea snails, sponges, starfish, fishes, shore birds, many others. Covers appearance, breeding, growth, feeding, much more. 305pp. 5¼ x 8¼.   23366-9

ATTRACTING BIRDS TO YOUR YARD, William J. Weber. Easy-to-follow guide offers advice on how to attract the greatest diversity of birds: birdhouses, feeders, water and waterers, much more. 96pp. 5³⁄₁₆ x 8¼.   28927-3

MEDICINAL AND OTHER USES OF NORTH AMERICAN PLANTS: A Historical Survey with Special Reference to the Eastern Indian Tribes, Charlotte Erichsen-Brown. Chronological historical citations document 500 years of usage of plants, trees, shrubs native to eastern Canada, northeastern U.S. Also complete identifying information. 343 illustrations. 544pp. 6½ x 9¼.   25951-X

STORYBOOK MAZES, Dave Phillips. 23 stories and mazes on two-page spreads: Wizard of Oz, Treasure Island, Robin Hood, etc. Solutions. 64pp. 8¼ x 11.   23628-5

AMERICAN NEGRO SONGS: 230 Folk Songs and Spirituals, Religious and Secular, John W. Work. This authoritative study traces the African influences of songs sung and played by black Americans at work, in church, and as entertainment. The author discusses the lyric significance of such songs as "Swing Low, Sweet Chariot," "John Henry," and others and offers the words and music for 230 songs. Bibliography. Index of Song Titles. 272pp. 6½ x 9¼.   40271-1

MOVIE-STAR PORTRAITS OF THE FORTIES, John Kobal (ed.). 163 glamor, studio photos of 106 stars of the 1940s: Rita Hayworth, Ava Gardner, Marlon Brando, Clark Gable, many more. 176pp. 8⅜ x 11¼.   23546-7

BENCHLEY LOST AND FOUND, Robert Benchley. Finest humor from early 30s, about pet peeves, child psychologists, post office and others. Mostly unavailable elsewhere. 73 illustrations by Peter Arno and others. 183pp. 5⅜ x 8½.   22410-4

YEKL and THE IMPORTED BRIDEGROOM AND OTHER STORIES OF YIDDISH NEW YORK, Abraham Cahan. Film Hester Street based on *Yekl* (1896). Novel, other stories among first about Jewish immigrants on N.Y.'s East Side. 240pp. 5⅜ x 8½.   22427-9

SELECTED POEMS, Walt Whitman. Generous sampling from *Leaves of Grass*. Twenty-four poems include "I Hear America Singing," "Song of the Open Road," "I Sing the Body Electric," "When Lilacs Last in the Dooryard Bloom'd," "O Captain! My Captain!"—all reprinted from an authoritative edition. Lists of titles and first lines. 128pp. 5³⁄₁₆ x 8¼.   26878-0

THE BEST TALES OF HOFFMANN, E. T. A. Hoffmann. 10 of Hoffmann's most important stories: "Nutcracker and the King of Mice," "The Golden Flowerpot," etc. 458pp. 5⅜ x 8½. 21793-0

FROM FETISH TO GOD IN ANCIENT EGYPT, E. A. Wallis Budge. Rich detailed survey of Egyptian conception of "God" and gods, magic, cult of animals, Osiris, more. Also, superb English translations of hymns and legends. 240 illustrations. 545pp. 5⅜ x 8½. 25803-3

FRENCH STORIES/CONTES FRANÇAIS: A Dual-Language Book, Wallace Fowlie. Ten stories by French masters, Voltaire to Camus: "Micromegas" by Voltaire; "The Atheist's Mass" by Balzac; "Minuet" by de Maupassant; "The Guest" by Camus, six more. Excellent English translations on facing pages. Also French-English vocabulary list, exercises, more. 352pp. 5⅜ x 8½. 26443-2

CHICAGO AT THE TURN OF THE CENTURY IN PHOTOGRAPHS: 122 Historic Views from the Collections of the Chicago Historical Society, Larry A. Viskochil. Rare large-format prints offer detailed views of City Hall, State Street, the Loop, Hull House, Union Station, many other landmarks, circa 1904-1913. Introduction. Captions. Maps. 144pp. 9⅜ x 12¼. 24656-6

OLD BROOKLYN IN EARLY PHOTOGRAPHS, 1865-1929, William Lee Younger. Luna Park, Gravesend race track, construction of Grand Army Plaza, moving of Hotel Brighton, etc. 157 previously unpublished photographs. 165pp. 8⅞ x 11¾. 23587-4

THE MYTHS OF THE NORTH AMERICAN INDIANS, Lewis Spence. Rich anthology of the myths and legends of the Algonquins, Iroquois, Pawnees and Sioux, prefaced by an extensive historical and ethnological commentary. 36 illustrations. 480pp. 5⅜ x 8½. 25967-6

AN ENCYCLOPEDIA OF BATTLES: Accounts of Over 1,560 Battles from 1479 B.C. to the Present, David Eggenberger. Essential details of every major battle in recorded history from the first battle of Megiddo in 1479 B.C. to Grenada in 1984. List of Battle Maps. New Appendix covering the years 1967-1984. Index. 99 illustrations. 544pp. 6½ x 9¼. 24913-1

SAILING ALONE AROUND THE WORLD, Captain Joshua Slocum. First man to sail around the world, alone, in small boat. One of great feats of seamanship told in delightful manner. 67 illustrations. 294pp. 5⅜ x 8½. 20326-3

ANARCHISM AND OTHER ESSAYS, Emma Goldman. Powerful, penetrating, prophetic essays on direct action, role of minorities, prison reform, puritan hypocrisy, violence, etc. 271pp. 5⅜ x 8½. 22484-8

MYTHS OF THE HINDUS AND BUDDHISTS, Ananda K. Coomaraswamy and Sister Nivedita. Great stories of the epics; deeds of Krishna, Shiva, taken from puranas, Vedas, folk tales; etc. 32 illustrations. 400pp. 5⅜ x 8½. 21759-0

THE TRAUMA OF BIRTH, Otto Rank. Rank's controversial thesis that anxiety neurosis is caused by profound psychological trauma which occurs at birth. 256pp. 5⅜ x 8½. 27974-X

A THEOLOGICO-POLITICAL TREATISE, Benedict Spinoza. Also contains unfinished Political Treatise. Great classic on religious liberty, theory of government on common consent. R. Elwes translation. Total of 421pp. 5⅜ x 8½. 20249-6

MY BONDAGE AND MY FREEDOM, Frederick Douglass. Born a slave, Douglass became outspoken force in antislavery movement. The best of Douglass' autobiographies. Graphic description of slave life. 464pp. 5⅜ x 8½. 22457-0

FOLLOWING THE EQUATOR: A Journey Around the World, Mark Twain. Fascinating humorous account of 1897 voyage to Hawaii, Australia, India, New Zealand, etc. Ironic, bemused reports on peoples, customs, climate, flora and fauna, politics, much more. 197 illustrations. 720pp. 5⅜ x 8½. 26113-1

THE PEOPLE CALLED SHAKERS, Edward D. Andrews. Definitive study of Shakers: origins, beliefs, practices, dances, social organization, furniture and crafts, etc. 33 illustrations. 351pp. 5⅜ x 8½. 21081-2

THE MYTHS OF GREECE AND ROME, H. A. Guerber. A classic of mythology, generously illustrated, long prized for its simple, graphic, accurate retelling of the principal myths of Greece and Rome, and for its commentary on their origins and significance. With 64 illustrations by Michelangelo, Raphael, Titian, Rubens, Canova, Bernini and others. 480pp. 5⅜ x 8½. 27584-1

PSYCHOLOGY OF MUSIC, Carl E. Seashore. Classic work discusses music as a medium from psychological viewpoint. Clear treatment of physical acoustics, auditory apparatus, sound perception, development of musical skills, nature of musical feeling, host of other topics. 88 figures. 408pp. 5⅜ x 8½. 21851-1

THE PHILOSOPHY OF HISTORY, Georg W. Hegel. Great classic of Western thought develops concept that history is not chance but rational process, the evolution of freedom. 457pp. 5⅜ x 8½. 20112-0

THE BOOK OF TEA, Kakuzo Okakura. Minor classic of the Orient: entertaining, charming explanation, interpretation of traditional Japanese culture in terms of tea ceremony. 94pp. 5⅜ x 8½. 20070-1

LIFE IN ANCIENT EGYPT, Adolf Erman. Fullest, most thorough, detailed older account with much not in more recent books, domestic life, religion, magic, medicine, commerce, much more. Many illustrations reproduce tomb paintings, carvings, hieroglyphs, etc. 597pp. 5⅜ x 8½. 22632-8

SUNDIALS, Their Theory and Construction, Albert Waugh. Far and away the best, most thorough coverage of ideas, mathematics concerned, types, construction, adjusting anywhere. Simple, nontechnical treatment allows even children to build several of these dials. Over 100 illustrations. 230pp. 5⅜ x 8½. 22947-5

THEORETICAL HYDRODYNAMICS, L. M. Milne-Thomson. Classic exposition of the mathematical theory of fluid motion, applicable to both hydrodynamics and aerodynamics. Over 600 exercises. 768pp. 6⅛ x 9¼. 68970-0

SONGS OF EXPERIENCE: Facsimile Reproduction with 26 Plates in Full Color, William Blake. 26 full-color plates from a rare 1826 edition. Includes "The Tyger," "London," "Holy Thursday," and other poems. Printed text of poems. 48pp. 5¼ x 7. 24636-1

OLD-TIME VIGNETTES IN FULL COLOR, Carol Belanger Grafton (ed.). Over 390 charming, often sentimental illustrations, selected from archives of Victorian graphics—pretty women posing, children playing, food, flowers, kittens and puppies, smiling cherubs, birds and butterflies, much more. All copyright-free. 48pp. 9¼ x 12¼. 27269-9

PERSPECTIVE FOR ARTISTS, Rex Vicat Cole. Depth, perspective of sky and sea, shadows, much more, not usually covered. 391 diagrams, 81 reproductions of drawings and paintings. 279pp. 5⅜ x 8½. 22487-2

DRAWING THE LIVING FIGURE, Joseph Sheppard. Innovative approach to artistic anatomy focuses on specifics of surface anatomy, rather than muscles and bones. Over 170 drawings of live models in front, back and side views, and in widely varying poses. Accompanying diagrams. 177 illustrations. Introduction. Index. 144pp. 8⅜ x11¼. 26723-7

GOTHIC AND OLD ENGLISH ALPHABETS: 100 Complete Fonts, Dan X. Solo. Add power, elegance to posters, signs, other graphics with 100 stunning copyright-free alphabets: Blackstone, Dolbey, Germania, 97 more–including many lower-case, numerals, punctuation marks. 104pp. 8⅛ x 11. 24695-7

HOW TO DO BEADWORK, Mary White. Fundamental book on craft from simple projects to five-bead chains and woven works. 106 illustrations. 142pp. 5⅜ x 8. 20697-1

THE BOOK OF WOOD CARVING, Charles Marshall Sayers. Finest book for beginners discusses fundamentals and offers 34 designs. "Absolutely first rate . . . well thought out and well executed."–E. J. Tangerman. 118pp. 7¾ x 10⅝. 23654-4

ILLUSTRATED CATALOG OF CIVIL WAR MILITARY GOODS: Union Army Weapons, Insignia, Uniform Accessories, and Other Equipment, Schuyler, Hartley, and Graham. Rare, profusely illustrated 1846 catalog includes Union Army uniform and dress regulations, arms and ammunition, coats, insignia, flags, swords, rifles, etc. 226 illustrations. 160pp. 9 x 12. 24939-5

WOMEN'S FASHIONS OF THE EARLY 1900s: An Unabridged Republication of "New York Fashions, 1909," National Cloak & Suit Co. Rare catalog of mail-order fashions documents women's and children's clothing styles shortly after the turn of the century. Captions offer full descriptions, prices. Invaluable resource for fashion, costume historians. Approximately 725 illustrations. 128pp. 8⅜ x 11¼. 27276-1

THE 1912 AND 1915 GUSTAV STICKLEY FURNITURE CATALOGS, Gustav Stickley. With over 200 detailed illustrations and descriptions, these two catalogs are essential reading and reference materials and identification guides for Stickley furniture. Captions cite materials, dimensions and prices. 112pp. 6½ x 9¼. 26676-1

EARLY AMERICAN LOCOMOTIVES, John H. White, Jr. Finest locomotive engravings from early 19th century: historical (1804–74), main-line (after 1870), special, foreign, etc. 147 plates. 142pp. 11⅜ x 8¼. 22772-3

THE TALL SHIPS OF TODAY IN PHOTOGRAPHS, Frank O. Braynard. Lavishly illustrated tribute to nearly 100 majestic contemporary sailing vessels: Amerigo Vespucci, Clearwater, Constitution, Eagle, Mayflower, Sea Cloud, Victory, many more. Authoritative captions provide statistics, background on each ship. 190 black-and-white photographs and illustrations. Introduction. 128pp. 8⅞ x 11¾. 27163-3

LITTLE BOOK OF EARLY AMERICAN CRAFTS AND TRADES, Peter Stockham (ed.). 1807 children's book explains crafts and trades: baker, hatter, cooper, potter, and many others. 23 copperplate illustrations. 140pp. 4⅝ x 6.   23336-7

VICTORIAN FASHIONS AND COSTUMES FROM HARPER'S BAZAR, 1867–1898, Stella Blum (ed.). Day costumes, evening wear, sports clothes, shoes, hats, other accessories in over 1,000 detailed engravings. 320pp. 9⅜ x 12¼.   22990-4

GUSTAV STICKLEY, THE CRAFTSMAN, Mary Ann Smith. Superb study surveys broad scope of Stickley's achievement, especially in architecture. Design philosophy, rise and fall of the Craftsman empire, descriptions and floor plans for many Craftsman houses, more. 86 black-and-white halftones. 31 line illustrations. Introduction 208pp. 6½ x 9¼.   27210-9

THE LONG ISLAND RAIL ROAD IN EARLY PHOTOGRAPHS, Ron Ziel. Over 220 rare photos, informative text document origin (1844) and development of rail service on Long Island. Vintage views of early trains, locomotives, stations, passengers, crews, much more. Captions. 8⅞ x 11¾.   26301-0

VOYAGE OF THE LIBERDADE, Joshua Slocum. Great 19th-century mariner's thrilling, first-hand account of the wreck of his ship off South America, the 35-foot boat he built from the wreckage, and its remarkable voyage home. 128pp. 5⅜ x 8½.
40022-0

TEN BOOKS ON ARCHITECTURE, Vitruvius. The most important book ever written on architecture. Early Roman aesthetics, technology, classical orders, site selection, all other aspects. Morgan translation. 331pp. 5⅜ x 8½.   20645-9

THE HUMAN FIGURE IN MOTION, Eadweard Muybridge. More than 4,500 stopped-action photos, in action series, showing undraped men, women, children jumping, lying down, throwing, sitting, wrestling, carrying, etc. 390pp. 7⅞ x 10⅝.
20204-6 Clothbd.

TREES OF THE EASTERN AND CENTRAL UNITED STATES AND CANADA, William M. Harlow. Best one-volume guide to 140 trees. Full descriptions, woodlore, range, etc. Over 600 illustrations. Handy size. 288pp. 4½ x 6⅜.   20395 6

SONGS OF WESTERN BIRDS, Dr. Donald J. Borror. Complete song and call repertoire of 60 western species, including flycatchers, juncoes, cactus wrens, many more—includes fully illustrated booklet.   Cassette and manual 99913-0

GROWING AND USING HERBS AND SPICES, Milo Miloradovich. Versatile handbook provides all the information needed for cultivation and use of all the herbs and spices available in North America. 4 illustrations. Index. Glossary. 236pp. 5⅜ x 8½.
25058-X

BIG BOOK OF MAZES AND LABYRINTHS, Walter Shepherd. 50 mazes and labyrinths in all—classical, solid, ripple, and more—in one great volume. Perfect inexpensive puzzler for clever youngsters. Full solutions. 112pp. 8⅛ x 11.   22951-3

PIANO TUNING, J. Cree Fischer. Clearest, best book for beginner, amateur. Simple repairs, raising dropped notes, tuning by easy method of flattened fifths. No previous skills needed. 4 illustrations. 201pp. 5⅜ x 8½. 23267-0

HINTS TO SINGERS, Lillian Nordica. Selecting the right teacher, developing confidence, overcoming stage fright, and many other important skills receive thoughtful discussion in this indispensible guide, written by a world-famous diva of four decades' experience. 96pp. 5⅜ x 8½. 40094-8

THE COMPLETE NONSENSE OF EDWARD LEAR, Edward Lear. All nonsense limericks, zany alphabets, Owl and Pussycat, songs, nonsense botany, etc., illustrated by Lear. Total of 320pp. 5⅜ x 8½. (Available in U.S. only.) 20167-8

VICTORIAN PARLOUR POETRY: An Annotated Anthology, Michael R. Turner. 117 gems by Longfellow, Tennyson, Browning, many lesser-known poets. "The Village Blacksmith," "Curfew Must Not Ring Tonight," "Only a Baby Small," dozens more, often difficult to find elsewhere. Index of poets, titles, first lines. xxiii + 325pp. 5⅝ x 8¼. 27044-0

DUBLINERS, James Joyce. Fifteen stories offer vivid, tightly focused observations of the lives of Dublin's poorer classes. At least one, "The Dead," is considered a masterpiece. Reprinted complete and unabridged from standard edition. 160pp. 5$\frac{3}{16}$ x 8¼. 26870-5

GREAT WEIRD TALES: 14 Stories by Lovecraft, Blackwood, Machen and Others, S. T. Joshi (ed.). 14 spellbinding tales, including "The Sin Eater," by Fiona McLeod, "The Eye Above the Mantel," by Frank Belknap Long, as well as renowned works by R. H. Barlow, Lord Dunsany, Arthur Machen, W. C. Morrow and eight other masters of the genre. 256pp. 5⅜ x 8½. (Available in U.S. only.) 40436-6

THE BOOK OF THE SACRED MAGIC OF ABRAMELIN THE MAGE, translated by S. MacGregor Mathers. Medieval manuscript of ceremonial magic. Basic document in Aleister Crowley, Golden Dawn groups. 268pp. 5⅜ x 8½. 23211-5

NEW RUSSIAN-ENGLISH AND ENGLISH-RUSSIAN DICTIONARY, M. A. O'Brien. This is a remarkably handy Russian dictionary, containing a surprising amount of information, including over 70,000 entries. 366pp. 4½ x 6⅛. 20208-9

HISTORIC HOMES OF THE AMERICAN PRESIDENTS, Second, Revised Edition, Irvin Haas. A traveler's guide to American Presidential homes, most open to the public, depicting and describing homes occupied by every American President from George Washington to George Bush. With visiting hours, admission charges, travel routes. 175 photographs. Index. 160pp. 8¼ x 11. 26751-2

NEW YORK IN THE FORTIES, Andreas Feininger. 162 brilliant photographs by the well-known photographer, formerly with *Life* magazine. Commuters, shoppers, Times Square at night, much else from city at its peak. Captions by John von Hartz. 181pp. 9¼ x 10¾. 23585-8

INDIAN SIGN LANGUAGE, William Tomkins. Over 525 signs developed by Sioux and other tribes. Written instructions and diagrams. Also 290 pictographs. 111pp. 6⅛ x 9¼. 22029-X

ANATOMY: A Complete Guide for Artists, Joseph Sheppard. A master of figure drawing shows artists how to render human anatomy convincingly. Over 460 illustrations. 224pp. 8⅜ x 11¼. 27279-6

MEDIEVAL CALLIGRAPHY: Its History and Technique, Marc Drogin. Spirited history, comprehensive instruction manual covers 13 styles (ca. 4th century through 15th). Excellent photographs; directions for duplicating medieval techniques with modern tools. 224pp. 8⅜ x 11¼. 26142-5

DRIED FLOWERS: How to Prepare Them, Sarah Whitlock and Martha Rankin. Complete instructions on how to use silica gel, meal and borax, perlite aggregate, sand and borax, glycerine and water to create attractive permanent flower arrangements. 12 illustrations. 32pp. 5⅜ x 8½. 21802-3

EASY-TO-MAKE BIRD FEEDERS FOR WOODWORKERS, Scott D. Campbell. Detailed, simple-to-use guide for designing, constructing, caring for and using feeders. Text, illustrations for 12 classic and contemporary designs. 96pp. 5⅜ x 8½. 25847-5

SCOTTISH WONDER TALES FROM MYTH AND LEGEND, Donald A. Mackenzie. 16 lively tales tell of giants rumbling down mountainsides, of a magic wand that turns stone pillars into warriors, of gods and goddesses, evil hags, powerful forces and more. 240pp. 5⅜ x 8½. 29677-6

THE HISTORY OF UNDERCLOTHES, C. Willett Cunnington and Phyllis Cunnington. Fascinating, well-documented survey covering six centuries of English undergarments, enhanced with over 100 illustrations: 12th-century laced-up bodice, footed long drawers (1795), 19th-century bustles, 19th-century corsets for men, Victorian "bust improvers," much more. 272pp. 5⅜ x 8¼. 27124-2

ARTS AND CRAFTS FURNITURE: The Complete Brooks Catalog of 1912, Brooks Manufacturing Co. Photos and detailed descriptions of more than 150 now very collectible furniture designs from the Arts and Crafts movement depict davenports, settees, buffets, desks, tables, chairs, bedsteads, dressers and more, all built of solid, quarter-sawed oak. Invaluable for students and enthusiasts of antiques, Americana and the decorative arts. 80pp. 6½ x 9¼. 27471-3

WILBUR AND ORVILLE: A Biography of the Wright Brothers, Fred Howard. Definitive, crisply written study tells the full story of the brothers' lives and work. A vividly written biography, unparalleled in scope and color, that also captures the spirit of an extraordinary era. 560pp. 6⅛ x 9¼. 40297-5

THE ARTS OF THE SAILOR: Knotting, Splicing and Ropework, Hervey Garrett Smith. Indispensable shipboard reference covers tools, basic knots and useful hitches; handsewing and canvas work, more. Over 100 illustrations. Delightful reading for sea lovers. 256pp. 5⅜ x 8½. 26440-8

FRANK LLOYD WRIGHT'S FALLINGWATER: The House and Its History, Second, Revised Edition, Donald Hoffmann. A total revision—both in text and illustrations—of the standard document on Fallingwater, the boldest, most personal architectural statement of Wright's mature years, updated with valuable new material from the recently opened Frank Lloyd Wright Archives. "Fascinating"—*The New York Times*. 116 illustrations. 128pp. 9¼ x 10¾. 27430-6

PHOTOGRAPHIC SKETCHBOOK OF THE CIVIL WAR, Alexander Gardner. 100 photos taken on field during the Civil War. Famous shots of Manassas Harper's Ferry, Lincoln, Richmond, slave pens, etc. 244pp. 10⅝ x 8¼. 22731-6

FIVE ACRES AND INDEPENDENCE, Maurice G. Kains. Great back-to-the-land classic explains basics of self-sufficient farming. The one book to get. 95 illustrations. 397pp. 5⅜ x 8½. 20974-1

SONGS OF EASTERN BIRDS, Dr. Donald J. Borror. Songs and calls of 60 species most common to eastern U.S.: warblers, woodpeckers, flycatchers, thrushes, larks, many more in high-quality recording. Cassette and manual 99912-2

A MODERN HERBAL, Margaret Grieve. Much the fullest, most exact, most useful compilation of herbal material. Gigantic alphabetical encyclopedia, from aconite to zedoary, gives botanical information, medical properties, folklore, economic uses, much else. Indispensable to serious reader. 161 illustrations. 888pp. 6½ x 9¼. 2-vol. set. (Available in U.S. only.) Vol. I: 22798-7
Vol. II: 22799-5

HIDDEN TREASURE MAZE BOOK, Dave Phillips. Solve 34 challenging mazes accompanied by heroic tales of adventure. Evil dragons, people-eating plants, blood-thirsty giants, many more dangerous adversaries lurk at every twist and turn. 34 mazes, stories, solutions. 48pp. 8¼ x 11. 24566-7

LETTERS OF W. A. MOZART, Wolfgang A. Mozart. Remarkable letters show bawdy wit, humor, imagination, musical insights, contemporary musical world; includes some letters from Leopold Mozart. 276pp. 5⅜ x 8½. 22859-2

BASIC PRINCIPLES OF CLASSICAL BALLET, Agrippina Vaganova. Great Russian theoretician, teacher explains methods for teaching classical ballet. 118 illustrations. 175pp. 5⅜ x 8½. 22036-2

THE JUMPING FROG, Mark Twain. Revenge edition. The original story of The Celebrated Jumping Frog of Calaveras County, a hapless French translation, and Twain's hilarious "retranslation" from the French. 12 illustrations. 66pp. 5⅜ x 8½. 22686-7

BEST REMEMBERED POEMS, Martin Gardner (ed.). The 126 poems in this superb collection of 19th- and 20th-century British and American verse range from Shelley's "To a Skylark" to the impassioned "Renascence" of Edna St. Vincent Millay and to Edward Lear's whimsical "The Owl and the Pussycat." 224pp. 5⅜ x 8½. 27165-X

COMPLETE SONNETS, William Shakespeare. Over 150 exquisite poems deal with love, friendship, the tyranny of time, beauty's evanescence, death and other themes in language of remarkable power, precision and beauty. Glossary of archaic terms. 80pp. 5³⁄₁₆ x 8¼. 26686-9

THE BATTLES THAT CHANGED HISTORY, Fletcher Pratt. Eminent historian profiles 16 crucial conflicts, ancient to modern, that changed the course of civilization. 352pp. 5⅜ x 8½. 41129-X

THE WIT AND HUMOR OF OSCAR WILDE, Alvin Redman (ed.). More than 1,000 ripostes, paradoxes, wisecracks: Work is the curse of the drinking classes; I can resist everything except temptation; etc. 258pp. 5⅜ x 8½. 20602-5

SHAKESPEARE LEXICON AND QUOTATION DICTIONARY, Alexander Schmidt. Full definitions, locations, shades of meaning in every word in plays and poems. More than 50,000 exact quotations. 1,485pp. 6½ x 9¼. 2-vol. set.
Vol. 1: 22726-X
Vol. 2: 22727-8

SELECTED POEMS, Emily Dickinson. Over 100 best-known, best-loved poems by one of America's foremost poets, reprinted from authoritative early editions. No comparable edition at this price. Index of first lines. 64pp. 5³⁄₁₆ x 8¼. 26466-1

THE INSIDIOUS DR. FU-MANCHU, Sax Rohmer. The first of the popular mystery series introduces a pair of English detectives to their archnemesis, the diabolical Dr. Fu-Manchu. Flavorful atmosphere, fast-paced action, and colorful characters enliven this classic of the genre. 208pp. 5³⁄₁₆ x 8¼. 29898-1

THE MALLEUS MALEFICARUM OF KRAMER AND SPRENGER, translated by Montague Summers. Full text of most important witchhunter's "bible," used by both Catholics and Protestants. 278pp. 6⅝ x 10. 22802-9

SPANISH STORIES/CUENTOS ESPAÑOLES: A Dual-Language Book, Angel Flores (ed.). Unique format offers 13 great stories in Spanish by Cervantes, Borges, others. Faithful English translations on facing pages. 352pp. 5⅜ x 8½. 25399-6

GARDEN CITY, LONG ISLAND, IN EARLY PHOTOGRAPHS, 1869–1919, Mildred H. Smith. Handsome treasury of 118 vintage pictures, accompanied by carefully researched captions, document the Garden City Hotel fire (1899), the Vanderbilt Cup Race (1908), the first airmail flight departing from the Nassau Boulevard Aerodrome (1911), and much more. 96pp. 8⅞ x 11¾. 40669-5

OLD QUEENS, N.Y., IN EARLY PHOTOGRAPHS, Vincent F. Seyfried and William Asadorian. Over 160 rare photographs of Maspeth, Jamaica, Jackson Heights, and other areas. Vintage views of DeWitt Clinton mansion, 1939 World's Fair and more. Captions. 192pp. 8⅞ x 11. 26358-4

CAPTURED BY THE INDIANS: 15 Firsthand Accounts, 1750-1870, Frederick Drimmer. Astounding true historical accounts of grisly torture, bloody conflicts, relentless pursuits, miraculous escapes and more, by people who lived to tell the tale. 384pp. 5⅜ x 8½. 24901-8

THE WORLD'S GREAT SPEECHES (Fourth Enlarged Edition), Lewis Copeland, Lawrence W. Lamm, and Stephen J. McKenna. Nearly 300 speeches provide public speakers with a wealth of updated quotes and inspiration–from Pericles' funeral oration and William Jennings Bryan's "Cross of Gold Speech" to Malcolm X's powerful words on the Black Revolution and Earl of Spenser's tribute to his sister, Diana, Princess of Wales. 944pp. 5⅜ x 8⅜. 40903-1

THE BOOK OF THE SWORD, Sir Richard F. Burton. Great Victorian scholar/adventurer's eloquent, erudite history of the "queen of weapons"–from prehistory to early Roman Empire. Evolution and development of early swords, variations (sabre, broadsword, cutlass, scimitar, etc.), much more. 336pp. 6⅛ x 9¼. 25434-8

AUTOBIOGRAPHY: The Story of My Experiments with Truth, Mohandas K. Gandhi. Boyhood, legal studies, purification, the growth of the Satyagraha (nonviolent protest) movement. Critical, inspiring work of the man responsible for the freedom of India. 480pp. 5⅜ x 8½. (Available in U.S. only.)   24593-4

CELTIC MYTHS AND LEGENDS, T. W. Rolleston. Masterful retelling of Irish and Welsh stories and tales. Cuchulain, King Arthur, Deirdre, the Grail, many more. First paperback edition. 58 full-page illustrations. 512pp. 5⅜ x 8½.   26507-2

THE PRINCIPLES OF PSYCHOLOGY, William James. Famous long course complete, unabridged. Stream of thought, time perception, memory, experimental methods; great work decades ahead of its time. 94 figures. 1,391pp. 5⅜ x 8½. 2-vol. set.
Vol. I: 20381-6   Vol. II: 20382-4

THE WORLD AS WILL AND REPRESENTATION, Arthur Schopenhauer. Definitive English translation of Schopenhauer's life work, correcting more than 1,000 errors, omissions in earlier translations. Translated by E. F. J. Payne. Total of 1,269pp. 5⅜ x 8½. 2-vol. set.
Vol. 1: 21761-2   Vol. 2: 21762-0

MAGIC AND MYSTERY IN TIBET, Madame Alexandra David-Neel. Experiences among lamas, magicians, sages, sorcerers, Bonpa wizards. A true psychic discovery. 32 illustrations. 321pp. 5⅜ x 8½. (Available in U.S. only.)   22682-4

THE EGYPTIAN BOOK OF THE DEAD, E. A. Wallis Budge. Complete reproduction of Ani's papyrus, finest ever found. Full hieroglyphic text, interlinear transliteration, word-for-word translation, smooth translation. 533pp. 6½ x 9¼.   21866-X

MATHEMATICS FOR THE NONMATHEMATICIAN, Morris Kline. Detailed, college-level treatment of mathematics in cultural and historical context, with numerous exercises. Recommended Reading Lists. Tables. Numerous figures. 641pp. 5⅜ x 8½.
24823-2

PROBABILISTIC METHODS IN THE THEORY OF STRUCTURES, Isaac Elishakoff. Well-written introduction covers the elements of the theory of probability from two or more random variables, the reliability of such multivariable structures, the theory of random function, Monte Carlo methods of treating problems incapable of exact solution, and more. Examples. 502pp. 5⅜ x 8½.   40691-1

THE RIME OF THE ANCIENT MARINER, Gustave Doré, S. T. Coleridge. Doré's finest work; 34 plates capture moods, subtleties of poem. Flawless full-size reproductions printed on facing pages with authoritative text of poem. "Beautiful. Simply beautiful."—Publisher's Weekly. 77pp. 9¼ x 12.   22305-1

NORTH AMERICAN INDIAN DESIGNS FOR ARTISTS AND CRAFTSPEOPLE, Eva Wilson. Over 360 authentic copyright-free designs adapted from Navajo blankets, Hopi pottery, Sioux buffalo hides, more. Geometrics, symbolic figures, plant and animal motifs, etc. 128pp. 8⅜ x 11. (Not for sale in the United Kingdom.)   25341-4

SCULPTURE: Principles and Practice, Louis Slobodkin. Step-by-step approach to clay, plaster, metals, stone; classical and modern. 253 drawings, photos. 255pp. 8⅛ x 11.
22960-2

THE INFLUENCE OF SEA POWER UPON HISTORY, 1660–1783, A. T. Mahan. Influential classic of naval history and tactics still used as text in war colleges. First paperback edition. 4 maps. 24 battle plans. 640pp. 5⅜ x 8½.   25509-3

CATALOG OF DOVER BOOKS

THE STORY OF THE TITANIC AS TOLD BY ITS SURVIVORS, Jack Winocour (ed.). What it was really like. Panic, despair, shocking inefficiency, and a little heroism. More thrilling than any fictional account. 26 illustrations. 320pp. 5⅜ x 8½. 20610-6

FAIRY AND FOLK TALES OF THE IRISH PEASANTRY, William Butler Yeats (ed.). Treasury of 64 tales from the twilight world of Celtic myth and legend: "The Soul Cages," "The Kildare Pooka," "King O'Toole and his Goose," many more. Introduction and Notes by W. B. Yeats. 352pp. 5⅜ x 8½. 26941-8

BUDDHIST MAHAYANA TEXTS, E. B. Cowell and others (eds.). Superb, accurate translations of basic documents in Mahayana Buddhism, highly important in history of religions. The Buddha-karita of Asvaghosha, Larger Sukhavativyuha, more. 448pp. 5⅜ x 8½. 25552-2

ONE TWO THREE . . . INFINITY: Facts and Speculations of Science, George Gamow. Great physicist's fascinating, readable overview of contemporary science: number theory, relativity, fourth dimension, entropy, genes, atomic structure, much more. 128 illustrations. Index. 352pp. 5⅜ x 8½. 25664-2

EXPERIMENTATION AND MEASUREMENT, W. J. Youden. Introductory manual explains laws of measurement in simple terms and offers tips for achieving accuracy and minimizing errors. Mathematics of measurement, use of instruments, experimenting with machines. 1994 edition. Foreword. Preface. Introduction. Epilogue. Selected Readings. Glossary. Index. Tables and figures. 128pp. 5⅜ x 8½. 40451-X

DALÍ ON MODERN ART: The Cuckolds of Antiquated Modern Art, Salvador Dalí. Influential painter skewers modern art and its practitioners. Outrageous evaluations of Picasso, Cézanne, Turner, more. 15 renderings of paintings discussed. 44 calligraphic decorations by Dalí. 96pp. 5⅜ x 8½. (Available in U.S. only.) 29220-7

ANTIQUE PLAYING CARDS: A Pictorial History, Henry René D'Allemagne. Over 900 elaborate, decorative images from rare playing cards (14th–20th centuries): Bacchus, death, dancing dogs, hunting scenes, royal coats of arms, players cheating, much more. 96pp. 9¼ x 12¼. 29265-7

MAKING FURNITURE MASTERPIECES: 30 Projects with Measured Drawings, Franklin H. Gottshall. Step-by-step instructions, illustrations for constructing handsome, useful pieces, among them a Sheraton desk, Chippendale chair, Spanish desk, Queen Anne table and a William and Mary dressing mirror. 224pp. 8⅛ x 11¼. 29338-6

THE FOSSIL BOOK: A Record of Prehistoric Life, Patricia V. Rich et al. Profusely illustrated definitive guide covers everything from single-celled organisms and dinosaurs to birds and mammals and the interplay between climate and man. Over 1,500 illustrations. 760pp. 7½ x 10⅛. 29371-8